Unseasonable Youth

MODERNIST LITERATURE & CULTURE

Kevin J. H. Dettmar & Mark Wollaeger, Series Editors

Unseasonable Youth

Modernism, Colonialism, and the Fiction of Development

Jed Esty

OXFORD
UNIVERSITY PRESS

UNIVERSITY PRESS

Oxford University Press is a department of the University of Oxford.
It furthers the University's objective of excellence in research, scholarship,
and education by publishing worldwide.

Oxford   New York
Auckland   Cape Town   Dar es Salaam   Hong Kong   Karachi
Kuala Lumpur   Madrid   Melbourne   Mexico City   Nairobi
New Delhi   Shanghai   Taipei   Toronto

With offices in
Argentina   Austria   Brazil   Chile   Czech Republic   France   Greece
Guatemala   Hungary   Italy   Japan   Poland   Portugal   Singapore
South Korea   Switzerland   Thailand   Turkey   Ukraine   Vietnam

Oxford is a registered trade mark of Oxford University Press
in the UK and certain other countries.

Published in the United States of America by
Oxford University Press
198 Madison Avenue, New York, NY 10016

© Oxford University Press 2012

First issued as an Oxford University Press paperback, 2013.

Library of Congress Cataloging-in-Publication Data
Esty, Joshua, 1967–
   Unseasonable youth : modernism, colonialism, and the fiction of development / Jed Esty
      p. cm.—(Modernist literature & culture)
   Includes bibliographical references and index.
   ISBN 978-0-19-985796-8 (hardcover : alk. paper); 978-0-19-930723-4 (paperback)
   1. English fiction—19th century—History and criticism.   2. English fiction—20th century—
   History and criticism.   3. Modernism (Literature)—Great Britain.   4. Bildungsromans,
   English—History and criticism.   5. Youth in literature.   6. Adolescence in
   literature   7. Progress in literature.   8. Colonies in literature.   9. Imperialism in
   literature.   I. Title.
   PR878.M63E77   2012
   823'.1009—dc22   2011021174

Printed in the United States of America
on acid-free paper

For ARG

Contents

Foreword

Jed Esty's topic in *Unseasonable Youth* is simply stated – the novel of subject formation in the Age of Empire – yet complexly explored. What happens to the form of the novel, Esty asks, when the reciprocal allegories of nation-building and self-making that underwrite the nineteenth-century bildungsroman, or novel of education, no longer seem adequate to the representation of life in an increasingly globalized world? Novels charting the individual's development from youth to maturity tended to resolve, or at least to mitigate, the potential contradiction between the necessity of closure and the potentially endless process of growing up by positing an ideal of adulthood that was deeply entwined, Esty argues, with the notion of national destiny. To become an adult was to complete the passage from innocence – understood as a kind of ungroundedness – into citizenship, or full integration into the national community. But as the seeming stability of the nation as form is challenged by the less certain frame of reference produced by an emerging global system, what seemed the inevitable progress from youthfulness to adulthood, from individual to national subject, begins to break down, and the novel of development starts to fixate on a pathology that marks the perceived obsolescence of the nation: the trope of frozen youth, the stunted individual who cannot or will not grow up. Peter Pan may spring to mind, but think as well of the dilated adolescence of Dorian Gray, Conrad's Jim, Woolf's Rachel Vinrace, and Stephen Dedalus.

Committed to investigating how literary form mediates historical forces, Esty identifies the historical referent for the bildungsroman's dialectic of youth and maturity as the historical tension between the dynamic energy of capitalist modernity and the binding power of national identity. The argument necessarily, then, takes up not only metropolitan bildungsromane, such as *The Picture of Dorian Gray* and H. G. Wells' *Tono-Bungay*, and modernist exemplars, such as *A Portrait of the Artist as a Young Man* and Woolf's *The Voyage Out*, but also colonial novels of development, such as *Lord Jim* and Olive Schreiner's *Story of an African Farm*. Such novels are fundamental to the argument insofar as "colonial modernity unsettled the progressive and stabilizing discourse of national culture by breaking up cherished continuities between a people and its language, territory, and polity." Esty understands frozen youth as a defining feature of the core period of European modernism, but his historical and geographical range also takes in what he calls the modernist semi-periphery of Jean Rhys and Elizabeth Bowen, and, in his conclusion, Samuel Beckett and Flann O'Brien, Mulk Raj Anand and G. V. Desani, Vladimir Nabokov and Günter Grass, Salman Rushdie and William Golding, Tahar Ben Jelloun and Ben Okri, Ian McEwan and "Lad Lit." In addition to this genealogy of post-1930s novels of arrested development, Esty offers a detailed examination of important nineteenth-century models: *Wilhelm Meister*, conventionally thought to be literature's closest approximation to the mythic origin of the bildungsroman, the granddaddy of them all, and *The Mill on the Floss*, a Victorian anticipation of modernism's more far-reaching critique of the form.

Locating "the historical specificity of the modernist era . . . at the dialectical switchpoint between residual nineteenth-century narratives of global development and emergent twentieth-century suspicion of such narratives as universalist and Eurocentric," *Unseasonable Youth*'s main contribution is to modernist studies. And yet Esty's account of the still unfolding dialectic between developmental thinking and the discourse of difference – between the lingering appeal (and institutional power) of historicist metanarratives and the counterchallenge of alternative modernities – will also be of great interest to postcolonial and subaltern studies and to theorists of world literature. As one might expect of such a capacious argument, Esty is indebted to the work of Franco Moretti and Fredric Jameson, as well as to one of Jameson's intellectual heroes, Georg Lukács; at the same time, he also offers telling critiques of all three, unearthing the buried importance of national form in Moretti, rescuing the critical force of Conrad's style from Jameson's charge of ideological mystification, and most importantly, the value of modernism more generally against Lukács's imputation of quietism. Indeed, enlisting Adorno, Esty makes a frank and refreshingly unapologetic case for "the power of literary form as against propositional discourse" and for modernist formal experimentation in particular as a valuable conceptual resource in continuing to think our way through "the central contradiction of modernity": "modernity is a state of permanent transition."

Yet Esty's commitment is not to experimentation per se. Rather, he values "the residual realism of high modernism as against the more radical anti-developmental and counter-Hegelian modes of avant-gardist writing," for while "the counterdiscursive strikes against the ideology of progress" associated with, say, Surrealism or *Finnegans Wake*, are too easily assimilated, commodified or dismissed, modernist narrative's dialectical engagement with developmental thinking – via scrambled and distorted time schemes and ironic forms of arbitrary closure – more effectively challenges the hegemony of Eurocentric models of global development by refusing to ignore the lived experience of temporality and the historical fact that we live in a world "organized by modernization schemes that have outlived academic critiques of modernization theory."

Esty's work is thus profoundly formalist and historical at once. As for Jameson, form mediates history, and Esty shares Jameson's gift for recognizing structural similarities and for grasping as homologies what otherwise might seem mere analogies, that is, as signs pointing to a shared historical logic. But Esty's attention to structure is also complemented by a sharp eye for matters of syntax, diction, and tone – of style at a more granular level than one often sees in arguments equally attuned to broader narratives of genre, periodization, and historical change. Moreover Esty himself writes with admirable stylistic panache. It is tempting to indulge in a list of brilliant turns of phrase, from H. G. Wells's "gothic didacticism" to Stephen Dedalus's "bluff and rivalrous jackass of a father," or resonantly metaphoric formulations – modernist novels of stalled development "peel away the residua of romantic nationalism from the bildungsroman plot, compromising its ability to turn the chronos of open-jawed modernity into the kairos of national destiny" – but that would be an unnecessary exercise, given that readers of this foreword should not be compelled to wait any longer before enjoying the pleasures of *Unseasonable Youth* unburdened by Esty's gratefully superfluous editors.

Mark Wollaeger and Kevin J. H. Dettmar

Acknowledgments

Thanks are due to many friends, colleagues, students, and institutions who sustained this book through its own unseasonable youth and up to the time of publication. I want to acknowledge, with gratitude, the American Council of Learned Societies for a Charles Ryskamp fellowship that provided vital support at an early stage of the project. The University of Illinois also supported my research with great institutional good will, with fellowships at the Center for Advanced Study and at the Illinois Program for Research in the Humanities, and, most importantly, with its fostering of a warm and lively community of scholars. I was fortunate to find keen readers in Matti Bunzl, Antoinette Burton, Jon Ebel, Stephanie Foote, Lauren Goodlad, Jim Hansen, Matt Hart, Michael Rothberg, and Zohreh Sullivan. Joe Valente read most of these pages and made all of them better.

More recently, at the University of Pennsylvania, I have enjoyed the intellectual and professional company of new friends and colleagues who set the bar high for good and collaborative work. Among them, Rita Barnard, Nancy Bentley, Margreta de Grazia, Jim English, Amy Kaplan, Suvir Kaul, Zack Lesser, Ania Loomba, Heather Love, Jo Park, Jean-Michel Rabaté, Paul Saint-Amour, and Chi-ming Yang all made valuable contributions to this project. Rita, Jim, and Paul read the last chapter drafts and gave me the final push I needed, with wise counsel and sparkling insight. Zack, Ania, and Suvir have been valued friends and generous colleagues, two times over. Thanks, too, to Chris Nichols and Tamara Walker of the Race/Empire working group, and to Ariela Rosenberg, Shana Rusonis, and Christina Walter for excellent research assistance.

Along the way, these generous scholars and good friends shared their time and expertise with me: Nigel Alderman, Amanda Anderson, Dan Blanton, Ian

Baucom, Ericka Beckman, Richard Begam, Jessica Berman, Tim Bewes, Tobias Boes, Jim Buzard, Byron Caminero-Santangelo, Joe Cleary, Sarah Cole, Jay Clayton, Tommy Davis, Jay Dickson, Greg Dobbins, Simon During, Jonathan Eburne, Maria Fackler, Anne Fernald, Christine Froula, Nathan Hensley, Heather Hicks, Janice Ho, Emily Hyde, Pericles Lewis, Enrique Lima, David Lloyd, Maria Lima, Greg Londe, Colleen Lye, John Marx, Jesse Matz, Mike Mirabile, Michael Moses, Carl Niekerk, Emer Nolan, John Plotz, Nicole Rizzuto, Urmila Seshagiri, Joey Slaughter, Pam Thurschwell, Rebecca Walkowitz, and Laura Winkiel. I am grateful to all of them for questions and suggestions that helped me refine and redefine the project. Franco Moretti provided the initial inspiration for this book and offered encouraging words at the outset; my debt is larger even than it appears in these pages. I started thinking about this project in Eve Sedgwick's Victorian novel seminar years ago; her generous pedagogy has guided me ever since. More than they realize, Nancy Armstrong, Robert Caserio, Maria DiBattista, Luke Gibbons, Michael Levenson, and Jahan Ramazani have offered invaluable advice and encouragement. Janet Lyon and Doug Mao both asked the right questions at the right times, and have been steadfast supporters along the way. Bruce Robbins and an anonymous reader of the manuscript provided remarkably detailed, timely, and useful reviews, for which I am most grateful indeed.

Particular thanks are due, too, to Mark Wollaeger and Kevin Dettmar for their editorial vision, speed, and sure-handedness; and to Shannon McLachlan and Brendan O'Neill at Oxford for their expert guidance and their inspiring commitment to this work. I would also like to thank Molly Morrison at Newgen and copy editor Stacey Hamilton for seeing the book through production with great professionalism and swift hands.

My intellectual and personal debts go beyond even this long catalogue, of course, and extend to all the readers, writers, and scholars named in the text and footnotes of these pages; to helpful interlocutors and audiences at Berkeley, Colorado, Johns Hopkins, Kansas, Maryland, Montreal, Notre Dame, Oklahoma State, Penn State, Princeton, Reed, Santa Barbara, Vanderbilt, Wisconsin, and Yale; and, especially, to all the students I've taught in the last seven years, graduate and undergraduate alike, at Illinois and Penn.

Finally, to Andrea, a partner for all seasons, this is for you.

. . .

A portion of Chapter 1 previously appeared in essay form under the title "Global Lukács," in *Novel* 42.3, pps. 366–372. Copyright 2009, *Novel*, Inc; reprinted by permission of Duke University Press. A portion of Chapter 5 previously appeared in *Modernism and Colonialism*, eds. Richard Begam and Michael Valdez Moses, pps. 70–90. Copyright 2007; reprinted by permission of Duke University Press. Grateful acknowledgment is also given to Ohio State University Press for permission to reprint material from an essay in *Narrative* for Chapter 2; to Indiana University Press for permission to reprint material from an essay in *Victorian Studies* for Chapter 3; and to Johns Hopkins University Press for permission to reprint material from an essay in *Modern Fiction Studies* for Chapter 6.

Unseasonable Youth

1. Introduction

Scattered Souls—The Bildungsroman and Colonial Modernity

The young man has become so homeless and doubts all concepts and all customs . . . a lord in the universal empire of history. If already as a boy he was "ripe," now he is over-ripe.

—Nietzsche, *Untimely Meditations*

The novel overcomes its "bad infinity" by recourse to the biographical form.

—Lukács, *The Theory of the Novel*

After the Novel of Progress

It is commonly observed that the bildungsroman, or novel of education, had its heyday in the nineteenth century and that modernism tended to avoid its generic dictates or to revise them out of recognition. Consider the landmark fictions of international modernism: Kafka's *Metamorphosis*, which short-circuits and hideously travesties the development of its young protagonist; Proust's *Remembrance of Things Past*, which not only displaces the plot of development with the story of recollection, but also distends its temporal frame over hundreds of pages; Mann's *The Magic Mountain*, which describes Hans Castorp wasting away and *un*becoming himself in an Alpine sanatorium; Musil's *The Man without Qualities*, which empties rather than fills the vessel of novelistic character; and Wilde's *The Picture of Dorian Gray*, which converts the aging process into a long and lurid adolescence.

Metamorphosis, dilation, consumption, evacuation, inversion: these stories spectacularly and conspicuously thwart the realist proportions of biographical time that had, from its inception, defined the bildungsroman. The range of great novels centered on frozen youth almost defines this period, from Melville's *Billy Budd* in 1891 to Alain-Fournier's *Le Grand Meaulnes* in 1914 through to Günter Grass's *The Tin Drum* in 1959.[1]

And this is not even to mention the stylized alternation between compression and expansion in the work of such definitive Anglophone modernists as Conrad, Woolf, and Joyce. In their fictions, characterization does not unfold in smooth biographical time but in proleptic fits and retroactive starts, epiphanic bursts and impressionistic mental inventories, in accidents, in obliquity, in sudden lyric death and in languid semiconscious delay. In *Lord Jim* (1900), *The Voyage Out* (1915), and *A Portrait of the Artist as a Young Man* (1916), Conrad, Woolf, and Joyce, respectively, rework narrative time via youthful protagonists who conspicuously *do not grow up*. What is less often noted is that all of these texts block or defer the attainment of a mature social role through plots of colonial migration and displacement. To put it another way, all three are antidevelopmental fictions set in colonial contact zones, where uneven development is a conspicuous fact of both personal and political life.

This observation suggests a geographical and historical framework for the commonplace notion that modernist fiction resists the tyranny of plot. One of our most stable definitions of international modernism rests on the idea that novels of the period find ingenious ways to cut and split what Forster called the tapeworm of story. They reorganize narrative data into lyrical, pictorial, mythical, thematic, aleatory, or elegiac shapes; they weave Freudian regression and Bergsonian flux into the warp and woof of social realism; and they mount bohemian, queer, non-white, and feminist challenges to the stale dictates of bourgeois socialization or the grooved contours of nineteenth-century characterization.[2] The remapping I propose in this book begins in the novelistic heartland of the European nation-state but moves outward to Conrad's Asian straits, Woolf's South American riverway, and Joyce's Irish backwater. These are places where imperialism—in its late and bloated form—unsettles the bildungsroman and its humanist ideals, producing jagged effects on both the politics and poetics of subject formation. Those early achievements of Conrad, Woolf, and Joyce exemplify a central, yet surprisingly underexplored nexus between modernist aesthetics and modern colonialism: the disruption of developmental time in reciprocal allegories of self-making and nation-building. They make up the core of an argument that extends to other novels by Rudyard Kipling, Olive Schreiner, Oscar Wilde, H. G. Wells, Elizabeth Bowen, and Jean Rhys, whose "English" fictions cast doubt on the ideology of progress through the figure of stunted youth. Modernism exposes and disrupts the inherited conventions of the bildungsroman in order to criticize bourgeois values and to reinvent the biographical novel, but also to explore the contradictions inherent in mainstream developmental discourses of self, nation, and empire.

This hypothesis first emerged not as a theoretical deduction, but as an empirical observation. Teaching a course called "Fictions of Empire" several years ago, I prepared some remarks about the bildungsroman as a way to introduce, first, Schreiner's *Story of an African Farm*, then *Kim*, then *Lord Jim*. But each week I realized that the novels in question did not narrate the passage into adulthood. In fact all three seemed designed precisely to avoid it. It is not just that—as in so many novels of the late Victorian era—there are few happy endings here, or even that we have a swerve into interiority alongside a steepening arc of social disillusionment, but that the experimental novels *and* the so-called imperial romances of the epoch so purposefully break the temporality of the classical bildungsroman plot. In open and sustained violation of the developmental paradigm that seemed to govern nineteenth-century historical and fictional forms, such novels tend to present youthful protagonists who die young, remain suspended in time, eschew vocational and sexual closure, refuse social adjustment, or establish themselves as evergreen souls via the tender offices of the *Kunstlerroman*.[3]

Many outcomes across many different kinds of novels, some less obviously connected to metropole-colony relations than others: but from a structural perspective, it is striking that all of the novels in question so fully excise the connective tissue between youth and age, so systematically omit the process of maturation itself. At one level, perhaps it is not surprising that a group of colonial and imperial fictions from the period of 1880 to 1920 should put figures of unseasonable youth in the foreground. Such a trope would seem to conform nicely to the wish-fulfilling aspects of imperial romance and adventurism in the era of *Peter Pan* (1904) and *A Little Princess* (1904).[4] However, the novels I propose to examine are not simple wish-fulfilling romances nor mere documents in a banal national cliché of the British cult of youth. Their antidevelopmental temporality suggests a more complicated and interesting story, one that casts colonial fiction as integral to the emergence of the modernist art novel rather than as a middlebrow detour.[5]

This book proceeds from the idea that a formal and historical analysis of the bildungsroman at this turning point in literary history yields insights into the fate of developmental thinking more broadly during the breakdown of nineteenth-century positivist historicism and the massive but strained expansion of European political hegemony. To pursue this hypothesis, we can begin with Franco Moretti's

provocative argument that the European bildungsroman's historical vocation was
to manage the effects of modernization by representing it within a safe narrative scheme. During the golden age of European realism, Moretti suggests, youth
was the master trope of modernity itself, signifying the constant transformation
of industrial society and the growing interiority and mobility of middle-class
subjects. However, "to become a 'form'":

> youth must be endowed with a very different, almost opposite feature to
> those already mentioned: the very simple and slightly philistine notion that
> youth "does not last forever." Youth is brief, or at any rate circumscribed, and
> this enables or rather *forces* the a priori establishment of a formal constraint
> on the portrayal of modernity. Only by curbing its intrinsically boundless
> dynamism, only by agreeing to betray to a certain extent its very essence,
> only thus, it seems, can modernity be *represented.*
>
> (*Way* 6)

The young protagonist's open development is ultimately and rather artificially contained by the imposition of a static state of adulthood. "A *Bildung* is truly such,"
writes Moretti, "only if, at a certain point, it can be seen as *concluded*: only if youth
passes into maturity, and comes to a stop there" (*Way* 26). In Moretti's model, the
bildungsroman reflects a deep counterrevolutionary impulse embodied in Goethe
and Jane Austen, whose works turn on their ability to reconcile narrativity and
closure, youth and adulthood, free self-making and social determination. In their
originary hands, the genre both reflects and produces social consent, for it negoti-
ates a flexible and wily compromise between inner and outer directives in subject
formation.

   But if this standard novel of socialization figures modernity's endless revolution
in the master trope of youth, then what is the historical referent for the countertrope
of adulthood? If capitalism never rests, what symbolic equivalence can explain the
capacity of adulthood to put the brakes on developmental time, preventing the bildungsroman from becoming a never-ending story? Here we arrive at a possibility
that remains somewhat oblique in Moretti: that the discourse of the nation supplies the realist bildungsroman with an emergent language of historical continuity
or social identity amid the rapid and sweeping changes of industrialization. What
Moretti's model leaves unexplored is the crucial symbolic function of nationhood,
which gives a finished form to modern societies in the same way that adulthood
gives a finished form to the modern subject. With this central premise in place,
we can begin to track the changing nature of the soul-nation allegory as it faces
increasingly globalized conditions after 1860.

To lift out the somewhat buried role of national form in Moretti (and, beyond that, in the narrative theory of Georg Lukács), I want to suggest that the tension between the open-ended temporality of capitalism and the bounded, countertemporality of the nation plays out in fictional or symbolic form as a vivid struggle between youth and adulthood—and this would be a formative condition of both the classic (national-era) and the modernist (global-era) bildungsroman. From the beginning, of course, the concept of *Bildung* evolved within the intellectual context of romantic nationalism; the genealogy of the term begins with Goethe, Schiller, Lessing, and Herder and the philosophical milieu of late eighteenth-century Germany. This lineage establishes the genre's roots in a burgeoning nationalism based on an ideal of organic culture whose temporality and harmony could be reflected in the developing personality at the core of the bildungsroman. A historically specific notion of *becoming* enabled the formalization of *Bildung* as a literary device and defined culture as an ideal process: the "aesthetic education" of the subject (Schiller) and the emergence of the folk into the historically meaningful form of the nation (Herder).

M. M. Bakhtin codified the literary-critical adaptation of the *Bildung* concept to fiction when he claimed that a true (and thus truly modern) bildungsroman presents "an image of *man growing* in *national-historical time*" ("The *Bildungsroman*" 25; his emphasis). For Bakhtin, a narrative that fuses individual experience and sociopolitical development requires a tacitly masculine and explicitly national form of emergence. These are the premises woven into Bakhtin's taxonomic and teleological account of the bildungsroman's pride of place in the history of realism:

> Along with this predominant, mass type [the novel with the "ready-made" hero], there is another incomparably rarer type of novel that provides an image of man in the process of becoming. . . . The hero himself, his character, becomes a variable in the formula of this type of novel. Changes in the hero himself acquire *plot* significance. . . . Time is introduced into man, enters into his very image, changing in a fundamental way the significance of all aspects of his destiny and life. This type of novel can be designated in the most general sense as the novel of human *emergence*. . . . Everything depends upon the degree of assimilation of real historical time.
>
> ("The *Bildungsroman*" 21)

"National-historical time" allows the Goethean bildungsroman to reconcile the unbounded time of capitalist modernity and the bounded or cyclical time of tradition. Only national time is, in that sense, for Bakhtin, real; hence his emphasis on the "concrete perception of the locality" that undergirds Goethe's deep historical vision ("The *Bildungsroman*" 34). Bakhtin specifically excludes from Goethe's concrete and realistic historical imagination, and thus from the purview of the bildungsroman, the far-away realms of the exotic, the sublime, and the wild.

This foundational gesture (and its logic of exclusion) allow us to sketch the defining historical tension between the realism of the bildungsroman (bounded by national time) and the potentially unbounded forms of temporality associated with supranational forces that emerged in the era of the French and Industrial revolutions. Those expansionist and portable forces—whether identified as political rationality or economic hegemony—threatened the concept of culture itself insofar as they threatened to spill outside the borders of the European nation-state. In the British sphere, Burke and Coleridge consolidated this central opposition between a national culture (in which restrained or proportionate social and personal growth can occur) and a multinational civilization (in which unrestrained growth or modernization has no organic checks or balances). If the nation was the proper cultural container for the bildungsroman's allegory of development, then modern imperialism was a culture-diluting practice that violated "national-historical time" and set capitalism loose across the globe in ways that would come to disturb—indeed still do disturb—our dreams of inevitable, and yet measured, human progress.

I am hypothesizing that the developmental logic of the late bildungsroman underwent substantial revision as the relatively stable temporal frames of national destiny gave way to a more conspicuously global, and therefore more uncertain, frame of social reference. What we conventionally understand as the transformation of the bildungsroman into the naturalist fiction of disillusionment (with its logic of fixed social hierarchies, broken destinies, and compensatory but socially eccentric artistic visions) may also have had a geopolitical dimension, one that is especially visible in the British novel tradition. The imagined harmony between culture and the state, taken as a way to manage and to narrate the uneven development of capitalism, came under pressure as a new phase of empire-building revealed modernization to be unpredictable and unending. Colonial modernity unsettled the progressive and stabilizing discourse of national culture by breaking up cherished continuities between a people and its language, territory, and polity. It is in this sense that empire throws the Goethean formula of novels out of joint, cracking the alignment between biographical and "national-historical" time while exposing both to the logic of historical paralysis and regression.[6] But the course of capitalist modernization never did run all that smoothly, and the allegory of progress embedded in the bildungsroman was, in fact, unstable from the beginning (in Scott, in Dickens, in Balzac), so perhaps we should say that what happened was a shift in scale, where the thematics of uneven development attached increasingly to metropole-colony relations within the global frame rather than to urban-rural relations within the national frame.[7] As a matter of empirical literary history, the problem of uneven development became more conspicuous and more colonially coded in the period between 1880 and 1920, and vividly so in fictions of unseasonable youth.

The figure of youth, increasingly untethered in the late Victorian era from the model and telos of adulthood, seems to symbolize the dilated/stunted adolescence of a never-quite-modernized periphery, and thus to register the global asymmetries of capitalism in terms of what Hannah Arendt calls a "permanent process which has no end or aim but itself" (137). Unseasonable youth condenses into the language of character and plot this new, open-ended phase in imperial/finance capitalism. Modernist writers were not, of course, constrained by history to revise the coming-of-age motif nor do modernism's experiments in the disruption of *Bildung* need to be understood exclusively in terms of colonial allegories of failed development. After all, modernist writers were hardly the first to stretch or vex the developmental plot (as a mere mention of *Tristram Shandy* reminds us), and the temporal logic of the bildungsroman has always been more stable in theory than in practice. But the intertwined tropes of frozen youth and uneven development represent something more than just a handy symbolic affinity. As motifs of failed progress, they play a crucial role in the emergence of modernist fiction and in the reimagination of colonial space at the fin de siècle. To begin to develop the argument from a more empirical and inductive base, let us take up the glaring—if somewhat anomalous—example of Kipling's *Kim*, perhaps the most famous novel of imperial adolescence in the English canon.

· · ·

Kipling's Imperial Time

Kim (1900) straddles the nineteenth and twentieth centuries, the frontiers of childhood and adulthood, the worlds of East and West, and the domains of modernist and middlebrow fiction. As an imperial picaresque, Kipling's novel seems to join the rowdy ranks of popular boys' fiction of the late Victorian period. One might well read it as a fantasy of perpetual boyhood, the projection of imperial innocence onto a hero held forever at the threshold of sexual and social adulthood. However, like its contemporary *Lord Jim* (1899), *Kim* is a generically layered text that explores the symbolic and political limits of the coming-of-age plot in the colonial sphere. The absence of a fixed destiny or moral arc for Kim has always raised questions about the end of the novel: is there a genuine resolution or simply a stopping point? Is the novel driven and organized by the conflict-resolution model common to modern realist fiction or is it pieced together as an end-to-end romp, its bravura scenic energy distracting us from pat ideological reconciliation and psychological wish-fulfillment?

These are the questions still under dispute among Kipling critics and readers, who continue to wonder whether Kim's destiny lies in serving as Colonel Creighton's spy in the imperialist Great Game or as the lama's *chela* in a cross-cultural spiritual quest. The debate about *Kim* runs from Cold War scholarship (Wilson, Howe, Annan) to recent postcolonial approaches (Suleri, Said, Parry), suggesting that ideological indeterminacy is an essential feature of the novel's construction.[8] Like so many other early twentieth-century novels, *Kim* refuses to clarify the symbolic status of youth and maturity, refuses to make plot legible as a drive toward moral adulthood. To the running question, "Who is Kim?"—a question fraught with multiple markers (white or not-white? Western or Asiatic? Irish, English, or Indian? boy or man? native or alien? teen-spy or acolyte?)—the novel gives no final, synthetic answer.[9]

Looking back at the end of *Kim* now, Kipling's method for avoiding symbolic closure seems like a clunky bit of misdirection. He shifts attention from Kim's fate to the lama's beatific vision: "I saw all Hind . . . beyond the illusion of Time and Space and of Things" (239). What Zohreh Sullivan calls the "luminous freeze-frame" of this final scene dispels any hint of social division from the fantasy of imperial adolescence (Sullivan 177). It recapitulates the technique central to the whole operation, the subsumption of the narrative into a static and spatial representation of India itself, a pan-subcontinental "vision" that is the ultimate end of both the espionage plot and the religious quest. Kim's identification with the spectacle moots the question of his political affiliation and short-circuits his identity crisis. Presenting India as a knowable, navigable space is Kipling's tactic for managing the antagonisms to which *Kim*, and Kim, are heirs, the perfect way to imply that Pax Britannica is the guarantor, not the enemy, of Asian multiculturalism. From start to finish, the conceit of Kim as a "Little Friend of all the World" makes imperial adolescence the master trope of conflict deferred.

Kipling's use of the boy hero echoes the nostalgic and racially placatory devices central to *Huckleberry Finn* (an homage that makes sense given the young Kipling's devotion to Mark Twain).[10] Like Kim, Huck is an Irish rogue who resists the entwined imperatives of self-cultivation and wealth-accumulation, of storing experience in the coffers of the developing personality. Huck's story ends with a contrived paragraph in which "lighting out for the territory" seems to defer the ideological burdens of adulthood for Huck in much the same way that Kim's promise of endless motion thwarts the logic of closure. One of the costs of this picaresque contrivance is to produce an oddly static plot in both novels: what seems exciting becomes repetitive, then ends with a bit of a thud. Kim's adventures, colorful as they are at the level of dialogue and description, tend to bore readers who crave psychological nuance. When Kim changes in the novel, it is by dint of stagecraft and spy craft; racial transvestism displaces inner development.

With an arrested hero and a static (but kaleidoscopic) representation of India, it would seem that *Kim* fulfills Bakhtin's formula for the bildungsroman by inversion: neither the hero nor the nation emerges into history as a self-possessed entity. Kipling's commitment to the imperial "illusion of permanence" gives shape to a distended plot of adolescence, frozen at the moment of Raj ascendancy, just as Twain gives us a freeze-frame of pre–Civil War America.[11] Such a reading accords with Edward Said's claim that *Kim* is more spectacle than narrative; Said argues that spatial plenitude breeds historical poverty in *Kim*, giving us a nostalgic and tendentious—though not simply jingoistic—view of Anglo-Indian life.[12]

But there is another, more critical side to the text's timelessness, one that becomes more obvious when we read Kim's imperial adolescence alongside other figures of recalcitrant youth in Wilde, Conrad, Joyce, and Woolf. Such a reconstellation shifts the interpretive register away from Kipling's apparent political intentions and toward a consideration of the ideological dimensions of the novel's form. The episodic and ahistorical structure might, in other words, be taken not just as an imperialist fantasy but also as an exposé of the basic contradictions of Anglo-India in 1900—a society held on the brink of national self-possession. Along these lines, Sara Suleri has suggested that Kim's youth testifies to the ultimate futility of the imperial project, which must confront "the necessary perpetuation of its adolescence in relation to its history" (111). Suleri links the most obvious formal and political features of the text:

> Here "imperial time" demands to be interpreted less as a recognizable chronology of historic events than as a contiguous chain of surprise effects: even as empire seeks to occupy a monolithic historic space, its temporality is more accurately characterized as a disruptive sequence of a present tense perpetually surprised, allowing for neither the precedent of the past nor the anticipation of a future. . . . Kipling's narrative internalization of

the superficiality of imperial time engenders both the adolescent energy of his tales and—in a text like *Kim*—the immanence of tragic loss, of an obsessively impelled discourse that lacks any direction in which to go.

(113)

Even before Suleri's, traditional readings of the novel had pointed to the link between Anglo-India's frozen present and Kim's spectacular youth. In *Origins of Totalitarianism* (1951), for example, Hannah Arendt comments on the novel's lack of temporal dynamism. Since the essence of the imperial system is "aimless process," Arendt suggests, it is fitting that the novel's spies and bureaucrats are subsumed into the endless maneuvers of the Great Game. The best symbol of that endless logic is the boy hero himself; after all, "purposelessness is the very charm of Kim's existence" (216–17). Similarly, Noel Annan, in his landmark 1960 essay, "Kipling's Place in the History of Ideas," proposes that the broad realism of *Kim* reflects the new sociological theories of the day (chiefly linked to Weber and Durkheim), which tended to depict order and equilibrium among social groups rather than dynamic historical change or social transformation (Annan 326–27).

The flattened temporality of *Kim*—whether understood as spatial form (Said), imperial time (Suleri), aimless process (Arendt), or static society (Annan)—jibes with a long-standing critical truism about Kipling, which is that he is a skilled storyteller but a flawed novelist, a writer who gives us the immediate journalistic spectacle of Anglo-Indian life, but not the deep motive forces of history.[13] Indeed, Annan's original insight continues to resonate now because it helps explain the depiction of race and caste in *Kim* not so much as barracks-room cliché, but as an effect of the novel's commitment to the present tense, so that difference is registered within a static sociological or anthropological grid. Such a view helps account for the somewhat unsettling fact that Kipling seems both to relativize culture (native ways are as valuable and meaningful as Western ways) and to absolutize race ("No native training can quench the white man's horror of the Serpent," 40). Since political and biographical criticism of Kipling has tended, in the main, to define *Kim* as an imperialist novel, it is important to consider the possibility that the novel's form exceeds the political limitations of its author and lays bare the motif of immaturity as a problem rather than a solution, a self-confessing rather than a self-concealing ruse of the Raj imagination.[14]

Indeed the ahistorical or antidevelopmental logic of the text, manifested in the central motif of immaturity, lays itself bare from the start. *Kim* operates as a set of generic modules, pieces of the "narrative of development" now isolated and objectified so that they are no longer connected or animated by the driving historical pulse of the classic bildungsroman. In this, *Kim* anticipates the other novels examined in later chapters. Destiny becomes a sequence of mutually exclusive prophecies; education is compressed into a few scenes of schooling; ethical growth is displaced from the start by a fixed and spontaneous set of moral instincts; the ideal of self-possession is estranged by the Buddhist concept of self-dispossession; and vocational and sexual closure is, as we have noted, permanently postponed.[15]

These observations are made not simply to restate the limits or virtues of Kipling's "present tense" writing, but to suggest that the novel encourages readers to see that adolescence cannot last forever, and that Kim's fixed youth therefore underwrites a narrative with a surprisingly complex political charge. *Kim* represents colonial India in terms of endless youth; it attaches its hero's maturation to the same receding horizon as India's political modernization. Furthermore, Kim's adolescence—held in narrative abeyance—does not just violate the time scheme of national emergence that is the trademark of the bildungsroman after Goethe, but it also undoes with an almost diagrammatic clarity the formula of vocational/ spiritual compromise lodged at the heart of the classic novel of socialization. Kim's non-choice between spy and *chela* at the end evokes the Goethean ethos—the young hero must freely reconcile inner desires and outer demands, but postpones its fulfillment. Within the narrative frame, Kim never reconciles the competing logic of commerce and culture; he cannot achieve the fundamental synthesis of action (espionage) and contemplation (Buddhism) that was the hallmark of the bourgeois hero. Familiar plot points are thus present, but in an estranged and attenuated form.[16] As a literary device, then, Kim does not simply fall outside the generic conventions of the bildungsroman, but he embodies their transformation in the age of empire.

The colonial arena seems to promise a space for Kim to restore the heroic production of character per se, but the logic of symbolic reconciliation between soulmaking and rationalized work fares no better in colonial precincts than in the industrialized zones of high naturalism. In fact, it is not just the youthful Kim but an entire roster of father figures in the novel who appear to struggle with the Goethean balance of action and contemplation. Each of them—the late Sgt. O'Hara, Col. Creighton, Mahbub Ali, Hurree Babu, Father Bennett, Lurgan Sahib, and the lama—seems either too rash or too passive. No wonder Kim cannot choose a single mentor. Still less does he choose a home that would stabilize the plot—another sharp departure from the classic Victorian orphan plot as typified by, say, *David Copperfield* or *Jane Eyre*. In the place of social mobility understood as a discrete, terminable process within a dynamic class society, Kipling presents social mobility as a potentially endless yet entirely static process.[17]

Within this replotted (deplotted) frame of the bildungsroman, the motif "Who is Kim?" recurs, ostinato, from beginning to end. Adventures pile up, but Kim never really trades disorientation for self-possession. A swooning identity crisis strikes in chapter 7, recurs in chapter 11 ("Who is Kim—Kim—Kim?") and remains unresolved through the final chapter. Even with his mission fulfilled, a feverish Kim cannot stably locate himself within the social machinery of Anglo-India:

> All that while he felt, though he could not put it into words, that his soul was out of gear with its surroundings—a cog-wheel unconnected with any machinery, just like the idle cog-wheel of a cheap Beheea sugar-crusher laid by in a corner . . . "I am Kim. I am Kim. And what is Kim?" His soul repeated it again and again.
>
> (234)

Kipling then tries to reattach his subject-hero to the object-world:

> Roads were meant to be walked upon, houses to be lived in, cattle to be driven, fields to be tilled, and men and women to be talked to. They were all real and true—solidly planted upon the feet.
>
> (234)

The passage marks not so much a symbolic compromise between self and society but a return to mere perception of the ambient spectacle, a fact literalized in the tautologies and passive grammatical constructions ("to be . . . to be") on display. The world of Kim is essentially given, not made and not transformable. The pile of infinitives in the passage ratifies the untensed quality of the whole text and of the closing scene in particular, which becomes a kind of phenomenological paroxysm shared by *chela* and *lama*, lovely in its timeless verity but emptied of historical depth.

All along, Kim is tutored in the art of self-negation by the lama, who campaigns against the ego-centered model of development. It is hard to miss the contrast between the lama's holy Wheel and the linear imperative of self-cultivation enshrined in *Bildung*. The lama fosters the eternal adolescent in Kim, teaching him to strip away not just the accoutrements of whiteness and Britishness, but the impedimenta of subjectivity and desire (162).[18] Even Kim's European mentors—though they may seek to reattach him to his racial (and sexual) privilege as a self with an individual destiny—serve a Great Game whose defining quality is its endlessness. Thus the contest over Kim between Eastern and Western father figures is finally less significant than the fact that Kipling builds the novel so that both sides of the cultural divide represent quests-without-end in a world of sheer adolescent narrativity.

Little wonder, then, that the closural process seems strained and artificial. Kipling uses the logic of arrested development to shape the representation of India as a nation perpetually coming of political age, of the Great Game as an infinite mode of British rule, and of Kim as an open-ended human project. In this constantly shifting but never fundamentally changing political landscape, as Said's reading has reminded us, Indian nationalism is occluded. The novel's fantasy of imperial-adolescent time is predicated on the lack of national-historical time. And yet the fragility of imperial time is finally, if slyly, exposed by the very impossibility of an endless youth. After all, even when closure is eschewed, endings happen, so long as novels come with a terminal period and a last page. This is not just a mundane fact; it is a matter of the novel's inherited relationship to the narrativization of history itself. As I will suggest in more detail in later chapters, the modernist bildungsroman in particular comes with specific closural stakes that are invoked even when the closural plot of adulthood is banished from the text. Even in Kipling's idealized vision of India, antidevelopmental or episodic time must find a way to coexist with some quantum or concept of linear time. Kim's story exposes a tension between developmental and antidevelopmental time that is as germane to the world of the colonial periphery as to his own lingering youth. It is not so much an antibildungsroman converting the linear plot of growth into its opposite (the plot of degeneration) as it is a metabildungsroman laying bare the contingent elements of a progressivist genre formed inside the framework of the nineteenth-century European nation-state.[19]

The meta-generic effect of *Kim* does not, in other words, utterly explode the historical and biographical emplotment devices of classic realist fiction, but rather disrupts the naturalized relationship between souls and nations understood as co-subjects of an allegory of progress. That disruption of the soul-nation allegory runs through all the novels to be examined here, though each has its own idiosyncratic relation to colonial politics and to modernist style. The convergence on the figure of frozen youth by writers as dissimilar as Kipling, Schreiner, Conrad, Wilde, Wells, Woolf, Joyce, Rhys, and Bowen reveals, then, an interlocking set of effects: in this cluster of texts, the perpetuation of adolescence displaces the plot of growth; the inability to make a fortune or stabilize an adult ego displaces the fulfilled vocational and sexual destiny; the mode of sociological or anthropological realism (à la Annan) displaces evolutionary historicism; the static, regressive, and mixed time schemes of the colonial sphere displace the plot of national progress as a normative story of modernization; and the "making strange" of uneven development as a stubborn problem of global or colonial relations replaces its customary naturalization as a feature of national life in industrializing Europe.[20]

To put it concretely, Kipling's antidevelopmental bildungsroman—spatial, episodic, picturesque, above all, adolescent—literalizes the problem of colonialism as failed or postponed modernization, giving an aesthetic form to what Dipesh Chakrabarty calls the endless "not yet" (the permanent deferral of self-rule and self-possession) of imperial history and Western historicism (8). And Kipling's story is only the beginning of a larger one; as it turns out, many canonical works of the late Victorian and modernist period feature colonial themes of backwardness, anachronism, and uneven development that provide the symbolic basis for an anti-teleological model of subject formation. This is the very model of social delay and narrative distension that will, in the hands of Conrad, Joyce, and Woolf, open up space for the novel of consciousness and thereby become the hallmark of modernist style.

. . .

Genre, History, and the Trope of Youth

The case of *Kim* sets in place interpretive strategies used in the rest of this study and raises methodological questions that need to be addressed at some level of generalization. Let me enumerate four areas for initial reflection:

1) The Politics of Genre: What does it mean to argue that changes in literary form and style register or reflect broader or deeper changes in history? How does the trope of frozen youth—in *Kim* or any other novel—address the shape of uneven development within the colonial world-system? If we grant that the bildungsroman was *already* a complex and ambiguous form even in its so-called classic phase, is the shift in scale from national to international development enough to trigger a reorganization of the genre?

2) Questions of Periodization: Is it plausible and productive to isolate a short phase within the longer narrative of European colonialism? By what critical method can we meaningfully link the "age of empire" to the complex literary-historical phenomenon of modernism? How exactly, beyond historical coincidence, do the crisis of European realism and the shifting temporal contours of the bildungsroman intersect with the rise of the new imperialism?

3) Sexuality and Gender: How are the traditional closural plots of the bildungsroman, particularly heterosexual coupling and marriage, affected and inflected

by feminist and queer experience? Even within the restricted domain of British/ Anglophone fiction, can the varieties of frozen and failed adolescence (some tragic, some not; some male, some female) be referred to the same literary-historical account?

4) The Soul-Nation Allegory: Are the novels examined here describing a breakdown in the allegorical function of the coming-of-age plot itself or are they extending its allegorical function into an era of globally uneven development, wherein progress is no longer symbolically safeguarded by the promises of organic nationalism? What, in other words, does it look like to allegorize uneven development in a world-system rather than in a national container?

The Politics of Genre

To begin to answer the first set of questions, let us take *Kim* as both an exemplary and an anomalous case. Unlike many of the youthful protagonists at the center of this study, Kim is a mixed-race character. Neither he nor his author (an Anglo-Indian) fits neatly into a colonizer-colonized binary. As Kim roams freely over the subcontinent, one can attribute the author's command of detail either to an arrogant colonialist sense of possession or to a naturalized sense of belonging. In this sense, Kipling seems an odd case, the arch-imperialist who is also a colonial native.[21] Yet most of the writers examined in this book also resist the interpretive schema of colonizer-colonized, particularly if one takes into account the variety not just of national origins but also of apparent political attitudes toward the British Empire. In the chapters that follow, we will find the narrative logic of arrested development in works by semi-English imperialists (Kipling), English anti-imperialists (Woolf), English semi-imperialists (Wells), non-English anti-imperialists (Jean Rhys), non-English semi-imperialists (Olive Schreiner), non-English part-time anti-imperialists (Conrad), as well as in Catholic Irish and Anglo-Irish writers of disparate backgrounds, views, and temperaments (Wilde, Joyce, Bowen).

The trope of unseasonable youth runs across the colonial divide, though its meaning and function vary according to the particular experience of empire described or represented. For example, Joyce's brand of social critique is shaped by an Irish history of colonial domination in a way that Woolf's surely is not, but Joyce and Woolf nevertheless share a suspicion of imperial patriarchy rooted in British power. In *Kim*, as we have noted, the temporal logic of deferral and dilation structures the entire text; it is not ascribed to people or social relations on one side or the other of the Anglo-Indian line. The versatility of the trope of adolescence in the colonial contact zone makes historical as well as symbolic sense.[22] As many commentators have noted, imperialism generally casts its subject peoples not as radically different, but as an underdeveloped or youthful version of their rulers, not quite ready for self-government. But imperialism also casts its own agency as youthful and rejuvenating; its beneficiaries are rendered young outside the finite markets and social constraints of the Old World. Perhaps especially in the British sphere, colonialism involves not just the Hegelian dehistoricization of the colonized as backward or timeless but also the dehistoricization of the European subject as juvenescent. Hannah Arendt describes the sociology of imperial youth with particular regard to the English experience:

> Only those who had never been able to outgrow their boyhood ideals and therefore had enlisted in the colonial services were fit for the task. Imperialism to them was nothing but an accidental opportunity to escape a society in which a man had to forget his youth if he wanted to grow up . . . the colonial services took them away from England and prevented, so to speak, their converting the ideals of their boyhood into the mature ideas of men. Strange and curious lands attracted the best of England's youth since the end of the nineteenth century, deprived her society of the most honest and the most dangerous elements, and guaranteed, in addition to this bliss, a certain conservation, or perhaps petrification, of boyhood noblesse which preserved *and* infantilized Western moral standards.
>
> (211)

This petrified boyhood *noblesse* no doubt forms a crucial and visible part of the ruling ideology propagated among elite institutions in Victorian Britain. Empire was, after all, the raison d'être of the "character factory" of the British educated classes: its neotraditional notion of soulmaking offered a cover story for the grubbier work of imperial rule (Rosenthal). One can also see the logic of petrification writ large in the influential formulations of the historians Tom Nairn and Perry Anderson, who have argued that empire retarded the political and cultural modernization of Britain altogether (Nairn 57; Anderson 24).

In *Kim*, of course, it is India's modernization that appears stuck while the Great Game cycles on, promising constant activity and no structural change. For this reason, Kipling's Great Game stands as a peculiarly apt motif to introduce the literary crux of my analyses: the fact that endless youth signifies both absent change (no growth) and constant change (continuous transformation). Unseasonability in my book's title refers to youth out of joint—endlessly adolescent or suddenly aged, sophomoric or progeriac, subject to what Nietzsche called with almost uncanny

Eurocentric aptness the "tropical tempo" that manifests a "fateful simultaneity of spring and autumn" (qtd. in Marshall Berman 22). Turned loose in modernist texts, the trope of autonomous youth reveals the contingent, even fragile, logic of the old bildungsroman in which soul and nation grow together, then stop. Once that formula is destabilized, it becomes difficult to distinguish between no change and constant change. So, for example, Kipling's India does not assume the form of an organic nation pegged to teleological time, but rather an endlessly morphing multicultural state with no clear or final political form. Everything is always changing in this game, but the game itself does not change. This is the quality of imperial time that stands behind both Francis Hutchins's "illusion of permanence" and Frantz Fanon's description of the "immobility to which the native is condemned," planted in a "motionless Manicheistic world, a world of statues" (51).[23] My guiding thesis, then, is that colonialism introduces into the historicist frame of the bildungsroman the form-fraying possibility that capitalism cannot be moralized into the progressive time of the nation.

The case of *Kim* suggests some of the wider implications of this argument: the novel seems, on the one hand, to express a pro-British fantasy of endless rule and benign interculturation packaged in the marketable story of a shape-shifting, code-switching, eternally boyish hero. On the other hand, *Kim* discloses the basic temporal contradiction of the Raj: It wants to go on forever but cannot. It encodes both an imperialist fantasy about the "immature" colonial world and a countervailing critical insight into the temporal paradox of empire. Because these two substrates of the text coexist, and particularly in view of Kipling's fallen reputation, it makes sense to adopt a formal approach to the text rather than an identitarian or intentionalist approach to its author, characters, or readers.[24]

A formalist approach immediately raises the question of definition: what stabilizes the term *bildungsroman* across eras of literary history and across different national traditions? The genre can be loosened to include almost any novel where experience trumps innocence or tightened to a fine point where no novel fits. If we follow the latter, stricter impulse, we will look in vain for a *true* bildungsroman, tumbling quickly backward through literary history from Rushdie and Morrison, to Woolf and Joyce, to Hardy and Eliot, to Dickens and Brontë and Balzac, to Austen and Scott and Fielding, and, finally, even to Goethe himself, whose *Wilhelm Meister*, most Germanists now agree, appears to violate most of the generic rules invoked in its honor.[25] The fact that the genre is both ubiquitous and "missing" has been well established by Jeffrey Sammons and further explored in a superb book by Marc Redfield, who argues that the bildungsroman is a "phantom formation." Redfield's poststructuralist ghosting of the genre makes sense, but the concept of *Bildung* has shaped literary criticism and practice for generations—a fact not altered by its nonfulfillment in any given text.²⁶ Indeed, genres are almost always empty sets that shape literary history by their negation, deviation, variation, and mutation. Such deviations can themselves be tracked, grouped, and historicized.²⁷ Although the bildungsroman's unmaking is always coeval with its making (in literary history writ large as well as in individual texts), it remains worthwhile to try to see patterns in the process of its unmaking and even—at a metacritical level—to explain why a phantom genre is such a recurrent object of literary and theoretical desire.

For the purposes of my larger argument, then, I take the bildungsroman as a generic ideal more than an empirical object or set in literary history, though I do not reject the positivist genre history of Bakhtin-Lukács altogether. After all, even complex and internally self-divided genres age over time, and it is the aging of the bildungsroman through and past the era of the emergent nation-state that motivates my inquiry. In what follows, the generic target encompasses texts with youthful protagonists whose growth is central and conspicuous, either as a narrative presence or a genuinely marked absence. Thus, for example, *Lord Jim* fits better than does *Heart of Darkness*. In the traditional bildungsroman, youth drives narrative momentum until adulthood arrives to fold youth's dynamism into a conceit of uneventful middle age.²⁸ In the set of youth-fixated novels I have identified, though, youth retains its grip on the center of the text, disorganizing and distending the plot.

In that way, the belated and revisionary *bildungsromane* of modernism bring to a logical extreme some of the familiar contradictions of the genre. One such hoary contradiction stems from what Thomas Pfau calls (in the spirit of Redfield's argument) the epigenetic quality of *Bildung*, its designation of "what has been brought forth and likewise what is in the process of being brought forth" (141). Modernism, perhaps because it is so obviously an epigenetic and self-begetting movement in its own right, seems to accentuate this contradiction in the bildungsroman. Modernist novels of unseasonable youth violate a progressive logic that they presume to have existed, resist a linear historicism that is in part projected back onto Victorian realism by writers eager to assume the mantle of an experimental literary future. Moreover, since this study confines itself largely to famous books—visible islands in a vast sea of unread novels, as much recent literary history and sociology has reminded us—the patterns of genre change apprehended here tell us as much about canon formation as about the empirical reading practices or distribution of texts in either the Victorian or modernist period. Canonical selection reveals our ongoing reinvention of modernism as a redress to Victorian historical consciousness as well as to modernism's own prejudicial account of the Victorian mind as slavishly historical. But even if we recognize the extent to which modernist studies continues even now to require a transcended Victorian/realist other, it is nonetheless worth stating that modernism's own anxiety of Victorian influence seems to have activated new and splendid possibilities for the English novel. And we can use genre history to identify the special capacity of modernist texts to give literary form to the collapse of progressive historicism as an organizing idea of European modernity and therefore of the European novel.

This project takes shape at a moment of resurgent interest in the bildungsroman, particularly within twentieth-century studies, where scholars have been concerned to think about its history as both a Western and non-Western genre.[29] Franco Moretti has written a new conclusion to *The Way of the World*, covering the early phases of modernism. Gregory Castle, too, has published a systematic study of the bildungsroman, arguing for the renewed vitality of the genre in the early twentieth century. In a strong series of essays, Tobias Boes has begun to replot the modern bildungsroman in German and English against a late nineteenth-century crisis of historical experience. Working out of the same German philosophical tradition, Joseph Slaughter has tracked the enlightenment ideal of the individual's "free and full development" into both the contemporary postcolonial novel and the modern discourse of human rights law (4). And in *Fateful Beauty*, Douglas Mao offers an elegant historicization of the increasing, multidisciplinary interest in the environmental shaping of young souls during the late Victorian period, with many implications for the changing shape of the coming-of-age novel after 1860.

Mao's work, building on Patricia Spacks's classic account of literary youth, establishes an intellectual and social-scientific context for the late Victorian novel of development, in particular the newly codified concept of adolescence embodied in G. Stanley Hall's 1904 compendium *Adolescence*.[30] For Mao, the professional and scientific, medical and juridical languages of adolescence emergent in the period are strongly resonant with aestheticist accounts of the environment's shaping power over the young mind. In both kinds of discourse, every social input, every exquisite detail, counts in the subject-forming process:

> We might say that the novel of formation had to reach a watershed when development became a matter of continuous shaping by the totality of one's surroundings, of often silent and invisible molding by factors human, inhuman, and quasi-human. The traditional bildungsroman, with its dependence on crisis, example, reflection, and socialization, could hardly have seemed adequate to this understanding of growth.

(96–97)

Mao's account suggests from a different angle of analysis why the problem of an endlessly unfolding youth was so central to the late bildungsroman: It was coming to seem a process without (narratable) bounds, either spatial or temporal.

The power of reification and social determinism to reshape the discourse of self-development is a central premise for Mao as it is for Moretti and for Castle.[31] All three cite the general rationalization and institutionalization of youth as a challenge to the bildungsroman's aesthetic viability.[32] But where Castle and Mao emphasize the new and often rich narrative strategies imagined in response to these circumstances, Moretti proposes a more Darwinian thesis, according to which modernism had to abandon the bildungsroman and seek new formal possibilities for the novel. For him, the genre no longer presides over the symbolic adjustment of protagonists to their place in bourgeois society, nor does it sustain the master allegory of modernization that was so successfully inscribed in the nineteenth-century bildungsroman. Youth "looks now for its meaning within itself," suggests Moretti, so that the "relevant symbolic process is no longer growth but regression" (*Way* 231). In addition to the growing power of school, state, and mass media to cut into the old Schillerian ideal of a self-cultivating aesthete, Moretti argues that World War I finally shattered an already dying genre by destroying the fabric of intergenerational exchange and evacuating the residual heroic elements from the European concept of the rite of passage.[33]

Questions of Periodization

This book largely pivots on the year 1900 (the date of *Kim*'s publication) with its core decades corresponding roughly to what Eric Hobsbawm calls the "age of empire" (1875–1914). Hobsbawm, like Hannah Arendt in *Origins of Totalitarianism*, focuses on the quickening and formalizing of European colonialism in the 1870s and 1880s—a global process for which the Berlin Conference of 1884–1885 stands as a concrete marker. Arendt defines high imperialism in terms of the eclipse of national by international capitalism (135). The centuries-long history of exploitative slave and colonial economies notwithstanding, Arendt's characterization of this era as inaugurating a new phase of unrestrained capitalist relations outside the national boundaries and moral limits of middle-class progress proves, I think, quite telling for literary history in general and for the bildungsroman in particular.[34] Arendt's account—taken alongside any number of literary studies such as Edward Said's *Culture and Imperialism* or Fredric Jameson's "Modernism and Imperialism"—provides a suggestive colonial gloss on what Lukács described as a

European "crisis of bourgeois realism" rooted in the failure of the 1848 revolutions (85, 174).[35] Lukács's account overlaps with Arendt's not just chronologically but in its explanatory logic, suggesting in broad terms that the crisis of realism in the novel is coterminous with the end of the national-industrial phase of European modernization. What mediates between his history of forms and her history of socioeconomic structures is the faltering concept of progress driven by the middle classes of the Western nations, a concept whose fictional incarnation was the bildungsroman.

Arendt and Lukács also converge in their analysis of the imperial era as the moment when a certain kind of racialized thinking became entrenched within European capitalism, with broad ideological repercussions that disrupt the middle-class commitment to social mobility. For Arendt—particularly in her analysis of colonial South Africa—and for Lukács—particularly in his analysis of Darwinian and Nietzschean thought, the regressive logic of racialism, a biologized apotheosis of instrumental reason and social hierarchy, began in the later nineteenth century to replace the progressive elements of the European bourgeoisie's project of modernization (Arendt 159; Lukács, *Historical Novel* 175).[36] Lukács translates this left-liberal thesis about a rigidifying and regressive bourgeois ideology into literary history as a crisis in the novel, which was drained of its socially representative protagonists, left without the dynamic plot of social mobility, and emptied of the historical depth associated with classic realism. Many rightly view the Lukácsian story as schematic, and its provenance and chronology are clearly more continental than Anglophone or global. Nonetheless, if we understand its effects to unfold gradually in the several decades after 1850, it begins to resonate with what most English-oriented literary historians would see as the displacement of the realist social novel by naturalist elements and, more specifically, the displacement of socially integrative Victorian *bildungsromane* such as *David Copperfield* and *Jane Eyre* by the plot of disillusionment and alienation.

Arrested development is such a vital trope for modernist fiction because it travels across several intellectual domains in the late Victorian period, from psychological theories of the subject to biopolitical theories of social antagonism to economic theories of industrial stagnation to anthropological theories of structuralized difference to geoeconomic theories of colonial immiseration. The faltering developmental logic in these various realms or zones can be defined in terms of the historiographical crisis in the narrative of progress and the interlocking political crisis of imperial legitimacy. For the remainder of the book, I will use the phrase "age of empire" to signal this multipronged discursive model centered in the 1880–1920 period.[37] The 1880s also mark, of course, the beginning of the end of

European expansion with the African scramble and the Berlin Conference. Only three decades later, V. I. Lenin famously remarked that "for the first time, the world is now divided up, so that in the future *only re-divisions* are possible" (70). We can thus conceive of this period not just as a fin de siècle, but as a *fin du globe*, in which imperial growth, which had become by then the spatial confirmation of Western progress, reached its earthly limits.[38] With no new territory to annex, the European powers faced new pressure to cast the extant colonies as eternally adolescent, always developing but never developed enough.

Sexuality and Gender

The intellectual contours of the larger crisis of progress sketched earlier are well documented in political and cultural histories of the late Victorian period; literary analysis allows us to examine them in relation to fine textual details and intimate vocabularies of identity. As we interpret the inner life of youthful characters in modernist writing, it helps to remember that arrested development discourse in the period applied to a raft of social others, such as women, natives, and queer subjects.[39] These putatively immature subjects stand out in relief against residual but still normative progress narratives and resonate with emergent counternarratives of degeneration, decadence, and rebarbarization. In this volatile discursive field, queer and colonial versions of underdevelopment or "backwardness" intersect, as a variety of minority subjects—what we might call Europe's internal and external others—are concatenated together in a more insistently global field of culture. Indeed the project of exploring failed or frozen *Bildung* in the Anglophone novel could be pursued under the aegis of queer studies (or gender studies) as well as colonial discourse studies. Most of the novels of colonial adolescence examined here resist or forestall the traditional plot of libidinal closure in the bildungsroman (heterosexual coupling and reproduction) and feature instead story lines driven by homoerotic investment, sexual indifference, homosexual panic, and same-sex desire.[40] Sorted together, sexually dissident protagonists such as Lord Jim (Conrad), Rachel Vinrace (Woolf), Lois Farquar (Bowen), Dorian Gray (Wilde), and Stephen Dedalus (Joyce) suggest a deep epochal link between the queer/adolescent and the colonial/native as twin subjects of arrested-development discourse.

Neville Hoad has examined that convergence in some detail, charting the alignment between colonial discourses of the native/savage and sexological discourses of the homosexual. Hoad zeroes in on the fact that, during the age of empire, so-called immature subjects came to represent much larger problems of uneven development:

> The understanding of "homosexuality" as the marker of western decadence par excellence may also suggest ways in which the person laying claim to homosexual identity in an era of global capitalism can be made to carry the anxieties surrounding the social ruptures produced by economic development.
>
> (152)

If we combine Hoad's analysis of arrested development and Heather Love's account of historical backwardness with Michael Warner's challenge to "repro-narrativity" and Lee Edelman's brief for queer (non)futurity, we can adduce a composite model of the queer figure who holds a position outside dominant discourses of progress at the level of individual self-formation and of social reproduction. From this point of view, the novels examined here comprise a colonially inflected subset of the larger modernist group in which the marriage plot is marginalized, and in which even heterosexual romance is queered so that it no longer stands as the allegorical basis for reconciling social antagonisms or projecting a national future. That larger set would include a number of queer and belated coming-of-age novels by England-based writers such as Lawrence, Forster, Ford, H. D., Radclyffe Hall, and Sylvia Townsend Warner.[41]

Of course the troubling of the marriage plot was already a fixture of the female bildungsroman in the nineteenth century. Woman-authored and woman-centered texts in the British canon often deviate from and disrupt the generic template, checkering the history of the bildungsroman. Several scholars have recounted that gendered history in rich detail: Rita Felski (*Beyond Feminist Aesthetics*), Susan Fraiman (*Unbecoming Women*), Sandra Gilbert and Susan Gubar (*Madwoman in the Attic*), Elaine Showalter (*A Literature of Their Own*), Patricia Spacks (*The Adolescent Idea*), and the editors of the collection *The Voyage In* (Elizabeth Abel, Marianne Hirsch, and Elizabeth Langland).[42] Building on their work, my readings explore the ways in which a feminist critique of the representative soul becomes more conspicuous in the late Victorian period and takes on a more global dimension in the age of empire. Many novels of rebellious girlhood and fixed youth in the period seem to be fueled by a joint critique of patriarchal and imperial norms of development. In the chapters to come, I follow a trajectory from George Eliot in 1860 to Olive Schreiner in 1883 through to the early 1900s with modernists such as Jean Rhys, Virginia Woolf, and Elizabeth Bowen, tracking a gendered logic of provincial failure from its national to its international expression.[43]

The Soul-Nation Allegory

The great novels of that lineage of women writers expose the ideological under-pinnings of the bildungsroman as a genre of male destiny and heroic moderniza-tion. For example, in Schreiner's *African Farm* and in Rhys's *Voyage in the Dark*, provincial or colonial girls meditate on the implausibility of conceiving the indi-vidual self as some kind of avatar for national destiny. Their gendered suspicion of allegorization itself underscores a crucial dimension of this book's larger argu-ment, which is that there are two distinct strategies used to expose the conven-tional alignment between personal destiny and national eschatology: 1) the broken allegory, in which the link between individual and collective is untethered and laid bare rather than naturalized as a principle of composition; and 2) the negative alle-gory, in which individuals continue to represent collective or national destinies, but not necessarily in the upward direction of moral or historical progress. The first explodes the very possibility of allegory, the second preserves it but peels it away from the tenets of what David Lloyd calls "developmental historicism" (*Irish Times* 75). In practice, of course, the two strategies overlap. The bildungsroman's biographical form was for generations yoked to a progressive concept of national destiny, so that to emplot a nonprogressive version of national-historical time is almost automatically to trouble the inherited allegorical platform of the genre. If the generic ideal implies, per Bakhtin, a plot of masculine self-formation that both shapes and is shaped by national historical time, then a novel that disrupts prog-ress also casts doubt on the basic symbolic adequacy of the individual life span to the representation of (national) history. The novels to be examined in this study freely trade between these two strategies of metageneric critique in order to high-light the waning vitality or plausibility of the old bildungsroman formulae and their organic conceptions of self and nation.

As the genre transforms and adapts to new historical conditions, a central ques-tion is whether it still performs what Moretti sees as its two classic functions: to make modernity's endless revolution narratable and to secure middle-class consent through a realist narrative of vocational-spiritual compromise. The modernist pres-sure on bildungsroman conventions goes beyond raising the possibility that the genre can no longer serve those functions; it also raises the possibility that it never did. This is the point driving Thomas Pfau's subtle approach to the genealogy of the *Bildung* concept in modern fiction. Pfau isolates a cluster of modern German writ-ers, including Spengler and Mann, to argue that "modernism effectively reverses the epigenetic and developmental confidence of nineteenth-century narrative," bringing out "the long-repressed implications of Goethean organicism" (155).

Organicist logic is also the central concern in Pheng Cheah's compelling study of the bildungsroman as a global and postcolonial genre with its origins in German idealism. Taken together, Pfau and Cheah establish a philosophical genealogy of *Bildung* that clarifies the literary-historical trajectory of the bildungsroman as it becomes an increasingly global fictional genre. Building on their insights, we might say that modernism accentuates the inherent contradiction of an organicist logic whose role was to stabilize (temporally and epistemologically) the course of history by representing it in terms of the human biography or life story. Why, Moretti wonders about the classic bildungsroman, did "modern Western civilization discard such a perfect narrative mechanism"? (*Way* 72). My hypothesis is that the function of the national frame within that narrative mechanism was crucial, but was also as time-limited as the German-idealist notion of self-cultivation. As the national referent was increasingly embedded in the matrix of colonial modernity, the destinies of persons, and the peoples they represent, had to include not only the story of progress, but also stories of stasis, regression, and hyperdevelopment. Modernism's untimely youths—Woolf's Rachel Vinrace, Conrad's Lord Jim, Joyce's Stephen Dedalus—register the unsettling effects of the colonial encounter on humanist ideals of national culture that had always, from the time of Goethe and Schiller, determined the inner logic of the bildungsroman. Separating adolescence from the dictates of *Bildung*, modernist writing created an autonomous value for youth and cleared space for its own resistance to linear plots while registering the failure of imperialism as a discourse of global development. The genre-bending logic of uneven development—never wholly absent from the genre—thus takes on a new and more intense form in modernism as it fixes its etiolated and broken allegories to the uncertain future of a colonial world-system.

. . .

Modernist Subjectivity and the World-System

The types of unseasonable youth in modernist fiction are as various as the novels themselves, and each novel to be considered in the chapters ahead reveals in its turn a different facet of the formal and historical problematic outlined so far. In what remains of this introduction, I will present a critical overview of those different facets and conclude by contextualizing this research within debates about Eurocentrism, political formalism, and the new modernist studies. To unfold the book's larger argument requires a detailed account of how Bakhtin's concept of national-historical time works as a matter of emplotment in both nineteenth- and twentieth-century fiction. I develop that argument in chapter 2 by stepping back in my timeline to investigate a major Victorian novel, George Eliot's *Mill on the Floss* (1860). Because Eliot is often taken to mark the end of the bildungsroman's "classic" phase and because she is also a key disseminator of German thought into British letters, I concentrate on her work, but briefly consider other Victorian novels by, for example, Dickens and Charlotte Brontë.

The central premise that emerges from that return to the Victorian period, and that organizes much of the subsequent interpretive work on modernist-era texts, is that a national-cultural system in the emergent phase of European industrialization could mediate between unevenly developed regions (e.g., city and country) in ways that, during a later phase, neither a multinational imperial state nor a capitalist world-system could.[44] By anchoring the bildungsroman in a Goethe-Schiller origin story, we do not simply rehearse shopworn genealogies, but remind ourselves that the history of the novel enfolds and overlaps with the emergent power of national culture to manage the symbolic relations between otherwise antagonistic regions and classes. Nations contain and naturalize the problem of uneven development by appeal to a common culture, language, and destiny; their organicist claims underlie a reciprocal allegory of development with the representative soul. As I suggest in the chapters that follow, such claims cannot really be sustained by the inorganic entities of the modern state, the baggy empire, or the acultural world-system.

The return to George Eliot (or Dickens) also supplies a critical test case for my hypothesis that the national referent was, however tacitly at the level of content or theme, vital to the nineteenth-century bildungsroman's ability to bring its story to closure. Adulthood and nationhood were the twin symbolic termini for the endless and originless processes of self-formation and social transformation. To kick that formula into historical motion, then: If the chronotope of national *Bildung* loses force as a symbolic device toward the end of the Victorian age, what kind of closural plot becomes operative, particularly in the face of an open-ended process of socioeconomic modernization spreading ever wider on the planet? Naturalist fate is one grim solution to the narrative problem. The modernist figure of unseasonable youth is another, one that keeps secular historicism at the core of the modern novel yet unsettles the protocols of a genre that can no longer restrict the story of progress to the symbolic confines of the nation-state.

Without the national frame securely in place, modernist novels confront afresh the challenge of circumscribing an unbounded capitalist modernity. The interlocking narrative and geopolitical problems of the late bildungsroman can thus be said to circle around the specter of Hegelian "bad infinity." Hegel develops the concept of the "spurious infinite" (*schlecht Unendlichkeit*) in his *Science of Logic*. The essence of his point is that a spurious infinity is one defined in direct and full contradistinction to the finite, so that it could be exemplified by a numerical series that goes on forever or, indeed, by a temporally blank conception of history as moments unfolding into the future without end. This technical discussion in Hegel becomes more relevant in Marx, who assigns to capitalism itself something of the nature of spurious infinitude.[45] Still more relevant is Lukács's adaptation of the concept in *The Theory of the Novel*: he argues that the novel lacks the self-sufficient and organic enclosure of the epic and so must lean on the biographical form or individual "life story" to create a finite span as a hedge against the potential endlessness of modern secular narrative. In the passage taken as this chapter's epigraph, Lukács summarizes his point: "The novel overcomes its 'bad infinity' by recourse to the biographical form" (81). This maneuver underlies what Moretti describes as the basic counterrevolutionary impulse of texts that find a way to arrest the revolutionary energies of nascent capitalism and political democracy in order to secure and stabilize bourgeois society. More specifically still, we might say that the classic realist novel used the organic finitude of biographical form and national form alike to enclose the bad infinity of a narrative that would otherwise have no objective limits. Such a formulation gives some political grounding to the philosophical formalism of Lukács's *Theory of the Novel*, and thereby gives us a way to extend the Lukácsian models (including Moretti's) into the era of globalization/modernism. The trope of unseasonable youth defines modernism's historical encounter with the problem of bad infinity at the existential and geopolitical levels, establishing the conditions for a provisional aesthetic solution—the metabildungsroman, which encodes the impossibility of representing global capitalism's never-ending story via the offices of finite biographical form.[46]

To freeze and stylize youth is to write the novel of modernity as permanent revolution. It gives a new kind of symbolic justice to the open metanarrative of globalization; put otherwise, it announces the growing obsolescence of national allegory as a device for inscribing European nation-state formation as the end of history.[47] Without the moralizing time of the soul-nation allegory, the bildungsroman becomes the story of modernity's unfinished project condensed into the trope of endless youth. As the example of *Kim* would indicate, frozen youth (no change) is often narratively isomorphic with endless youth (constant change): Both refuse the bildungsroman ideal of smooth progress toward a final, integrated state. So too at the level of social transformation: Without the temporal frame of nationhood, collective change cannot be grasped in a stable epistemological context (so long, that is, as historiographical knowledge continues to be shaped by its Enlightenment roots). In the readings that follow, the problem of static or insufficient development thus mirrors and is entailed by the problem of constant or hyper-development.

The problem of uneven development troped as unseasonable youth is made concrete in novels of the new global frontier such as *The Story of an African Farm* and *Lord Jim*, which I examine in chapter 3. The two novels are separated by a gendered logic featuring the colonial woman and imperial man as the failed subjects, respectively, of provincialism and cosmopolitanism. Yet both describe protagonists who cannot age, and whose fatal immaturity seems to align with a demoralized, nonprogressive temporality. In this pairing of novels, we see that both local traditionalism and global capitalism, without the mediating political and symbolic force of nationality, can seem like parallel versions of historyless-ness. Once cut free from its embedded teleologies, the trope of adolescence reveals the cruel lesson, made vivid in Schreiner's *African Farm*, that endless youth is merely the obverse of sudden death. Without age—or, to be more precise, without aging—youth mutates from a figure of vitality into the very sign of lifelessness. For Lord Jim, too, languishing unmoored in the extranational tropics, life is a sentence of bad infinities: either all youth (the narrative never ends) or sudden death (the narrative only ends).

In *Lord Jim*, the traditional protagonist who embodies a progressive or linear model of history is eclipsed by a protagonist who registers the contradictions of an era split into multiple and conflicting temporalities of under- and overdevelop-ment. Jim is an Edward Waverley for the early twentieth century: not the national hero, but the postnational anti-hero, the overripe lord identified by Nietzsche in the epigraph to this chapter.[48] In what is a dichotomy rather than a dialectic of youth-and-age, Marlow has assimilated the endlessness of imperial capitalism in the form of salty pragmatism, always already mature, and Jim has assimilated that same endlessness in the form of saccharine idealism, forever immature.

For the protagonists of *Story of an African Farm* and *Lord Jim*, situated at the colonial frontier and on the early cusp of modernism, the problem of vocational failure translates into a narrative short-circuit from youth to death. The split between empire disguised as a higher calling and empire exposed as capitalism in the raw exacerbates the main contradiction papered over by the old Goethean spiritual-vocational compromise, revealing that soulmaking and wage-earning are no easier to reconcile abroad than at home. Whether they end with a frozen corpse or a frozen youth (or both) at their center, these novels conspicuously evade the closural plot of adulthood and the harmonic social integration it implies. The problem of arrested development as a marker of modernist selfhood thus cuts two ways: It denotes a certain kind of metropolitan privilege, but it also denotes a split subjectivity unable to integrate or reconcile opposing forces. Colonial plots of frozen youth reflect and intensify the fissile logic of high modernism, in which subject formation is simultaneously more and less free than ever before— beholden at once to a Proustian logic of deep interiority and a Kafkaesque logic of cold objectivity.[49]

The trope of frozen youth guides us into modernist fictions of failed development in both colonial contact zones and metropolitan core territories of the world-system. In the cases of Schreiner and Conrad, the non-accumulation of wealth at the colonial periphery provides an obvious analogue for stalled *Bildung*, but in the novels of Oscar Wilde (*The Picture of Dorian Gray*, 1891) and H. G. Wells (*Tono-Bungay*, 1909), we find new economic phenomena—high consumerism, rabid marketing, and financial speculation—spooling out of all proportion to any stable narrative of production or of self-production. In these two London-based novels, plots of exorbitant immaturity play out against the backdrop of a spectacular new phase in imperial-finance capitalism. By framing the *metabildungsromane* of Wilde and Wells within the problematic of bad infinity, we can see the displacement of aesthetic education and self-cultivation in the Goethean tradition by uneven processes of consumption and commodification—processes that are, even in their metropolitan contexts, clearly linked to both the endless imperial expansion of capitalist markets and the endless cycles of new consumer desires. Both Dorian Gray's hollow consumption and George Ponderevo's spurious production require a global frame of economic reference.

The somewhat unusual pairing of Wilde with Wells in chapter 4 expands, I think, the standard approach to *Dorian Gray*, which tends to refer the novel's supernatural conceit to the symbolic demands of bohemian, aestheticist, cosmopolitan, and queer subject formation.[50] The protomodernist Wilde and semimodernist Wells represent different angles of remove from the nineteenth-century bildungsroman: Neither Wilde's residually aristocratic values nor Wells's emergent lower-middle-class values quite fit into the story line of the realist coming-of-age plot; and neither Wilde's aphoristic and lurid neogothic tale nor Wells's prolix and didactic "anti-novel" conforms to the tonal discipline of classic or Jamesian realism. Both writers self-consciously take apart the narrative pieces of the bildungsroman (education, courtship, apprenticeship, disillusionment, adventure, journey, self-doubt, bankruptcy). Both describe crippled egos who are disintegrated into mere functions rather than integrated into a harmonious personality. These plots of slow decay and sudden overdevelopment give us an unusually clear glimpse of the bildungsroman in the process of mutating from a genre of middle-class consent to a genre of unreconciled social contradictions. Wilde and Wells embed the motif of broken *Bildung* in a wider story of the disjunction between capitalist dynamism (consumerist lust, rampant financial speculation, bottomless energy needs) and national tradition. At the thematic level, they activate the tension that was always latent in the bildungsroman between youth-as-plot and adulthood-as-closure. At the allegorical level, they activate a similarly latent tension between modernization processes that never stop and national discourses that posit origins and ends.[51]

The pairing of works by Wilde and Wells cuts across the Anglo-Irish line, as does the subsequent pairing of Woolf and Joyce in chapter 5. The early fictions of Woolf and Joyce bring us to the eve of World War I, one of several key moments we can use to punctuate this history of the late bildungsroman. At the threshold of high modernism, we find not just the bristling, blustery emergence of the poetic "men of 1914," but also a strikingly high concentration of major novelists publishing stories of unseasonable or doomed youth, all in the same three-year span: Proust (*Du côté de chez Swann*, 1913), Lawrence (*Sons and Lovers*, 1913), Alain-Fournier (*Le Grand Meaulnes* in 1913), Woolf (*Voyage Out*, 1915), Maugham (*Of Human Bondage*, 1915), Kafka (*Die Verwandlung*, 1915), Ford (*The Good Soldier*, 1915), and Joyce (*Portrait of the Artist*, 1916).[52] To this list we might add Freud's *Totem and Taboo* (1913) and Lukács's *The Theory of the Novel* (written 1914–1915), both of which concern the question of developmental narrative as well as the regression and adolescence of the metropolitan subject, as if to foretoken the outbreak of the Great War that would demystify the European tradition of heroic youth.[53]

Most accounts of the cultural history of World War I emphasize the profound destruction it visited upon young bodies and on the intergenerational transmission of European culture—in particular, on the humanizing, spiritualizing images of education so central to the canonical novel of youth.[54] Moretti remarks of the postwar literary world:

> The trauma introduced discontinuity within novelistic temporality, generating centrifugal tendencies toward the short story and the lyric; it disrupted the unity of the Ego, putting the language of selfconsciousness out of work. . . . In the end, nothing was left of the form of the *Bildungsroman*: a phase of Western socialization had come to an end, a phase the *Bildungsroman* had both represented and contributed to.
>
> (*Way* 244)

In addition to Moretti's claim that World War I dealt a death blow to a genre already moribund by the 1890s, we have Walter Benjamin's influential essay "The

Storyteller," which casts the war as the definitive event that broke the chain of experience carried by stories across generational lines.[55] Peter Osborne summarizes Benjamin's point:

> Relations between generations are no longer the medium of historical continuity here, but of crisis, rupture and misunderstanding. Youth is no longer a sign of apprenticeship, or even hope, but of an empty infinity of possibilities, disorientation and potential despair.
>
> (135)

No doubt the war and its traumatic aftermath form a crucial part of the "crisis of the bildungsroman" (Moretti's term), but for Woolf and Joyce working in the prewar decade, the genre's inherited conventions were already strained. In *The Voyage Out* and *Portrait of the Artist*, moreover, the problem of failed or frozen development—and the motif of adolescence—subsist within the less cataclysmic and more global context of the late British empire. This pairing of texts allows us to consider the unseasonable youth of an English girlhood and Irish boyhood in the same analytical frame, as differently refracted aspects of a formal and historical problem native to this epoch of colonial modernity.[56]

Both Joyce and Woolf position their texts within a dialectic of national and global forces, casting the journey of expatriatism or exile as a provisional line of escape from national closure. However, both indicate that breaking free of social and novelistic conventions, especially those associated with developmental time, can be only a partial or Pyrrhic victory. If Rachel Vinrace occupies a kind of null function in *Voyage Out*, Stephen Dedalus raids the symbolic center of the bildungsroman with an almost opposite strategy: Where she evacuates the concept of destiny, he overfills it. Where she deflates the plot of becoming, he supercharges it; where she feels blocked by her lack of access to a proper education, he becomes paralyzed by the insights of his elite training. Just as important as these differences, though, is the fact that from opposite directions and from either side, as it were, of the colonial divide, both fixate on stalled personal and socioeconomic development. And yet, as we will see, neither Woolf nor Joyce can expunge the temporal imperatives of biographical (organic) time, of narrative closure, or, finally, of colonial modernity. This facet of the larger problem—how even an antidevelopmental bildungsroman still confronts the temporality of closure—becomes increasingly important as we move from colonial and pre–World War I contexts to the postcolonial and devolutionary contexts of interwar modernism.

To assess this interwar period, I turn in chapter 6 to two semicanonical, semiperipheral modernists, Jean Rhys and Elizabeth Bowen. The protagonists of their influential early novels *Voyage in the Dark* and *The Last September* are exiled girls who cannot reach maturity; they carry the symbolic weight of two different plantation classes that cannot realize their own modernity. Long histories of colonial dispossession inform the failed processes of self-possession in Rhys, as in Bowen. The texture and style of their novels are quite distinct, and there are obvious differences between the Caribbean and Irish histories evoked in their texts. Yet Rhys and Bowen come to the predicament of the Anglophone plantocracy at the end of empire, and to the aesthetic problem of the novel at the end of Victorian social realism, armed with certain overlapping perspectives. Both delve into the vulnerable social situation of the belated offspring of the colonial plantocracy—orphaned and disinherited children with a precarious foothold in a class that itself has a precarious foothold in history.

The novels of Rhys and Bowen bring to the fore a facet of the late bildungsroman not emphasized in previous readings. In them, the logic of cultural difference seems increasingly to structure antidevelopmental plots at the level of both individual and collective destiny; indeed *Voyage in the Dark* and *Last September* upend the old bildungsroman story of upward social mobility. Reading them together as contact-zone fictions highlights the features of generic modulation, from developmental to antidevelopmental plots, which in turn indexes a broader shift in the modernist era as social antagonisms are increasingly coded in terms of cultural (especially racial) difference.[57]

Broadly speaking, fictions centered on entrenched modes of cultural or biological difference cut against older, humanist models not just of development as a narrative device, but of development as an ideological principle implying fixed or universal standards. The instance of Rhys's *Voyage* requires us, I think, to consider an incipiently posthumanist and indeed a biopolitical modernism (in which the key conflicts turn on the play of racial and sexual difference); the instance of Bowen's *Last September* requires us to consider a devolutionary and increasingly anthropological modernism (in which essentialized cultural differences help define social boundaries in the post–World War I world). Taken together, they highlight the pressure put on realist fiction by late Victorian professional and scientific discourses of race, sex, and identity that tended to delegitimate, or at least to deromanticize, middle-class progress narratives.[58] The colonial setting may provide a particularly clear sense of the historical forces behind this process—and the trope of frozen youth a particularly visible sign of its narratological entailments—but there are many kinds of modernist text that encode this broader translation of difference into the increasingly rigid race-culture-nationalism language of twentieth-century devolution.

This account of the modernist bildungsroman thus helps explain the partial displacement of nineteenth-century historical concepts of progress by twentieth-century anthropological concepts of difference as the major frame of reference for the novel.[59] What replaces the historical metanarratives of the Victorian era (with their evolutionary and developmental time frames) seems to be a more static anthropological grid of cultural differences. As James Clifford puts it:

> An intellectual historian of the year 2010, if such a person is imaginable, may . . . look back on the first two-thirds of our century and observe that this was a time when Western intellectuals were preoccupied with grounds of meaning and identity they called "culture" and "language" (much the way we now look at the nineteenth century and perceive there a problematic concern with evolutionary "history" and "progress").
>
> (95)

Since I am myself writing in Clifford's imagined future year 2010, it seems fitting to take his cue and investigate the (relative, gradual) displacement of historical-progressive thinking by anthropological-structural thinking in modernist fiction, where the figure of youth seems less and less to symbolize "history and progress" and more to refer to the messy conceptual overlapping of developmental historicism with a- or anti-historicist logics of cultural difference.[60]

To set this kind of general context for the novel of unseasonable youth, I have sketched an alignment of several strands of fin de siècle intellectual history: the historiographical critique of progress, the anthropological critique of social evolution, the colonial critique of Eurocentrism, the philosophical critique of the sovereign subject, the psychoanalytic critique of the integrated ego—all taken as intertwining challenges to nineteenth-century "developmental" thinking. Such tectonic shifts never happen neatly or instantly of course, and part of the special power of literary genres is to record, in what Fredric Jameson has memorably described as a kind of formal sedimentation, the presence of earlier epistemes even as they adumbrate new intellectual dispensations, new social conjunctures, and new aesthetic possibilities. The novels examined here carry the tenets of their genre forward into the twentieth century, recirculating its sticky ideological content even as they interrogate and revise that content. The signature topoi of modernist fiction—stream of consciousness, epiphany, delayed decoding, and ekphrastic interlude, for example—are signs not of a wall-to-wall triumph of antinarrative form, but of a reorganized novel framework that can bracket or marginalize, but never fully purge, the progressive flow of narrative or existential time. More particularly, since a specific kind of national-historical time was knitted into the primal generic/genetic origins of the bildungsroman, it was of course extremely difficult to deactivate all of the temporal and allegorical traces of its presence. Nonetheless, if, as Moretti suggests, the classic bildungsroman brings us the "triumph of meaning over time," the novel of unseasonable youth brings us to a stalemate between meaning and time (*Way* 55). Time's raw power as *chronos* is no longer so easily channeled into the shapely bounds of *kairos*.[61]

The ideological substrata of the modernist bildungsroman are mixed; so too are its spatial bases and origins. It is difficult, then, to separate the canonical and central texts of modernism from its so-called peripheral and minor texts, at least not without forcing rigid core/periphery distinctions onto a fluid set of cultural and historical relationships that were, increasingly, integrated at the level of the world-system. To take the example of Rhys, a transatlantic migrant writer claimed for both modernist and postcolonial canons: Clearly our interpretive models of center and margin, or colonizer and colonized, cannot contain or explain her work. Better to conceive of aesthetic experiments in European modernism as crosshatched by global uneven development than to divide center and margin, even in the name of marginal or insurgent new modernisms. Literary histories that aim to minimize inherited Eurocentric habits can inadvertently produce, in other words, an exoticizing effect by reifying the concept of Western core and non-Western periphery as if these two had constituted fully separate cultural zones. If we instead compare Western and non-Western modernisms together in the same cultural system it may be easier to explore what Jahan Ramazani calls the "mutually transformative relations" between "metropole and margin" (308). It is not that the old high modernism was European until the "new modernisms" came along to challenge and reshape it: The old high modernism was always a formation shaped globally and by forces that included, from the start, the economics of colonialism and the politics of anticolonialism.[62]

This book examines the Anglophone novel from a metropolitan and formalist perspective, but it is worth remembering that at the material core of this genre history lies the challenge raised by colonial difference.[63] We should not imagine that Western culture had all of its autocritical and anti-imperial resources in place before the anticolonial movements (and later postcolonial studies) came along to challenge European power/knowledge effects, but neither should we imagine that modernist literature was fully or easily conscripted into Western triumphalism and ethnocentrism. One aim of my research is to say something specific about the language and meaning of British-sphere modernism within a wider global history of the novel in general and the bildungsroman in particular. But one might easily extend some of the lines of inquiry opened here into the postwar, postcolonial period; in chapter 7, I therefore consider the fate of the genre after 1945. A number of interesting genealogies of autonomous or frozen youth emerge in the period, crossing between both Western and non-Western literary zones, running from Beckett to Ishiguro, Lessing to Dangarembga, Grass to Rushdie.

Given what I have suggested about the splintering of developmental discourses emanating from Enlightenment Europe, perhaps the most pressing question about the contemporary bildungsroman is whether and how it functions, post-1945, as a vital genre in the "new nations" of the postcolonial world. Do the Bakhtinian principles of realist emergence at the biographical and national levels hold in the post-, anti- and neocolonial territories of the novel in the global South? The question opens up a large research agenda beyond the scope of this study, but scholars such as Pheng Cheah and Joseph Slaughter have begun to assess the afterlife of the European bildungsroman in postcolonial literature of the last several decades. Cheah considers Asian and African writers such as Pramoedya and Ngũgĩ in order to assess the contemporary uses and limits of German-idealist thought, particularly its organicist substrate, for national cultural and literary projects; Slaughter adduces a number of contemporary novelists, including, for example, Marjorie Oludhe Macgoye and Michael Ondaatje, as he examines the role of the bildungsroman's developmental ideals in the formation of a putatively universal language of human rights.

It is notable in this connection that Cheah and Slaughter both start from an eighteenth- and nineteenth-century German philosophical base, explore the widening European influence of the *Bildung* concept, then turn to postcolonial writing of the later twentieth century, where that concept is generally adapted to critical or counterdiscursive purposes. These compelling narratives share a common feature: They leapfrog over the modernist period and therefore miss what I see as a crucial mediating generation (in both literature and philosophy) and a fascinating set of mediating texts—the modernist novels under examination here, in which neither the older developmentalist ideals of *Bildung* nor the newer, post-Hegelian rejections of *Bildung* hold full sway. One way to conceptualize the historical specificity of modernism itself, in fact, is to locate it at the dialectical switchpoint between residual nineteenth-century narratives of global development and emergent twentieth-century critiques of universalist and evolutionist thought.

Because its formal and stylistic registers—down to the most intimate devices of characterization—are shot through with this specific historical predicament, the modernist novel stands as a rich resource for getting us beyond what may now be a theoretical impasse between development and difference. In the humanities and social sciences of the last decade, one can sense the development/difference binary mapping onto a fairly pervasive and entrenched dichotomy that pits a "singular modernity" against multiple or alternative modernities.[64]

In chapter 7, I return to this debate as an intellectual context for current interpretive work in global modernist studies. There I propose a provisional connection between the politics of time in avant-garde aesthetics and postcolonial theory, and identify the risk of a temporal or narrative repression in the more obviously "spatial" (in the sense of alternative territories) or "antidevelopmental" (in the sense of counter-Hegelian temporalities) forms of both. That complex genealogy of anti-Hegelian art and thought, even when drastically telescoped, as it is here, helps explain the fact that the novels of Woolf, Conrad, Joyce, and other Anglophone modernists retain their artistic fascination and political relevance even now.[65] These texts are not just counters in a Bourdieu-style game of modernist prestige, but engaged narrative experiments that throw into question—without seeking fully to banish or destroy—linear time as the organizing principle of form, biography, and history. With their mixed and vexed time schemes, modernist novels offer, I think, a better and more dialectical rejoinder to the Hegelian developmental imperative than have the more fiercely iconoclastic modes of the historical and theoretical avant-garde, whose counterdiscursive strikes against the ideology of progress have been in the long run assimilated as encapsulated outbursts at the margin or, perhaps worse, commodified into radical chic.

To put the same point another way, modernist plots of stalled and/or accelerated *Bildung* generate an inside-out critique of, rather than a frontal attack on, developmental historicism (taken as the time scheme of imperialist thought). The novels in question activate the negative fantasy of frozen youth to symbolize failed or incomplete modernization, but do not project a premature or a permanent escape route from the material effects of modernization theory as (neo)colonial discourse. Viewed in this way, modernist forms do not serve as a kind of direct counterdiscourse to imperial metanarratives of modernity (the West civilizes the rest), nor as their docile, apologetic partner, but expose modernity's temporal contradictions, particularly in zones of colonial encounter. The trope of adolescence, once conceived of as entailing the telos of maturity (and, by allegorical extension, the telos of modernization), comes to refer both to that developmental process *and* to its multiple sites of failure or incompleteness.

If Balzac, Tolstoy, and Scott capture the concrete crises of emergent nationhood in the world-system of the nineteenth century, then Conrad, Joyce, and Woolf capture the concrete crises of residual nationhood in the world-system of the twentieth. From this perspective, it is possible to argue that the bourgeois novel of the modernist period finally (belatedly) transfers the narrative of uneven modernization from a national frame of reference to a global one, diminishing in the process the operative symbolic power of Lukácsian or liberal norms of universal progress.[66] In the specific form of the metabildungsroman (mixing antidevelopmental and developmental narrative units), the modernist novel encodes the objective conditions of a world-system based on endless capitalist innovation yet still informed and legitimated by a now-fragile ideology of developmental historicism. With the semicollapse of the universalist and evolutionist discourses of the Western Enlightenment, with the faltering of historical positivism, with increased political recognition of anticolonial struggle, with the obviously strained resources of European hegemony in the tropics, and with the rise of anthropological concepts of difference, it becomes difficult to imagine, at the turn of the twentieth century, a realism that could in any straightforward way conform to evolutionary or teleological models of world history. But it is not impossible to imagine a critical realism—call it modernism—that registers a heterochronic model of world-historical temporality, one that combines underdevelopment, uneven development, and hyperdevelopment across the global system.[67] Modernist novels of unseasonable youth project the narrative of modernization understood as constant revolution without or despite the symbolic backstop of national tradition. As eminently historical texts, they represent global capitalism, with special fidelity, as an apparently "permanent process which has no end or aim but itself" (Arendt 137).[68]

From the perspective of normative Marxist narrative theory, such novels mark the end of the bildungsroman proper as they fixate on youth and defer, distort, or distend the essentially progressive resources of realist fiction. Although I have for the purposes of argument here adduced a positivist notion of the genre derived from that critical tradition, my reading breaks from the Lukács lineage in one crucial respect. I read novels like *Lord Jim* and *The Voyage Out* as something more than the *disjecta* of a postrealist age in which the bourgeois novel, folded in on its own subjectivity, could no longer synthesize the inner and outer world, no longer project the true shape of history. These dilatory, adolescent novels manage to encode antidevelopmental time into the very language of human interiority and to objectify the deep-structural allegory binding the development of souls and nations. They stand as the narrative art of an era in which state forms and capitalist flows spilled out of their national-cultural borders in increasingly globalized and interdependent ways, an era in which the time of modernization seemed both *hyper* and *retro*, futurist and barbaric. Where the classical novel of education was shaped by the eschatology of nineteenth-century industrialization and nation-building, the modernist version assimilates the temporality of an imperial era when the accelerating yet uneven pace of development seemed to have unsettled all narratives of progress, on the ground and in the mind. In this sense, unseasonable youth manages, in fact, and against all odds, to fulfill the original aesthetic function assigned to the bildungsroman by Bakhtin: the assimilation of "real historical time."

2. "National-Historical Time" from Goethe to George Eliot

The novel must proceed slowly and the feelings of the hero must, in some way or other, restrain the tendency of the whole to its development.

—Goethe, *Wilhelm Meister*, Book V

For the happiest women, like the happiest nations, have no history.

—Eliot, *The Mill on the Floss*

One central premise of the previous chapter was that the classic or nineteenth-century bildungsroman in Europe aligned nationhood and adulthood in order to create a manageable narrative about modernization. According to this premise, adulthood and nationhood served as mutually reinforcing versions of stable identity; they were the fixed states of being that gave form and meaning to an otherwise chaotic and unending (or unnarratable) set of personal and social transformations. Such a line of analysis isolates the tacit historical logic of Lukácsian novel theory in Franco Moretti's *Way of the World* and allows us to extend and elaborate that logic into the age of empire, where the national bildungsroman modulates into modernist and colonial fictions of youth. In this chapter, I propose to explore these opening premises more fully, moving back into the nineteenth-century novel in order to investigate the allegorical co-implication of nationhood and adulthood in the biographical novel. A detailed reading of George Eliot's *The Mill on the Floss* will anchor an otherwise brisk genealogical survey of the bildungsroman centering on its ideal of bounded progress as, first, a German philosophical concept and, second, a British literary practice.

The progressive ideals under examination here took classic or canonical shape within a historical context of emergent nationhood, romantic historicism, and early industrialization. They were forged in and of the contradiction between the endless transformations of market capitalism on the one hand and the cultural politics of origins-and-ends nationalism on the other. These two metanarratives of modernity—one unbounded (capitalization) and one bounded (nationalization)—were not always at odds; in fact, they were functionally coarticulated in both the literary and philosophical discourses of the Enlightenment. Early capitalism worked within the national frames of eighteenth-century Europe and, to a certain degree, reinforced them.[1] From the age of Goethe into the early nineteenth century, the novel could both describe and facilitate the transition from feudal to modern social relations, and could subsist on biographical narratives of the representative individual and organic national culture, without fully confronting the bad infinities of capitalist modernity (to invoke the Hegelian terms outlined in chapter 1).[2]

But the period of the "classic bildungsroman," as Moretti's account of the genre implies, was a brief and a special one—a short season in Europe's political, economic, and literary history between the ancien régimes and the age of mass culture.[3] Its core decades fall during the post–French revolutionary era, the age of Scott and Austen, Goethe and Stendhal, in which the soul-nation allegory of emergence could function, at a socially symbolic level, as a metanarrative of the bourgeoisie's rise to maturity. In its prime (1790–1860), the bildungsroman was a supple and synthetic form, able to narrate and produce middle-class consent by presenting the cold dictates of socialization as if they were the warm inner promptings of the soul's "subjective growth" (Moretti, *Way* 233). The Victorian and modernist afterlives of this novel type suggest, however, that it did not simply wither on the vine of high naturalism, but transformed itself into a story of frozen or fatal colonial adolescence. That story, centered on the years 1860–1930, begins with the recognition that the genre's formal adaptation to the age of revolution required reorganization, not abandonment, in the age of empire.

In its original form, the bildungsroman stabilizes the protagonist's aging process within and against the backdrop of the modern nation. However, since stable national frames and endlessly transforming societies do not always consort in harmony, this core imaginative device—the plot of national closure—was a fragile one. The conflict between youth and adulthood was often put to rest in final chapters that now seem arbitrary, artificial, or pat. In later iterations of the novel of youth, the ideological fantasy of bounded growth—of restive youth bent to the asymptote of stable adulthood—becomes more conspicuous as a problem and thus becomes subject to dramatic estrangement and startling revision. Its more unrealistic elements—sudden tragic death, natural disaster, deus ex machina, multiple fairy-tale couplings, pure social reconciliation—are gradually exposed and textually isolated as the genre's own age begins to show after 1860. And in more obviously global fictions of development, we often find the trope of youth running *without* the countertrope of adulthood; as a consequence, young protagonists come to embody not the compromise of national destiny and capitalist dynamism, but the contradiction between them. From the belated perspective of modernism, the form of the classic bildungsroman—with adulthood synched to nationhood—is a dialectical precursor calling out not just for distant appreciation, but for close reinvestigation.

Infinite Development versus National Form

Goethe retains his mystique as a canonical genius of European and even of world literature because his writing registers both the thrilling crisis of modernity's infinite and international horizons (in a work like *Faust*) and the historical shapeliness of the nation-state as a cultural container (in a work like *Italian Journey*). Viewed from either angle—as the prophet of open horizons or of national forms—Goethe stands in literary history, and particularly in the tradition of materialist narrative theory, as the master technician of developmental discourse. Lukács cites Goethe's investment in the "free and full development of the human personality" (*Goethe* 39) as a central concept of German idealism.[4] Bakhtin, too, insists on the centrality of Goethean models of development to the German Enlightenment and to modern conceptions of historicism more generally. In Goethe, Bakhtin celebrates the true acme of the "artistic visualization of historical time"—the very essence of modern art and literature as the capacity to think and render the shape of linear, modern, historical time in concrete, sensuous, and spatial terms ("*Bildungsroman*" 27).[5] Both Lukács and Bakhtin emphasize Goethe's apparently limitless attraction to the inner life of developmental processes, be they botanical, geological, anatomical, or sociohistorical. But, as Bakhtin observes, Goethe's capacity to see history realistically is anchored and rendered lucid by spatial schemes rooted, as per his *Italian Journey*, in emergent, intra-European national distinctions.

More recently, Franco Moretti has also addressed Goethe's oeuvre as central to the story of modernization from both international and national perspectives, in the open-ended worldliness of Faust (in *Modern Epic*), and in the closed circle of Wilhelm Meister (in *Way of the World*). Returning to *Wilhelm Meister's Apprenticeship*, we can see that it manages to banish infinity—to anticipate as it were the diabolical immortality of Faust—by circumscribing its hero's life in the frame of the emergent German nation. This early biographical type of the realist novel, unlike the tragic and epic dimensions of *Faust*, uses the national chronotope to give shape to its social content. When Wilhelm self-inflates with passion and possibility, Goethe gives his aspirations solid form by resorting to national terms. In a single paragraph, Wilhelm soars "in loftier regions," into a world filled with "vistas of endless delight," but converts those diffuse energies into the romantic agenda of becoming "founder of a future National Theater" (16–17). In the ensuing struggle between theatrical hopes and bourgeois necessities, both culture and commerce seem to be, for the most part, national concerns. And when, toward the end of the novel, the wider world beckons in the form of Jarno's proposal to take Wilhelm with him to America, a national imperative once again takes precedence. Jarno describes the colonial development of the Tower Society as a way to manage the balance between national and international investment:

> We have therefore worked out a new plan: from our ancient Tower a Society shall emerge, which will extend into every corner of the globe, and people from all over the world will be allowed to join it. We will cooperate in safeguarding our means of existence, in case some political revolution should displace one of our members from the land he owns.
>
> (345)

At this point, Wilhelm inclines to the American adventure, but fate intervenes in the form of a marchese who needs a German interpreter to escort him around the country. Jarno reflects: "It will be a great advantage for him to get to know Germany in such good company and under such favorable conditions. He who does not know his own country has no yardstick with which to measure others" (347). The last phase of the plot appears to demand what Moretti calls a closed circle of life and of love, but also, of political geography. Wilhelm finds a vocation, a partner (Natalie), and a homeland in one fell turn; just as the global dimensions of a possible future are glimpsed, Wilhelm's open journey is converted into a circumscribed national one.

Goethe's realist aesthetic thus entails the measured chronotope of national development as opposed to the older chronotope of cyclical time, and as opposed to a more global chronotope of endless futurity. It is the Goethe of national time that Lukács and Bakhtin enshrine as modern and realist.[6] Nationalism becomes the epistemological and cultural frame for a theory of the novel: "The second half of the eighteenth century in England and Germany is characterized," Bakhtin writes, "by an increased interest in folklore," inspiring, "a new, powerful, and extremely productive wave of national-historical time that exerted an immense influence on the development of the historical outlook in general and on the development of the historical novel in particular" (52). Likewise for the concept of aesthetic education developed by Schiller in rough parallel to the Goethean prototype of the novel of development: If it was directed formally at a universal human race, it nonetheless depended for its coherence on national-cultural institutions and frameworks.[7]

The developmental thinking associated with the Goethean bildungsroman and with Schillerian education emerged within the context, in other words, of the Herderian Revolution, which established "a necessary link between nation and language" (Casanova 75). Of course, there are deeper roots for the novel of national-historical time than just Herder's *volksgeist*. One such root runs in the direction of Vico, whose *New Science* proposed an "ideal eternal history traversed in time by the history of every nation in its rise, development, maturity, decline and fall" (qtd. in Jay 34).[8] Even within the German milieu, a detailed genealogical account of national time as the basis for the modern novel of development would need to account for the influence of Wilhelm von Humboldt as well as Herder. It was Humboldt who insisted that individualism is not merely a matter of autonomous self-development, but an expression of harmonic relations with humanity and its collectives—of which Herder's national culture is but one (Løvlie, Mortensen, and Nordenbo 32).[9] Gregory Castle has argued that Humboldt in effect paved the way for the reorientation of *Bildung* from a rarefied process of aesthetic education plotted by Goethe and Schiller into a more socially pragmatic account of socialization dominant in the English and French realist novels of the nineteenth century (39–47).[10]

Even with their variations in philosophical emphasis, Goethe, Schiller, Herder, and Humboldt helped form a discourse of national development integral to modern historical consciousness itself, a turn that becomes still more clear in the work of Fichte and Hegel. For Fichte and Hegel, collective historical life implied both national tradition and the state form. Of the two, Fichte offers the more intensive focus on a unified, organic national culture; for Hegel, states can be multicultural and polyglot. However, as Pheng Cheah suggests in his detailed and pointed genealogy of the bildungsroman as a national form, Hegel provides the more systematic philosophical infrastructure for the nineteenth-century novel of development: "The universal which emerges and becomes conscious within the state, the form to which everything in it is assimilated, is what we call in general the nation's

Bildung" (*Lectures on the Philosophy of World History*, qtd. in Cheah 171). Cheah's major argument is that an "organismic ontology" underlies this entire German tradition (in both its national and cosmopolitan iterations), thus embedding into the substrata of the bildungsroman a conceptual ruse that conflates biological and political life (2).[11] Thomas Pfau, too, reads the inner logic of *Bildung* as an attempt to give stable and organic life to "an irreducibly contingent and volatile world to which humans never had a biologically stabilized, organic relationship" (152). Cheah traces the organismic metaphor that runs through so much modern political theory and that organizes the narrative presentation of time-as-development in the form that I have called the soul-nation allegory.[12]

With that symbolic infrastructure in place, novels of national emergence can finesse the problem of mortality or finitude, but they immediately face an embedded and corollary problem: They must register the raw historical nature of souls and societies (always changing), yet also arrive at the formal stasis implied, in the end, by nationhood and adulthood. The bildungsroman is thus a special kind of time machine that organizes personal and historical experience into the loaded motif of bounded growth. In the mainstream bildungsroman, the existential fixity of the mature individual and the modern nation are not just analogies for each other, but mutually reinforcing ideological constructions. Their symbolic exchange gives the nation the organic coherence of a person and gives the individual the apparently objective continuity of a nation. This is German idealism's legacy for the bildungsroman: a core device that enshrines cultural development (national-historical time) as against older cyclical concepts of time, but one whose assimilation of progressive historicism requires it always to confront a set of open-jawed or "bad" infinities, that is, the demoralized, empty, and acultural temporalities of the rationalized society, the hegemonic state, and the free market.

In the developmental discourse of *kultur-bildung* originating in German idealism, then, the representative man embodies a universal and potentially infinite process that requires boundaries provided by national history. Translated from philosophical and speculative discourse into realist fiction, this means that if youth was, as Moretti claims, a master metaphor for modernization in the European novel, it was a trope of always-incomplete modernization, of modernization processes cut at both the symbolic and political levels by the continuity-discourses of national destiny. In a series of studies on this problematic, David Lloyd has described aesthetic culture as a foundational concept for narratives of the representative man and for allegories of both European nation-state formation and imperial hegemony. In *Nationalism and Minor Literature*, for example, Lloyd observes that nationalist rhetoric in early nineteenth-century Europe tended to promote

an education that will cultivate in the individual those moral principles that
are the repetition in the finite individual of the eternal principles of the
divine essence of life, or, on yet another level, a repetition in the individual
of the national spirit, which in himself he represents. The whole man, the
man of integrity, becomes thus the man who is integrated with and reproduces the spirit of his nation.

(70)

This is the moral-allegorical logic of the national subject as a philosophical ideal.

When, however, that ideal is translated into fiction, in the shift from *Bildung*
to bildungsroman, the buried conflict between universal processes of cultivation or education (set in cosmopolitan modernity) and bounded histories of
self-formation (set by national origins and ends) takes shape as a formal tension
between narrativity and closure. The national novel requires biographical closure;
it cannot project (as in, say, the epic of Goethe's *Faust*) a global or universal story.
To achieve the temporal stabilization of national closure, then, novels of youth
require the bounded time of adulthood to arrest development. Along these lines,
Simon Gikandi has analyzed the signal importance of national time in the history
of the novel:

> The relative stability we seem to detect in the great "realistic" narratives of
> the nineteenth century arises from the writers' confidence in the stability
> of the world they represent, its sense of time, and its cartography; this style
> is predicated on the hope that the crisis of culture and consciousness trig-
> gered by radical historical change can be redetermined in narrative form.
> And thus, *until colonialism enters the period of crisis* . . . [i.e., circa 1880], no
> one doubts what England signifies and what its relation to the rest of the
> world is.
>
> (172–73; emphasis added)

Gikandi's redetermination in narrative form of unmediated historical time is
another name for the function I identify here with the phrase "national closure,"
and, like Gikandi, I think it faces new and different historical pressures in the age
of empire.[13] The term *national closure* helps us apprehend the shift in the late Victorian period when the novelistic formula of bounded nationhood (embodied in
the adulthood that transcends youth) reorganizes itself in response to global forces
(embodied in endless or autonomous youth).

Such a periodizing claim should not be surprising since we are still, in literary studies, operating under the influential framework of Benedict Anderson's

Imagined Communities with its essential linkage between realist fiction and national narrative—not to mention Homi Bhabha's later exploration of colonial discourse as a disruptive force brought to bear on both. Surveying the intertwining of personal and national narratives beginning in the age of Goethe, Anderson notes the basic asymmetry between the organicism of human existence and the pseudo-organicism of the nation:

> As with modern persons, so it is with nations. Awareness of being imbedded in secular, serial time, with all its implications of continuity, yet of "forgetting" the experience of this continuity—product of the ruptures of the late eighteenth century—engenders the need for a narrative of "identity." . . . Yet between narratives of person and nation there is a central difference of employment. In the secular story of the "person" there is a beginning and an end.
>
> (205)

Modern novels inherit a narrative problem as well as a narrative solution: Representing the continuous transformations of societies and selves, they use artificially complete concepts of nationhood and adulthood to create discrete narrative spans of time.[14]

This contradiction embedded in novel history explains why Lukács's studies of Goethe in particular and of the novel in general—alert as they are to the besetting problem of narrative infinitude for realist fiction—center so consistently, if implicitly, on the national frame for the modern novel. In the mainstream of Lukács's thought, a specific model of European national-industrial emergence shapes the moving forces of history into the humanist idiom that he calls critical realism. The nation acts as the social referent for the modern novel as a genre of collective destiny—whether Russian or French, British or Italian. In *The Historical Novel*, he states that historical thinking depends on "the awakening of national sensibility" (25). Walter Scott, the key figure of that book, characteristically addresses a "given, concrete . . . crisis of national history"; so, too, Manzoni's love story in *I Promessi Sposi* rises to the level of great historical realism when it squarely represents the Italian people's "state of national degradation and fragmentation" (70). And in *The Theory of the Novel*, centered in a German intellectual tradition, the historical idiom of Lukács's Romantic anticapitalism is, as Gareth Stedman Jones has noted, a distinctly national one (30). One might in fact refine Lukács's terms by describing the historical novel as a distinct subset of the larger category European realism; the former type of novel makes the national frame explicit, the latter keeps it relatively tacit (though no less necessary to the narrative organization).[15]

The original premise of *The Theory of the Novel* holds that the bounded world of epic gets displaced in the modern novel by a peculiar openness to history, to the ever-unfolding dynamism of the Hegelian historical process itself. What gives closure to this post-epic form, the signature genre of modernity, is the nation-state, though Lukács does not elaborate the point in much detail. The nation-state stabilizes the bourgeois revolution into a narratable form. Think of the impossible, never-ending story of modernization without the mythogenic power of the nation undergirded by the administrative power of the state.[16] That is a crucial but largely tacit Hegelian premise of *The Theory of the Novel*, and it allows us to grasp why Lukács's historical fiction would be challenged by the increasingly multinational and supra-state forces at work in the later nineteenth and early twentieth centuries.

The problem of national closure persists in Franco Moretti's *The Way of the World*. In the classical bildungsroman, Moretti observes, "just as in space it is essential to build a 'homeland' for the individual, it is also indispensable for time to stop at a privileged moment" (26). Moretti uncovers two countervailing motifs of national time and imperial untimeliness in his brief discussion of *Robinson Crusoe*. Defoe must abolish "the problematic of temporality" in the end of the Crusoe series, making for an arbitrary closural device brought down on the potentially endless sequelae of a novel dedicated to the open chronotope of colonial capitalism. This is why Moretti describes Goethe's bildungsroman as an "Anti-Robinson Crusoe": It resolves the problem of growth into the logic of the soul-nation allegory in a way that Defoe's "novel of capitalism" cannot (26).[17] Moretti establishes an opposition here between national citizen and cosmopolitan merchant; the former reflects, in his happiness and proportionate growth, the bounded time of the nation. Working on the classic bildungsroman, Moretti rightly restricts the question of national time to the Goethean idiom of the homeland: "To reach the conclusive synthesis of maturity," he writes, the protagonist "must learn first and foremost, like Wilhelm, to direct 'the plot of [his own] life' so that each moment strengthens one's sense of belonging to a wider community. Time must be used to find a homeland" (19). This idea of homeland—it would be a bit anachronistic to call it a nation in Goethe's case—becomes increasingly nationalized in nineteenth-century literature, first in British and French, then in U.S. and Russian realism. By this I mean that the *kairos* of national-historical time becomes the semivisible guarantor that the *chronos* of modernity can be made meaningful in the bildungsroman's grammar of plot.

The nation's role as spatial and political container for developmental historicism, already observable in Goethe, becomes more visible and explicit as German concepts migrate into British cultural life in the nineteenth century. If there is one thinker who represents the adaptation of the *kultur-bildung* concept to the British sphere, particularly as an intellectual hedge against the revolutionary force of political and economic modernization, it is Edmund Burke. For Burke, both revolution and empire threaten to produce the wrong kind of development, the kind unchecked by tradition and traditional forms of identity.[18] Burke helps establish a British philosophical and humanist line of thought that poses the bounded and harmonic model of national growth against a more revolutionary chronotope; he represents the possibility that cultural discourse can absorb and temper the blunt force of modernization—a belief analyzed at large in studies such as Raymond Williams's *Culture and Society* and Martin Wiener's *English Culture and the Decline of the Industrial Spirit*.

For Moretti, Burke sets the tone for a conservative streak in the British novel, one that resists the more radical and radically modern implications of Enlightenment and Revolution alike.[19] In keeping with the Nairn-Anderson thesis that Britain experiences a long developmental delay in the modernization of its politics and society, Moretti frames the British variant of the bildungsroman as particularly given to static rather than transformative social plots (*Way* 181–228).[20] Intellectual historians such as Raymond Williams and Francis Mulhern (in *Culture/Metaculture*) have charted the larger idea that a national-cultural discourse of bounded and tempered modernization tended to diffuse revolutionary energies in English society during the nineteenth century. Tracking the absorption of the German *kultur-bildung* discourse into the bloodstream of British letters, Williams and Mulhern follow English culturalist thinking from Burke and Coleridge through Mill and Carlyle to Arnold and Eliot.[21] As I suggested in chapter 1, this Burke-Coleridge lineage consolidates a running opposition between a national culture (in which restrained or proportionate social and personal growth can occur) and a multinational civilization (in which unrestrained growth or modernization has no organic checks or balances). Coleridge, for example, imagined that national forms could mediate between "Permanence" and "Progression" (xi). His interest, moreover, in noninstrumental practices of education and cultivation for the clerisy domesticated the Schiller ideal and depended quite explicitly on national institutions.

The concept of national development codified by the German idealists gives both a conceptual language and, in Goethe at least, a literary plot for what would become an English cultural project of wrestling imperial and industrial modernity into shapely form. As Williams and Mulhern suggest, the discourse of culture gains prestige in the Victorian age not just because of its ultimately universal aspirations, but also—and perhaps preeminently—because of its restricted ethnonational dimensions. In thinkers like Matthew Arnold, the discourse of culture opposed more universalist traditions such as German metaphysics or French political rationality. British culturalist discourse in the nineteenth century thus qualifies and modifies the forces of rampant modernization with the chronotope of national time, and establishes a shaping intellectual context for the production and reception of the novel of youth. Carlyle's translation of *Wilhelm Meister's Apprenticeship* in 1824 marks an early landmark in that process, as do Scott's *Waverley* fictions, with their intertwined plots of personal and national emergence. In Scott, youth and nationalism are partially eclipsed, partially recuperated by the advance of the multinational Anglophone empire.[22]

The movement of the *Bildung* concept from England and Germany was not just an international migration of a philosophical ideal, but an ongoing modulation of that ideal into a mainstream English narrative practice. In the *Waverley* model, a folkloric or Herderian discourse of the nation infuses the developmental form of the bildungsroman, and this combination continues to influence the British novel of education well into the mid-Victorian work of Dickens, Thackeray, and the Brontës. Although it oddly neglects Scott, Susanne Howe's 1930 study *Wilhelm Meister and His English Kinsmen* established the British bildungsroman as a recognizable subgenre of modern realism. Howe's original corpus included Carlyle, Bulwer-Lytton, Disraeli, and, later in the nineteenth century, Meredith. Her book paved the way for Jerome Buckley's equally influential *Season of Youth* (1974), which ranges from Dickens to the mid-twentieth century. Both Howe and Buckley have been significantly revised in the last few decades by critics who have doubted the genre's stability and centrality as a Victorian practice. Susan Fraiman, for example, not only challenges the positivist definition of bildungsroman but offers a feminist and metacritical account of its tendentious canonization in U.S. academic criticism.

As Fraiman notes, Howe's book solidifies the Goethe origin story, producing a critical myth centered on male narratives of self-determination as against both feudal and capitalist determinations of vocation and labor (3–5). But choice, mobility, interiority—the sacred motifs of masculine coming-of-age—were all exposed as sheer fictions by powerful practitioners of the female novel of youth in the English nineteenth century. Fraiman (and other feminist scholars such as Showalter and Gilbert and Gubar) use the marginalization of Victorian women from narratives of masculine/national destiny to lay bare the ideological strains written into the classic bildungsroman—in particular its ability to stage the paradigmatic compromise between inner desires and social conventions. Following their lines of analysis forward, I suggested in chapter 1 that novels of unseasonable youth after 1860 use colonial plots to tease out the abiding generic tension between shapely national progress and untimely modernization.

Even more than the feminist argument outlined by Fraiman, the colonial argument advanced here requires a specifically British frame of reference within the larger history of the bildungsroman. The novels of colonial adolescence that anchor subsequent chapters of this study represent an intensification, perhaps even a transvaluation, of what Franco Moretti sees as the English difference all along (*Way* 181). For Moretti, the peculiarity of the British novel, compared especially to its French counterpart, was that it was always transfixed by the possibility of a wish-fulfilling romance that ignored the contradictions of capitalism. The British tradition of the bildungsroman in particular seemed to privatize politics and extend the legacy of Goethean compromise to the point where the dynamism of youth became a fantasy of liberal innocence. In Moretti's terms, this manifests itself in the English bildungsroman's addiction to stability: its story of fairy-tale heroes with a childlike moral or juridical structure, designed to sacrifice youth to adulthood, freedom to happiness. The governing themes of the present study, empire and youth, are so prevalent in late Victorian Britain that their convergence in canonical fictions of colonial adolescence appears to confirm their historical role as modernist foils to that inherited doublet of closural motifs, nationhood and adulthood.

The national closure hypothesis runs in two directions. If closure happens in the form of adulthood and social reconciliation, it tends to proceed at both thematic and symbolic levels as an interlocking alignment between soul and nation. Alternately, if traditional closure is deferred or blocked, it tends to happen in relation to denationalized global or commercial space lacking the moralized features of national-historical time. Even Edward Said's strong rereading of Austen's *Mansfield Park* in terms of the economic and political significance of overseas wealth, or Gayatri Spivak's rereading of *Jane Eyre* in terms of the cultural and allegorical centrality of the colonial madwoman in the attic (or, for that matter, Fredric Jameson's reading of the dark Irish sources of capitalist and libidinal energy embodied in the Heathcliff of *Wuthering Heights*) do not change the national reframing and recontaining that occur in the closural process of the novels in question. In the novels of Austen or the Brontës, the colonial substrate may well be narratively present and historically fascinating, but the text's closural process drives home the underlying idea that animating conflicts (at the thematic level) and contradictions (at the socio-symbolic level) are resolved through an alignment between the protagonist's end-narrative in time and the nation's boundary-limit in space.[23]

Consider in light of this claim *David Copperfield* (1850) and *Jane Eyre* (1847), perhaps the two most exemplary and canonical instances of the high Victorian bildungsroman. In both, the fulfillment of the protagonist's maturity interlocks with the reconsolidation of the national boundaries. The process unfolds in two steps in *David Copperfield*. First, the Micawbers have to clear the national space: "You are going out, Micawber, to this distant clime [Australia] to strengthen, not to weaken, the connexion between yourself and Albion," says Mrs. Micawber (879). Second, the hero himself stabilizes his long cycle of slow growth and punctual trauma by leaving the English circle and then returning to it: His major plot inverts the Micawbers' minor plot (885–87). "I went away from England," he reports, to overcome loss. However, his recovery and social reconciliation remain fully bound up in his return to the stable frame of the nation, fusing Copperfield back into "England, and the law" (894). *Jane Eyre*, too, engages in a long process of traumatic purification, transforming the protagonist and equipping her to close out the novel with full symbolic reconciliation in a nationally representative space. Along the way, Brontë describes a banishing of non-English elements even more clearly than does Dickens: The dangers of wandering and delirium, the purging of threats from both imperial man (St. John Rivers) and colonial woman (Bertha), the trials by fire, and the symbolic castration of Rochester all pave the way for the ultimate insertion of Jane into a stabilized and socially sanctioned English container at Thornfield Hall. As Buzard observes of *Jane Eyre*, "The framework of the universal and colonial must 'die' so the national culture can live" (165). Like Scott, though without the folk-cultural theme of nationalism at the fore, Dickens and Brontë show the nation as mediating between various regions of under- and overdevelopment. In urban and rural registers, respectively, they develop a model in which narrative obstacles are cleared, and modernization plots arrested, via the protagonists' reconciliation to national time and space.[24]

Moving forward to 1860–1861, to Dickens's *Great Expectations* and George Eliot's *The Mill on the Floss*, we find another urban-rural pairing of English *bildungsromane* in which the classic Stendhal-Balzac plot of the provincial youth's migration toward the capital receives something of a twist: a tragicomic reversal (Dickens) or a tragic undoing (Eliot). Patricia Spacks:

> Eliot and Dickens . . . both demonstrated clear awareness of society's corruptions without accepting the corollary that adolescence should triumph. The wisdom their protagonists acquire in transcending their adolescent state does not enable them to lead viable lives; neither does it enable them to avoid, or even consciously to wish to avoid, the responsibilities of adulthood. Eliot and Dickens, consequently, like Scott, and for some of the same reasons, had trouble with their endings.
>
> (204)

In *Great Expectations* and *Mill on the Floss*, we can see the signs of generic aging; the soul-nation allegory that had defined the core ideology of the classic bildungsroman begins to fray and unravel. As 1860 texts, they mark what for many critics is already a late stage in the bildungsroman's dominance as a realist subgenre.[25] Both show the residual power of the national closure plot, but signal that it is beginning to disintegrate. Eliot's deliberately failed bildungsroman in particular stands as a good transitional or precursor text for any discussion of the modernist-era bildungsroman—not just because its heroine dies rather than truly comes of age, but because the impossibility of her aging process is so thoroughly framed in terms of the symbolic uncertainties associated with expanding geographical scales.

For Dickens and Eliot (as, I think, for Thackeray in *Vanity Fair*), overseas empire serves as a plot function (a possible source of wealth or opportunity for feckless men, for example). But it also begins to make deeper inroads into the terrain of national closure. The Magwitch plot in *Great Expectations* seems to distend and retard Pip's growth and in this sense to foreshadow modernist novels of new-imperial capitalism such as *Tono-Bungay*. But even with its wider geographical frame of empire, *Great Expectations* still reaches final resolution through an alignment between Pip and an English destiny. The Magwitch plot admits to England a source of outside capital, and Pip's emergence into adulthood is deferred by the conceit of Miss Havisham as shadow-patron screening his (and our) awareness of Magwitch's money. Havisham, as the not-Magwitch, represents a principle of stopped time ("this arrest of everything, this standing still" [60]) in direct counterpoint to Magwitch, who embodies the principle of ruthless progress and unstopped time. In the end, Magwitch has to be cleared from national space; as in *David Copperfield* this is both a legal and a symbolic requirement of the national closure plot.[26]

Magwitch's crash landing into, and later willing expulsion from, the novel's English force field defines Pip's ability to reach social reconciliation: The elements of danger, of wealth, of unpredictability that Magwitch represents—these have to be introduced into and then jettisoned from the national container. As a figure, Magwitch underscores the structural dependence of the Victorian middle class (or Victorian realist fiction) on colonial wealth, but also the symbolic dependence of the biographical plot on the relatively artificial borders of the nation-state. Even at the end, Pip must go abroad to seek fortune, and his bildungsroman of restless growth and transformation can only come to an end when he *returns*, when the circulation of hero and capital is renationalized (*Great* 480–81).

The attenuated and compressed narration of the final few pages of *Great Expectations*, though, indicate that Dickens himself senses the strain in the twin plot of nationhood-adulthood. Such strain is even more apparent in the historical frame of *Mill on the Floss*, where Maggie Tulliver's story is embedded in a tale of social and economic reorganization that takes us, in a single narrative, from the pre–Reform Bill agrarian world of St. Ogg's to the frontiers of global traffic and commerce. Provincial growth, so long embodied in the hero or heroine of the bildungsroman, shifts, in this later phase of the Victorian period, from a national to an international frame. Plots no longer simply slough off extra bodies or finished adults into the extranational territory of out-migration, but also assimilate an increasingly global logic of economic transformation into the very texture of the protagonist's emergence. This forces—or proceeds apace with—a reconception of earlier principles of composition and novel construction that were embedded in the national bildungsroman. To examine that reconception in textual detail, we can turn to Eliot's *The Mill on the Floss*.

Nationhood and Adulthood in *The Mill on the Floss*

George Eliot is not in any simple way a writer of *bildungsromane*, though a number of her books have titles that imply the old biographical plot (*Adam Bede, Silas Marner, Felix Holt, Daniel Deronda*). Her works are generally multiplot fictions based on secularized and modernized networks of social relations rather than single-protagonist narratives of emergence. However, Eliot was a key translator into English of German historical concepts that were central to the intellectual context of the bildungsroman in theory and practice. Eliot and G. H. Lewes (her longtime companion) were two important transfer agents for German concepts into Victorian literature.[27] Eliot translated Feuerbach's *The Essence of Christianity* [*Das Wesen des Christentums*] in 1854; Lewes published his *Life of Goethe* a year later. Both were strongly influenced by German thinkers such as Goethe, Schiller, and Fichte, especially in the second half of the 1850s. Written at the end of that decade, *The Mill on the Floss* examines the generic inheritance of the "novel of development" from the ironic point of view of an educated woman; elements of classic German *Bildung* are present along with a critique that is not only squarely feminist, but incipiently late Victorian in its attunement to the problem of national-historical time. The novel affords us an archeological view of the allegorical forms and organic rhetorics with which a leading Victorian writer tried to make narrative sense of endless capitalist transformation. Seen in this light, *The Mill on the Floss* offers new perspectives about the recuperative work done by nationalism during England's industrial period and new insights about the way that novels of education have always been entangled with the eschatologies of national myth.

It is one of George Eliot's most distinctive achievements that her novels seem to combine liberal meliorism and romantic nostalgia—and to represent the combination of these strands of Victorian historicism (one progressivist, one not) within the emergent secular nationalism of her own epoch. Bathed in Eliot's sympathy, English communities like Middlemarch reach tragically mixed conclusions: a sad loss of grandeur paired with a gentle recuperation of value. In her fiction, development happens according to the familiar if paradoxical logic whereby individual and social essences remain constant despite deep and drastic changes. Yet in many ways, *Mill* challenges the model of historical and psychological continuity that we otherwise associate with Eliot. It stands out among Eliot's works as an unusual case—prickly, undigested, immature (as F. R. Leavis dismissively called it in *The Great Tradition* [46]). Its resistance to historical, generic, and psychological conventions of development is what defines the novel's intractability, its "portion of radical discontent" (Fraiman 123). Eliot does not simply cast doubt on the idea that societies or individuals *improve* over time, but asks the more radical question of whether societies or individuals can be said to possess any kind of continuous identity over time.

By choosing to set the novel's action back into the 1820s, Eliot no doubt follows autobiographical promptings, but the decision also locates Maggie Tulliver in the breach between two societies with competing value systems. The narrator quickly establishes and rigorously maintains a fault line between the premodern village life of St. Ogg's and the modern conditions of mid-Victorian England. Rather than narrate the continuous development of Victorian capitalism out of a traditional agricultural and trading economy, Eliot implies the dramatic difference between the two.[28] By describing drastic changes (not smooth transitions), the text unsettles recuperative, organic versions of English history wherein the land and the folk remain mystically constant despite the complete reorganization of their economy. Of course, Eliot is ambiguous on this point: Victorian readers are asked to recognize that they are on the near side of a historical divide from the rural English past, but they are also invited to feel a symbolic connection to the villagers of St. Ogg's.[29]

The novel's setting, Dorlcote Mill, constitutes a *locus classicus* of English yeomanry. Owned by the economically autonomous Tulliver family, the mill is both a domestic and a productive site. Uncle Glegg, a wool stapler, and Uncle Pullet, a prosperous farmer, also belong to the yeoman class. But the early agrarian capitalism that gave rise to such yeomen changed dramatically during the

1830s and 1840s as a result of enclosures and other concentrations of land and capital (Williams, *Country* 97–100). This economic transformation, a fait accompli for Eliot's readers, can barely be glimpsed by the characters in the novel. Faced with inevitable modernization, the St. Ogg's families are "constituted . . . a race" by dint of their archaic economic habits (188). Eliot attributes a quaint mercantilist understanding of commerce to the village merchants, who share the precapitalist assumption that trade is a zero-sum game in which the participants dicker face to face. The inhabitants of St. Ogg's do not fully understand the abstract, anonymous, legal-financial capitalism that is overtaking them. Mr. Tulliver's loss of Dorlcote Mill to lawyer Wakem—the crisis that triggers the novel's plot—is a paradigmatic instance of the yeoman fallen prey to modernization.

Modernization in this novel kills off central characters and social practices, making them victims ripe for historical obscurity. While Eliot's general position on historical commemoration certainly allows for recovery of the past, this particular novel demands the recognition that some losses are absolute. The narrator admits to a "cruel conviction" that the Dodsons and Tullivers "will be swept into the same oblivion with the generations of ants and beavers" (362). The Dodsons and Tullivers may be irrelevant to, or at least drastically discontinuous from, the modern world of her readers. By proposing that elements of the past become radically unavailable to the present, *The Mill on the Floss* pays tribute to an unblinking historicism that cuts deep into the connective tissue of national myth.

For Eliot, one of the chief differences between Victorian England and premodern St. Ogg's is historical consciousness itself: "The mind of St. Ogg's did not look extensively before or after. It inherited a long past without thinking of it" (184). *Mill* is a novel about people who have no need for historical novels. Eliot makes an implicit comparison between the village and her own society, which, rather than enjoy a tacit assumption of shared origins, must construct its collective (national) past. Moreover, the narrator takes pains to suggest that St. Ogg's cannot in any simple way be imagined as the "inner child" of modern England. Rather than describe an eternal connection between land and *ethnos*, Eliot's local history tells a story of colonization and cultural intermingling among Romans and Saxons, Normans and Danes (181). And when Eliot does evoke the national myth of the yeoman, she draws attention to its fictive and conventional quality—warning off literal-minded readers who might take St. Ogg's as the essence of modern England.

Throughout the novel, the narrator's self-consciously modern voice brims with authority about a rural existence that is nonetheless distant from it and its metropolitan audience. In regard to its provincial subjects, the novel adopts an ethnographic tone that reflects the difference between modernized observer and premodern object. But the narrator is no naive tourist; in fact, Eliot, often recognized for her excellence as a domestic historian, might also be considered a prescient anthropological theorist. She notes, for example, that a modern writer needs irony in order to describe "unfashionable families." Moreover, she identifies irony as the product of a "national life" imagined in explicitly metropolitan-rural terms.[30] In a fascinating passage, Eliot recognizes that the nation, predicated on economic injustice and the inclusion of unfashionable rustics, supports both the material and representational needs of "good society." As a political container for regional and class heterogeneity, the nation allows for the "gossamer wings of light irony" that leaven the Victorian novelist's treatment of her archaic country cousins (385).

At such moments, Eliot acknowledges that metropolitan representations of the rural often depend on a rhetoric of nationhood that yokes together diverse populations otherwise separated by class and religion as well as by space and time. She undermines romantic nativism by insisting on the historical incommensurability between 1820s St. Ogg's and the modern industrial nation of 1860. Eliot's strong commitment to historicism—the idea that different epochs are irreducibly different—requires the novel to execute a complicated double maneuver. First, the text shows that modernization generates absolute losses both materially and epistemologically: There are objects, documents, people, values, experiences, and knowledge that can neither be preserved nor re-collected from the past. Second, the novel exposes and challenges the recuperative rhetoric of nationalism that seeks to deny those losses and to emphasize the survival of a rural English core. This double movement—which is integral to the novel's representation of social history—also informs its representation of Maggie Tulliver's coming-of-age plot. The process of maturation generates absolute losses for Maggie: There are moods, sensations, relationships, and experiences that cannot survive into adulthood. And the novel challenges the rhetoric of development that seeks to deny those losses and to posit instead a continuous self that remembers, preserves, and endures it all.

The novel challenges, in other words, the organicist logic of the bildungsroman that I have identified as the soul-nation allegory. What this novel and others to follow in this study suggest, when read synoptically, is that the bildungsroman can and usually does project an array of overlapping chronotopic possibilities: the local, bounded space of tradition (in which historical time is displaced by a more static scheme featuring the time of frozen youth and the space of provincial or colonial life); the radically open and unbounded space-time of empire and globalization (glimpsed at the horizon by Eliot, in which capitalism is constantly transforming the social world, and in which collective and individual identities are dissolved into endless revolution); and the mediating, reconciling chronotope of the nation (in which harmonious growth is projected as the normative temporal mode for both subjects and societies). In *Lord Jim*, for example, England figures for Marlow as a residual spatiotemporal mean between the bad finitude of Jim's tropical entrepôt and the bad infinity of global commerce. As Jim's eternal adolescence suggests in vivid and concrete ways, both colony and empire are spaces of relative historylessness marked respectively by the torpid absence of progress and by the brutal eternalization of change. By contrast, national time is shapely because it moves forward, but not forever and ever. Eliot's bildungsroman represents, I think, a transitional point in this history of residual and emergent forms. It still honors the logic of the soul-nation allegory as the heart of the genre, but presents it in etiolated and ultimately negative form, subjecting it—along with everything else—to the quietly devastating logic of a historicism without recuperation.

It only makes sense, then, that Eliot represents the passage from childhood to adulthood as more disjunctive than additive. For example, although the narrator describes memories of youth as the "mother tongue of our imagination," this Wordsworthian sentiment quickly gives way to the recognition that childhood experiences are in fact frustratingly inaccessible (94). Memories of youth carry such drastically different emotional value from the original experiences that they seem almost to belong to another person. Just as the novel implies a lack of self-presence in the modern nation, it also casts doubt on the mature self's supposed relationship of identity to its childhood incarnation.

Historical and individual nostalgia recurs throughout the novel, each cast by Eliot in terms of the other. In the Wordsworthian passage cited earlier, for instance, the narrator describes personal memory in ethno-linguistic terms ("mother tongue of our imagination") and indicates the unsatisfactory quality of recollected youth by declaring that no "tropic palms" could thrill the same fibers as a May day in England (94). Conjuring images of the colonies, this passage establishes an analogy whereby the far-flung empire represents a lapsed national adulthood, no longer even imaginable as connected to the native setting of its English childhood. This figurative hint about the eroding logic of self-continuity under the pressure of scalar expansion (region to nation to empire) recurs in the text.[31] Quite a bit later, for example, Eliot addresses the metropolitan reader whose experience of home cannot match that of the legendary yeoman:

> Our instructed vagrancy which has hardly time to linger by the hedgerows, but runs away early to the tropics . . . [and] which . . . stretches the theatre

of its imagination to the Zambesi can hardly get a dim notion of what an old-fashioned man like Tulliver felt for this spot where all his memories centred.

(352)

The modern economy of industry and empire has forced England to develop into something quite different from what romantic nationalism identified as its core. The political entity "Britain" was never really coextensive with its founding *ethnos*, but it was increasingly removed from that national mythic core as it extended itself globally; the extent of that distance or discontinuity is measured here metaphorically by the psychological rupture between child and adult.

The maturation of the protagonist and the modernization of the nation unfold as parallel narratives—a convention that Eliot both observes and objectifies as she breaks its progressivist assumptions. Indeed, the novel's deviation from bildungsroman formulae depends on the thematic power of Eliot's turn on these reciprocal allegories of growth and her corresponding commitment to motifs of disjunction and of loss. But modernization is not only a figurative parallel to maturation: The two stories also intersect causally. England's economic changes play a direct role in arresting the development of Maggie (and Tom) Tulliver. The economic transformations that Eliot documents (including, for example, the loss of Dorlcote Mill) leave Maggie stranded in the historical gap between old St. Ogg's and modern England. *Mill* disrupts the soul-nation allegory so that a narrative of historical change impedes, and ultimately prevents, the adjustment of Maggie Tulliver.

Modernization in *The Mill on the Floss* has different effects on women than on men and creates different narrative problems for Maggie Tulliver than for her brother Tom. It is the novel's female hero who, for the most part, reveals *Bildung* to be a disjunctive and tragic process. At one point, quoted in this chapter's epigraph, the narrator acknowledges that there would be neither reason nor means for telling Maggie Tulliver's story were Maggie not trapped in the class and provincial margins of pre-Victorian England, "for the happiest women, like the happiest nations, have no history" (494). Maggie and her society operate in parallel to illustrate the idea that narrative itself is an index of unhappiness. In Eliot's postlapsarian epigram, ideal or innocent states give way to historical awareness. After the fall, grown women, like modern societies, can only tell and retell their histories in an impossible attempt to reinhabit imaginary, innocent sites like premodern St. Ogg's or the girlhood of Maggie Tulliver.

If unhappy women are (in Eliot's broad figurative sense) similar to modern nations, they are also (in Eliot's keen historical view) subject to certain new limitations of power within modern nations. Modernization reorganizes the culture of St. Ogg's, converting yeomen into wage-earners and dividing domestic from productive space. These conversions, along with the rise of professions and bureaucracies, move normative power from the local community to national institutions. They also transfer such power from women to men. In old St. Ogg's, women like the Dodson sisters enforce the rules of conduct, which, though rooted in domestic life, are not limited to household matters. Although the village is no feminist utopia, Eliot's account of the Dodson Aunts as *policières des moeurs* shows that distinct powers accrued to women in the kinship systems of rural England. Aunt Glegg's expertise in matters of tradition gives her sway over an extended family that includes the Tullivers. But with power relocated in the male-run nuclear family, Glegg will have considerably less influence.[32] By registering the potential losses for women when male institutions replace female-regulated customs, Eliot gives special relevance to the obscurity of a "generation of ants [aunts]."

As for Maggie Tulliver, she lives in the liminal zone between traditional and modern arrangements of gender and power. Local customs, regulated by Glegg of St. Ogg's, are the binding force at the center of young Maggie's life—signaled it would seem by the Anglo-Saxon velar stop (gg) at the center of her name. But she does try to break away from that social network at various points in the novel. One early escape attempt—Maggie's flight to the gypsies—serves as a good example of how Eliot coordinates gender and national identity. In the scene, Maggie rebels against the prospect of sexual and economic development—processes that threaten to alienate her from brother Tom and to replace her Edenic childhood at Dorlcote Mill with a "fallen" modern/adult world. When Tom and his cousin Lucy Deane form a bond that excludes her, Maggie flees the constraints of her tribe and joins the gypsies. At this point, Tom conforms to the kinship rules and customary expectations of St. Ogg's in a way that Maggie cannot. Discovering that life as a reformist queen of the gypsies is not possible, however, Maggie returns home and signals acceptance of her identity by evincing a new attachment to a girlish bonnet she had earlier spurned. She pays the price in a gender adjustment for the reassurance of belonging to a familiar, if constraining, community.

The gypsy episode prefigures Maggie's attempt to escape down the river Floss with Stephen Guest, a journey that is equally abortive. After Maggie returns, the women of St. Ogg's ostracize her for what is apparently a sexual transgression. But the older women are not simply punishing a libidinal crime; they are also reclaiming their power to regulate the behavior of village youths. By floating out of the sphere of St. Ogg's on their way to establish a nuclear family, Maggie and Stephen threaten to erode the power of the kinship system. The consequences of this escape are more than just sexual, but so is Maggie's interest in Stephen Guest. In fact, Maggie's desire for Stephen runs through channels that are created by her predicament as an unhappy provincial woman. Maggie cannot adjust to the values of old St. Ogg's (especially insofar as those values are losing historical viability), but neither can she find a line of escape. Stephen seems to offer Maggie a potential pathway to a more modern existence not only through his family's capitalist success, but also through his pedagogical wooing. As Mary Jacobus and Nancy Miller have suggested, education represents all that Maggie cannot have; she is recurrently and painfully excluded from male-dominated chambers of culture. Thus when Stephen courts her "as if he had been the snuffiest of old professors and she a downy-lipped alumnus," he seems to answer Maggie's fervent desire for intellectual exchange (489). She acquiesces to the illicit journey with Stephen, making a grab for modernity and for the metropolitan privileges of literate culture. But the attempt fails; Maggie does not and cannot escape from St. Ogg's.

Even if Maggie could surmount the constraints of her backward and provincial circumstances, however, she would find herself in a metropolitan culture dominated by men. This is another ambiguity in the novel: Eliot seems to indicate that Victorian Englishwomen have gained a certain amount of intellectual freedom even if they have lost the customary powers enjoyed by Aunt Glegg. For example, the narrator describes the 1820s as

> a time when ignorance was much more comfortable than at present . . . a time when cheap periodicals were not, and when country surgeons never thought of asking their female patients if they were fond of reading but simply took it for granted that they preferred gossip: a time when ladies in rich silk gowns wore large pockets in which they carried a mutton bone to secure them against cramp.
>
> (185)

Victorian women have at least been spared by their relative modernity from quackery and medical condescension. But, the passage also suggests with gentle irony, advances in women's status have only really afforded them access to cheap periodicals. Does this compensate for the quarantining of middle-class women in the domestic space? Clearly, Victorian society does not represent a paradise for emancipated women any more than does old St. Ogg's. Maggie thus inhabits a middle zone between two almost equally—if not monolithically—unattractive historical options for women of her region and class.

Marrying neither the local Philip Wakem nor the outsider Stephen Guest, Maggie is barred from entering into either traditional or modern gender arrangements.

The absence of a marriage plot for Maggie is the most important index of the novel's break from bildungsroman conventions: Without a husband, she cannot be recognized as a fully formed woman. In at least one important way, Eliot's uncompromising historical logic determines that neither Maggie nor Tom will be able to marry and reproduce. After all, if modernization consigns the yeoman to history's ashcan, it makes sense that the yeoman class—as represented by the Dodson sisters and their families—cannot reproduce itself. Consider the statistics: The Pullets and Gleggs are childless; the Tullivers and Deanes have only three children between them. The only families in the novel whose procreative pace exceeds zero population growth (the peasant Mosses and the capitalist Guests) fall on either side of the class zone staked out by the dwindling Dodson clan.

In keeping with Eliot's ethnographic viewpoint, we might think of St. Ogg's as an endogamous village whose viability is suddenly threatened by modernization. The narrator implies that, under ordinary circumstances, the tribe would produce a marriage between Tom Tulliver and Lucy Deane. Economic changes, however, force the yeoman class into retrenchment, a condition expressed by Eliot in her extreme application of the rules of endogamy to the Tulliver offspring, who end up bound to each other. The loss of Dorlcote Mill causes an artificial and premature circumscription of the Tullivers, cutting them off from the larger Dodson clan. In a disastrous "premature birth" of the nuclear family, the Tullivers lose their status as members of an extended kinship system and become an economically fragile, socially independent unit. This crisis in turn precipitates the imploding family romance whose outcome is the final union and death-embrace of Tom and Maggie. The symbolic incest plot does more than simply thwart (by exaggerating) a heteronormative literary convention; it delivers an appropriately antidevelopmental conclusion to the historical crisis facing old St. Ogg's.

Tom's development, like Maggie's, is arrested by uneven modernization; he never passes through the conjugal and vocational rites that we expect in a bildungsroman. At first, Mr. Tulliver ships Tom out of the family circle and into the wide world of letters and commerce. But the crisis of the Wakem lawsuit intervenes, drawing a net of obligation and class insecurity tightly around the family. This turn of events initiates an odd trajectory for Tom, who begins moving toward a modernized education, then succeeds in a capitalist-style trading venture, but finally doubles back in a relentless drive to reinstate the economic life of the yeoman and reinhabit Dorlcote Mill. In the process, Tom not only foils his father's oedipally driven economic scheme to remove him from the scene of the mill, but he also effectively bars himself from sexual or reproductive possibilities outside the family. Facing a similar familial and historical trap as his sister, Tom has no access to the relatively unfettered character formation of the conventional *bildungsheld*. The novel's refusal of *Bildung*, largely organized by gendered factors particular to Maggie, crosses over into Tom's narrative line.

When brother and sister are united in a final moment of hyper-endogamy, the novel accepts the implications of its unblinking historicism. Given the figurative links between personal and social development, Eliot needs an outcome in which the losses suffered by a given class are also suffered by its particular representatives. Along the same lines, Lukács praises Walter Scott for remaining faithful to the logic of historical necessity by killing off sympathetic characters whose death represents the demise of an obsolescent way of life (*Historical* 55). The exogamous plot (Maggie marries Stephen Guest)—or even the appropriately endogamous one (Tom marries Lucy Deane)—cannot occur because such marriages would provide an allegorical basis for the yeoman community to "mature" smoothly into the social fabric of modern England. Such an outcome would run counter to the novel's emphasis on the ruptures of national history. The commitment to rupture is the marker of the kind of modernization narrative I see as coming to definitive expression in the modernist/colonial novel, in which capitalist transformations become still less manageable via the offices of organic nationalism—and in which youth persists without age or aging as the progressive elements of the bildungsroman appear in a state of disintegration.

But *Mill* is a transitional text; the force of the soul-nation allegory is still a shaping force in the generic apparatus inherited by Eliot. The novel makes a belated concession to an integrative national history by hinting, in a kind of epilogue, at the marriage between Stephen Guest and Lucy Deane (656). Such a marriage establishes—though to be sure only at the outer margins of the narrative arc—a family unit that provides the missing bourgeois resolution. The linkage of Lucy (the blond Dodson force of custom) with Stephen (the dark Guest force of capitalism) creates a developmental pathway leading from old St. Ogg's to modern England. It is precisely the resolution Eliot refuses for Maggie and Tom Tulliver. And, on the allegorical level, it is precisely the resolution whose synthetic and recuperative version of national history the novel otherwise eschews.

In discussing the historical factors that condition Maggie Tulliver's suspension on the threshold of womanhood and modernity, I have implied that her arrested development is an unfortunate narrative outcome. In a certain sense, however, it would be still more unfortunate to see Maggie's energies, desires, and talents subordinated to the strictures of womanhood in either St. Ogg's or Victorian England. Heroines like Maggie challenge the norms of *Bildung* because those norms so often imply a kind of social adjustment that restricts women's freedom. In *The Mill on the Floss*, Eliot manages to short-circuit the generically ordained process of social adjustment.

It is especially surprising for readers of the "mature" Eliot to consider *Mill* in this light. Where the exquisitely wrought narrative machinery of *Middlemarch* grinds out an accommodation between characters and their social environment, this novel does not, finally, subject Maggie to her Victorian norms of class, gender, region, and religion.[33] Other Eliot heroines grow up and make their peace with social exigencies, but *Mill* represents Maggie's childhood in and for itself, not as mere prelude to the demands of full Victorian womanhood. *Mill* refuses the socialization plot in order to forestall the conversion of Maggie into a mature "angel of the house." From this perspective, we can endorse F. R. Leavis's identification of the novel as an "immature" work while reversing its valuation. The novel's immaturity is neither accident nor flaw, but the necessary formal premise and thematic goal of its entire operation.

Of course, given that Maggie dies in the novel's climactic flood, readers may legitimately wonder whether she—socially adjusted or not—is an apt vehicle for feminist expression. Taken in the context of the novel's general critique of development, however, her watery death has formal justification. In the first place, it seems a fitting device given that Eliot so regularly deploys the language of hydraulic currents and pressures. In fact, the flood confirms Eliot's investment in a rich figurative system built around images of land and water, of Mill and Floss. The language of flows and currents dominates the novel's representation of desire and becomes quite literal when Maggie and Stephen drift downstream. The river Floss plays an equally important role in the novel's wider historical scheme, where it acts as the conduit for economic modernity into St. Ogg's. Merchant ships from beyond the village borders open the gates to the capitalist economy and disrupt the traditional yeoman world.

Bearing the seeds of economic change, the river runs like an epistemological fault line through St. Ogg's. As Raymond Williams suggests, nineteenth-century capitalist dynamism tends to produce fractures in the "knowable community" and to place strains on literary realism (*Country* 165). In this figurative scheme, the flood serves as the ultimate figure for modernization itself—for the drastic transformations wrought by capitalism. The waterways of global trade and imperial expansion loom large in the modernist novels discussed later in this book, from Conrad and H. G. Wells to Woolf and Joyce, all occupying a later and more intense stage of global integration into the world-system.[34] Eliot depicts modernization as a rather brutal force that renders an entire cast of characters literally antediluvian. In a different novel, one whose historical logic were to conform more to our stereotypes of Victorian liberalism, modernization might figure as a controlled form of progress that gradually improves conditions for these provincial Britons. However, instead of humanist and recuperative bourgeois realism, *Mill on the Floss* expresses the stern fatalism of classical tragedy, with the flood as its deus ex machina.

Mill concludes with a final indication that, although nature and society can rebuild themselves after the flood, some losses are absolute: "If there is a new growth, the trees are not the same as the old, and the hills underneath their green vesture bear the marks of the past rending. To the eyes that have dwelt on the past, there is no thorough repair" (656). Critics of Eliot's tendency to thwart female characters have pointed out that Maggie Tulliver, to all appearances a fictional self-portrait, is denied the options enjoyed by George Eliot herself.[35] Despite the parallels between the fictional Maggie Tulliver and the real Marian Evans, the latter gained access to metropolitan privileges denied the former: intellectual achievement, escape from sexual and social conventions (the nonmarriage to G. H. Lewes), escape from national rootedness (the extended continental travels), and escape of a kind even from assigned gender roles (the assumption of the male pseudonym). And yet, as the pseudonym cannot help but remind us, these advances for Eliot also entailed a certain drastically self-alienating process, a process from which Maggie Tulliver is spared by death.[36]

Eliot's investment in Maggie's girlhood runs athwart the generic ethos of maturity and eschews the standard method for ending a bildungsroman. In the ordinary (male-centered) novel of socialization, the protagonist's achievement of maturity provides the necessary symbolic closure, preventing the novel from becoming an endless story of change. But the modernization process itself never reaches an endpoint—a fact that is ordinarily swept under the carpet by the bildungsroman's symbolic foreclosure of youth into an artificially static adulthood. By refusing the genre's telos of adulthood, Eliot fully and honestly assimilates the logic of capitalism and accords genuine power to modernization as a constant, ruthless process. The novel does not ratify adulthood as a final and static form, nor does it provide an allegorical basis for believing that English society had or has arrived at its final, stable form. Just as moral and psychological change proceed without regard to received ideas about the "mature self," social and economic change proceed without regard to romantic illusions about national permanence.

After Eliot: Aging Forms and Globalized Provinces

The Mill on the Floss combines feminist complaint with conservative lament in complex and paradoxical ways. Nostalgia for girlhood fuses with nostalgia for traditional community in a joint rejection of the progressivist assumptions of the male-oriented bildungsroman and of modern triumphalism in both its national-industrial and global-financial forms. As a woman surveying these transitions in nineteenth-century England, Eliot occupies the same kind of tragic, nonaligned position that Lukács ascribed to Walter Scott. According to Lukács, Scott's perspective on the bourgeois revolution was unbiased because he knew that his class (the provincial low aristocracy) was doomed no matter what the outcome. If *Mill* evinces an especially clear-eyed vision about the losses that result from ceaseless modernization, perhaps it is because Eliot knew that women were unlikely to share equally in the spoils of Victorian capitalism. The next four chapters extend this argument to later writers such as Olive Schreiner, Jean Rhys, and Elizabeth Bowen—all of whom were in a way provincialized cosmopolitans, and all of whom used narratives of stunted girlhood or aborted adulthood to register suspicion of masculine destiny and national progress.[37]

Taking a long view of nineteenth- and twentieth-century fiction centered on women protagonists, Rita Felski has offered a useful way to distinguish between two main types of female bildungsroman. The first, generally "historical and linear in structure," depicts a realist process of social adjustment and compromise. The second, less linear, less realistic, and less progressively organized, works "as a process of awakening to an already given mythic identity or inner self and frequently occurs in nature or in a generalized symbolic realm from which the contingent social world has been excluded" (*Beyond* 126–27).[38] The second type, Felski notes, does not narrate self-discovery "as a historical process," but tends instead toward visionary and individuated resolutions to the problem of alienation or repression (142).

Felski's general account tends to skip modernism itself and to draw most of its examples from nineteenth-century classics (more realist) or from women's writing of the last sixty years (more visionary). To give a clear model of the emergence of the feminist bildungsroman in the contemporary period, she organizes her thesis around the possibility of a mediating "female community" (*Beyond* 138–39). Most of the women's novels at the center of the modernist tradition—despite the context of suffrage and sexual liberalization—tend not to feature that mediating female community. They tend rather to operate in the form of critique or negation, to point to the absence of such a community. In a sense, the modernist novel's historical importance is that it mixes modes between the Victorian novel of social compromise or social foreclosure and the post-1945 novel of visionary or communal feminist resolution. In the metabildungsroman of women's modernism, the problem of arrested development indexes a symbolic and ideological refusal to endorse either a dystopian or a utopian model of gender relations. What is more interesting still (though in a sense not surprising) is that so many of the key feminists in the wider British tradition—from Schreiner, Woolf, Rhys, and Bowen to Doris Lessing and Janet Frame—end up modeling the problem of uneven development in terms of the colonial world system.

With that cluster of novelists in mind, the trope of frozen youth offers a specifically colonial and feminist angle on the relation between modernist literary aesthetics and the modern world-system. As we will see in the following chapters, the provincial woman protagonist, for whom progress and development themselves are framed in terms of the integration of the periphery into the advanced stages of finance-imperial capitalism, becomes a richly symbolic figure. We can track that figure from the nineteenth-century intranational scene of provinciality, typified here in Eliot's Maggie Tulliver, to the more international sites of provinciality, occupied, for example, by a Creole migrant such as Jean Rhys's Anna Morgan. By framing this problem in terms of a gendered critique of development immanent to the genre's own traditions, a critique that is at least partially coextensive with the broader problem of the underdeveloped and ahistorical hinterlands, we can build the case from the Victorian precursor forward, gaining conceptual traction on what is both a general crisis in the discourse of progress and a generic crisis in the novel of progress.

After Eliot, the fissile logic of the bildungsroman becomes more and more apparent as it breaks down and pulls apart the entwined narrative *telê* of personal maturity and social modernization. If we cite Eliot as a turning point in literary history, a mediating figure between Victorian and modernist epochs, though, we have also to acknowledge the intervening wave of feminist social and cultural revolt associated with the figure of the New Woman (a movement in which Olive Schreiner, to whom we will next turn, played a direct and significant role during the 1880s and 1890s). And we have to recognize changing literary styles and markets in those decades, particularly the proliferation of genre fiction, on the one hand, and the rise of naturalism, on the other. With regard to the latter, feminist critics such as Felski and Alice Gambrell have noted with some irony that the turn to a more deterministic or naturalist type of fiction—one that tends to strip protagonists of free will and social agency—occurred just as women in British and American society were beginning to assert their rights of self-determination. The novel of unseasonable youth and high naturalism is an alternative response to the growing aesthetic inadequacy of the novel of progress in the age of imperial-finance capitalism and of increasingly bureaucratized and institutional forms of middle-class socialization. Perhaps the crucial differences lie in their geographical frames of reference (unseasonable youth plots seeming to flourish in the space of colonial encounter and to mix domestic-naturalist plots with picaresque and adventure elements) and in their critical modes (unseasonable youth plots preserving perhaps a higher index of dialectical—as opposed to purely antinomial—investment in the still-progressive elements of middle-class realism).[39]

In the decades just after *The Mill on the Floss*, in fact, Eliot's marking of the bildungsroman as a fragile, contradictory, and possibly outmoded genre seems to have converged with a number of aesthetic, literary, political, and philosophical developments that were both signs and causes of morbidity in the "novel of progress." Late Victorian intellectuals of various stripes took account of the ebbing dynamism of bourgeois enterprise, and their discourse of decadent historicism filtered into the realist novel, shouldering aside narratives of progress and emergence once embodied in the national hero. Along these lines, Regenia Gagnier, in her detailed account of economic history's shaping influence on the late nineteenth-century novel, tracks the widespread "displacement of ideas of *progress*, which implied moral and political progress as well as economic growth, by ideas of development, which implied only an inevitable trajectory toward high mass consumption" (94; her emphasis).[40] Gagnier examines influential economic thinkers of the 1870s and 1880s such as August Bebel, who began to envision the eclipse of national interests by global markets (84). She notes: "It seems clear now that the great age of literary realism was also that of industrial production and Malthusian reproduction" (169). The realist novel of progress is part of a productive, industrializing, and nationalizing phase of European history succeeded by a consumerist era linked to imperial adventurism and speculative finance. Nineteenth-century ideals of worldwide development and historical progress came up against stubborn signs of underdevelopment and uneven development in and beyond Europe, just at the same moment that post-Darwinian racial sciences and proto-Freudian sexological discourses lent ever greater prestige and influence to the idea that certain forms of human difference could not be mitigated by would-be civilizing or progressive forces. In such an epoch, as economic and cultural differences appeared to rigidify against the imperial ideal of global convergence, the equipoise of nation-based and controlled-growth capitalism also began to disappear. The social referent of the bildungsroman shifted from the shaped time of national destiny to the unshapely time of capitalism-without-borders, at once underdeveloped and overdeveloped, static and accelerated.[41]

These various developments—the philosophical critique of progress, the naturalist plot of disillusionment, the global market's incursions into national territory, the broader shift from production-oriented to consumption-oriented discourses in economics and aesthetics—all form part of the multipronged contextual model proposed in chapter 1 for the reorganization of the bildungsroman plot after 1860.[42] This chapter's rough trajectory, from Dickens and Eliot to Schreiner and Conrad, defines the contours of mainstream British novel history in terms of what Christopher GoGwilt calls the "collapse of nineteenth-century assumptions about the coordination of natural, individual, national, human, and ultimately universal processes of development" (19). As the cases of *Robinson Crusoe* and *Mansfield Park* already suggest, the late Victorian era does not mark the starting point for colonial influences on English realism, but it does mark a more comprehensive shift in which the global problem of uneven development fuses into the coming-of-age plot, disrupting the standard narrative of growth and emergence in biographical/national fiction. With that disruption, we find new and uncertain allegorizations of collective destiny that tend, at the least, to denaturalize the generic alignment between maturing subjects and modernizing nation-states. As the nineteenth century wore on, it became increasingly difficult to sustain the illusion of a national culture coextensive with its language and territory and coterminous with a progressive, yet bounded, future. The concurrent expansion and disintegration of the European imperial states from 1880 to 1920 made it obvious that a developmental model of history rooted in romantic nationalism was less and less tenable, politically or symbolically. The bildungsroman's generic capacity to reconcile the perpetual motion of modernization with the stabilizing claims of nationalism thus becomes attenuated in the later nineteenth century, as a new era of global empire challenged the pretense of an organic relationship between culture and the state.[43]

In Britain, the period of the New Imperialism corresponded not only to an intensifying pace of economic and technological development, but also to an increasing symbolic schism between the political commitments of liberalism and imperialism. The centrality of empire to British national identity after Disraeli forced a crisis in the national myth of a freedom-loving people. At the same time, imperialism tended to rigidify the mythology of English liberty, turning a general liberal compromise formation with the state into a more triumphant variation of the nation-state's destiny.[44] High imperialism also precipitated a crisis in national self-identity since the constituent cultures of the British state were increasingly separated from each other geographically and culturally. As we shift from Eliot and Dickens in 1860 to Schreiner and Conrad in the late Victorian period, the communities of the English novel become less and less knowable, to adapt Raymond Williams's phrase. What remains mostly oblique or partially concealed about empire in the mainstream Victorian novel—the ways in which colonial labor and wealth support elite English mores, the contradiction between liberalism and imperialism—moves increasingly to the fore.

And, as I began to illustrate with the case of *Kim* in chapter 1, colonial allegories of untimely youth lay bare the inbuilt ideology of personal and national growth that defined the classic bildungsroman. They do so by taking the ideology of progress apart and exposing it to plots of stasis, regression, and endless revolution. In this historical context, the temporal meaning and social vocation of the bildungsroman undergoes a comprehensive shift, as the history of the novel indexes the gradual displacement of historical-progressive thinking by anthropological-structural thinking in the age of empire. In texts like Schreiner's and Conrad's, as we will see in chapter 3, the trope of autonomous youth asks readers to confront with fresh eyes the growing symbolic frailty of nationhood/adulthood as symbolic backstops for what are, after all, the endless and originless processes of self-transformation and world-modernization.

In Schreiner's *African Farm* and Conrad's *Lord Jim*, and in other cases to follow, there is no single plot template for the motif of arrested development. Some protagonists seem prematurely aged, some endlessly juvenile; some develop rapidly and others remain stuck in a psychosocial groove; some die suddenly, some never age. In some cases youth is stylized and dilated, in others it is truncated and stunted; some novels feature youth as consciousness, some as consumerism, some as romanticism, some as provincialism. All of these variants, though, share in foregrounding their departure from the master plot of harmonic growth. All negate and estrange, in one way or another, the soul-nation allegory enshrined in the philosophic conception of *Bildung*. The original magic of the genre, which was to assimilate work into a narrative of education—to harmonize, as it were, production and self-production—comes under strain in colonial settings that appear to reenchant this formula, only to disenchant it with a vengeance. The contest between capitalism (work) and culture (aesthetic vocation) so effectively knitted together by the symbolic mechanisms of the classic bildungsroman (with its implicitly national telos) is instead exacerbated and formalized as a contradiction in the high imperial age.

In modernist novels of unseasonable youth, both the local region/backward colony, on the one hand, and the expanding world-system, on the other, function as non-national spaces, subject to the historylessness of an eternal past or a horizonless future. Those spaces comport equally with the symbol of youth-without-age; youth represents what never fully modernizes *and* what is always modernizing. In both cases, and in both spaces (sub- and supranational), the danger of narrative infinity or endless youth prevails over the stable (and national) temporal concept of bounded progress. In that spirit, we can reexamine *African Farm* and *Lord Jim* as globally mimetic texts whose stunted protagonists point to an uneasy generic grafting of New World–historical knowledge into an older national-historical model of the realist bildungsroman. What is presented to readers in these texts as an immediate and often moving set of unresolvable existential or social conflicts also indexes the structuring contradiction between an imperial ethos of worldwide modernization and the stubborn facts of uneven development and underdevelopment in the colonial periphery. Such a double crisis is, I want to suggest, definitive of Conrad's and Schreiner's relationship both to emergent modernist form and to the New Imperialism. The novel's capacity to use unseasonable youth as the concrete embodiment of failed modernization, within and beyond Europe, will be the focus of the next chapter.

3. Youth/Death: Schreiner and Conrad in the Contact Zone

And sometimes what is more amusing still than tracing the likeness between man and man, is to trace the analogy there always is between the progress and development of one individual and of a whole nation; or again, between a single nation and the entire human race. . . . It is the most amusing thing I know of; but of course, being a woman, I have not often time for such amusements.

—Olive Schreiner, *The Story of an African Farm*

He dominated the forest, the secular gloom, the old mankind. He was like a figure set up on a pedestal, to represent in his persistent youth the power, and perhaps the virtues, of races that never grow old, that have emerged from the gloom. I don't know why he should always have appeared to me symbolic.

—Joseph Conrad, *Lord Jim*

This chapter aims to test the interpretive scheme suggested in chapters 1 and 2 by extending the geographical frame of the discussion out to the colonial frontiers, first of Africa, with Olive Schreiner's *The Story of an African Farm* (1883), and then of Asia, with Joseph Conrad's *Lord Jim* (1900). Both Schreiner and Conrad present us with thwarted and preternaturally youthful subjects set against the background of a languishing colonial periphery. But the non-European world is no mere background here: These paradigmatic colonial novels narrate the failure of development in both characterological and geopolitical registers; taken together, they help us elaborate a working model for the changing meaning of the bildungsroman in the age of empire.

Of course, if Schreiner's *African Farm* shares with *Lord Jim* a particular relation between problematic acculturation and uneven accumulation in the colonial contact zone, its feminist concerns would seem to differentiate it rather sharply from the work of Conrad. After *African Farm*, Schreiner went on to a major career as a "New Woman" writer, attacking both the politics and economics of the prevailing gender system, particularly in her landmark treatise, *Woman and Labour*. In the epigraph to this chapter from *African Farm*, Schreiner's protagonist Lyndall declares an ironic feminist perspective on the entire allegorical procedure that ties the progress of "one individual" to the progress of the "whole nation": That procedure, she recognizes, depends on a male prerogative to expand the soul's domain by analogy to the development of nation and species.[1] Lyndall's outsider perspective recalls the unsettling of developmental allegory we have already observed in Eliot's *Mill on the Floss*, and it anticipates the interlocking critique of patriarchy and imperialism to be found in modernist novels by Virginia Woolf, Jean Rhys, and Elizabeth Bowen.[2]

However, one might equally read *Lord Jim* as a novel about the limits and contradictions of imperial masculinity. Obviously Jim himself, after jumping ship in the first half of the novel, becomes the living embodiment of a failed code of honor and service. By his mere presence, he threatens to expose the grubby deeds of colonial exploitation hiding just beneath the ennobling rhetoric of civilizing mission and seafaring valor. And Jim is not exceptional. Conrad patiently reveals that several other men in the story (much like the masculine exempla in *Kim*) suffer from their own crippling version of a disjunction between chivalric values and social function. The iteration and echo of Jim's conflict across the male characters is clearest of course in the case of Marlow, a figure of practical maturity who cannot quite let go his romantic idealism. Marlow's refrain, "he was one of us," recurs like an emotional tic because Jim can neither be included in, nor excluded from, Marlow's charmed circle of masculine, professional, and racial solidarity. Jim is a code-breaking exception. Thus the plot of *Lord Jim* directly inverts the Goethean plot of social adjustment established by Wilhelm Meister's entry into the Tower Society. In Jim's case, the dream/reality gap structuring middle-class destiny not only cannot be mediated by the elite homosocial group, but it actually threatens to compromise the social function of the group and to shatter its self-conception.

As a result, we find in Conrad's novel a series of male figures more or less stuck in one station or another of the youth-age continuum, but no real transit from station to station. Between callow youth and anxious age, there is no *aging*. Without a narrative presentation of psychic or social change, Conrad organizes his plot into a series of prismatic and perspectival tableaux, a pinwheel of blurry stories collated by Marlow into an array of social perspectives. As in the mature fictions of the decade that followed *Lord Jim* (*Nostromo*, *The Secret Agent*, and *Under Western Eyes*), Conrad uses a structured relay of embedded male narrators to produce an oddly static blueprint for a novel. With perspectival narration as the organizing device, the divorce of action from contemplation is assimilated into the form, echoing and deepening the guiding theme of Jim's passivity. As he perfects that structure in the first stage of his career, Conrad begins to outdo even the original master of bathos, Flaubert, stripping the momentum of plot from the modernist novel, peeling novelistic futurity away from the progressive logic of national allegory.

Schreiner and Conrad thus converge in plots of arrest and stasis organized around broken allegories of progress. Schreiner's Anglo-African woman cannot liberate herself, to be sure, but neither can Conrad's Anglo-Asian man. Lyndall and Jim both slip into the dangerous darker side of their respective gender stereotypes: the dying mother/fallen woman and the broken hero/macho redeemer. The gender codes operative in those plots are all the more binding as they play out across not just national but colonial space. Picking up where George Eliot and Thomas Hardy leave off, Schreiner extends the naturalist motif of the trapped provincial woman into the colonial context. Conrad, too, exhibits streaks of cruel naturalism: In both *African Farm* and *Lord Jim*, we find the striving idealisms of youth viewed from a clinical distance by narrators who cast them as the puny, futile efforts of insects (beetles and butterflies echoing the "ants and beavers" of *Mill on the Floss*). Without modernization and maturation in place as the familiar tandem engines of story line, these novels trace a short circuit from frozen youth to sudden death. Where one might expect to find at the colonial frontier the last redoubt of heroic idealism or free self-making for the Anglophone novel, one finds instead modes of rationalization and reification even more unyielding than the ones back home. As Marlow himself sagely notes: "In no other kind of life is the illusion more wide of reality—in no other is the beginning *all* illusion—the disenchantment more swift—the subjugation more complete" (137). Hence both novels produce rapid swings between romance and naturalist modes.

Conrad and Schreiner frame a *colonial* divide between the dream of soul-making and the brute facts of work, breaking open an encapsulated imperialist romance with its temporal obverse: the naturalist code of death. Schreiner's characters are playthings of fate, not Goethean self-makers; their growth is both too fast and too slow for the *Bildung* ideal of concrete, measured emergence. The original magic of the genre, which was to assimilate work into a narrative of education—to harmonize, as it were, production and self-production—comes under strain in a colonial setting that appears to reenchant and globalize this formula, only to disenchant it with a vengeance. In other words, when we begin to explore these novels in detail, we can see what it looks like when the definitive modern conflict between capitalism (work) and culture (aesthetic vocation)— the conflict that is, ideally, knitted together by the symbolic mechanisms of the bildungsroman—is instead exacerbated, revealed, and given newly visible form as a contradiction in terms.

Outpost without Progress: Olive Schreiner's *Story of an African Farm*

If there is one thing upon which Olive Schreiner's readers and critics now generally agree, it is that *The Story of an African Farm* is an odd duck in terms of genre and style—a kind of literary platypus whose ungainly combination of parts and functions seems to flummox both classification and periodization. To describe the novel to new readers requires an entire glossary of both exotic and familiar generic categories; it is one part South African *plaasroman* (farm-novel), one part New Woman fiction, one part Dickensian farce (featuring pale, sentimental orphans and ruddy, sadistic adults), one part naturalist tragedy (with a merciless rising sun and a pitiable fallen woman), one part colonial gothic, one part Victorian melodrama (featuring hopeless love and missed letters), one part allegorical tale, one part satire of provincial manners (with its dusty Boer wedding scene), one part spiritual autobiography, one part neotranscendentalist novel of ideas. Moreover, *The Story of an African Farm* now holds a firm place in both British and South African literary canons and, despite its nineteenth-century date of publication (1883), seems to anticipate a number of modernist fictional techniques. Combining these problems of periodization, literary geography, and stylistic taxonomy, this chapter reads Schreiner's sui generis African novel in relation to the history of yet another genre, the European bildungsroman.

The combination of gender and colonial concerns that animates Schreiner's first novel no doubt partly accounts for its initial success in the 1880s and 1890s and its renewed prominence in the 1980s and 1990s, when feminist and postcolonial approaches raised its profile in North American curricula and critical debates. Of course, as both John Kucich and Anne McClintock have recently noted, *African Farm*'s open design—what some critics have seen as its immature or haphazard quality—imparts to the text a high level of ideological indeterminacy, so that it has been read variously as counterfeminist and feminist, anti-imperial and imperial, nonracist and racist.[3] In part for this reason, my reading brackets the question of political intention and concentrates instead on the problem of narrative form. The novel's force stems, I think, not from Schreiner's avowed views—hopelessly mixed and perhaps impossible to correlate definitively to the book we have—but from its systematic assimilation of a certain uneven and markedly colonial temporality into its plot structure, characterization, and figurative language. Its conspicuously awkward temporal scheme not only challenges the formal dictates of the Goethean bildungsroman (with that genre's accrued or conventional sense of teleological and masculinist destiny), but also registers the deep contradictions of colonialism itself—contradictions growing more conspicuous during the age of empire.

Perhaps the best way to define the age of empire as a context for Schreiner's novel is not to cite Eric Hobsbawm's book (though his dates, 1875–1914, would align rather neatly with the contours of this study), but to recall Hannah Arendt's account of modern imperialism, which assigns a significant place to 1880s South Africa. Arendt focuses on the quickening, formalizing, and globalizing of European colonialism in the 1870s and 1880s—a vast process for which the Berlin Congress of 1883–1884 often stands as a concrete historical marker. Arendt defines high imperialism as the eclipse of national by international capitalism, noting the increasing intensity and instability of speculative-financial and colonial-extractive modes of wealth creation (as against more traditional lines of industrialization) (135). She focuses special attention on South African colonialism, starting with the breakneck growth generated by the opening of the Kimberley diamond mines just at the time of *African Farm*'s publication. Arendt traces the origins of apartheid back to the Kimberley boom and to the imperial project defined by Cecil Rhodes. In Rhodes's South Africa, she suggests, the "so-called laws of capitalism were actually allowed to create realities" without any kind of backstop from national politics (136–37). As a result, "normal capitalist development" was forestalled and avoided (203). If South Africa stands as a special case of racialized labor exploitation and unfettered capitalism, it also, for Arendt, signals the beginning of a crisis and a condition that was not just peripheral or colonial, but also European and even global, in which the modernizing ethos and self-reliant bourgeois dynamism that drove Western industrialization began to dissipate. The Boers, she claims, were the "first European group to become completely alienated from the pride which Western man felt in living in a world created and fabricated by himself" (194).[4]

The centuries-long history of exploitative slave and colonial economies notwithstanding, Arendt's characterization of this era as inaugurating a new phase of unrestrained capitalist relations outside the national boundaries and moral limits of middle-class progress proves, I think, quite telling for literary history in general, for the bildungsroman as the genre of progress, and for *African Farm* in particular. Few texts are as well positioned to help us assess the speculative links outlined so far between the rise of the new imperialism, the crisis of European realism, and the new temporal contours of the bildungsroman. In *African Farm*, we can track the shift from realism to naturalism, from self-made protagonists to environmental victims, from regional to global maps of uneven development, from narratives of (at least apparent) class mobility to narratives of racialized class stasis—all as part of the history of the Victorian novel of education transplanted into the world of fin de siècle imperialism.[5]

The point of such a reinterpretation is not so much to finesse the Victorian/ modernist borderline, nor even—though this merits consideration—to argue that colonial fiction was central to the innovations of the late Victorian novel of consciousness. The point is, rather, to situate *African Farm* within a particular conceptual, historical, and generic crisis in the discourse of progress, and to estab-lish the fissile logic of the bildungsroman as it breaks down and breaks apart the entwined narrative *telê* of personal maturity and social modernization. What kind of novel, we might ask, can keep faith with the complex interaction of European narratives of progress and their manifest faltering on the colonial periphery, with the unsteady tempo of modernization in a fully extended yet unevenly developed world-system? The answer, of course, lies in the narrative form and linguistic texture of *African Farm* itself; it is what makes the novel's generic variety and non-realist technique fascinating even today. This is what a coming-of-age story looks like when its social referent is the very frontier of imperial capitalism, when it addresses a form of modernization with no national boundaries and few political limits, a form corresponding to what Arendt calls "a supposedly permanent pro-cess which has no end or aim but itself" (137).

Schreiner's *African Farm* embeds and entwines the Kipling plot of endless colonial youth (as described in chapter 1) with the Eliot plot of feminine self-renunciation and sudden death (as described in chapter 2). In both kinds of plot—youth extended and youth truncated—the missing element is aging, that is, the process of development itself. When we read *African Farm*, we can see right away that failed or absent development is the governing motif of Schreiner's imagina-tive response to colonial life in Africa. Her utterly provincial protagonists are as distant from the metropole as they are sealed off from the inner life of Africans, who feature here only as domestic and agricultural labor. *African Farm* is, as J. M. Coetzee puts it, a "microcosm of colonial South Africa: a tiny community set down in the midst of the vastness of nature, living a closed-minded and self-satisfied existence." "The farm," Coetzee observes, "is pettiness in the midst of vastness" (65). Its little world reflects the intra-European rivalries of southern Africa, with sympathy attached to English stepchildren living in a Boer household.

To focus my reading of the novel, I am going to concentrate on the separate bildungsroman plots of the novel's orphan trio: Waldo, Em, and Lyndall, young sufferers who endure the slapstick violence of the Dickensian villain Bonaparte Blenkins in the first half of the story. The second half begins with a kind of spiritual biography pertaining mostly to Waldo, then shifts attention to Lyndall and gains momentum as a feminist novel of ideas and a provincial tragedy along the lines of Hardy's *Tess*. Stolid Em follows the lit pathway toward marriage; Lyndall, a precocious embodiment of New Woman aspirations, leaves the farm in search of a worldly education; and Waldo, dreamy son of the deceased German overseer, seeks an otherworldly education while tending to the farm. Each develops outside the protocols of realistic linear time—a fact that is highlighted by explicit commentary, by the patterned imagery, and of course by the unorthodox narrative pacing and structure. Sandra Gilbert and Susan Gubar (among other readers) have noted that the novel's two halves are rather disjointed, so that the protagonists' "youth, presented in the first book, is completely discontinuous with the adulthood they have mysteriously managed to attain in the second" (*No Man's Land* 56). This oddity of construction, quite akin, I think, to the famous bifurcated structure of *Lord Jim*, is in fact only the most obvious manifestation of an antidevelopmental logic that shapes the novel at every level and subplot. Em, for example, matures so rapidly that she is in effect domesticated from the start, leaving her to wonder "if all people feel so old, so very old, when they get to be seventeen" (219).

In the cases of Waldo and Lyndall, the tempo of growth is more complicated and dilated. The novel opens with an agonizing scene in which a ticking clock torments Waldo; time haunts him from beginning to end. In the middle, Schreiner meditates on Waldo's growth in a somewhat jarring first-person plural voice, so that his intensely idiosyncratic thoughts are presented as the normal phases of childhood cognition that "we" all pass through. This description occupies its own, anomalous chapter, entitled "Times and Seasons," and is lodged at the pivot point of the novel very much in the manner of Virginia Woolf's "Time Passes" section in *To the Lighthouse*. The sequence—now much commented upon—is dominated by the notion that the soul's private time is discrete and incremental:

> They say that in the world to come time is not measured out by months and years. Neither is it here. The soul's life has seasons of its own; periods not

found in any calendar, times that years and months will not scan, but which are as deftly and sharply cut off from one another as the smoothly-arranged years which the earth's motion yields us.

(137)

In "Times and Seasons," Schreiner restricts Waldo's development to the spiritual and intellectual plane. The peculiarly asocial nature and syncopated time of Waldo's development takes shape in relation to the remote colonial setting of the farm; he is not subject to everyday realist temporality, but instead models his subjectivity on deep and inhuman forms of zoological, geological, and metaphysical time. Just as Conrad's Jim is suspended between the high ideals and low practices of empire, Waldo dwells in a peripheral zone somewhere between beautiful absolutes and brutal facts. He grows up well outside the civilized "hum and buzz" of Lionel Trilling's middle-class mores (106). That is, he does not grow up, for despite the outward elongation of his limbs, Waldo remains a pious ragamuffin, an ageless, curly-haired cherub of Germanic intellection.[6]

Waldo's passion for homespun and purple metaphysics, flowering in what Schreiner codes as the vast cultural emptiness of the African veldt, cuts directly against the Goethean formula of concrete historical thinking. The colonial setting allows Waldo to encounter instead abstract existential concepts and the hard facts of merciless nature. Thus Waldo's governing time is both more and less abstract than the profoundly civilized and realist time ascribed to Goethe by Bakhtin, Lukács, and Moretti. The conventional aspects of Waldo's entire *Bildung* plot are compressed into a single letter, a miniature scale model of a provincial novel of development: boy leaves farm, goes to town, seeks fortune, meets good souls and bad, tastes new tastes, sees corruption and earns companionship, learns trade, gains informal education, then returns to the farm. Whereas in a conventional novel we follow the hero through each episode, here the story of Waldo's way in the world is delivered in skeletal, retrospective, and indirect form—an effect that intensifies the novel's quite rigid restriction of the action to the farm setting.

Waldo's circumscribed destiny is both determined and figured by the colonial conditions, especially insofar as the farm is a vulnerable settlement that does not, itself, develop. The land is dry and unforgiving, the livestock bare-ribbed, and the crops scant; the only wealth gained in the novel comes through marriage or inheritance. Schreiner matches this curious absence of production with a notably anemic rate of reproduction among the settler class. If we assess Waldo's absent plot of emergence against this backdrop, we can see that his failure to develop moves in parallel to the nonemergence of a genuine culture or society in this fictionally distilled reflection of colonial South Africa. Waldo's African farm is—like the Patusan of *Lord Jim*—an "outpost of progress" in which there is no real progress, only local realignments of limited resources and quite arbitrary power. The modernization of economic and social life fails in both *African Farm* and *Lord Jim*; both consistently refer its failure to the impermanent and fragile quality of colonial settlement. Near the start of *African Farm*, Waldo observes the following as he contemplates the passing of the Bushmen (Khoikhoi): "And the wild bucks have gone, and those days, and we are here. But we will be gone soon, and only the stones will lie on here" (50). By restricting itself to members of a marginal settler class (a class that, to be sure, manages to dispossess the indigenous peoples), Schreiner's novel emphasizes the futurelessness of life eked out on the edge of the veldt.

However, despite—or perhaps because of—the hardscrabble boundaries of Waldo's life (paralleled in the dank jungle privations of Jim's reign in Patusan), there is in *African Farm* a brief romance of colonial innocence based on a vision of virgin land and unalienated labor, of colonialism without the contradictions of European capitalism. But these romances—Waldo's and Jim's—are in fact fully encapsulated by the novelistic structures that surround them. In the end, their colonial bubbles of pastoral or neofeudal social harmony are burst by the reassertion of modernity; both European man-boys, once astride Asian and African Nature, must then trade lyrical contentment for sudden death. Like Jim, Waldo expires after a brief frontier episode of inner and outer harmony and remains a walking figure of nondevelopmental time.

Lyndall's separate journey is equally compressed and fatal: She leaves the farm, attends school, encounters the world, takes a lover, becomes pregnant, returns to the farm, leaves again, gives birth, and dies, all the while fiercely attempting to throw off the coils of Victorian womanhood and offering a cogent dismissal of marriage as a degrading property arrangement. At one point, Lyndall reviews for Waldo the ideological burdens of a girl's education:

> The curse begins to act on us. It finishes its work when we are grown women, who no more look out wistfully at a more healthy life; we are contented. We fit our sphere as a Chinese woman's foot fits her shoe. . . . In some of us the shaping to our end has been quite completed.

> (189)

This kind of education works, like the *Bildung* of Moretti's darkest Lukácsian vision, by securing the consent of the subordinated, causing them freely to accept unfreedom. However, this is not the story *of* the novel; it is a story encapsulated *within* the novel, objectified as the kind of female bildungsroman whose generic mold the novel breaks.

Schreiner ironizes by literalizing the motif of the bound Chinese foot, framing Lyndall in terms of her own tiny hands and feet. Lyndall's size does not represent her subjection to womanhood, but her willful refusal to mature. Still, if Lyndall's plotline is not the story of social compromise with "women's roles," neither is it an emancipation story. Lyndall's precocious political sensibility spurs her toward freedom, but her critique of contemporary gender arrangements cannot provide a public role or social resolution equal to her private sense of destiny. Often Schreiner presents Lyndall as immured within her own vision, stuck within a closed circuit of introspection: "I am so weary of myself! It is eating my soul to its core—self, self, self!" (241). Lyndall's consumption of soul by self marks the process wherein development has disintegrated. Just as for Waldo's metaphysical lust, so for Lyndall's freethinking ambition; these inner drives can be described but they are not, as in the classic bildungsroman model, integrated into the logic of a socially realized character. *African Farm* thus offers a colonially inflected example of what is in fact a familiar pattern in Victorian fiction, where female protagonists complicate or violate the masculine vocational and sexual model of middle-class consent, leading to what feminist critics have seen as a necessary refusal of *Bildung*, a dissenting "voyage in," or a tragic plot of self-renunciation.[7]

As we have already noted, the case of Schreiner is a tricky one for both feminist and postcolonial analysis. A formalist approach to *African Farm* helps us avoid political reductions of the text, warding off a predictable but inapt focus on the thematics of alterity or the reciprocal allegorization of woman and native. *African Farm* resists the interpretive frame of colonial otherness, of cross-cultural identification and marginalization, in large part because it so thoroughly commits itself to the logic of colonial failure and provincial tragedy. In this way, it resists the model described by Gayatri Spivak with respect to Victorian novels like *Jane Eyre*, in which white women establish a kind of subjective freedom by obscuring, displacing, or demonizing a racialized figure, a native, so-called (121). Schreiner's commitment to representing the problem of colonial development translates into a shrunken estate for Lyndall's subjective destiny. That commitment entails the failure of both cultural and biological reproduction at the periphery, putting the novel quite at odds with the gendered project of imperial humanism that Spivak identifies both in her reading of Brontë and at large in her *Critique of Postcolonial Reason*.

The novel's colonial and feminist concerns converge most fully in Lyndall's monologues on the problem of the educated provincial woman's limited capacity to abstract herself into universal narratives of human or civilizational progress.

Consider, for example, the following passage in which Lyndall seems to weave classical and colonial vignettes into an expansive transcultural perspective:

> I like to realize forms of life utterly unlike mine . . . I like to crush together, and see it in a picture, in an instant, a multitude of disconnected unlike phases of human life—mediæval monk with his string beads pacing the quiet orchard, and looking up from the grass at his feet to the heavy fruit-trees; little Malay boys playing naked on a shining sea-beach; a Hindoo philosopher alone under his banyan tree, thinking, thinking, thinking, so that in the thought of God he may lose himself; a troop of Bacchanalians dressed in white, with crown of vine-leaves, dancing along the Roman streets . . . a Kaffir witch-doctor seeking for herbs by moonlight . . . I like to see it all; I feel it run through me—that life belongs to me; it makes my little life larger; it breaks down the narrow walls that shut me in.
>
> (214–15)

This global fantasy of males freely harvesting the fruits of nature and culture establishes Lyndall's shrewd views about the privileges of imaginative self-projection. The passage assumes a more pointed meaning when we recall that Lyndall's secret pregnancy is emerging at just this point, establishing a fine counterpoint between two modes of self-extension. Its placement in the text underscores Lyndall's restriction to, on the one hand, private fantasies of mobility, cultural prestige, and social vocation and, on the other, the prospect of a delimited public role as handmaid and nursemaid to male destiny.

What makes this example of Lyndall's sophistication such a potent thematic note in the novel is that it comes, in a sense, to define her as an authorial surrogate who provides oblique commentary on the gendered abstractions that drive the classic bildungsroman with its "typical" hero figuring the fate of the collective. At one point, in fact, Lyndall all but declares that the problem of allegory is a feminist one:

> And sometimes what is more amusing still than tracing the likeness between man and man, is to trace the analogy there always is between the progress and development of one individual and of a whole nation; or again, between a single nation and the entire human race. It is pleasant when it dawns on you that the one is just the other written out in large letters; and very odd to find all the little follies and virtues, and developments and retrogressions written out in the big world's book that you find in your little internal self. It is the most amusing thing I know of; but of course, being a woman, I

have not often time for such amusements. Professional duties always first, you know. It takes a great deal of time and thought always to look perfectly exquisite, even for a pretty woman.

(198–99)

Lyndall's arch tone points to the bitter fact that women bear a blocked relation to a mode of self-representation whose narrative equivalent is allegory and, even more particularly, to the bildungsroman as a symbolic device that binds subject to nation in a shared trajectory of "progress and development." Her remarks testify to the pleasure of making these symbolic narratives, but she seems also to be mocking their substance. In fact, Schreiner's self-conscious approach to *Bildung*—a critique that is both colonial and feminist—presents allegory itself as an *adolescent* or naive form of representation.[8] In the "Times and Seasons" chapter, the narrator describes it as a passing preoccupation of youth: "For an instant our imagination seizes it; we are twisting, twirling, trying to make an allegory" (143). This is a juvenile and male prerogative associated—not incidentally for my purposes—with that hermetic German-idealist Waldo. Here is Schreiner's irony of allegory: that Goethean developmental thinking is, after all, underdeveloped thinking.

Lyndall's plot does not merely parallel but implicitly comments on Waldo's, casting skepticism on his youthful idealism, on his Goethean penchant for seeing and seeking the drama of progress in all things. In "Times and Seasons," Waldo conducts a series of experiments geared to finding metaphysical and narrative meaning—systematically *developmental* meaning—in every phenomenal cranny of his little universe, from the geological to the zoological. He cracks eggs "to see the white spot wax into the chicken" and dissects "dead ducks and lambs," looking for traces of ontogenetic symmetry and phylogenetic design in their viscera, avid to confirm that "all is part of a whole," that progress and development cast their sheltering meaning over the barnyard and across the stratified earth of the Karoo (152–54). This, reflects the narrator, is how the mystified youthful mind tries to shore the evidence of nature against the "weltering chaos" of experience. The principles of unification and development, which, as many have noted, allude quite directly to Schreiner's own formative encounter with Herbert Spencer's *First Principles*, provide a foil for the novel's dramatic revision of developmental allegory. Schreiner thus presents allegorical thinking as a passing phase in the life of her German-romantic boy hero but also in the history of European ideas. The narrator explicitly locates herself in an era of rational skepticism about all forms of historical or developmental design, whether derived from philosophy, religion, or science.

With the erosion of these bases for allegorical and teleological thinking, Schreiner creates a metageneric level in the text, in which the naturalized Goethean motifs of developmental fiction are exposed as contingent and outmoded. She organizes (or disorganizes) her novel according to a more random and cruel form of temporality, a naturalist clock whose uneven, unpredictable strokes cut across any sense of pure progress, whether individual or civilizational.

In setting her naturalist clock against the romance of imperial progress, Schreiner also establishes a formal pattern that Conrad repeats, with variations, in *Lord Jim*, equally a story of colonial removal and frozen adolescence. The two novels share the arch-naturalist motif of the puny human insect: Schreiner's beetle, rolling dung, symbolizes "a striving, and a striving, and an ending in nothing," thus establishing the epigraphical keynote for Waldo and Lyndall in Book Two (107; 135); likewise, Conrad's remote patron Stein sees Jim, with his futile romanticism, as a perfect specimen of the fragile, sad human Lepidoptera. More tellingly, *African Farm* shares with *Lord Jim* the two-phase plot, highlighting its refusal or incapacity to narrate growth, to fuse the objective and subjective conditions of soulmaking.

The point of establishing *Lord Jim* as an intertext for *African Farm* is not to argue for direct influence, but to analyze related instances of late Victorian fiction that encode uneven development into protagonists who cannot mature and into colonies that cannot modernize. Conrad's Jim fails to accumulate experience just as his colonial enterprises fail to accumulate wealth; the old bildungsroman link between *self*-production (the hero who creates his own personality) and production per se still obtains, but in an inverse or negative form. Jim is not so much a psychologically dynamic character as a walking principle of imperial time, a colonial Dorian Gray to Marlow's Picture, since Marlow appears to take on all the sad, sagging weight of self-doubt that Jim seems to shrug off. When Jim dies, he remains inside a bubble of supervirginal egoism, just as Kipling's Kim remains in the neverland of imperial adolescence, and just as Lyndall seems to trap the mature political consciousness of a New Woman in a tiny, charming body that cannot age until it dies.

"A free and wandering tale": Conrad's *Lord Jim*

Work is the domain wherein Conrad's Jim has an initial advantage over Schreiner's Lyndall. Despite Lyndall's education, her exclusion from "the great world of earnest labour" is never in doubt and is in fact exacerbated by her location in the provincial agrarian world of Boer South Africa (194). Jim by contrast begins his career as a promising mate in the merchant marine, though of course through Marlow's eyes we can see right away that, for Jim, fantasies of derring-do have displaced Lyndall's "world of earnest labour." Unlike Kipling, who genuinely narrates work itself, Conrad's Marlow preaches the saving grace of the Protestant work ethic (above all in arenas of colonial enterprise), but seems to have a bottomless philosophical appetite for talking about vocation rather than doing it.[9] The novel follows the logic of Marlow's priorities (soul status over labor value): Once Jim's character is devalued, he can no longer find redemption through work no matter how far he travels the wide imperial waterways of the East, no matter the privilege of his race, gender, and class. In one small but telling episode, Marlow huffily rejects the idea of stationing a disgraced Jim with a group of indentured Asian laborers on a deserted guano island where he can act as coolie-master and "supreme boss." Chester, the island's would-be birdshit capitalist, insinuates to Marlow that Jim is a walking version of the guano island: a pile of golden waste that cannot really be salvaged or developed (167).

The need to rescue Jim vocationally is a long-term, novel-shaping problem for Marlow (and Conrad) as it is for Jim himself. Without redemptive work, the imperialist enterprise reveals itself as merely exploitative. It is not surprising to find a novel from this period (the era of Hardy, Dreiser, Zola) in which no fortunes are made, but Conrad takes particular pains to underscore the failure of imperial accumulation and to align it with the static quality of Jim's existential development. As in *African Farm*, there is a notable dearth of both production and reproduction; indeed these are not just missing features but central and conspicuous lacks reciprocally indexed to the master trope of underdevelopment, Jim's youth. Jim, Marlow announces, is the, "youngest human being now in existence" (204). He appears to defy the laws of time and the conventions of *Bildung*, remaining a Teflon-coated fair-haired boy despite the episodes of moral and professional failure that kick the novel into gear in chapter 3.

Jim is not just a moral or psychological type; he's also an idealized ethnic English type. During the years before and after *Lord Jim*, Conrad seems to have been preoccupied with the figure of the English idealist, whom he criticizes for naive sentimentality, celebrates for moral integrity, and frames in terms of arrested development.[10] The three Marlow tales that Conrad published during the 1898–1900 period, "Youth," *Heart of Darkness,* and *Lord Jim,* show Marlow encountering three different forms of idealism. In "Youth," Marlow recounts the heady days of his first Eastern voyage (as second mate on the *Judea*) and his admiration for the *Judea's* captain—an iteration of the Jim character, a strangely adolescent Englishman whose clear blue eyes were "amazingly like a boy's, with that candid expression some quite common men preserve to the end of their days by a rare internal gift of simplicity of heart and rectitude of soul" (10). This blue-eyed hero contrasts with Kurtz the corrupted idealist; both contrast in turn with Jim, who lays claims to ideals that he cannot embody or redeem.

The opening chapters of Lord Jim establish Jim's heroic fantasies as at once reminiscent of the Goethean bildungsroman (insofar as he feeds his notions of destiny a steady diet of heroic literature) and quite obviously divergent from the generic model (insofar as we can already see that Jim's dreams are callow and fraudulent, divorced from action). When the opportunity to act emerges, Jim fails, though Marlow notes with grim irony that Jim ardently recuperates his own passivity: "He had enlarged his knowledge more than those who had done the work . . . he exulted with fresh certitude in his avidity for adventure" (49–50). The novel recurrently probes the gap between knowledge and action, widening it as Jim spirals into disgrace after abandoning the Patna, closing it temporarily in the Patusan episode, then blasting it back open in the denouement. The generic languages of the novel keep modulating, because Jim is a romantic hero stuck in a naturalist plot: The social conditions are calculated to break his heroic self-conception, but he perversely refuses their lesson. Marlow can never decide if it is appalling or admirable to see such dogged will attached to such unsound actions (109).

To talk about the problematic of endless youth in Lord Jim then is not just to reckon with Jim the existential or moral adolescent, but also to consider the dilatory and recursive organization of the novel itself as a coded reflection on both the history of the novel and on the historical context of late empire.[11] Famously enough, Lord Jim began life as a short tale and ballooned into the "free and wandering tale" that we now have (43).[12] One might well imagine that the plotlessness is most salient in the romantic Patusan portion of the text, but in fact both the colonial outpost (Patusan) and the merchant ship (Patna) are sites of stasis. Conrad's technique for plot-stalling a shipboard tale is already visible in both The Nigger of the "Narcissus" and "Youth." In the latter story, the expository section mirrors that of Lord Jim, with Marlow playing the role of the young mate avid for adventure. Exclamation points and fervid interjections pile up as Marlow recalls his own state of mind shipping out on the Judea:

> O youth! The strength of it, the faith of it, the imagination of it! To me she was not an old rattle-trap carting about the world a lot of coal for a freight—to me she was the endeavour, the test, the trial of life.

(17)

But this high feeling is suspended and dissolved by a long legal wrangle that keeps the *Judea* portbound and forces youth to stew in its own potentiality (20). Marlow's Eastern adventure becomes Conrad's experiment in adventurelessness; in it, souls are formed in contemplation and retrospect rather than in act and will.[13] Colonial journeys in most Conrad texts—certainly in *Lord Jim*—do not deliver men from the enforced passivity of domesticated masculinity in the industrial age. Instead they provide a stark contrast-medium for discovering and disclosing the impossibility of adventure.

Of course, such bathetic spectacles of fortunes unmade and destinies unmet present an artistic problem to a novelist: How to advance a narrative that has adventurelessness at its core? How to organize the pattern of scene, set, and episode without conceding—as Conrad did not—to a fully naturalist inversion of narrative Providence into tragic, deterministic fate? In "Youth," we can see Conrad figuring out how to balance action and stasis on a small scale by rotating points of view and mulling over impressions while action is held at bay. This tells us a great deal about the mechanics of plot in Conrad, because he so faithfully reproduces the problem of construction in the overt content of the tale. Coal smolders in the cargo bay while the story and the ship are held still, but we know (as we know in *Secret Agent*) that an explosion will come and that the narrative will therefore end. Explosions are not just topical referents for Conrad; they also literalize the trigger-function needed to kick a stalled plot back into forward motion—even when, as in the rigged silver mine of *Nostromo*, the dynamite stays unexploded. Explosive devices define, in a sense, the displacement of destiny by accident in fiction, and it is precisely that displacement that defines, in turn, modernism's most fundamental revision of the bildungsroman.

In "Youth," when the smoking cargo explodes, it blows Marlow off the ship: "I seemed somehow to be in the air" (26). The evacuated agency of the line anticipates Jim's jump off the *Patna*: "I had jumped. . . . It seems" (125). Conrad frays and spreads the syntax here in order to underscore the passive nature of the anti-hero caught among forces too large or unknowable to contest. That motif of the paralyzed hero overtaken by invisible or invincible forces that suddenly break the crust of a stalled narrative recurs not only across Conrad's works, but across quite a number of recursively organized modernist novels of youth: It marks the arrested development of the protagonist.[14] Thus the object that sinks the *Patna* in *Lord Jim* remains an unseen, underwater dark mass, "something floating awash," a "whatever it was." In *Kim*, we find the Shamlegh pit, a bottomless, sexualized, Asiatic maw that Kim must evade in order to preserve his imperial innocence. In Woolf's *The Voyage Out*, a number of invisible phallic creatures populate the depths of Rachel

Vinrace's psyche and of the sea, "white, hairless, blind monsters lying curled on the ridges of the sand" that threaten Rachel's long girlhood (16). Stephen Dedalus, the hero of Joyce's *Portrait of the Artist as Young Man*, not only entertains grisly spectacles of hell as an infinity of suffering, but has unsettling dreams "peopled by apelike creatures" (124). At such moments, working from a depth beyond telling, these images are not just metaphors tapping the psychosexual unconscious, they are also self-exposing figures that announce their own necessity to a plot of stalled action; they reactivate the story when characters are mired in psychic or ethical stasis. These uncanny figures also signal—in their thematic links to infinitude and depth—the allure of actionlessness, of the stall that never ends. More specifically, they seem to operate as variations on the theme of an Hegelian "bad infinity"—an infinity associated with both frozen youth and imperial depth/death.

In the case of Conrad, bad infinity seems always to demand its chronotopic opposite: a site of bounded space and stopped time. On an isolated ship (the *Judea*, the *Narcissus*, the *Patna*) or in an isolated colony (Sulaco in *Nostromo*; Patusan in *Lord Jim*), time is trapped into an almost airless lack of motion.[15] Bogged down in cycles of failed modernization, colonial spaces such as Sulaco and Patusan provide the setting for Conrad to cycle through episodic bouts of speculation and spectatorship, philosophical chatter and moral inertia. Into these pocketed worlds of muffled action and stalled development comes the violent accident or intrusion that Conrad uses to drive time forward. Oscillating between the distended time of narrative recycling and the instant accidents that bring historical or linear time back into play, Conrad manages to create the narrative framework for what we generally call his impressionist style.[16] *Lord Jim* establishes a fairly legible relationship between the slowness or languor of the style and the lingering youth of the protagonist; Conrad's language has the same "gorgeous virility" and "charm of vagueness" that his hero does (58). To put the point more simply, Conrad aligns his own emergent technique for breaking the action with Jim's penchant for inaction.

This link is nowhere more clear than in the fateful moment of Jim's jump from the sinking *Patna*. The jump is a jump-cut, vaulting the reader forward from the deck of the *Patna* to the inquest a month later. Conrad's use of deferred climax and delayed decoding finds perfect correspondences in Jim's brief confession (itself postponed for several chapters *after* the opening of the public inquest): "I had jumped. . . . It seems" (125). At a stroke, Conrad hollows out the act with a past-perfect verb tense that reflects Marlow's layered retrospect, with an ellipsis that matches the untold narrative gaps, and a haze of "seeming" that clouds the space between subject and action, event and reader. Jim's nonadventure might well be described as a perfect inversion of the "rite of passage"—not just because it marks a wrong action, but because Jim preserves "through it all a strange illusion of passiveness, as though he had not acted" (123). The jump-cutting in Marlow's story brings readers to and through a middle portion of the text in which Jim's geographic mobility produces not the awaited ethical maturity and social integration, but a discontinuous set of failed episodes through which Jim does not grow. After his disgraceful exit from the *Patna*, Jim cannot really rejoin the fraternal subsociety of the merchant marine, but must remove himself endlessly toward the horizon of the known empire, stuck in a loop of rebirth and shame in each new port. Finally, through the offices of the trader Stein, Marlow manages to remove Jim to Patusan, the remote Bornean trading colony where the remainder of Jim's story plays out.

Most readers of *Lord Jim* take note fairly quickly of the fact that Marlow and Stein choose Patusan, an outpost at the far edge of imperial modernity, as a place where Jim can redeem his neofeudal dreams of heroism and adventure. In keeping with the delayed maturity of his protagonist, Conrad presents a colonial space defined by arrested modernization: "The seventeenth-century traders went there for pepper, . . . but somehow, after a century of chequered intercourse, the country seems to drop gradually out of the trade . . . nobody cares for it now" (209–10). To fill out the picture of an impossible, premodern social world in Patusan, Conrad also provides for Jim a baldly allegorical romance with a beautiful half-Asian woman named Jewel. Of course, we do not expect much from Conrad in the depiction of romantic love or of women's experience, but Jewel is even more a cipher than her blue-eyed lover. She is the exotic and faithful mate who fixes Jim into a fantasy of cross-cultural "marriage" and innocent colonial wealth-extraction.[17] This love-story-cum-buried-treasure plot is a pat combination of imperial romance motifs, and it underscores Conrad's somewhat desultory decision to allot Jim a complete imperial-hero fulfillment kit: "He had the gift of finding a special meaning in everything that happened to him. This was the view he took of his love affair; it was idyllic, a little solemn, and also true, since his belief had all the unshakeable seriousness of youth" (267). Almost droningly now, Marlow hits the note of Jim's permanent youth, though by this point in the text we understand that whether his inner desires are denied or fulfilled, Jim will not mature. In fact, the bildungsroman track now runs in reverse, bringing "Lord" Jim from hard experience to (fantastic) innocence.

But the fantasy entails its own impermanence; as Jim and Jewel (and Marlow and Stein) always know, Patusan cannot function as a home or homeland for Jim. So much is clear from the hard-wired tragic elements of the novel, but what is worth investigating in some detail is Conrad's implication that Patusan cannot ground a realistic reconciliation plot because it is non-national space. From this point of view, the novel seems organized to illustrate by negative example the logic of national closure outlined in chapter 2. If in the classic or Goethean model of the bildungsroman, historical time and social transformation are shaped by the fixed states of adulthood and nationhood, then Jim's story gives us the counter or revisionary narrative in which historical time cannot be shaped by the nation-hood-adulthood plot. In Jim's Patusan, the time of emergence—of Bakhtin's "national-historical time"—is absent all around.[18]

At the level of plot, this means that only homecoming can redeem Jim. At the level of form, this means that only the anchoring chronotope of the nation can contain a narrative of endless youth by converting it into a narrative of social reconciliation. If, in *Great Expectations*, Pip must return to the domestic-national space to achieve symbolic closure, here Jim must suffer the impossibility of closure (adulthood) in the form of permanent exile from England. Marlow makes this fairly explicit when he indicates that the ennobling ideas that justify his existence, the animating spirits that justify all action in the imperial arena, are national ones:

> Those who return not to a dwelling but to the land itself, to meet its disem-bodied, eternal, and unchangeable spirit—it is those who understand best its severity, its saving power, the grace of its secular right to our fidelity, to our obedience. Yes! few of us understand, but we all feel it though, and I say *all* without exception because those who do not feel do not count.
>
> (206–7)

Marlow understands the abstract and imaginary rules of national belonging: "I do not mean to imply that I figured to myself the spirit of the land uprising above the white cliffs of Dover, to ask me what I . . . had done with my very young brother" (207). Marlow does not conjure England up in his mind like a mirage, but he nev-ertheless sees that the problem of Jim's redemption lies in the fact that he can never belong to the "spirit of the land" rising over Dover. We are used to being reminded in the Marlow texts of Conrad's preference for the liberalism of the British empire as against other, more rapacious European colonialisms. But here the symbolic role of Englishness is of a subtler kind, less often noticed. The spirit of the land is historical existence itself: It guarantees and imparts historical being to its sub-jects—the grace of a secular belonging, to paraphrase Marlow.[19] Marlow's soaring speech invokes the national geography as the ground and source of identity itself ("those who do not feel it do not count").

Marlow grasps the importance of national belonging because he too has fallen outside its shelter. Marlow seeks sheltering conceptions—racial solidarity, masculine honor, the Protestant work ethic—that can replace the territorial and political guarantees supplied by national belonging.[20] Recognizing Jim as a fellow untethered being, Marlow seeks to anchor Jim in his fraternal-professional code; the novel is a long meditation on that failed effort. Indeed Jim cannot be assimilated to the global order of Marlow's overseas life any more than he can be assimilated to the permanent life of Patusan and that is why the trials of what Nico Israel calls his "exilic bildungsroman" never end, short of death (58). Stuck in these extranational territories outside England, Jim experiences a temporal sentence that is either all youth (the narrative never ends) or sudden death (the narrative only ends).

England works for Marlow—and for Conrad—as the stable spatiotemporal mean between the bad finitude of the colony and the bad infinity of empire. Read back against the model of the classic bildungsroman, *Lord Jim* reveals a chronotopic array of possibilities: the local, bounded space of tradition and romance (in which historical time is displaced by the static time of romance and frozen youth); the radically open and unbounded space-time of empire and globalization (in which capitalist modernization is constantly transforming the social world and in which collective and individual identities are dissolved into endless revolution); and the mediating, reconciling chronotope of the nation (in which harmonious growth is projected as the normative temporal mode for both subjects and societies). National time is shaped or narratable time because it progresses, but not forever. The nation, particularly as enshrined in the classic or realist novel, mediates between a bounded and a boundless chronotope, achieving a spatiotemporal compromise that allows for the reconciliation of tradition and modernity. By contrast, both the pocket-colony and the expanded world-system are extranational spaces of historylessness marked, respectively, by the utter absence of progress (all tradition) and by the endless expansion of progress (all modernity). In both cases, and in both spaces, the danger of narrative infinity or endless youth prevails over the stable (and national) temporal concept of aging-into-closure.

This split temporality of the premodern and the hypermodern marks the absence of modernization, maturation, and development from the middle of *Lord Jim*, and finds its spatial counterpart in Patusan, an enclave outside national-historical time. It is shaped by both local political force and global economic forces, but not mediated by a nation-state form, even as a formal tributary or colony. Both in the historical source material centered on Sarawak (present-day Indonesia) and in Conrad's composite rendering of that material, Patusan is an odd kind of stateless colony. As Michael Moses has described it, Patusan functions as a peculiar premodern space almost akin to the *polis* of Greek tragic drama (*Novel* 85). Indeed Patusan has the enclosed quality of a tragic space: Both *polis* and prison, it sets the limits on Jim's imperial subjectivity. A captive master in Patusan, Jim represents the torn halves of the bildungsroman compromise: Where the classic hero in the Goethean model reconciles desire with law, Jim embodies the contradiction between them.

Dwelling outside the zone of modernization, Jim serves not just as a symbol of English idealism, but as a totem for Patusan and its people, who are—as Marlow would have it—without history:

> He dominated the forest, the secular gloom, the old mankind. He was like a figure set up on a pedestal, to represent in his persistent youth the power, and perhaps the virtues, of races that never grow old, that have emerged from the gloom. I don't know why he should always have appeared to me symbolic.

> (238)

This tableau of Marlow gazing at Jim's persistent youth against the native background of "the old mankind" seems to me to define the novel's core. Immediately one senses the tension between "old mankind" and "races that never grow old," though it is perhaps a familiar paradox of imperial discourse to cast both Europeans and non-Europeans as ageless: a youthful yet advanced modernizing race encountering an ancient yet childlike one. The atemporal or bipolar logic organizing this double trope organizes much of *Lord Jim*, beginning with the presentation of Jim/Marlow as a youth/maturity doublet rather than a moving dialectic of growth and transformation. The missing existential and narrative tissue between youth and age in this text corresponds to the missing historical being of two different "races that never grow old"; that is, of a racialized colonial encounter that troubles the language of development itself. To put the matter more concretely, we might think of Jim as the ironic modernist version of a Walter Scott protagonist. If, as Lukács has it, the Scott hero embodies the emergent force of national history, then Jim embodies the frozen, uncertain, or heterochronic dimensions of postnational history.

But what are the political implications of using an arch-imperialist "Lord" like Jim to represent not just the shiny dynamism of European empire-making, but also, and at once, the stripped historical being of Asian peoples? As with Kipling and Schreiner before, we have to ask whether the adolescence of the colonizer (however symbolically inflected) can plausibly be interpreted as a device for acknowledging the lost history of the colonized. The answer begins with Marlow, who already tries in the previously cited passage to establish some distance from his fantasy of Jim's representativeness: "I don't know why he should always have appeared to me symbolic." But it is part of the text's artistic power that those

Marlovian projections of a romantic youth barely touched by time, and of an exotic colony barely touched by Westernization, coexist with Marlow's awareness that history can leave neither Jim nor Patusan alone.[21] Going a step further into this Conradian fun house of ironized ironists, we can see that Marlow himself is only half-aware of the problems inherent in framing Jim's adolescence as a version of the natives' backwardness, but the novel thus registers that its double allegory of underdevelopment is not merely an inert device. Just as Schreiner voices, through Lyndall, her suspicion of the representative protagonist in the passage cited in the epigraph to this chapter, Conrad voices, through Marlow, his suspicion of the representative protagonist. Jim's agelessness represents for Marlow the historylessness of Patusan's ancient races, but the text does not credit this act of representation as true so much as use it to unfold and disclose the embedded contradictions of both the inherited allegory of progress attached to the European bildungsroman and the civilizational discourse of progress attached to the new imperialism.

The political fantasy underwriting Marlow's presentation of the Patusan episode is that Jim is a natural leader whose charismatic Englishness fairly breathes integrity to the corrupt and fractious local powers in Patusan: It is a fantasy of British hegemony without domination. On the other hand, Jim's presence does not change much in this highly stultified local ecology of power.[22] As in the case of Kipling's Anglo-India, social forces are distributed in more or less fixed equilibria—a constantly shifting but never fundamentally changing "Great Game" in which the British are honest brokers but not makers of an emergent, modern nation-state. In *Kim*, as in *Lord Jim*, a notable lack of "national-historical time" underwrites a tendentious fantasy of juvenile imperial subjectivity. But in both texts, the ideological fantasy's impossibility is exposed precisely by the biological/biographical imperatives attached to the condition of youth.

Lord Jim uses mixed temporalities and ironic frame narratives to encode and to debunk the colonialist dream of endless youth, giving us a self-detonating fantasy that reveals itself as a coded critique of imperial time-regimes along the lines of Johannes Fabian's *Time and the Other*. The exoticized and dehistoricized position of the native has been the focal point, naturally, for a number of recent postcolonial readings of the novel, too, though such readings must contend with the fact that Conrad has already thrown doubt upon Marlow's fantasy of native life. In a recent positioning of *Lord Jim* within the long history of globalizing and abstracting discourses in Southeast Asia, Sanjay Krishnan pays close and welcome attention to the elements of the text that appear to rehistoricize native subjectivity by decentering the model of interiority "as the sole marker of historical being" (334). In a sense, of course, the model of European subjectivity remains at the center of the text, but is subjected to a devastating historical critique by the arrest, revision, and objectification of the inherited progressivist logic of the bildungsroman. As Krishnan notes, the novel does not end up "drawing Patusan into the normative horizon of a foregone modernity"—the foregone modernity that Conrad at some level seeks to expose as the false Hegelian idol of imperialist discourse (347).[23] Conrad's flexible shuttling of the motif of underdevelopment across colonizer/colonized lines does the work of unsettling Western/non-Western modes of historical being. Moreover, when the text exposes the fantasy of endless youth (underdevelopment) to ironic demystification, it creates an interference pattern between the idea of Patusan as an exotic land outside history and Patusan as a resource colony already subject to colonial regimes of modernization. In that interference pattern, the novel reveals the central contradiction of the new imperialism: that it seeks to underdevelop and develop at the same time; and the long youth/sudden death motif of Jim himself is a fitting emblem for that exposed contradiction. Jim's missing adulthood makes clear what is missing at large in this colonial tale of broken *Bildung*—and in the tale of European imperialism's own "illusion of permanence" is the narrative of achieved self-possession, the time of emergence.[24]

Reading *Lord Jim* in this way means that the involuted and convoluted language of modernist subjectivity is not, finally, an evasion of the historical world, but a deeply realist method for describing the evasion of historical forces implied by neofeudal imperialism—and the inevitable return and backlash of those forces. Conrad uses tales of interiority to represent objective social conditions, but those conditions include an advanced stage of capitalist modernization in which neither the material signs nor the intellectual prestige of progress as a metahistorical motif could be guaranteed. Taken very simply, *Lord Jim* is a bildungsroman for its own age, in which we can see the traditional protagonist, one who embodies a progressive or linear model of history, getting eclipsed by the protagonist who registers the contradictions of an era split into multiple and conflicting temporalities of under- and overdevelopment. As the model of national-industrial emergence becomes obsolete in Europe, and is barely emergent in the global South, the novel as a form registers the faltering power of the nationhood-adulthood allegory to give shape to historical time and to social transformation. Lord Jim is an Edward Waverley for the early twentieth century: not the national hero, but the postnational anti-hero.

Given the magnetic power of Marlow's fantasy of endless youth—with its postponement of narrative closure, existential maturity, and historical modernization, the challenge for Conrad is to bring the Patusan episode to a meaningful close. One can sense the strain in the denouement of *Lord Jim*, even as one can appreciate the thematic symmetry of the Gentleman Brown subplot, in which the spell of Jim's semicharmed colonial life is broken. Brown is the right doppelgänger for Jim. Like Jim, he is a pseudo-aristocratic figure marooned at the ends of the earth; but unlike Jim, he represents the buccaneer spirit of empire—a life of pure action with little romantic self-contemplation or chivalric window-dressing. Conrad cannot resist the opportunity to split the atom of Goethean character once more and reveal to us the explosive and tragic results of this active/passive dyad (Brown/Jim). Brown confronts Jim at the point of Jim's weak integration into Marlow's code of imperial ruling-class values, and thereby makes Jim fall prey to the colonial forces he had hoped to redeem. As if taking its cue from the ruthless Brown, the narrative bangs along toward the end with a speed that is jarring after three hundred pages of Marlow's philosophical cud-chewing. As the windy narrator himself observes, in the final part of Jim's story, "events move fast without a check" (331). Destiny bursts into the temporal vacuum of Jim's Patusan life, and death comes quickly in a tragic sequence of battlefield miscues and cross-cultural blunders. Jim ends where Schreiner's Lyndall does: He cannot age, but neither can he step outside the flow of historical time, so he follows the same circuit from frozen youth to sudden death.

With the full sequence of events, from *Patna* to Patusan and afterward, in view, we can see that the romance of frozen colonial youth expresses a recalcitrance to the teleologies of maturity/modernity, but that these teleologies cannot be fully banished from the text. The novel seems to absolutize the (Hegelian) idea of historical teleology as predicated on the diffusion of European modernity, yet exposes that idea to a rigorous and ironic critique from within. At an earlier stage of the argument, I described Jim's youth as a sign of timelessness or absent history, but if history is missing from Marlow's depiction of Jim, it is not by any means missing from Conrad's depiction of Marlow. Reading *Lord Jim* now, from the vantage point of our moment in the long process of globalization, I think we can see the text as a document that records a certain kind of historical pressure on the individualistic novel as the master genre of modernity, and as a metageneric work of art that blends stalled and accelerated time-schemes in order to project the story of Westernization as both an impossible *and* an inevitable discourse of progress.[25]

To put this another way, we need to reclaim the critical realism of *Lord Jim* as a novel of globalization as against the Jamesonian claim that Conrad mystifies into style and subjectivity the actual conditions of the colonial world-system circa 1900. In a recent reinterpretation, John Marx reads the novel as continuous with the tradition of the industrial "condition of England" novel, insisting—I think persuasively—that it does not disguise or stylize labor and production into a modernist dazzle of absences, but shows them, as they are being transformed, by the objective processes of high imperialism (15). *Lord Jim* is a realist novel that does not so much occlude the global division of labor as draw attention to the standard languages and story lines by which that division of labor is hidden from Western eyes. The novel is also realist in the Bakhtinian sense that it assimilates to the hero "real historical time" just at the moment that a progressive or linear interpretation of world history centered in Europe was being eclipsed by a heterochronic and multipolar model of global history. The problematic of uneven (colonial) development—as figured in Patusan—is not just reabsorbed by Conrad into the metanarrative of progressive modernization, but begins to break down the fibers of that metanarrative, exposing its contradictions in the medium of an anachronic modernist style. In that spirit, we can take *African Farm* and *Lord Jim* as globally mimetic texts wherein the mix of antidevelopmental and developmental logic—revealed through the characterology of the stunted protagonist—points to an uneasy generic grafting of new metahistorical knowledge into older European models of the bildungsroman.

I have so far suggested that the troping of colonial anachronism (both underdevelopment in colonized spaces and uneven development across the colonial world-system) is a crucial dimension of *Lord Jim*, and that its ideological significance is considerably complicated by the ironic distance established by Conrad's use of Marlow as subnarrator. To describe in detail the branching effects of Conradian irony within this interpretive scheme, it is helpful to track Marlow as both a connoisseur of irony and an object of it. Moving out of Patusan proper and further into the frame narratives of *Lord Jim*, we get a clear blueprint of the newly charged meaning of bildungsroman conventions at the moment of their highly self-conscious redeployment in modernist writing and in the force field of the colonial contact zone. Reflecting on his own story, Marlow is aware that he has constructed Jim as a symbol not just of lost youth and lost ideals, but of an even more general interruption of historical time. Here Marlow describes the effect of leaving Patusan and its composed image of Jim and Jewel:

> I had turned away from the picture and was going back to the world where events move, men change, light flickers, life flows in a clear stream, no matter whether over mud or stones.

> (286)

Marlow sets the opposition between a static and pictorial timelessness (the Patusan chronotope) and the grim necessity of change and motion—an almost cinematic onrush of flickering light, frame giving way to frame without stop. And this flow of time bears down on the self hard enough to threaten the luxury of an ethical or philosophical calibration of experience ("whether over mud or stones"). Marlow, as Conrad's surrogate, appears to accept the mantle of an existentially conceived concept of history, and also to reflect that concept back into the formal struggle between style (static, pictorial, impressionistic) and the flow of history/plot. Through Marlow, Conrad reflects, in other words, on the tension between scene and story that is the basic literary code for all the larger oppositions between youth and age, illusion and disillusion, the colonial romance of Patusan as frozen time and the imperial reality of Patusan as raw material for inevitable modernization.[26]

As a character, Marlow has deeply ambivalent views that are themselves set off and framed by a further set of narrative displacements. Even before Marlow's viewpoint is qualified externally, we find him doubting his own claims and motives. No wonder, since, for example, he insists on hard work as the means to redemption, but appears to spend most of his time and energy on ministering rather quixotically to Jim's destiny. He virtually declares his self-division on every page as he wants to discipline Jim to the wheel of history but also seems to enjoy and even to inflate Jim's florid romantic idealism. Marlow uses Jim as a screen to prevent himself from realizing his own naïveté, that is, from confronting the fact that he has maintained an enchanted worldview by transferring his romantic impulses from the individual hero to a masculine collective whose ethos is the "solidarity of the craft" (139). Although Marlow plays the role of grizzled pragmatist, his illusions in many ways are deeper and more durable than are Jim's own; one might say that it is Marlow's innocence that is most at stake in *Lord Jim*.

Marlow's ambivalent oscillation between pragmatism and romanticism has a distinctively imperial cast to it, and bears out some of Hannah Arendt's observations about imperial service in the age of Rhodes. Arendt claims that imperialism produced an effect whereby specific economic or political goals were increasingly displaced by ceaseless self-justifying expansion, a law of endless development:

> No matter what individual qualities or defects a man may have, once he has entered the maelstrom of an unending process of expansion, he will, as it were, cease to be what he was and obey the laws of the process, identify himself with anonymous forces that he is supposed to serve in order to keep the whole process in motion; he will think of himself as mere function, and eventually consider such functionality, such an incarnation of the dynamic trend, his highest achievement.
>
> (Arendt 215)

Marlow seems to have assimilated just these laws of imperial capitalism in the form of a functionalist pragmatism, always already mature, and Jim seems to have assimilated the same laws of endless motion in the form of a romantic idealism, forever immature.

But of course the reason Marlow cannot countenance Jim's idealism is not, finally, that it represents an opposite value, but that it so closely mirrors his own disguised idealism, which threatens to destabilize his professed pragmatism.[27] Marlow's structure of feeling (anxiety because he cannot integrate idealism and pragmatism) gives us the subjective or emotional correlate to the problematic of colonial (under)development. Identifying schizophrenically with both the urge to celebrate Jim/Patusan as signs of an alternative to Western modernity and to acknowledge their final vulnerability to the discipline of history (qua Western modernity), Marlow must be understood as a figure who embodies colonial contradictions rather than a detached mind who observes them.

Conrad sets Marlow's illusions inside a chain of related figures (youth, idealism, colonial space, arrested development) for which Jim is the standard-bearer. But the more significant romantic is Marlow, and we can hear this quite clearly in the major chords of the earlier Marlow story, "Youth: "For me all the East is contained in that vision of my youth. . . . Only a moment; a moment of strength, of romance, of glamour, of youth!" (43). The conceptual overlapping of "the East . . . that vision . . . my youth" captures the distinctive flexibility of arrested development as a political (East), stylistic (vision), and existential (youth) term. Youth and Asia are thematic pretexts for a text of impressionist style, as Conrad reveals with greater depth moving from "Youth" to *Lord Jim*, where Marlow's idealism occasions an autocritical assessment of the limits of modernist style framed in terms of colonial youth. Thus the operative fantasy of a colonized "people without history" figured in the hero's immaturity is not the soft ideological underbelly of an imperialist novel but rather the subject of the novel's ironization of Marlow.

Lord Jim revises the bildungsroman not by inverting its logic into a European romance of white lordship, but by laying bare the tension between old allegories of progress in the European novel and new facts of radically uneven development in the colonial world-system. That complex double act becomes more apparent as the novel pushes beyond Marlow's unsatisfactory language of sentimental education and *illusions perdues* and turns to two other viewpoints that outflank Marlow's: those of the "privileged man" and Stein.[28] The transfer of narrative perspective from Marlow to the "privileged man" is a traditional point of interest for formal analyses of *Lord Jim*. By effecting that transfer, Conrad qualifies Marlow's viewpoint and deepens the meaning of Jim's Patusan existence. For the privileged man is a skeptic, who doubts that Patusan could have redeemed Jim. "You said also," Marlow writes to him, that "giving your life up to them" (*them* meaning all of mankind with skins brown, yellow, or black in colour) "was like selling your soul to a brute." You contended that "that kind of thing" was only endurable and enduring when based on a firm conviction in the truth of ideas racially our own, in whose name are established the order, the morality of an ethical progress.

(293)

"Ideas racially our own": a volatile phrase secreted inside a web of prepositions (an ethos based *on* a conviction *in* the truth *of* an idea), its grammatical position as complex as its narratological one (the phrase is relayed *to* an unnamed subnarrator *by* another unnamed subnarrator, the privileged man, *from* a letter addressed *to* the latter by Marlow who is, in turn, reproducing the privileged man's words from an earlier conversation). It is hard to imagine a more indirect pathway from author to reader for such important words. The highly filtered presentation of Marlow's voice reveals a deep ideological strain in Conrad's thinking about race, empire, and the politics of "ethical progress." Marlow wishes to read Jim as redeeming a notion of heroism that he, Marlow, barely credits but cannot abandon since it glorifies the motivations underlying his own imperial career. The privileged man refuses to view Jim's Patusan life in terms of progress, since it appears to have been a temporarily charmed exercise in intercultural and interracial romance, a demodernizing of "Tuan Jim" rather than a modernization of the native subject.

Bewildered, Marlow falls back on his blanket skepticism ("I affirm nothing"). He sidles up interrogatively to an alternative viewpoint, not quite breaking faith with the progressivist values of the privileged man: "The point, however, is that of all mankind Jim had no dealings but with himself, and the question is whether at the last he had not confessed to a faith mightier than the laws of order and progress" (293). Does Jim, at the last, embody a faith beyond the laws of order and progress? In what would such a faith consist, for Marlow? It is here that we reach the tender points of Marlow's mind, the place where his own sense of contradiction is almost—almost!—as acute as the novel's. He has submitted himself to a logic of linear history naturalized as existential time, and to the goals of imperial trade and modernization naturalized as masculine action itself. But he has collected a secret and explosive cargo of doubt, amounting almost to resistance or subversion. By crediting Jim's immaturity as a meaningful alternative to the "laws of order and progress," as a kind of anachronistic romance of the heroic soul, he identifies with the underdeveloped periphery as a zone outside the existential and political purview of European modernity. However, even if peripheral colonies such as Patusan temporarily resist the forces of modernity/historicization, they are finally swept into those metanarratives. *Lord Jim*, precisely in its objectification of the soul-nation allegory, spotlights its inability to reconcile the demands of the romantic soul (allegorized in Patusan as the exotic remainder of colonial difference) and the demands of the social code ("ideas racially our own" understood as a faith in secular progress).

Lord Jim takes pains to objectify all of its elements: first, the romantic narrative of Jim's self-image, then the faux-skeptical view of Marlow's narrative of Jim's image, and, finally, its own framing devices, taken as a way to give aesthetic form to the copresence of two conflicting value systems. Marlow works at a synthesis that cannot be realized, and the privileged man arrives to articulate its impossibility. The fundamental historylessness of Jim-in-Patusan as a colonial romance does not square with the force of historical progress embodied in imperialism. But the novel does not want to give the final word to the privileged man's Eurocentric concept of order and progress either. To the battle between synthesis and non-synthesis we have a guided response in the form of Stein, who appears to stand for an ironic narrativization of the stalled dialectic between developmental and antidevelopmental time in the novel.

Stein is the one figure in the novel who seems to have stabilized his own identity in terms of the demands of action and of contemplation, of passionate idealism and mature pragmatism. More to the intertextual point, he is a German associated by direct reference to the literary antecedent of Goethe (and to the 1848 revolutions—which Lukács takes as the threshold event that brings the curtain down on European realism). Stein's authority in the text stems in part from the fact that he has lived the jungle adventures and intercultural love plots of Jim and traversed them, progressed through them, to arrive at a mature standpoint. Only Stein in that sense could be said to mediate or to modulate across the competing temporalities of delayed and enforced development. Stein idealizes neither the idealism of permanent youth, nor the disillusionment of resigned adulthood—unlike Marlow, who idealizes both. Citing Goethe's play *Torquato Tasso*, Stein describes to Marlow a moment when he felt that he held the meaning of his own existence unambiguously in his own hands. He embodies, for Marlow and for us, the paradigmatic fulfillment of the Goethean bildungsroman, but he also sees that fulfillment as temporary, as part of the narrative of a life, not as an artificially eternalized moment of closure. Paul Kirschner has persuasively tracked the thematic resonances of Goethe's *Tasso* in the Stein portion of the text. The Goethean theme, as Kirschner notes, is the battle between strong imagination and the actual terms of existence, a battle resolved in the bildungsroman of *Wilhelm Meister* by a compromise between the two. Stein's fusion of practical intellect and romantic idealism defines the residual element of a functional Goethean plot of self-formation and self-integration in *Lord Jim*. It is the device that recurs at the end of the novel to throw into relief the stalled dialectic of the main plot, where the oppositions between youth and age, revolutionary change and historical meaning, remain unreconciled.

The final triangulation of Marlow and Stein around the deliquescent figure of Jim's youth gives the close of *Lord Jim* a strong echo of an intertext even more immediate than any Goethean resonance: Oscar Wilde's *The Picture of Dorian Gray*. It is surprising that few critics have directly compared *Lord Jim* to *Dorian Gray* since Conrad is so clearly mining some of the same territory of an eroticized homosocial transaction organized around the figure of an eternally fair-haired English youth who serves to embody the projected desires and lost illusions of two older men. Beyond the obvious morphological correspondences between these two canonical fictions of exorbitant youth, there is a deeper set of relations in which the development of modernist style, emergent in the aestheticized language of both Wilde and Conrad, works in close relation to the figure of an eroticized and idealized English youth. Both situate their golden youths in the middle of an increasingly global system of commercial exchange and commodification, and in both youth itself stands for the slow unwinding of the soul-nation allegory of progress. Turning to chapter 4, we move from the Afro-Asian contact zone back to the Anglophone metropolis of London in order to track the motif of endless youth first in the gothic protomodernism of Wilde and then in the satirical semimodernism of H. G. Wells.

4. Souls of Men under Capitalism: Wilde, Wells, and the Anti-Novel

No life is spoiled but one whose growth is arrested.

—Wilde, *The Picture of Dorian Gray*

I am, in a sense, decay.

—Wells, *Tono-Bungay*

What does a novel look like when its protagonist engages in permanent self-development with no obvious end, no external aim, no vocational or libidinal closure, no horizon of bourgeois self-discipline or social compromise? How does such a novel, a tale of endless becoming, function as a narrative? The Kipling, Schreiner, and Conrad texts examined in previous chapters provided some answers, revealing various subgeneric combinations and encapsulated narratives, all organized in relation to the geography of the frontier within the colonial world-system. Meanwhile, other late nineteenth- and early twentieth-century Anglophone writers were reconceiving, even deforming, the biographical plot of the bildungsroman from within that system's metropolitan zone. Oscar Wilde's *The Picture of Dorian Gray* (1891), for example, gives the motif of frozen youth its archetypal expression, depicting a man charmed into boundless beautiful youth until the horrifying moment when the conceit crumbles and—as in *Lord Jim* and *The Story of an African Farm*—snaps back into sudden death.

Wilde's novel has come to stand for an entire fin de siècle shift away from the social realism of the mainstream Victorian novel and toward various gothic, decadent, sensational, or naturalist forms. In fact, Wilde himself, in "The Critic as Artist," an essay written almost contemporaneously with *Dorian Gray*, speculates on the branching path of English fiction: "He who would stir us now by fiction must either give us an entirely new background, or reveal to us the soul of man in its innermost workings" (*Complete Works* 1054). Wilde goes on to say that while there remains "much to be done in the sphere of introspection" ("innermost workings"), Kipling's 1880s Indian fiction had already begun to give the "entirely new background," with its "superb flashes of vulgarity" (1055). Here Wilde describes the forked future of English fiction in precisely the terms that Lukács—or Edmund Wilson for that matter—would use to model the situation of the modernist turn: He proposes, that is, a binary model posing objective, journalistic, or naturalistic works against subjective or symbolist works.[1]

As noted in the previous chapter, the Lukácsian notion of a "crisis of bourgeois realism" retains a certain explanatory force in English studies—despite its normative continental account of the 1848 revolutions as *the* turning point and despite its inattention to sex and gender—because it partially confirms the shape of a late Victorian gothic/naturalist canon now largely enshrined in Anglo-American literary studies. Lukács's account of this literary-historical shift holds that novelistic realism breaks down into two strains—the naturalist-objectivist and the romantic-subjectivist—as European writers register a broad philosophical and intellectual faltering in the concept of progress.[2] The robust productive life of the bourgeois revolution weakens and dissipates, just as the robust materialist concept of combined and uneven development splits into two inadequate parts: on the one hand, the self-congratulatory dream of endless, Whiggish forward motion and, on the other, the irrationalist discourse of decline and degeneration (*Historical Novel* 85, 174). Where the great realists Goethe, Scott, Balzac, and Tolstoy managed to produce heroes who incarnated Lukács's Marxist-humanist concept of social progress, the heroes of the late bourgeois novel become playthings of determinist social principles or—on the flip side—mere eccentrics trapped in the cell of the mind.

Oscar Wilde straddles the poles of this binary model of fin de siècle literary subjectivity, working at the contradictions between commodified social relations and the utopian possibilities of an aesthetically grounded existence. The paradoxes and antinomies that Wilde gathers up, in all of his writing, between action and contemplation, or between production and consumption, animate and organize the gothic didacticism of *The Picture of Dorian Gray*. While *Dorian Gray* initially gives its plot over to a fantasy of eternal youth and permanent Hellenic indulgence in sensory pleasure, it is in many ways—as critics have often observed—an almost moralistic text driven by an uncompromising sense that Dorian's experiment cannot but end in disaster.[3] The beautiful Dorian of Basil Hallward's imagination, a living icon of youth and beauty, becomes in the end a kind of subject-object monster of reification. Or, to put it another way, in keeping with the economic logic of Wilde's aesthetic, the soul who begins to live as a pure and ageless artwork ends up embodying the logic of pure commodification, hollowing out his will, and collapsing into a dead thing.

What would it be like, though, to organize a novel from the opposite end of this trajectory, so that the very premise of the text is the idea that the protagonist's inner life is already fully shaped by the logic of reification? Where the commodified soul was not revealed to itself in gothic paroxysm at the moment of closure, but taken as the center of a biographical plot in a tale dedicated from the start to the unstable laws of modern marketing, a life story shaped by the boom-and-bust of capitalist speculation, where characterization and commodification cannot be separated? In fact, we have such a book: H. G. Wells's *Tono-Bungay*. In this novel of ideas, a self-styled "Romance of Commerce" (73), the protagonist, George Ponderevo, tells his life story as the story of the prototypical modern commodity, a fake tonic named Tono-Bungay. Like its real-life source, Coca-Cola, Tono-Bungay is an elixir that floods the market on a crest of advertising hype and that dissolves the social bonds and psychic rites of passage that organize traditional biographical fictions. Our hero, Ponderevo, subordinates himself to the cause of Tono-Bungay, becoming the man of commercial action stripped of orderly self-cultivation. Like Dorian Gray, but from the opposite direction, Ponderevo transforms the pedagogical ideal of self-making into a deformed plot of arrested development. A scientific young man with artistic pretensions, Ponderevo mutates into a corporate hack who can sustain neither relationships nor vocations; even at the end, he cannot reconcile his inner needs with operative social conventions. Ponderevo's lower-middle-class science becomes as corrupted as Dorian's upper-middle-class art, generating parallel records of antidevelopmental life stories, one based on the formless failure of continual self-production and one based on the formless failure of continual production.

Although Wilde and Wells are seldom analyzed in a comparative frame, then, their signature fictions, *Dorian Gray* (1891) and *Tono-Bungay* (1909), taken as a pair, capture the disintegration of realism into subjective (aestheticist) and objective (naturalist) modes. In these two novels of stunted youth, modern consumer culture fully penetrates the plot of socialization, unraveling the culture-commerce compromise of the classic bildungsroman with particular clarity and throwing overboard the heterosexual marriage plot as the presumed center of social reproduction.[4] The comparison makes further sense given that both writers were, during the 1890s, working in the mode of post-Darwinian gothic didacticism. Given their shared interest in degeneration, it may not be surprising that Wilde's Dorian Gray and Wells's George Ponderevo can be taken to represent the torn halves of the nineteenth-century bildungsroman, the fission of the Goethean compromise between sensitive soul and dutiful citizen. As a deformed subject, the art-man Dorian Gray ends up quite neatly anticipating the commodity-man George Ponderevo: Both lives engender plots of arrested development, of delay and decay, of rise and fall, of vicious or absurd closure. In both cases, the failed synthesis between commerce and culture is the subject of the text, not just an incidental feature. In that sense, these two antidevelopmental texts together expose an unmediated contradiction between the subjective world of cultural aspiration and the objective sphere of commodified social relations.[5]

But what is even more striking than the thematic convergence of Wildean decay and Wellsian half-life on the figure of the anachronic hero is the historical convergence of the two novels as pictures of consumption and production in the age of empire. Wilde's cosmopolitan decadence and Wells's global marketing give us what we might call the two faces of postnational narrative, rendered in terms of an overt crisis in the allegorization of the maturing soul linked to the modernizing society. In the cases of Schreiner and Conrad, the nonaccumulation of wealth on the underdeveloped colonial periphery provided an obvious analogue to stalled *Bildung*, but in the novels of Wilde and Wells, we find a different kind of economic logic: overconsumption and hyperproduction, respectively. The fascinating part of the immediate Wilde-Wells comparison is that both of these economic problems sink contextual and thematic roots right down into the colonial world-system and both find vivid literary expression in the motif of stunted/endless youth. Faced with the swamping of national histories by the boundless energy of capitalism's global revolution, no wonder modernist fiction turned the inverted or exploded plot of progress to such trenchant symbolic ends. In the comparative analysis that follows here, we see Wilde and Wells ring their changes on the antidevelopmental plot and reveal, from the perspective of the metropole, the increasing displacement of national by global frames of reference for the British novel.

"Unripe Time": Dorian Gray and Metropolitan Youth

In *Dorian Gray*, Wilde sets an antidevelopmental fable within a specifically metropolitan and global economy, taking his cue from the exoticizing consumerism of Huysmans's *À Rebours*. We open in Basil Hallward's studio, redolent of roses, dotted with "Persian saddle-bags" and silk curtains designed to "produce a kind of momentary Japanese effect" (23). This kind of description has the effect of pausing or stalling the narrative: Wilde's paragraphs often luxuriate in long sumptuous litanies of descriptive detail, directing the reader's attention to sensory inventory rather than to plot, action, or even characterization. The combination of lyrical description, epigrammatic discourse, and dramatic dialogue that we find in the opening chapter is characteristic of the entire text—one reason it can be understood as a kind of anti-novel. The term *anti-novel* in my chapter's title has this restricted meaning of a novel organized, at the level of syntax and structure, as well as the level of plot and character, to delay and distort the linear temporality and narrative logic of biographical realism.[6] Many critics have, naturally, attended to the basic antidevelopmental structure of *Dorian Gray*, but it is less often noted that the text's Orientalist tropes cluster and thicken just at the points where Wilde needs to break with the realist mode of presentation or the linear demands of traditional plotting.[7] In establishing the central supernatural conceit of Dorian's gothic alteration, for example, Wilde produces an ambience of exotic indolence: "The warm air seemed laden with spices. A bee flew in, and buzzed round the blue-dragon bowl" (123). These Asian motifs are echoed in the opiated demimonde of Dorian's London dockside prowls, the seedy underbelly of metropolitan commerce of which Basil's studio is the perfumed, West End incarnation.

Wilde perhaps sets a precedent here for Virginia Woolf, who, seeking to introduce a break from realist conventions and Aristotelian unities in *Orlando*, also makes use of Orientalist imagery to reroute narrative time into descriptive delay, to challenge and bend the organic conceits of the biographical plot. She plunges her reader into temporal disorientation and gender ambiguity during the most Orientalist portions of the text, set in Constantinople (and inspired by Woolf's vicarious investment in Vita Sackville-West's journeys in Turkey and Persia). Shifting Orlando from male to female body, Woolf offers a riposte to the fiction of masculine imperial adventure. Exoticizing distance seems to afford Woolf the necessary experimental license with the boundaries of fictional and sexual convention to shrug off the imperatives of domestic realism. It is not hyperbolic to say that a pair of Turkish trousers is the pivotal device that allows Woolf to pull off her gender-shifting plot with a subtle nonchalance.

Wilde likewise sustains his conceit of prolonged youth without experiential depth by glutting Dorian Gray's senses with a continual parade of aesthetic stimulation, drawing substantially on what Regenia Gagnier calls "the exotica of the world outside the West" (110). Following the arrest of Dorian's aging, the long descriptive interludes that constitute the novel's middle offer a serious artistic challenge to Wilde: how to keep the story interesting. In fact, as Jeff Nunokawa has aptly and tersely noted, "the book is boring" (71). *Dorian Gray* is boring for the same reason that both *Kim* and *Lord Jim* (despite *their* exotica) are boring: Their plots are static and antidevelopmental. For readers trained to expect strong emplotment and characterological progress of the kind typically found in Austen, Brontë, or Dickens, the transfer of interest to symbolic, linguistic, ideological, and descriptive registers cannot fully make up for the stalled development of a passive hero.

Dorian's long experiment in urban delectation requires, on the supply side, a rich world city and the form of cultural privilege that Raymond Williams has called metropolitan perception, that is, the "magnetic concentration of wealth and power in imperial capitals and the simultaneous cosmopolitan access to a wide variety of subordinate cultures" (*Politics* 44). Describing Dorian's years of protracted hedonism, Wilde emphasizes the multicultural stimuli and underscores the appropriative (imperialist) dimension of Dorian's consumerism: When he studies perfumes, he turns to "burning odorous gums from the East"; when music grabs his attention, he stages concerts featuring "mad gypsies," "yellow-shawled Tunisians," "grinning Negroes [who] beat monotonously upon copper drums," and "slim turbaned Indians" (165). He gathers "from all parts of the world the strangest instruments that could be found, either in the tombs of dead nations or among the few savage tribes that have survived contact with Western civilizations, and loved to touch and try them" (165–66). Dorian's senses crave the variety of world music, and his long sensory bath requires—or at least unfolds most meaningfully within—the urban environment of the imperial metropolis, where the wealth of dead nations and savage tribes filters in and remains available for consumption.[8]

Orientalism and metropolitan perception are cultural predicates for the key ideas of pleasure, beauty, and consumption in the novel; ideas such as Hellenism, hedonism, aestheticism, and individualism (the last borrowed from Wilde's own lexicon in "The Soul of Man under Socialism").[9] Such anti-utilitarian doctrines are both practiced and embodied by the ageless Dorian Gray, who literalizes some of the throwaway dicta uttered by Lord Henry Wotton. "You have the most marvellous youth, and youth is the one thing worth having," says Lord Henry. He continues:

> Time is jealous of you, and wars against your lilies and your roses. . . . Ah! realize your youth while you have it. . . . A new Hedonism—that is what our century wants. You might be its visible symbol. With your personality there is nothing you could not do. The world belongs to you for a season.

(45–46)

"For a season": This connoisseur of youth, unlike his deluded pupil, recognizes that youth's value and its impermanence cannot be prized apart. As Douglas Mao puts it: "One of the lessons of the novel thus seems to be that it is easy to mistake an impoverishing *failure* of becoming (a lack of growth) for a fruitful *resistance to* becoming (an evasion of narrowing and ossification)" (93). Indeed Lord Henry will later give voice to what amounts to the moral of the tale: "No life is spoiled but one whose growth is arrested" (102). Wilde's conceit is to set experience and sensual pleasure free from the limits of biographical and psychological accumulation, indeed from existential time itself: "Eternal youth, infinite passion, pleasures subtle and secret, wild joy and wilder sins—he was to have all these things" (135). As he explores the narrative outcome of this Faustian bargain, Wilde gives us the canonical and archetypal late Victorian account of the dangers of this "bad infinity," precisely the dream-cum-nightmare of infinite self-transformation that was dissolved by the realistic compromise of the Goethean bildungsroman. Even if, as Lord Henry opines, "the aim of life is self-development," one cannot realize one's youth except by letting it come to an end (41).

If Lord Henry maintains a Goethean-Schillerian ideal of self-cultivation and self-fulfillment, then Dorian stands as an object lesson in the warping of that ideal.[10] Wilde too associates the ideal of self-making with German romanticism; in "The Critic as Artist," he insists on self-cultivation as against any kind of institutional education: "Self-culture is the true ideal of man. Goethe saw it, and the immediate debt that we owe to Goethe is greater than the debt we owe to any man since Greek days" (*Complete Works* 1043–44). Goethe's pattern for the bildungsroman depended on the integration of apparently incompatible value systems and time schemes into a single narrative frame organized around the pattern of development or growth. Dorian cannot reconcile or even countenance the intermixing of progress and decay, the integration of acculturation and decadence into a single organic body or narrative form: "Culture and corruption," he says at one point, "I have known something of both. It seems terrible to me now that they should ever be found together. For I have a new ideal, Harry. I am going to alter. I think I have altered" (248). Dorian's "alteration," like Gregor Samsa's metamorphosis, is a narrative device that opens up antidevelopmental potential, displacing the organicist allegory of individual and social growth with an unnatural and unclockable process of overripening and underripening. The result—in Kafka as in Wilde—is a failed synthesis that displaces the lynchpin temporal compromise between youth and adulthood, freedom and social constraint, narrativity and closure.

A novel that fixates on youth can only draw attention to its own quixotic effects, its own estrangement from the inherited nineteenth-century techniques of the coming-of-age tale. Dorian has, in a morally probative way, taken the notion of permanent youth rather too literally. Wilde has, in an artistically potent way, taken it just literally enough to reveal the compositional weakness of the old bildungsroman as a symbolic device—the arbitrariness of its closural forms, the ideological patchwork of its way of rounding off existential time into adulthood (understood as a kind of plateau)—and, as I have suggested in earlier chapters—rounding off constant social transformation into the shapely time of nationhood. With the Dorian Gray conceit, Wilde manages to lay bare the negative potential of a never-ending story of self-development by steering it away from the telos of adulthood and from the spatiotemporal containment of the nation.

For this reason it is useful to zero in on the Orientalist tropes that help Wilde suspend novelistic time: The cultural coding there hints at the symbolic value of a *culturally mediated* break from the great English tradition of realist fiction. Certainly *Dorian Gray* codes developmental imperatives (in all their normative and heteronormative force) as mainstream, middle-class, English ideology. That is, Wilde's narrator—like Wilde himself in "The Soul of Man under Socialism"— seems to oppose the compromise between bourgeois convention and aristocratic cultivation, hoping to see the latter sprung free from a particularly English insistence on work and wealth. Lord Henry gives voice to this view in a brief bit of repartee with the Duchess of Monmouth, where he derides the bourgeois practicality and narrow-mindedness of England. The duchess replies:

> "I believe in the race," she cried.
> "It represents the survival of the pushing."
> "It has development."
> "Decay fascinates me more."
>
> (232)

Here is the core dyad of the novel—decay versus development—and Wilde frames the temporal crux of the matter in terms of English self-construction as the leading edge of modernization, a "race" of producers and developers.

This understanding of progress as an English fetish—for both world-making and novel-making—may help explain why Wilde, and in his Irish wake, Joyce, Beckett, Flann O'Brien, and Elizabeth Bowen, offered implicitly critical or distanced views on classic English realism and contributed so much to the larger modernist project that I have described here as the antidevelopmental novel.[11] Vicki Mahaffey has proposed that Wilde's attraction to youth and underdevelopment, so central to the organization of *Dorian Gray*, stems not just from a moral, sexual, and aesthetic fascination with innocence but also from his view of Ireland as "a country whose beauty is unnaturally preserved in a green and frozen youth" (53). The preservation of a green and frozen Ireland occurs of course through the discursive and material effects of a colonial regime, subsequently transferred in part to the self-antiquating offices of many postcolonial Irish nationalisms. At the level of narrative structure, the trope of greenness or unripeness yields interesting new results when grafted into the realist novel. Like his followers Joyce and Bowen, Wilde gravitated toward the French model of Flaubert, that is, toward highly stylized scenes of bathos and enervation as against the more linear and robustly progressive models embodied by Stendhal and affirmed by Lukács. Wilde's investment in the flaneur/aesthete figure taken from French modernism also sets the pattern for Joyce's Stephen Dedalus, who follows Dorian Gray and oscillates between appreciating the fugitive beauty of the city and delving into the grisly racks of "sordid sinners" and "splendid sins" (*Dorian Gray* 73).[12] As Dorian shuttles between contrition and delectation, his inability to integrate moral and sensual experience anticipates much of the adolescent middle of Joyce's *Portrait*.

As powerful as recent insights into the "Irish Wilde" have been, it remains important to tread delicately in this territory of national identification, especially when it comes to the attribution of literary qualities or ideological positions to one side or another of the Irish/Anglo divide. For one thing, though I have already begun to suggest that Wilde, like so many Irish intellectuals of his time, associated England with philistine, utilitarian, and grubbily materialist thought, he also insists—in *Dorian Gray* and elsewhere—on a strongly materialist understanding of even the most ethereal and aestheticized human endeavors.[13] For another, the influence of urban decadent styles and motifs distilled from Flaubert and Baudelaire extends to English and American modernisms as well as to Irish; the rewriting of the nineteenth-century realist "action hero" into the passive subject of naturalist and modernist fiction is an event with wide literary-historical application, and our investigation of the colonial antidevelopmental fiction is but one part of that history.

Moreover, since it is so difficult a biographical task to sort out Wilde's own ironic mix of Anglo-Irish attitudes and affiliations, we should perhaps concentrate our attention on the form of *Dorian Gray* in order to avoid both schematic political intentionalism and ethnic or postcolonial pigeonholing. One effect of pairing Wilde with Wells in this chapter is to suggest that the formal problematic of the stalled *Bildung* plot runs across—and indeed renders blurry—national lines in modernism, from English (Woolf, Wells) to Creole (Rhys) to Anglo-German-South African (Schreiner) to Anglo-Polish (Conrad) to Anglo-Indian (Kipling) to Anglo-Irish (Wilde, Bowen) to Irish (Joyce).[14] All of the writers listed here experimented with a radically uneven temporality assimilated into their narrative compositions, indeed into the very language of human interiority—and all of them produced antidevelopmental fictions that seem to encode the historical and geographical dissonances of the age of empire.

My guiding claim to this point is that Wilde's *Dorian Gray* conspicuously exposes the progressive logic of the realist novel, using the trope of youth that does not age in the proper temporal order. That exposure of outmoded and contradictory generic conventions is, in Wilde's text, shot through with historical traces of Anglo-Irish colonialism and wider reference to uneven development in the imperial world-system (remember the "tombs of dead nations"). It is not that Wilde uses Dorian's golden youth to assert the value of the Irish imagination and its spiritualized backwardness against the materialized progress of the English mind, nor even that he champions Dorian's bohemian flight from existential time and bourgeois values. In fact, as readers can fairly plainly see, Wilde narrates the vengeance of clock time on the decadent conceit of Dorian Gray's magical youth. Here is the moral self-recrimination of the final chapter, in which Wilde voices Dorian's thoughts about his error, and implies the necessity of organic time:

> Ah! in what a monstrous moment of pride and passion he had prayed that the portrait should bear the burden of his days, and he keep the unsullied splendour of eternal youth! All his failure had been due to that. Better for him that each sin of his life had brought its sure, swift penalty along with it. . . . What was youth at its best? A green, an unripe time, a time of shallow moods and sickly thoughts. Why had he worn its livery? Youth had spoiled him.
>
> (260)

Dorian Gray ends with the revelation that the logical endpoint of an experiment in pure hedonism is not freedom but its opposite. When people indulge in sensual excess, they "lose the freedom of their will. They move to their terrible end as automatons move. Choice is taken from them" (226). The narrator triply reiterates the point here, betraying a certain amount of eagerness to balance the novel's sensualism with a moralizing kick. The dream of a life lived with unregulated desire, outside the reified world of work, social obligation, and social convention, produces not a beautiful soul, but a sensual robot. The fatal concluding scenes remind us that *The Picture of Dorian Gray* is not a decadent novel but a book about a decadent novel: Huysmans's *À Rebours*, the infamous "novel without a plot" that bedevils Dorian (156).[15] In that sense, Wilde's gothic novel of ideas seems to affirm Lukács's model of the narrative crisis of bourgeois realism: Both the underdetermined self and the overdetermined self, the would-be free aesthete and the mere naturalist plaything of fate, reflect the same erosion of the balance between individual desire and social conditions.[16]

Wilde's plot, like the bifurcated ones we saw in both Schreiner and Conrad, is neither a bildungsroman nor an antibildungsroman, but an unorthodox combination of conflicting narrative principles set into a kind of interference pattern. Plot returns to claim sovereignty over the fate of Dorian Gray's body, just as it does in the final pages of *Lord Jim*. The suppression of existential and historical force that is operative in the middle of the novel produces a kind of temporal rebound effect, so that even with the nonmimetic or gothic energies of the novel taking center stage for so long, the form manages to accommodate both nonprogressive and progressive temporalities. Wilde's combination of time schemes thematized in the form of the art novel sets a precedent for any number of high modernist *Kunstlerromane* by figures as diverse as Joyce and Stein, Maugham and H. D., Lawrence and Woolf, in which an ironic narrative voice manages both to champion and ironize the values of the marginalized aesthete. In the Anglophone modernist novel, bourgeois socialization is never quite defeated, one might say, by bohemian dissent. *Dorian Gray*—like the other stalled youth novels discussed so far—operates as a metageneric project that both deploys and objectifies bildungsroman conventions. It forces readers to confront what is most strange and contradictory about the biographical conceit as a way of organizing fiction, and about the ideological commitment to progress (for both subject and nation) that such a conceit seems traditionally to have entailed.[17]

What I described in the previous chapter as the return of historicist or developmental logic "with a vengeance" (a kind of reality principle that challenges the fantasy of endless youth) occurs here too, as objective social conditions make themselves felt in Wilde's text when organic-biographical time whips back into place, closing down the long urban adventure of Dorian Gray. However, the novel should not be understood as a mere encapsulation of endless youth; there is more here than just a realist text that has returned to absorb and sanitize the antiprogressive or antinarrative materials of gothic romance. Here, as in chapter 3's reading of *Lord Jim*, the critical concept of interference is perhaps more apt than the concept of encapsulation to describe the unresolved dialectic between youth and age. Both Conrad and Wilde ironize their own resident ironists, Marlow and Lord Henry.[18] Neither work is designed to be put to rest by an aging observer who neatly wraps up the folly of bloody youth; both unsettle the authority and legitimacy of the Marlow/Lord Henry position because they do not quite want to abandon the value of full-time, never-ending self-cultivation.

Few critics have explored Conrad's role as an inheritor of the Dorian Gray motif and a mediating figure between the Wilde of the 1890s and the Wells of the 1900s.[19] Both *Dorian Gray* and *Lord Jim* center on an eternally fair-haired boy, prototypically and phenotypically English, who becomes the object of fascination for ethically worn older men contemplating their own lapsed romanticism. Consider an early description from Wilde, which might well have been excerpted from the opening chapter of *Lord Jim*: "His frank blue eyes, his crisp gold hair. There was something in his face that made one trust him at once. All the candour of youth was there, as well as all youth's passionate purity. One felt that he had kept himself unspotted from the world" (39). The triangle of Marlow-Stein-Jim replicates in many ways the triangle of Lord Henry–Basil Hallward–Dorian—and in that sense it is Basil whose obsessive fascination matches Marlow's, with Lord Henry and Stein as the more remote, detached observers of the spectacle of youthful idealism.[20] Both of the "blank" fair-haired boys, Dorian and Jim, find rather blank doomed lovers—flatly depicted women with obvious allegorical names (Sibyl Vane and Jewel). Jim and Dorian are passive in their blemishless youth, acceding to a destiny that they can neither outrun nor accept. Both throw themselves upon the knife in the end as a way of bringing sudden closure to the potentially endless story of their lives, accepting fate's vengeance for having shrugged off the weight of experience.[21]

Of course, *Dorian Gray* does not commit to tragic closure with the same force as *Lord Jim* (or, for that matter, Schreiner's *African Farm*). Despite the fact that Wilde's narrator gives vent to some anti-Faustian pedagogy at the end, readers may still sense that the utopian longing behind Dorian's magic youth is more memorable than the hero's grisly end. In the Nietzschean vein of "Soul of Man under Socialism," Wilde sees the value of individual freedom as compromised and displaced by various forms of social thinking, including the charitable and the religious, and in *Dorian Gray* he releases a full fantasy of youthful openness while posing it against the sad necessity of experiential accumulation and existential limits.[22] Wilde's text has a radical or utopian critique of progress that makes itself felt even through the censure of Dorian's immaturity, whereas Conrad's tragic politics of time makes itself felt even through the ironic presentation of Marlow's closet idealism. It is difficult, of course, to peel these interpretive judgments apart from our received ideas of Wilde and Conrad as, respectively, a queer aesthetic provocateur and a conservative master craftsmen. But the juxtaposition of these golden-youth plots does seem like an object lesson in Sedgwickian queer analysis: Both of these are all-male philosophy-lab novels that explore the homosocial/homosexual line, with Conrad blurring the divide somewhat less than Wilde does.

Both texts use frozen youth, I think, to question developmental paradigms of all kinds, including what Lee Edelman has called "the absolute value of reproductive futurism" (3); however, Wilde's text advances the queer critique of progress and development with more intensity. The marriage plot is aborted and decentered with even more alacrity in Wilde than in Conrad. The adolescence/maturity binary operates in the texts as a coded version of the queer/straight binary, and Marlow's investment in the salvage ideology of professional solidarity cannot be separated from his strictly homosocial model of male bonding as a consummate sign of maturity. Those codes of implicitly celibate mastery or implicitly heterosexual maturity are designed to keep eroticism quarantined and to eclipse the allure of Jim's splendid youth. In *Dorian Gray*, Hallward's erotic investment in Dorian comes somewhat closer to the surface of the text than does Marlow's in Jim. But both Dorian and Jim clearly operate as objects of male desire, as devices that displace attention from the marriage plot, and as the center of a purposeful fantasy of adolescence that postpones and marginalizes all forms of bourgeois social adaptation, including mainstream heterosexual institutions.[23] In this sense, the two novels can both be glossed by Neville Hoad's useful discussion of the temporal and historical coding of queer figures in the age of empire: "The understanding of 'homosexuality' as the marker of western decadence par excellence may also suggest ways in which the person laying claim to homosexual identity in an era of global capitalism can be made to carry the anxieties surrounding the social ruptures produced by economic development" (152).

Indeed, though each of these two novels has its own temporal and sexual algorithm for balancing the imperatives of youth and age, both emplot a contest between developmental and antidevelopmental time as a way of representing a colonial crack in the discourse of European progress. In terms of the largest frame of analysis in this study, both *Dorian Gray* and *Lord Jim* expose the Goethean bildungsroman's traditional logic of national emergence and individual self-formation to the cold light of an adolescent *reductio ad absurdum*, in which shapely, progressive time becomes stalled *Bildung*. Historical and psychological becoming are turned into stasis and decay, punctuated by intermittent and violent bursts of narrative advance. And both writers unfold this program of narrative innovation and metageneric reflection in a postnational, semi-English space. Wilde and Conrad stand at different angles of remove from Englishness and from the English tradition of social realism, but their work, taken together here, manifests what we might see as the aging of the realist bildungsroman into an advanced stage of self-consciousness and of stylistic mutation.

If the residually aristocratic values of Wilde and Conrad destabilize bourgeois myths of moral and economic progress, so too do the emergent lower-middle-class values of H. G. Wells, chronicler of a disenchanted, institutionalized, mass-consumer English society. Even more, perhaps, than Wilde and Conrad, Wells records the dying days of an elite myth of education in English life and the transformation of neofeudal myths of empire into the twentieth-century realities of worldwide imperialism, crass consumerism, and unstable financial speculation. As we add H. G. Wells into the Wilde-Conrad equation, we can build on the insights of both Irish/postcolonial and queer approaches to *Dorian Gray* that allow fresh access to the historical traction of Wilde's brilliant decision to subtract the aging process from an otherwise verisimilar metropolitan milieu.[24]

Wilde's achievement, we might say, was to unwrap and expose the old *Bildung* conceit, which used nationhood-adulthood closure plots to arrest the ever-unfolding narrative of capitalist transformation. Wilde simply writes a novel that is unusual insofar as it commits more fully to the allegory of permanent self-transformation, showing by this narrative thought experiment how essential the recuperative motifs of adulthood/nationhood had been to the European novel. My speculation here is that Wilde's trope of endless youth—a symbol of the endless revolution of modernization—gained currency and resonance during the age of empire because the mediating power of the nation to produce political and social unity across zones of radically uneven development was giving way to a more globalized sense of inequality, unevenness, and culturalized or racialized difference. Regenia Gagnier has identified Wilde's centrality to our understanding of a broad shift from production to consumption as the symbolic center of economic activity in late Victorian Britain; moreover, her work has begun to suggest a contemporaneous shift away from the idea of a settled endpoint for national industrial economies (94).[25] In my analysis, such larger contextual stories resonate with the constellation of antidevelopmental texts in which the interlocking allegories of nationhood and adulthood seem to be attenuated in the power to effect "natural" narrative closure.[26]

When we pair the Wilde of *Dorian Gray* with the Wells of *Tono-Bungay*, we can begin to see all the more clearly the imploding and exploding forms of the British novel as indices of several related and massive transformations in Victorian economic and cultural life: mass consumerism, mass education, high imperialism, speculative finance, new media, and modern advertising. Moreover, Wilde and Wells each mark important turns in the modernization of sex in late Victorian Britain, with the heterosexual and reproductive family presented in their work as the object of queer and feminist critique. No coincidence, then, that cultural and biological reproduction—and the transmission of values from one generation to the next—emerges in their signature novels as problems or absences, shouldered aside by long investigations of interminable adolescence. In the case of Wells, we find several Edwardian novels (or anti-novels) driven by an expansive logic that resists containment and closure and that self-consciously rescripts the condition-of-England story for the age of global imperialism. *Tono-Bungay* in particular is a mock-epic fable of globalized commodity capitalism and, at the same time, a bildungsroman that has been turned inside out in ways that are, if less lurid than the story of *Dorian Gray*, no less intense in their challenge to the old humanist and progressive logic of the Goethean tradition.

An "unassimilable enormity of traffic": Commerce and Decay in *Tono-Bungay*

Given that so many Anglophone writers of the fin de siècle favored the plot of the "secret sharer," it is perhaps fitting that this chapter reads Wilde and Wells as opposites who turn out to be doubles. Our conventional understanding of these two writers—the Irish ironist and the English realist, the master of epigrams and prolix prosifier, the incipiently modernist Victorian and the residually Victorian modernist—conceals a deeper affinity that underscores some of the tectonic shifts that define the canon of 1890s British fiction. In that decade, both Wilde and Wells practiced what I have called gothic didacticism. Wells's famous fictions of the period—*The Time Machine* (1895), *The Island of Dr. Moreau* (1896), *The Invisible Man* (1897), and *The War of Worlds* (1898)—all trade in some version of the Darwinian fantasy of regression that inspired *Dorian Gray*. In Wells's "scientific romances," the twin specters of degeneration and invasion threaten the body politic.[27] *The Island of Dr. Moreau*, for example, stages a fantasy of species regression using the conceit of forced evolution: The mad vivisectionist Moreau cuts and flays the bodies of large mammals until he has roughed out new human forms, then reconditions their souls with the rudiments of law. This 1896 novel also anticipates the basic thematic and narrative structure of Conrad's *Heart of Darkness*, with the narrator Prendick in the role of Marlow, a reasonable Englishman who discovers a cruel and corrupted genius of European science at the outer reaches of civilization. Like the protagonists of *Heart of Darkness*, or *Dorian Gray*—or of other Victorian gothic doppelgänger texts, such as Stevenson's *Dr. Jekyll* and Stoker's *Dracula*—Wells's Prendick comes to see himself reflected in the degraded, irrational, and bestial sides of Moreau and his creatures. These secret sharers scandalize him and release potent anxieties provoked by Darwinian racial sciences and by the late Victorian historiography of Western decline.

Wells's thematic preoccupation with evolution/devolution itself, that is, the governing motif of progress-becoming-decline as both a social catastrophe and fictional contrivance, carries over from his 1890s gothic romances into his more "serious" and mainstream novels of the Edwardian era: *Tono-Bungay* (1909), *Ann Veronica* (1909), *The New Machiavelli* (1911), and *Marriage* (1912). In these, Wells rewrites the condition-of-England novel in terms of two revolutionary pressures on inherited values: the spread of the global economy and the modernization of sexual and gender relations. These are big novels, with expansive personalities and exploding forms, bulging as if in sympathetic response to the entropic and exponential growth of human knowledge, technological power, and the imperial system.[28] In *Tono-Bungay*, the best known of this group of novels, Wells invents a protagonist-narrator George Ponderevo whose coming-of-age plot gets hijacked by the unstable logic of commodity fetishism and the unpredictable rhythms of the business cycle. At the outset, George observes that modern social life has produced "unmanageable realities" that force him to record only "inconsecutive observations" rather than a seamless autobiography (11). He cannot, he confesses, arrange the details of his life "in any developing order at all" (37). "I must sprawl and flounder, comment and theorise," George insists (13). Impatient readers will find that he keeps his word! The case of bloat becomes more interesting when we consider the opening passage of the novel:

> Most people in the world seem to live "in character"; they have a beginning, a middle and an end. . . . But there is also another kind of life that is not so much living as a miscellaneous tasting of life. One gets hit by some unusual transverse force, one is jerked out of one's stratum and lives crosswise for the rest of the time, and as it were, in a succession of samples.
>
> (9)

The passage announces that *Tono-Bungay* is not, and cannot be, a shapely biographical novel, but will assemble itself as a set of miscellaneous episodes. It marks a self-conscious departure from the arc and curve of the coming-of-age plot. And it also introduces—though not by name—the global commodity Tono-Bungay, taken as an "unusual transverse force" that destabilizes the progressive and biographical plan of the national bildungsroman. Aside from his difficulties as the narrator of his own unruly life story, Ponderevo as the central actor in that story suffers from an ongoing failure to accumulate a functional, integrated personality.

More to the point, Wells sets this story of an unseasonable, discontinuous life into a specific phase in the decline of English class society and rise of global commodity capitalism.[29]

George Ponderevo starts out as a somewhat rootless, educated member of the lower middle class, his social desire mesmerized by the gentry values associated with his mother's employers at Bladesover estate, and his vocational ambitions vaguely directed at some kind of creative or scientific pursuit. But life only truly begins for George when his Uncle Edward, a glint-eyed, monomaniacal pharmacist, decides to market a tonic called Tono-Bungay (loosely based on the history of Coca-Cola), which then becomes a massive commercial success. As Uncle Edward's right-hand man, George goes along for the wild ride of Tono-Bungay's rise and fall in the marketplace. The fate of the magic elixir—driven by false claims, bogus science, financial speculation, and corporate voodoo—becomes inseparable from George's fate. The disposition of his soul, the inner desires of his heart, the intellectual promptings of his mind, are all sacrificed to the drama of Tono-Bungay's life cycle as a fad product. In the end, George can only look back at his life as a "story of activity and urgency and sterility. I have called it *Tono-Bungay*, but I had far better have called it *Waste*" (412). Just as Dorian Gray, seeking self-perfection, converts himself into a self-reifying object, so does George Ponderevo subordinate his self-formation to the erratic life of the commodity Tono-Bungay.[30] Just as Dorian sells his soul for eternal youth, beauty, and pleasure, so does George sell his soul for a privileged seat inside the belly of the corporate whale. And the result is the same at the level of narrative structure: George cannot grow or mature into an autonomous subject with a socially integrated self. Like Dorian, but in a different tonal key, George remains very much a moral and emotional adolescent—shallow, mercurial, callow, and obtuse. His life story reads, even to himself, like a looping, oscillating sine curve without clear resolution or growth.[31] George continually registers the fact that his life story seems to upend the expectations of the developmental plot, as in this pithy bit of self-diagnosis that might well have come straight from Dorian Gray: "I am, in a sense, decay" (413).

Tono-Bungay compresses and splits the normal code of compromise between bohemian urgings and bourgeois necessity at the heart of the Goethean bildungsroman: George the young man with creative ambitions suddenly becomes a hypertrophic business mogul with no soul, then slides sporadically back into a moody, puerile funk. Instead of social compromise, Wells describes a stalemate between irreconcilable states of mind. Once Tono-Bungay, the commodity, absorbs and displaces George as the protagonist of this novel, George's life becomes a spasmodic and self-trivializing affair, narrated not as a tale of emergence but as the offhanded passage of time without moral or psychological progress: "Nearly eight years slipped by. I grew up" (219).

Once Tono-Bungay enters its peak as a successful brand, the story of George's life can no longer be the story of England.[32] In the first third of the book, Wells, voiced through Ponderevo, anchors social fixity in the gentry stronghold of Blades-over, a stand-in for the English class tradition as a political container that gives rounded meaning to historical time. Enter Tono-Bungay, the global commodity that disrupts the spatiotemporal boundaries of class and nation, following the boundless energies of market capitalism. Summarizing the "tortuous" legal and financial maneuvers by which "we" (the Tono-Bungay corporate subject) "spread ourselves with a larger and larger conception," George himself observes that "that sort of development is not to be told in detail in a novel" (232). Novels tend not to narrate the tentacular and tortuous life of the corporation in part because it has no logical endpoint other than continued growth and expansion. When the logic of permanent expansion (global capitalism) displaces the logic of national growth (as symbolic counterweight to endless expansion), the specter of the Hegelian bad infinity appears, raising the possibility that the novel form will expand into a never-ending story of infinite details and numberless episodes.

But Tono-Bungay does not narrate the infinite expansion of capitalism itself, of course: It is the story of the rise and fall of a fad commodity whose life cycle deter-mines the jerky, episodic quality of the novel's composition. George Ponderevo, increasingly self-conscious about the problem of lost tradition, charges the loss of smooth progressive time to the depredations of newfangled capitalist opera-tions visited upon a stable English way of life centered on the old estate of Blades-over. He offers this picture of the condition of England: It is becoming a "country of great Renascence landed gentlefolk who have been unconsciously outgrown and overgrown" in an epoch defined as (in the words of his bombastic uncle) "a big Progressive On-coming Imperial Time" (107; 281).[33] Where once the English elites balanced scientific and industrial dynamism with the stabilizing values of a gentry-based national myth, the new ruling classes of the early twentieth cen-tury harbor, in Ponderevo's view, a "disorderly instinct of acquisition" with "noth-ing creative nor rejuvenescent" (70). Bladesover, the intact and integral estate of George's childhood, is replaced symbolically by Crest Hill, the failed estate of the nouveau riche Ponderevos, the house that Tono-Bungay couldn't quite, in the end, build. Crest Hill becomes, for George, "the compactest image and sample of all that passes for Progress, of all the advertisement-inflated spending, the aimless building up and pulling down, the enterprise and promise of my age. . . . 'Great God!' I cried, 'but is this Life?'" (376). Here *Tono-Bungay* makes manifest the breakup of national tradition and meaningful, productive economic relations as a predicate for the unclockable nonstory of George Ponderevo, whose maturation plot founders because it is assimilated to a modernization process with no symbolic or historical constraints. The novel encodes this problem thematically by depicting a widespread crisis of English wholeness when faced with the corrosive and uncontainable effects of mass commodity capitalism.

While he both laments and satirizes the lost productivity of the English ruling classes, George also embodies their etiolated and enervated state—not despite his role in the success of Tono-Bungay but because of it, since it is an empty commodity built on false value. With characteristic self-consciousness, George notes that the personal crisis of his uncle's hollow life/empty product is all too reflective of a crisis in national capitalism:

> Yet it seems to me indeed at times that all this present commercial civilisation is not more than my poor uncle's career writ large, a swelling, thinning bubble of assurances; that its arithmetic is just as unsound . . . that it all drifts on perhaps to some tremendous parallel to his individual disaster . . .
>
> (239)

The closing ellipsis in the text signals George's uncertainty about how to end a sentence, a paragraph, a narrative that is organized according to the rolling tempo of capitalist speculation. Everywhere the moral fervor of Wells shows through in this novel's saga of lost productivity: "It is all one spectacle," announces George at the end, "of forces running to waste, of people who use and do not replace, the story of a country hectic with a wasting aimless fever of trade and moneymaking and pleasure-seeking" (412).

The problem of failed productivity extends from Wells's portrait of capitalism run amok to the libidinal economies of George Ponderevo's life, where he indulges in a vain and self-blinded set of sour romances that he generally casts as the fault of "wasted and wasteful and futile" women. "What hope is there," he laments in his final reflections, "for a people whose women become fruitless?" (412). There is a kind of subtle feminist undercurrent running through speeches like this one, since George's callow understanding of women, sex, desire, and himself are all targets of Wells's irony. Indeed elsewhere in Wells's considerable body of fiction, we can find a much more developed criticism of the sex-property system in England; in novels like *The New Machiavelli*, for example, Wells offers a direct denunciation of the benighted puritanism of his times, particularly insofar as it blocks both women and men from romantic candor and sexual liberation.[34] Wells sees England's sexual mores as completely out of step with its scientific, technological, and economic modernity: They represent a national form of arrested development that recurs throughout his novels. In *Tono-Bungay*, the detached aesthete Ewart makes this clear to George: "We don't adolesce, we blunder up to sex" (186). Without an authentic or realistic path from youth to sexual adulthood, middle-class Englishmen develop unrealistic romantic goals and tastes.

Even more specifically in the case of George, romantic failures—too numerous and frankly tiresome to describe here—are driven by an irrational set of desires linked in Wells's diction to the economic irrationality of speculation and mass-marketing. "Love," Ponderevo observes, "like everything else in this immense process of social disorganization in which we live, is a thing adrift, a fruitless thing broken away from its connections" (372). In a fairly clear rewriting of the Pip-Estella subplot of *Great Expectations*, George misunderstands his own romantic destiny and channels his erotic energy through his nostalgic fixation on aristocratic values (Beatrice) and through his disavowed entanglement with consumerist gratification (Marion).[35] The results in either case are disastrous, and Wells frames the problem so as to accentuate the confusion between economic and sexual objects that bedevils his protagonist. The main bad-marriage plot in *Tono-Bungay* centers on Marion, whom George dismisses as too conventional: "It was the cruellest luck for Marion that I, with my restlessness, my scepticism, my constantly developing ideas, had insisted upon marriage with her. She had no faculty of growth or change" (197). Sexual life with Marion comes to signify both the immature Puritanism of the naive George and the compensatory restlessness of the corporate George, a game of ping-pong between frozen libido and boundless desire that mirrors the uneven growth processes of the novel's existential and economic registers.

Later, seeking comfort with his mistress Effie, George undergoes another round of disintegration and ennui: "I wondered if all the world was even as I, urged to this by one motive and to that by another, creatures of chance and impulse and unmeaning traditions" (214). This romantic crisis makes itself felt by George as a crisis of self-fashioning in post-traditional English society: Sex reduces him to a system of "appetites and satisfactions" rather than clarifying for him an integral model of desire and destiny centered in the maturing self (215). What is most radical about Wells's broken *Bildung* is perhaps this deromanticization and decentering of the marriage plot, something otherwise associated with the queer modernisms (and narrative innovations) of Wilde, Woolf, Forster, and Stein. And what is most distinctive about Wells's version of the decentered marriage plot is his insistence on the language of unstable subjectivity and unrooted desire as a mirror-effect of capitalism's endless motion. In the classic bildungsroman or realist novel, the marriage plot is the narrative and social convention par excellence for embedding subjects into the fixed state of adulthood, so the roving disrespect paid to that institution by Wells aligns nicely with his novels' expansive resistance to the standard signs and accoutrements of bourgeois maturity.

Tono-Bungay's vocabulary of corporate capitalism borrows heavily from the libidinal register (fruitless, wasted, sterile) in order to describe the crisis of bourgeois dynamism. That crisis takes the form of an alternating pattern between the hyperactivity of an enterprise driven by bogus technology, mass marketing, and rampant speculation on the one hand and the utter deflation of bankruptcy, economic collapse, and empty consumerism on the other. Wells's fable of late capitalism picks up the narrative I described in chapter 2 via Arendt and Lukács: that is, the collapse of the bourgeois revolution. The bourgeoisie, according to this model, no longer serve as the engine of social, economic, or cultural progress (moralized and stabilized through the political mediation of the multiclass nation). Ponderevo's governing theme as a narrator matches this story; he castigates the English ruling class and entrepreneurial class for their flagging energies and wasteful new practices. Both Arendt and Lukács take the expansion of imperialist activity after 1870 to be a sign of failed bourgeois dynamism—of the failure, not the success, of the European project of modernization. Here too Wells follows the same line of thinking: As Tono-Bungay enters a desperate stage of collapse and failure, the Ponderevos launch their own private scramble for African wealth. Uncle Edward dispatches George to Mordet Island off the African coast, to harvest a radioactive material called quap, a miraculous energy-commodity that will, they hope, save Tono-Bungay from imminent corporate death.

The quap episode marks a nadir in the fortunes of Tono-Bungay and in George's project of self-cultivation. In a Conradian drama of regression and rapacity, George enters the most brutalizing arena of global commerce, the tropical colony, and becomes a morally bankrupt European attempting to seize raw materials. Very quickly, the quap expedition devolves into an almost farcically compact and complete failure, as Wells anatomizes everything that can go wrong with the dream of colonial resources harvested for nothing. On board ship, George, who had preened himself on his own liberal tolerance, finds himself becoming a brutal racist taskmaster and, finally, a murderer: "I understand now the heart of the sweater, of the harsh employer, of the nigger-driver" (332). During the homeward journey, having swiped "heaps of quap," George discovers that its radioactivity is toxic. The men fall ill, and the ship begins literally to disintegrate. All is lost, predictably enough, and the Ponderevo fortunes, moral and financial, plummet further down the backdrain of failed capitalist ventures.

Reflecting on the trip, George writes: "That expedition to Mordet Island stands apart from all the rest of my life, detached, a piece by itself with an atmosphere all its own" (344). But in fact the episode is entirely consistent with the main plot at a thematic and symbolic level. It shifts attention from speculative and consumerist enterprise to plundering and imperialist enterprise, but keeps the focus on the underlying problem of nonproductivity in late capitalism. It illustrates the short circuit from a faltering national-industrial economy to a speculative finance-driven economy to a risky colonial-extraction economy, and dramatizes the racial and moral costs of high imperialism.[36] And the metaphoric value of quap is that it represents a kind of dangerous, disintegrative energy that has no bounds or limits: It is not just a fantasy of bottomless wealth, but a symbol of endless potential, endless becoming—the forces that define George's loss of moral integrity and the final deformation of his *Bildung* plot. George's regression and decay proceeds like the radioactive material he is chasing; he is developing backward, a half-life at a time. Wells makes this clear and ties soul decay directly to nation decay as the narrator declares that the break-up of the quap-laden ship represents "in matter exactly what the decay of our old culture is in society, a loss of traditions and distinctions and assured reactions" (355). Atomic decay becomes an overt metaphor for social disintegration, but also for the way that bad matter (associated with globalization) has displaced the moral fiber that should have defined the organic and humanist core of George's character.

Even more explicitly than *Dorian Gray*, *Tono-Bungay* links the unseasonable youth of its protagonist to the uneven developments of the age of empire. It enacts and describes the break-up of the bildungsroman and its soul-nation allegory of harmonious growth: Here both soul and nation are temporally disorganized, stuck in a rut yet driven too fast. Wells's commodity novel mirrors Wilde's art novel: When subjectivity is written in the language of pure commodity logic, it follows capitalism's endless forward motion and produces the plot of permanent adolescence. So too when subjectivity is written in the language of aestheticism— the language that seeks fully to disavow commodification and fully to arrest the forward momentum of time—the result is a plot of permanent adolescence. Endless self-development collapses into the absence of self-development because it cannot be converted into the narrative currency of achieved self-identity. Just as important, when the story of development spills out of the frame of national tradition, it foregoes the inherited symbolic resources of the bildungsroman, abandons its most naturalized technique for harnessing and halting the progressivist logic of modern realism and making the life of the individual and the life of the national the organic center of a representable (because not interminable) story of modernization. And Wells, ever the didact, makes it very clear to readers that the novel of global capitalism circa 1910 is the story of disproportionate growth and regression at once, a metabildungsroman that is in some crucial ways about the impossibility of biographical and national fiction in the post-Victorian world.[37]

We began, of course, with one of those impossibilities, as the narrator declared that he could not recount his life as a meaningful and organized sequence of events. We end, in *Tono-Bungay*, with the other, as the narrator observes that it has become equally impossible to describe the life of his nation as a meaningful and organized historical narrative. Tracking "the broad slow decay of the great social organism of England," Ponderevo states in the final chapter that the problem lies in the "tumorous growth-process" of the London metropolis (70, 418). He summarizes his views:

> That is the very key of it all. Each day one feels that the pressure of commerce and traffic grew, grew insensibly monstrous, . . . and jostled together to make this unassimilable enormity of traffic.
>
> (418)

The English novel, like the social system from which it arose, cannot assimilate such global traffic without losing its Jamesian sense of stylistic proportion and its Austenian sense of social composure. A multinational and metastatic process of modernization is unsettling the social referents of *Tono-Bungay* in neat parallel with the unsettled and unseasonable quality of George's prolonged moral adolescence. Or, to put it another way, George Ponderevo assimilates the "real historical time" (per Bakhtin) of a globalizing era driven by monstrous traffic—the same monstrous traffic, in a sense, that formed the backdrop to Dorian Gray's life of endless, listless consumption.[38] The results are only too legible in the protagonist's bustling yet unsatisfying existence, the boom-and-bust of a life that changes all the time but never improves.

Wells uses Ponderevo, with his evacuated agency and downward-spiraling destiny, to condense a multidimensional critique of modernity, focusing with special emphasis on the financial and imperial dynamos of the changing British economy. The wayward plot of *Tono-Bungay* exposes the English national myth of "traditionalists who modernize the world." Unharmonious times—both slow and fast, backward and forward—govern and shape the novel, making Ponderevo a figure for the failing, fissuring synthesis between national tradition and capitalist modernity. In a somewhat more discursive and less sensational way than the Irish Wilde, Wells takes apart the English self-image as the race that "has development" (in the words of Wilde's duchess, 232). Wells's anti-novel, like Wilde's, implicitly describes the limit points of realist narratability for young characters who embody capitalist modernization uncut and unharnessed by the stabilizing forces of national tradition. The limit points become legible to readers when we see the protagonist fail to develop an integrated personality while operating under the symbolic aegis of commodification, perpetual innovation, speculative finance, and high imperialism.[39] If the standard coming-of-age plot puts modernization into symbolic compromise with a moralized concept of national progress, the modernist novel of untimely youth removes the temporal checks and balances of that concept, giving us a heterochronic—though perhaps no less realist—form.

The resulting narrative forms take us beyond the familiar "novel of disillusionment" in which the hero's demoralization and alienation simply flip the socially affirmative poles of the bildungsroman. *Tono-Bungay* does not invert social-adjustment plots into tragedy and disillusionment, but folds open and objectifies the problem of the bildungsroman. Such a metageneric approach is both more and less radical than a fully exploded or inverted bildungsroman would be. On the one hand, it keeps certain nineteenth-century standards intact; no matter how much he falls short, George still measures himself existentially against clock time, psychologically against the interiority and fulfillment of the realist hero, and socially against the expectations of bourgeois adjustment. On the other hand, Wells disassembles the soul-nation allegory with such clarity that it is difficult to imagine the twentieth-century novel reassembling it, at least not in its relatively naturalized or "classic" form. The somewhat clunky pun in George Ponderevo's surname (revised by Wells from Ponderer to Ponderevo in order, it appears, to suggest the phrase "ponder evolution") points neither to an embrace nor to an outright rejection of evolutionary/developmental time, but rather to a project of pondering, of establishing historical and critical distance. The soul-nation allegory cannot simply be willed into oblivion by artistic fiat or modernist will-to-innovation; it must be tracked, dialectically, in a path toward social and symbolic obsolescence, its meaning changed by the eclipse of one phase in the history of modernization by another, more intensely global one.

The final passages of the novel concentrate our attention on the broken national frame of the story, and indeed of English experience in Wells's lifetime: "Again and again in this book I have written of England as a feudal scheme overtaken by fatty degeneration and stupendous accidents of hypertrophy" (417). "Degeneration" and "hypertrophy," accidents and bloat: an apt and vivid description indeed of the novel itself, unstrung into postnational, antidevelopmental time. The passage vividly captures the arresting-and-accelerating heterochrony that shapes the novel of untimely youth. And what brings England into disharmony is the boundless ocean of modern capitalism: The sea, with its "monstrous variety," bears the "flags of all the world" and drives London "beyond all law, order, and precedence" (417). Ponderevo's final thematic crescendo recalls George Eliot's riverine pathway to world trade in *The Mill on the Floss* and Conrad's merchant-marine waterways in *Lord Jim*. It depicts the global economy as an epistemological force that breaks the bounds of national territory, disrupting the ordered existence of both a person and a people. *Tono-Bungay*'s representation of London's monstrous traffic anticipates Virginia Woolf's *The Voyage Out*—a novel composed during the same years as *Tono-Bungay* and published in 1915. In *The Voyage Out*, Woolf begins where Wells leaves off, with a description of the London docks as a thematic gauge used to register the effects of the colonial world-system on national space and novelistic time. As we will see in the next chapter, Woolf's novel, too, unsettles the bildungsroman plot as it ventures out from England and into the seascapes and landscapes of uneven development.

In fact, the writers at the center of chapter 5, Virginia Woolf and James Joyce, both opened their careers as novelists by writing a version of the colonial metabildungsroman, in which underdeveloped or peripheral space grounds and allegorizes stubbornly youthful protagonists. These two writers (another English/Irish pair to match Wells and Wilde) define the very core of high modernist fiction. They share hypercanonical status now in part because their work exemplifies a signature modernist style, the "stream of consciousness." Unlike Wilde and Wells, Joyce and Woolf deemphasize the didactic and discursive narrator and assimilate commentary into the devices of interior monologue and free indirect discourse. As Benita Parry describes the Wells method, the "social and psychic turbulence" of *Tono-Bungay* is "described rather than syntactically inscribed" (150). If that feature—description, commentary, statement—allows Wilde and Wells to be all the clearer about their metageneric project (objectifying rather than deploying the conventions of the bildungsroman), it also helps account for their place as transitional figures between the Victorian and modernist canons—with Wilde a protomodernist and Wells a semimodernist. These are real differences in critical status, and they are matched by innumerable other stylistic, biographical, and ideological differences that separate Wilde from Wells from Woolf from Joyce. All the more striking then to discover the convergence of these four writers on the unaging protagonist as a device for exploring, from different angles of political perception, the problem of progress across the colonial divide. Like Wells, Woolf estranges both the coming-of-age plot and the condition-of-England frame as she transplants the story of Rachel Vinrace from southern England to South America. Like Wilde, Joyce picks up the Flaubertian thread of the urban anti-hero and uses it to write a definitive novel of Irish youth. It is, of course, a direct line of influence from Wilde's Picture to Joyce's Portrait, but we also should mark the difference in that Joyce's novel describes not the problem of the man-becoming-art, but the problem of the man-becoming-artist. That shift allows Joyce to address the worlds of commodification and reification—those forces that displace *Bildung* so comprehensively in Wilde and in Wells—with a somewhat subtler hand. As we will see in the next chapter, both Joyce and Woolf work through their own apprenticeships as novelists by decisively rewiring the plot of development and dropping it into the recursive, regressive groove of colonial adolescence.

5. Tropics of Youth in Woolf and Joyce

For the methods by which she had reached her present position, seemed to her very strange, and the strangest thing about them was that she had not known where they were leading her.

—Woolf, *The Voyage Out*

The economic and intellectual conditions of his homeland do not permit the individual to develop.

—Joyce, "Ireland, Island of Saints and Sages"

Edward Said's insistence on the "cultural integrity of empire" still offers a vital challenge to the humanities today, and particularly to literary scholars of the period 1880–1940, for whom Said's concept makes it at once more difficult and more necessary to reconceive the relationship between modernism and colonialism (*Culture and Imperialism* 97). The model of colonial culture established by Said identifies a flexible, often aesthetically complex, yet ideologically purposeful, discourse of colonialism that projected Western superiority, secular rationality, economic progress, and bourgeois triumphalism to the far corners of the earth. Yet the dominant models of aesthetic modernism describe it as a critical movement whose dissonant strains within European culture are unified by a deep suspicion of precisely those same projected narratives of Western superiority, rationalism, and progress. As we have already begun to see, these alternative propositions raise a key question for the politics of modernism: Do modernist works critique imperialism and its associated values or, alternatively, do they renovate Western art by exploiting the cultural and epistemological privileges that Raymond Williams has memorably described as "metropolitan perception" (*Politics* 44)? Of course the answers to this question are as various as modernism's disparate expressions in art, literature, music, and philosophy—and, by now, most scholars attempt to chart a middle course, eschewing both implausible claims of an ideological chasm between modernism and imperialism and equally implausible claims of direct ideological correspondence. Nevertheless, this somewhat Manichaean and moralistic framework continues to define much of the commentary on modernism and colonialism. As a result, many scholars restrict themselves to considering texts with obvious imperial content and, more to the point, end by charging or crediting particular modernists with pro- or anti-imperial views—even if the ratios of political intention are mixed, nuanced, and ever-shifting.

While Conrad stands as an obvious instance of a modernist writer whose relationship to colonialism has often been framed in largely intentionalist terms, the same problem has also shaped colonial discourse studies of, and postcolonial approaches to, the two most canonical modernists, Virginia Woolf and James Joyce. Such approaches have, for example, consolidated our understanding of Woolf's intertwined and impassioned suspicion of imperialism and patriarchy.[1] Jane Marcus's groundbreaking reading of *The Waves* established the initial bases of this interpretive position, arguing that that novel contains a veiled but unmistakable and cogent attack on the power/knowledge structures of British imperialism. In a subtle rejoinder to Marcus, Patrick McGee insists that *The Waves* offers an "implicit and partial critique," rather than an explicit denunciation of imperialism, drawing attention away from Woolf's own political attitudes and toward her form's symbolic mediations of the colonial context. McGee objects, in other words, to viewing Woolf as outside the ideology of imperialism that she anatomizes (and reproduces) in her fiction (631–32).[2] If we take Woolf's fiction as a key example of how modernism frames—both in terms of authorial intentions *and* formal effects—a historical relationship to colonialism, it is worth considering in more detail the literary devices that mediate between those two layers of textual meaning in the modernist novel.

Toward that end, this chapter begins by examining Woolf's most obviously colonial novel, *The Voyage Out* (1915), then moves to its near contemporary, Joyce's *Portrait of the Artist as a Young Man* (1916), taking the shared motif of stalled development as the master trope of both texts and as a device whose meaning outstrips author-based forms of *parti pris* ideology critique. A comparison of these two novels has limits from the outset, particularly with regard to the gender and nationality of the protagonists. But here, as in earlier cases of male-female or Anglo-Irish pairings (Conrad and Schreiner, Wells and Wilde), the overt differences between Woolf and Joyce sometimes obscure shared historical conditions and stylistic affinities.[3] From a gender-studies perspective, for example, one might say that Woolf's Rachel Vinrace exemplifies a late Victorian girl's blocked access to elite education while Joyce's Stephen Dedalus can join the ranks of the church, the university, or another site of masculine social prestige. But the path of Stephen's destiny is as compromised for Joyce as the path of Rachel's is for Woolf. If Rachel marks an early Woolfian effort to arrest a socialization process in which patriarchal authority limits women's freedom, Stephen likewise embodies a Joycean drama of rebellion against symbolic fathers and fatherlands. Where Rachel naively resists patriarchal authority by questioning its outcomes and opting out of its sexual arrangements, Stephen exposes its operations by acting as a kind of double-agent who raids its institutions, usurps its prerogatives, and exaggerates its intellectual habits. In her first novel, Woolf trains herself to purge the usual fundamentals of novelistic character and then to redistribute them extra-subjectively—an effort that later yields *Jacob's Room*, in which elegiac absence nullifies the heroic tale of *Bildung*. Joyce, it appears, is training himself to saturate the field of consciousness—an effort that later yields *Ulysses*, whose Stephen Dedalus still cannot quite think his way out of the vexed position of the antinational antihero. In their different ways, preintellectual Rachel and hyperintellectual Stephen must both assume a stubborn social passivity. And such passivity underscores the fact that these protagonists are built to serve a null function, to be fictional devices that disrupt the traditional coming-of-age plot, throwing into relief its masculinized and nationalized concepts of destiny.

Stalled development—or colonial adolescence—registers in both Woolf and Joyce, then, via a gendered critique of imperial authority. But these variations on the frozen-youth trope require interpretive responses that push through and beyond the avowed anticolonial politics of the two authors in question. In the opening case of Woolf, my discussion will not emphasize the postcolonial thematics of alterity (in the form of Rachel's oblique identification with colonized peoples) nor even the direct presentation of anti-imperial politics (in the form of Woolf's acerbic satire of the Dalloways and their fatuous jingoism), in part because the novel itself takes pains to establish the ineffectiveness of both cross-cultural identification and bourgeois dissent as types of counterdiscursive action. Instead, the reading will concentrate on the novel's assimilation of a certain uneven—and markedly colonial—temporality into its narrative and characterological language, which is to say, on the formal problem of how *The Voyage Out* undoes the generic protocols of the bildungsroman. This approach aims to bring together Woolf's characteristically modernist aversion to linear plots with her idiosyncratic representation of an ersatz Amazonian landscape in order to elaborate and extend this study's central claims about the structural link between modernist fictions of adolescence and the post-Berlin politics of European imperialism.

As in the previous chapter, I begin my analysis of Woolf with a straightforward question: How does the dissonance between hypermodernization in the metropolitan core and underdevelopment in the colonial periphery—a defining feature of the modernist world—make itself felt in the fabric of novelistic time? The question opens an equally pressing line of inquiry into *A Portrait of the Artist as a Young Man*. Indeed, in the case of Joyce, the last twenty-five years have witnessed a fairly comprehensive critical reorientation around questions of nation and empire, beginning with a first wave of "political" readings in the 1980s (Deane, Manganiello, MacCabe) and extending into a second wave of more recent postcolonial approaches (Attridge and Howes, Castle, Cheng, Duffy, Kiberd, Nolan, Valente). Here the critical literature runs a bit deeper than in the case of postcolonial Woolf, and includes many subtle elaborations of Joyce's own politics. Perhaps this is because it is notoriously difficult even to establish Joyce's political views, split as they were between his rejection of extra-Irish authority (whether British-imperial or Roman-Catholic) and his rejection of Irish authority (whether national or religious, cultural or political).

This chapter uses the pairing with Woolf and the emphasis on the symbolic utility of the metabildungsroman to try to establish a new critical angle on the postcolonial Joyce. Rather than dwell on the ambient irony produced by Joyce's anti-imperial-yet-also-antinational politics, I propose to concentrate on *Portrait* as a text that addresses colonial modernity by exposing the contradictions in what David Lloyd has termed "developmental historicism" (*Irish Times* 75).[4] Until now this study has been exploring various modernist breaks and traps in the standard coming-of-age plot, but we have now to confront a protagonist with his own fully elaborated theory of aesthetic stasis. Even in a modernist canon replete with arrested-development plots, Joyce's *Portrait* represents an additional turn of the screw. In it, the exposed contradiction between endless growth and shaped time works both as a symbolic and narrative principle and as a matter of thematized experience for the protagonist. Many of the structural back-eddies and symbolic flourishes of *Portrait*—not to mention the most searching political implications of the text—can be illuminated in light of a dialectical confrontation between the novel of pure adolescence on the one hand and the developmental imperatives of modernity and maturity on the other.

As we consider Joyce's modernization of the Goethean bildungsroman, we will see that it responds to the challenge of narrating artistic self-formation and Irish identity without simply replicating—nor simply dismissing—the dominant linear-progressive models of both the apprenticeship novel and the European nation-state.[5] *The Voyage Out*, too, set at a rather different angle of remove from the English great tradition, seeks to scramble the chronotope of the national bildungsroman. Where Joyce seems to write a novel of youth taken as an endless prelude, Woolf twists the coming-of-age plot into one long, spiraling denouement almost from the opening chapter. The overt narrative asymmetries mask an underlying formal symmetry in the two texts. And since Woolf and Joyce now occupy the very center of the twentieth-century canon, it is worth considering how foundational these two parallel texts of frozen youth were for writers who, having learned to invert and arrest the coming-of-age narrative during the age of empire, went on to conduct varied experiments in antidevelopmental and multiprotagonist fiction that have helped define not just their careers but the shape of literary fiction long after modernism.[6]

The "weight of the world": Woolf's Colonial Adolescence

The Voyage Out blends the tropical setting of imperial romance with the skeletal outline of a female bildungsroman, yet this combination of genres works to deromanticize the tropical setting of one and invert the temporal sequencing of the other. Readings of the novel have long turned on two broad interpretive questions that organize feminist and postcolonial approaches, respectively.[7] First, why does the novel initiate a trajectory of apparent self-determination, spiritual enlargement, or at least social adjustment for its protagonist Rachel Vinrace, only to close down those possibilities in a long spiral of illness, driving the plot into an antipatriarchal ground zero of death and renunciation? Second, why does Woolf stage this process in an obscure South American tourist colony? What narrative, symbolic, or stylistic purposes does the colonial setting serve? To put the two questions together: Since in the end the colonial distance from England only highlights the durability and portability of the social conventions that domesticate and threaten Rachel, why voyage out there in the first place?

My answer to this last question turns on the novel's capacity to shift the trope of development freely between psychic and political registers. *The Voyage Out* breaks from the narrative dictates of the bildungsroman, avoiding the baleful teleology of late Victorian womanhood with a twenty-four-year-old protagonist who remains stubbornly, insipidly young. Woolf describes the impression Rachel makes: "Her face was weak rather than decided . . . denied beauty, now that she was sheltered indoors, by the lack of colour and definite outline"; she seems "more than normally incompetent for her years" (13). Rachel's development in the novel is not so much absent as staccato: thrust in and out of her amorphous youthfulness by turns, she is now frustratingly pillowed in innocence, now suddenly alert to adult possibilities. More to the point, Woolf sets this story of fits and starts, of beckoned and deferred maturity, in an unevenly developed coastal enclave, Santa Marina, a misbegotten tourist colony that seems to have deferred its own modernity only to have it arrive belatedly.

Woolf invents a syncopated, suspended, then accelerated history of settlement for Santa Marina: First it is dimly Spanish, then briefly English, then Spanish again for three hundred years of apparent social stasis, then English again, made over into a holiday spot for the shabby genteel. Like Rachel, Santa Marina develops arrhythmically, first languishing, than suddenly catapulting forward, reeling with anachronism. Having failed to form itself into something firmly British and modern the first time around, Santa Marina appears as a cultural backwater. We learn that "in arts and industries the place is still much where it was in Elizabethan days" (80). And here, a few chapters earlier, is a description of Rachel Vinrace: "Her mind was in the state of an intelligent man's in the beginning of the reign of Queen Elizabeth" (26). To anticipate one additional point of resonance between *Voyage Out* and Joyce's *Portrait*: Both texts feature protagonists, the Elizabethan Rachel Vinrace and the medieval(ist) Stephen Dedalus, whose prolonged adolescence seems to correspond to a nonmodern temporality.[8] And there is another audible modernist resonance in Woolf's account of Rachel's backwardness: She persistently links her two subjects of arrested development—Rachel and Santa Marina—through the redoubtably Conradian motif of the "virgin land behind a veil" (79).

Conrad's importance to Woolf in the early stages of her career is not just apparent in the symbolic use of colonial territory to describe spoiled innocence, but extends to the level of diction and cadence. Consider this early description of the *Euphrosyne*, the ship carrying Rachel to her tropical destiny:

> An immense dignity had descended upon her; she was an inhabitant of the great world, which has so few inhabitants, travelling all day across an empty universe, with veils drawn before her and behind. . . . The sea might give her death or some unexampled joy, and none would know of it. She was a

bride going forth to her husband, a virgin unknown of men; in her vigour and purity she might be likened to all beautiful things, for as a ship she had a life of her own.

(24–25)

The Conradian homage in this passage seems to point back to *Heart of Darkness*, a clear intertext for *The Voyage Out* (which Woolf had begun to write only five or six years after Conrad's novella appeared in print).[9] Like *Heart of Darkness*, Woolf's novel begins on the banks of the Thames, moves to the edge of a distant continent, then traces a journey into unknown geographic and psychic territories, ending in death and a thwarted engagement. Moreover, Woolf's interest in women who are sheltered from the imperial way of the world echoes Marlow's insistence that women are "out of it" (*Heart* 26). Richard Dalloway, making his first appearance in Woolf's fiction, comes aboard the *Euphrosyne* to crystallize this point for Rachel Vinrace and for us: Women cannot have access to the dark realities of imperial rule, he pontificates, because it is impossible "for human beings, constituted as they are, both to fight and to have ideals" (*Voyage* 56). Men fight and compromise while women symbolize ideals for the men who have lost them in the fray. In Conrad, as in Woolf, a neochivalric gender ideology becomes the language of mystification for men living too close to the volatile contradictions between imperialist rhetoric and imperialist practice.

But the Conrad-Woolf resonances extend perhaps even more significantly—and in ways that have not been recognized in literary scholarship—from *The Voyage Out* to *Lord Jim*. The echo of Conrad in the ship-as-veiled-bride motif is perfectly apt since Woolf's Rachel is, much like Conrad's Jim, a virgin in a bubble of blushing egoism, a virgin not just to sex but to intersubjectivity, forced to face disillusionment but unable to live with it. She is, like Jim, a willfully adolescent adult whose refusal to age leads to death in an obscure colonial outpost. And, like Jim (and for that matter, Kipling's Kim), Rachel is a classic symbolic orphan, a many-parented figure who, as the object of other characters' projections and desires, stands as a kind of "semantic void," the null function that can carry the symbolic weight of *Bildung* as both a biographical and social process.[10] Using her stock exotica to full literary effect, Woolf casts Rachel's mind and the South American landscape as figures for each other, each prone to a certain formlessness. Here is Rachel on the cliff's edge with her suitor, the plump and hapless Terence Hewet:

> Looking the other way, the vast expanse of land gave them a sensation which is given by no view, however extended, in England; the villages and the hills there having names, and the farthest horizon of hills as often as not dipping and showing a line of mist which is the sea; here the view was one of infinite

sun-dried earth, earth pointed in pinnacles, heaped in vast barriers, earth widening and spreading away and away like the immense floor of the sea, earth chequered by day and by night, and partitioned into different lands, where famous cities were founded and the races of men changed from dark savages to white civilized men and back to dark savages again. Perhaps their English blood made this prospect uncomfortably impersonal and hostile to them, for having once turned their faces that way they next turned them to the sea, and for the rest of the time sat looking at the sea.

(194)

The protagonists' discomfort stems not just from the infinite space (which would invoke a familiar mode of the colonial sublime), but from the almost-glimpsed cities that are ruled by an unaccountable, nonlinear history, a round of racial leap-frog with no clear progress toward civilized, stable self-possession.[11] A lack of self-possession, in fact, stands as the most persistent motif linking Rachel to Santa Marina, "the sunny land outside the window being no less capable of analysing its own colour and heat than she was of analysing hers" (210). Cutting from psyche to setting, Woolf establishes a consistent figural scheme in which protagonist and colony share a generalized unboundedness and a resistance to purposeful or smoothly clocked development.[12]

The uncivilized South American landscape (however inauthentically rendered) serves as both figure and context for Rachel's ego dissolution. In the long passage cited earlier, the regress of the horizon disorients Rachel while signaling its actual—and her potential—alienation from English norms. The slow dematerialization of Rachel's selfhood in South America comes to language through its interconnectedness with those borderless vistas. Woolf underscores from the start a contrast between England's insularity, which allows for a kind of knowability, and the incomprehensible scale of the partially modernized, partially nationalized South American colonial territory. As they leave home in the opening chapters, Rachel and her shipmates gaze back as if they could see the "whole of England, from the bald moors to the Cornish rocks," grasped as a small and shrinking island, the spatial container of an entire way of life (23). But in her colonial adventure, Rachel can never quite orient herself—all the markers of national culture are missing, jumbled, or exaggerated; she feels, instead of the spatial coherence of the nation, the spatial incoherence of the global system. In the ambient imagery of the novel, that incoherence registers as what we have in earlier chapters called the specter of an Hegelian bad infinity: a spatial and narratological threat of endlessness that is the symbolic antitype of the bildungsroman (with its essential chronotope of national enclosure). The open, infinite horizon bears on Rachel Vinrace as a disorganizing force—ultimately, a fatal force. It feels like the "weight of the entire world"—and in a way it is (244). Woolf uses the motif of colonial travel to generate a language and imagery pattern for describing the self unbounded in time and space, and therefore unable to develop and stabilize itself within the frame of the realist novel. Or, better put: Woolf finds in non-European space the symbolic resources that allow her to keep Rachel in adolescent limbo, to postpone the process of sexualization and socialization more or less indefinitely.

Woolf never returns to modern colonial settings after *The Voyage Out* except by way of flashback or imaginary voyage; perhaps having used the scaffolding of the underdeveloped periphery so conspicuously in this initial work, she needs it only as a symbolic prop in later, more experimental novels of consciousness such as *The Waves*. From this point of apprenticeship forward, Woolf's fictions rework the conventions of the female bildungsroman in any number of ways. They generate new vocabularies for fractured time and recursive plotting rather than reproduce the conventions of linear time and chronological, sequenced plotting; they multiply protagonists and perspectives rather than organizing plot and focalizing voice through a single biographical device; they introduce sex and gender dissidence as well as vocational crisis rather than narrate a process of final socialization into work and love; they focus on death, loss, aging, and the failure of destiny rather than establish novelistic closure through the harmonic growth of a young protagonist; and finally, and crucially in this study, Woolf's novels tend to underscore problems of national and imperial ideology rather than tacitly reinscribe the stabilizing historical force of national belonging.[13]

In *The Voyage Out*, Rachel's identification with infinite space and uncouth nature becomes, for Woolf, a technique for indicating resistance to a mature identity, to the traps and trappings of bourgeois womanhood.[14] Woolf's experiment in suspending Rachel's identity formation depends on the colonial setting as both a figurative index and a causal agent in the mix. But what is in some ways most striking about the novel is the rapid, almost skittish permutation of figures established for Rachel: She is not just a lost colony or virgin land, she is also a ship, a river, a butterfly, a piano string, a breeze. The intermittency and inconsistency of these metaphors is not, as is sometimes thought, a flaw, but the point of a novel seeking to disrupt the momentum of *Bildung*. *The Voyage Out* displaces all the potential plots of development (Victorian social mobility, naturalist tragedy, bohemian compromise) by creating a narrative stasis or long threshold wherein Rachel does not so much develop an ego as accumulate metaphors.[15] She remains a bundle of crisscrossing libidinal vectors, a human nebula, poised between becoming and unbecoming herself, until she falls ill and dies.

The novel thus produces a systematic and astringent inversion of the Goethean ideal of male destiny, documenting Rachel's inability to cultivate her own self-hood through a set of linked images, through a set of averted narrative outcomes, and sometimes (as in the following passage) through explicit narratorial commentary:

> For the methods by which she had reached her present position, seemed to her very strange, and the strangest thing about them was that she had not known where they were leading her. That was the strange thing, that one did not know where one was going, or what one wanted, and followed blindly, suffering so much in secret, always unprepared and amazed and knowing nothing; but one thing led to another and by degrees something had formed itself out of nothing, and so one reached at last this calm, this quiet, this certainty, and it was this process that people called living.
>
> (297)

As the passage opens, the repetitive cadences almost evoke Gertrude Stein's characteristic method for forestalling narrative momentum, condensing into syntax the larger antidevelopmental logic of the text. Rachel's lack of self-knowledge at the level of plot also works at the level of language or style by generating an extreme mobility of perspective that slowly transforms itself from psychological quirk into narrative device. If a juvenile and estranged perspective on adult realities is a relatively common conceit (from Dickens's Pip to Faulkner's Vardaman to Günter Grass's Oskar Matzerath), Woolf actually dramatizes the migration of that youthfully coded viewpoint from its explicit source in a discrete character into a diffusely adolescent principle of narration. In other words, Rachel's character yields (to) a narrative trope of undevelopment, an erratic, semi-omniscient, semi-embodied third-person perspective from which Woolf's key writerly innovations emerge in the temporal vacuum left behind by the suspended coming-of-age plot. Rachel cannot interpret or describe the effects of her own self-dissolution, but Woolf absorbs the subject/object dissolve into an experimental fictional language. In a sense, style transforms and even displaces plot; that is to say, style *has* a plot, while the novel itself, dilating and distending arrhythmically for long stretches, often does not. As the chapters roll out, readers can sense Woolf testing the limits of her form: the unintegrated subject at the center (Rachel) making space for thematic digressions, animated objects and decor, rather loose figurative play, a good bit of minor-character-shuffling, and—most conspicuously—multipolar perspective.

This reading provides a more precise, and more specifically colonial, framework to explain what is a fairly common observation about *The Voyage Out*, which is that the failed bildungsroman of Rachel Vinrace is a pretext or precondition for the ultimately successful artistic development of Virginia Woolf—just as Stephen Dedalus's incomplete formation in *Portrait of the Artist* prepares the way for Joyce's mature achievement in *Ulysses*.[16] To elaborate our initial hypothesis about the connection between Rachel's ego dissolution in the colonial setting and the development of Woolf's modernist style, we might return to a comparison between *The Voyage Out* and Conrad's Marlow fictions. When Marlow encounters a socially or epistemologically unassimilable human figure (Mr. Kurtz or Lord Jim), he carries back some bounty of existential insight. But this two-man drama is feminized and internalized in *The Voyage Out*, where Rachel acts both parts, the peering protagonist and the blurry human figure. She cannot interpret or describe the effects of her own self-dissolution. Moreover, Rachel's stubborn innocence is repeatedly thematized as blocked knowledge about the imperial system itself, an incapacity to read the deep links between imperial capitalism and domestic humanism. This structuring motif, so crucial to the novel's shape and to its author's social experience, takes form in the words of Rachel's merchant father, who is shipping goats and other goods in the south Atlantic trading zone of Britain's informal empire: "'If it weren't for the goats [commerce] there'd be no music [culture], my dear; music depends upon goats'" (16).

Rachel's uncultivated selfhood is not just, in other words, figured in the colony as a metaphor; it is based quite directly and sociologically in the colonial system of exchange. Her failed education lies, after all, at the feet of an absent and inattentive father who is too busy abroad to superintend the cultivation of his daughter's mind. If we take Woolf's cue here, we can zero in on the mechanism that allows the trope of underdevelopment to shuttle between stylistic and generic registers on the one hand and colonial context on the other. For the novel addresses itself quite explicitly to the problem of women's incomplete access to knowledge about imperial economics and politics, while more slyly assimilating this foreclosed knowledge into its own revision of the bildungsroman's temporal imperatives. *The Voyage Out* invites us to consider its departure from generic conventions in terms of the unknowable geography of production in the imperial metropolis. In the opening scene, Rachel's aunt, Helen Ambrose, muses on the West End of London: "It appeared to her a very small bit of work for such an enormous factory to have made. For some reason it appeared to her as a small golden tassel on the edge of a vast black cloak" (6). Woolf foregrounds uncertain appearances ("It appeared to her . . . for some reason it appeared to her") and vast cloaked realities, gesturing toward the lost intelligibility that Fredric Jameson has conceptualized as part of life in modernism's "unreal cities," where key parts of the society's basic daily life take place out of sight.[17] Jameson's claim that colonialism's dispersed and unknowable forms of economic activity filter into modernist works at the level of style gains a certain force and specificity if we consider the Helen-Rachel doublet in its light. With *The Voyage Out*—a text conceived at roughly the same time as Forster's *Howards End*, which Jameson cites as his one key instance of British modernism's (imperial) political unconscious—Woolf gives us a case where the stylistic invention emerges alongside and even from the epistemological fault line produced by colonial modernity. The voyage out section of *The Voyage Out* establishes both the spatial crack between nation and empire and the ethical crack between culture and commerce. These unsynthesized divisions function as the thematic preconditions for Rachel's unformed (indeed unformable) subjectivity.

If Helen's bohemian and feminized image of the city's visible golden tassel marks out a gendered instance of the broad screens and epistemological decoys that are symptomatic of capitalist and colonial modernity, those screens are further highlighted as we shift focus from Helen to Rachel, the underdeveloped heroine who strains to see the lines of power and production connecting her own cultured inner life to the great world-spanning activities of men like her father and Richard Dalloway. In the southern latitudes of the novel, those lines are no easier to see though no less binding. Rachel embodies but cannot comprehend Woolf's keynote theme of nonsynthesis between aesthetic culture (your music) and mercantile capitalism (my goats). It is this nonsynthesis—framed explicitly in the text by global rather than national trade—that establishes Woolf's novel as a direct revision of the classic bildungsroman, the genre that aims to reconcile culture and capital by harmonizing self-production and production per se. As we have seen in earlier chapters, there is a long dissenting tradition in the female bildungsroman in which this symbolic reconciliation is not only not performed but is critiqued. Like Schreiner's *African Farm*, *The Voyage Out* embeds that feminist critique into the problematic of colonial development. Among the many reasons that Rachel cannot reconcile the rules of art and commerce is that she, like Conrad's cloistered women in *Heart of Darkness*, represents the gendering of the imperial unconscious, the split between civilizing and chivalric ideals on the one hand and the grubby deeds of empire men on the other.[18]

Even as the gendered dimensions of Woolf's project in *The Voyage Out*—or Schreiner's in *African Farm*—distinguish their plot of underdevelopment rather sharply from those of, say, *Kim* and *Lord Jim*, all of these novels share a common logic that structures the relation between acculturation and accumulation in the colonies. In them, the Goethe-Schiller model of aesthetic and inner education appears to displace the work of economic production, but that displacement is laid bare rather than naturalized at the level of plot. In *Lord Jim*, as we observed in chapter 3, Jim's failure to *accumulate* experience or to amass a personality is registered reciprocally by Conrad's colonial economy—in which the main preoccupation seems to be the production of character, not wealth. Of course, both production and self-production ultimately fail or remain stunted in Conrad's frontier spaces outside the chronotopic envelope of the nation-state. In the colonial fantasyland of Patusan, Jim's sense of an authentic and special destiny for himself aligns with the necessity of his removal to an obscure, unwanted outpost. But this alignment of inner and outer destinies, of the pedagogical project of soulmaking with the practical work of colonial administration, can only be temporary. In Patusan as in Santa Marina, the temporality of underdevelopment, shaping both adolescent heroes and colonial hinterlands, doesn't just prolong youth, it also snaps back into sudden death.

Like Jim, Rachel dies from a fateful encounter with a kind of native infection—an Amazonian virus in her case. Her death, like Jim's, is a Pyrrhic victory that symbolically affirms the value, and values, of the innocent protagonist even as the novel kills her off. A colonial romance lies buried in *The Voyage Out*, but it is an encapsulated romance (as in *Lord Jim*) whose logic is reversed by the closural process. In this sense, both novels expose the ideological romance of permanent adolescence by suggesting that neither human aging nor socialization nor modernization can be prevented, only deferred. In other words, Woolf and Conrad seem at first to reenchant the bildungsroman—to hold out hope for a reconciliation between the soul's private longings and its social obligations— but finally come to disenchant it with a vengeance. For Rachel, the voyage out to Santa Marina initially seems to promise some kind of enlarged possibility for semiautonomy within patriarchal social relations; her courtship with the fatuous Hewet seems, under the spell of the Amazon, to break from some of the rigid sexual conventions that threaten Rachel's happiness. However, when—at the heart of the novel's Amazonian darkness—Rachel looks into the eyes of the native women who are staring back at her, she recognizes that a vast and impersonal system, in which sex, gender, labor, and power are socially organized, will always impinge on her subjective and autonomous sense of self: "So it would go on for ever and ever, she said" (270).[19] Rachel's sense of entrapment in patriarchy, her lost myth of Goethean subjectivity and freedom, unspools in the language of horrifying stasis, the permanent absence of a special developmental destiny, as the gears of patriarchy grind on.

This moment of recognition at the uttermost, innermost remove from English civilization represents the core of *The Voyage Out*, where a never-ending generational chain and the stasis of arrested development converge to define the novel's revision of the bildungsroman. Woolf's novel puts pressure on the progressive logic of the genre, suggesting that it is not—or perhaps no longer—possible for subjects and nations to come of age in smooth, harmonic, morally affirmative lockstep; the special temporality of *Bildung* thus breaks down in two directions at once: into the instantaneous and the infinite. Those apparently opposed units of narrative time—the intensified, glorified "moment of being" and the vast, grand temporal registers lying beneath and beyond official history—have come to define the essence of Woolf's style as a Bergsonian modernist. What we learn from reading them back into Woolf's colonial metabildungsroman is that the enriched possibilities of modernist style derive in some detectable part from the fissure of the soul-nation allegory into isolated moments and endless procedures that thwart the logic of developmental historicism. Joyce too takes his part in a modernist dismantling of the progressive soul-nation allegory, fracturing its magical arc once more into two superficially opposed but logically complementary temporal registers, the epic and the epiphanic. If Rachel Vinrace—and through her, Virginia Woolf—escapes from the narrative conventions of *Bildung* on her voyage out, she must then face the profundities and uncertainties of time unmoored from its moralized and humanly scaled familiars (the life span of the self, the history of the nation). Hence the moment of being among the native women is also a showdown with eternity, with a particularly gendered and colonial nightmare of "for ever and ever," which is the moment when the freedom of endless becoming (frozen youth) is suddenly revealed in the dark nightmare of Hegelian bad infinity.

That scene has a close analogue in Joyce's *Portrait*. In a moment of climactic triumph toward the end of chapter 5, Stephen declares his epigenetic aspirations as an artist: "to recreate life out of life." He appears in that moment, moreover, to embrace the implications of a process that will go "on and on and on and on" (186). But there is, as Hugh Kenner aptly detects, an "ominous undertone" in the line—perhaps one "on" too many (Kenner cited by Levenson, "Stephen's Diary" 1020). Just as Rachel Vinrace confronts at her moment of truth a vision of eternal feminine labor and impaired subjectivity, of the endless process of gendered socialization that will make her its object, so too does Stephen glimpse the endless chain of gendered being—the dark side of his cherished self-image as the self-begetting man, the demon of pure potentiality. Later, he records in his diary an unsettling dream:

A long curving gallery. From the floor ascend pillars of dark vapours. It is peopled by the images of fabulous kings, set in stone. Their hands are folded upon their knees in token of weariness and their eyes are darkened for the errors of men go up before them for ever as dark vapours.

(272)

With the errors of men rising forever before the eyes of weary kings, this image collates the censers and icons of a patriarchal church with the bardic images of ancient Irish royalty, and even evokes the uncrowned king of modern Ireland, a weary Parnell. The vision troubles Stephen with its amorphous and portentous implication of an unending process of rising and falling, of fallenness itself eternalized, converting perhaps the Daedalian dream of flight into the dark, bodiless levity of the vapors. As soon as Stephen imagines prolonging his youthful ardor into the endless vocation of art, he must confront, perhaps more directly than any other character considered in this study, an equal and opposite danger, which is the endless life narrative as an eternal sentence with no period.

One might well extend the comparison between the unconscious life of Rachel Vinrace and Stephen Dedalus, since the gibbering and deformed little men of her shipboard dreams correspond so well with the goatish little creatures that people his enervated mind after the sermon in chapter 3 (and that recur as horrid little men in the bad dreams reported in his diary of 25 March). Both protagonists have their narratives of enlightened self-cultivation detained and derailed by manifestations of sexual trauma and of a distinctly undeveloping unconscious made vivid in the form of dream creatures who are regressed or primitive totems of raw masculinity. What Joyce and Woolf both seem to have discovered in the course of modernizing the bildungsroman against the backdrop of colonial modernity is the power of superimposing troubled sexual and gender rites of passage and scenes of confrontation with imperial authority. For example, in *The Voyage Out*, Rachel's bad dreams are triggered when Richard Dalloway, an archetypal Empire Man in this novel, presses a kiss on her and initiates her fall into sexual adulthood. This small-scale violation prefigures the entire plot, not just of tragic resistance to the institutionalization of desire as heterosexual marriage, but also of colonial self-dissolution as against an imperial and patriarchal stamping of the soul. Dalloway represents a conservative version of English history that involves swallowing "enormous chunks of the habitable globe" (43). He touts the world-historical mission of the British ruling class: "In one word—Unity. Unity of aim, of dominion, of progress. The dispersion of the best ideas over the greatest area" (55). When he kisses Rachel, he reveals himself as her antagonist, a threat to her freedom.

Shortly after his unwelcome sexual impression, a horrified Rachel sees "her life for the first time a creeping hedged-in thing, driven cautiously between high walls, here turned aside, there plunged in darkness, made dull and crippled for ever" (72). Already, then, before Rachel arrives in South America, the novel poses her unformed and dissolving adolescence against the entwined forces of maturation (understood as subjection to patriarchal power) and modernization (understood as subjection to imperial power).

The traumatic interlinking of sexual maturity with political visions of national conformity and progress shapes Stephen's youth as well, though in his case the nationalist cause is a second-order effect of British imperialism. Stephen's earliest sensations include, prominently, the green and maroon brushes of Parnell and Davitt, and the shaming, castrating taunt "Apologise, pull out his eyes"—both associated with the disciplinary nationalist Dante (3–4). Later, Stephen confronts a recurrent pattern of sexualized and gendered shaming interwoven with confraternal demands to join the circle of patriotic and patriarchal Irish manhood. The fallout from Stephen's cycle of cloaked sexual traumas—the narrative content that largely displaces the rite of passage in *Portrait*—has been well elucidated in queer criticism since the publication of *Quare Joyce*.[20] In Joyce's antidevelopmental novel, as in Woolf's, sexual normalization is disrupted from within and cannot proceed to a socially sanctioned closure point (i.e., marriage). As a result, Stephen cycles through traumatic exchanges that echo each other backward and forward; gilded with narcissistic fantasy and supported by self-conscious refusals of forced identity, that cyclical, or epicyclical, movement marks Stephen's adolescence as more or less permanent. He remains a swooning, listless, and passive spectator who queers even heterosexual desire and whose libidinal plots, all "elfin preludes," seem to suspend the double master plot of individual and national emergence.

"Elfin Preludes": Joyce's Adolescent Colony

Among the many urban settings Joyce uses to capture the dilatory mind and shifting moods of Stephen Dedalus in *A Portrait*, some of the most resonant are the Liffey-side quays and docks where our hero, the itinerant aesthete of Dublin, walks the margins of national space and courts the barely definable needs of his growing soul:

> A vague dissatisfaction grew up within him as he looked on the quays and on the river and on the lowering skies and yet he continued to wander up and down day after day as if he really sought someone that eluded him.

(69)

Stephen's dockside wanderings fill the middle spaces in a long narrative of becoming; they point to a durable symbolic connection between an inchoate adolescent selfhood, an uncertain and unsanctioned form of desire, and the quays and rivers that connote Stephen's own marginal or provincial place in a vast system of economic modernization. Such scenes, with their overtones of juvenile wanderlust, verge at times on banal romanticism. But they also recall a specific frame of literary reference: Beginning with Eliot's Maggie Tulliver and her fateful downstream journey on the Floss, we have encountered a series of protagonists whose coming-of-age plots have been disrupted by commerce and traffic running outside the symbolic boundaries of local or national territory. From Conrad's maritime empire and its dispersal of the soul-nation allegory to Wells's "unassimilable enormity of traffic" and its diffusion of the condition-of-England novel to Woolf's impenetrable London economy and its framing of Rachel's voyage out, we have been charting a close correspondence between antidevelopmental novels and a vast, disruptive global-colonial system of social and economic reorganization. We have been charting, in other words, symbolic tensions between the waterways of late Victorian or new Imperial capitalism and the territorialized spaces of national identity, tensions that seem to have altered the basic contours of the modern(ist) bildungsroman.

In *Portrait*, Joyce figures experience, especially traumatic experience, in a hydraulic system of images: pools and puddles, rivers and reservoirs, tides and currents, sweat and spittle, holy and profane liquids that wash over and run through Stephen.[21] Joyce sets the flow of sin and squalor against the elaborate bulwarks and levees of Stephen's own making: the patterning and ordering devices of arcane scholarship, churchly abstraction, aesthetic theory, and self-mythologization. Consider, for example, this typical passage, from chapter 2:

> He had tried to build a breakwater of order and elegance against the sordid tide of life without him and to dam up, by rules of conduct and active interests and new filial relations, the powerful recurrence of the tides within him. Useless.

> (104)

The tides of sexual awakening within and urban degradation without converge in Stephen's encounter with a Dublin prostitute. But the conflict is more than just sexual; it goes to Stephen's attempt to assert moral and temporal control over the process of his own formation; at a formal level, tides and breakwaters mark Joyce's attempt to manage the flow of time and story line. Water and waterways signify time in a generalized existential or purely narrative sense (the stream of consciousness, one might say), but here they also signify time in a more textured, perhaps even geopolitical, sense, since they open at both the literal and symbolic levels to the boundless world of modernization unchecked and unbalanced by the soul-nation allegory.

Like Rachel Vinrace, albeit in a more self-consciously dramatic way, Stephen oscillates between self-consolidation and self-dissolution; both resist the socialization process and value the fluidity of adolescence. As Rachel muses in free indirect discourse: "To be flung into the sea, to be washed hither and thither, and driven about the roots of the world—the idea was incoherently delightful" (281). In *Portrait*, the water imagery—right down to the "swirling bogwater" of Stephen's closing diary—flows across chapters, breaking up the plot with sensual repetitions that attune Stephen to alternative temporalities of drift, stasis, and regression.

If *Portrait* can be read as typical of a larger modernist problematic—in which subjective narratives of arrested development seem to cluster around themes of colonial backwardness and globally uneven development—it also stands apart from our earlier examples for at least two immediate and related reasons. First, it gives us a more thorough objectification of the bildungsroman: This protagonist not only embodies the displacement of action by thought, but he also theorizes an entire aesthetic program around the principle of stasis or arrested development. Joyce sets Stephen's ideas about aesthetic stasis into the historical context of emergent Irish nationhood, giving us a full demonstration of the ways in which modernist experimentation can denaturalize the soul-nation allegory of the Goethean novel.

Second, as we take up the case of Joyce, we move from ambiguously positioned exiles and dissidents within the British metropolitan or colonial sphere to a writer generally taken to represent the "colonized" population. Even so, we should recall the methodological caveats introduced by the editors of and contributors to *Semicolonial Joyce*, a book that refines our understanding of the postcolonial Joyce. Ireland represents a special case of what Joseph Valente has called "metrocolonial" status, and Joyce (or his alter ego Stephen) a special case of the highly educated and cosmopolitan Irish intellectual. If Stephen understands himself as partial heir to a baleful legacy of colonial impositions (witness the "tundish" scene), he also takes the iconic figure of the credulous Irish "peasant" to constitute the true subject of both British and "Roman" conquest. With this in view, we can say that Joyce's work appears here as a new variation on this study's governing theme, that is, the novel of subject formation in the age of empire. Reading Joyce and Woolf in semitandem, we can see important differences that can be ascribed to the divergent historical experiences of imperial and colonial cultures, but we can also appreciate the striking fact that, on both sides of the colonial divide, modernist fiction seems to challenge and scramble the Bakhtinian formula of "national-historical time."

Irish national emergence is obviously a problem of identity formation for Stephen and of aesthetic practice for Joyce. *Portrait* narrates a continuous tension between experiential flux and the time-shaping force of national identity. In the opening chapter, Stephen famously gives order to the (traumatic) disorder of experience by locating himself within a nested geography of classroom, school, town, county, nation, continent, planet, and universe (12). This signal moment of Ptolemaic self-assertion both reinterprets and, in a sense, travesties the soulmaking apparatus of the Goethean hero who builds a nascent intellect out of a kind of cultural global-positioning system always set to the cardinal point of the cosmopolitan self. Such devices—the most hoary conventions of the modern novel as a technology of self-fashioning—are deployed by Joyce but also torqued until they lay bare their own status as conventions. This one in particular, the location of the self within a concentric model of political geography, gets tested and exposed as Stephen doggedly exits the circles of family, church, school, and nation.

Joyce inventories the stock conventions of the bildungsroman in every episode of the novel, but some episodes in particular give us a deeper sense of how he interrupts the forward motion of the soul-nation allegory. Chapter 1, for example, takes up the motif of illness as an antidevelopmental tool (one used to fine effect by Woolf in *The Voyage Out*). Stephen's early illness at Clongowes Wood College, like Rachel's late illness in Santa Marina, seems placed in such a way as to suggest that it is a psychosomatic reaction to narrow ideologies of gender and class. First of all, his fever follows an early incident of sexual panic, echoing Rachel's retreat from the implications of compulsory heterosexuality. And his bout of unfitness ends, significantly, with the death of the national hero Parnell; it seems therefore to manifest a disorder not just of body but of spirit, a malady rooted in the problem of national destiny.

From this early point on, Stephen seeks to disburden himself of Irish icons while Joyce establishes a persistent tension between national spaces or traditions and the flow of subjective or private time. Whereas in the traditional bildungsroman, national territory and national history are often the narrative and epistemological containers that orient the hero in space and time, here the hero insists that he must break out of the cage of national identity in order to access some fresh, unfiltered knowledge of his place in the sensual and social universe. Read back against the history of the bildungsroman as the genre of European modernization, *Portrait* seeks to update and to objectify long-standing generic formulae, dislodging the soulmaking project from the moralizing time of national history by revealing the Irish national project as a belated, flawed, and often debilitating basis for Stephen's aesthetic education.

Like Woolf, with her feminist dissonance from traditional British ruling class education, Joyce in *his* apprenticeship-as-arrested-development fiction wages a campaign of revisionary reading and writing, always registering the particular problems of the Irish artist or what Seamus Deane has called the "provincial intellectual" (*Celtic* 75–91).[22] Traumatic repetition and ritualized behavior shape Stephen and give Joyce the occasion to expand the logic of serialized experience in several directions. His manner of cutting against the "tyranny of plot" differs from Woolf's; he assembles his *Portrait* as a series of recurring motifs that make each of the five chapters seem like retellings of the same story as much as phases in a single story. The contest between plot development and symbolic repetition— always on display in the novel to some extent, as J. Hillis Miller has demonstrated so elegantly—becomes more overt than usual here in Joyce's schematic plot. Joyce uses serialized motifs to undercut linear emplotment, just as Kipling uses episodic and spatial form, Schreiner allegorical interpolation, Conrad impressionist description, Wilde aphorism and dialogue, Wells discursive or didactic commentary, and Woolf lyric or elegiac interludes. Even now it is surprising how thoroughly Joyce uses repetition and recursion to make a novel whose end circles back to its beginning. If Hugh Kenner's celebrated reading of *Portrait* reveals that the first few pages of the text anticipate all that will follow, Michael Levenson's reveals that the final few pages recapitulate all that has come before ("Shape of a Life" 1026). Taken together, they remind us that Joyce's novel works by superimposing linear and circular form.[23]

Levenson notes that the diary form that takes over in the final chapter implies, by its very nature, that Stephen's life story is, page by daily page, a never-ending one (1019). Pericles Lewis offers a similar account of the novel's potentially infinite plot: "Joyce converts the disillusionment plot structure from a single, momentous event in the life of the protagonist into an indefinite process, coextensive with life itself" (30).[24] As Joyce prepares his hero to exit the nation, he shifts from a closed to an open genre (novel to diary). This gesture, like others we have observed in Conrad, Kipling, Wells, and Woolf, cinches the modernist novel's revision of national closure in the bildungsroman, throwing open the gates to the potential narrative infinities associated in all of these texts with colonial modernity.

The notions that Stephen's life is not a (linear) narrative and that Stephen's life is *only* narrative, that is, an infinite narrative with no closure, are, of course, mirror images of each other. *Portrait* thus stands as the clearest example of a met-abildungsroman in which the central, most indispensable device—developmental time—is subjected to a remarkably thorough articulation into two broken halves. All development, all the time, is the same, finally, as the absence of development. This is no mere narrative ruse or modernist gimmick, but also a deep, if deeply oblique, commentary on the postcolonial nation whose self-fulfillment is itself perpetually deferred because it is perpetually under development. The fissile logic of Stephen's coming of age, always happening and thus never happening, corresponds quite exactly to Joyce's vision of Ireland as a radically unfinished project. In "Ireland, Island of Saints and Sages," Joyce ventures the following conditional portrait of a true Irish cultural renaissance:

> It would be interesting, but beyond the aims I have set myself this evening, to see what the probable consequences would be of a resurgence of this people; to see the economic consequences of the appearance of a rival, bilingual, republican, self-centered and enterprising island next to England, with its own commercial fleet and its ambassadors in every port throughout the world; to see the moral consequences of the appearance in old Europe of Irish artists and thinkers, those strange souls, cold enthusiasts, artistically and sexually uninstructed, full of idealism and incapable of sticking to it, childish spirits, unfaithful, ingenuous and satirical, "the loveless Irishmen" as they are called.
>
> (*Occasional* 125)

Since the frame of reference for Stephen in *Portrait* is not the actual emergent postcolonial nation, but an idealized Ireland of an indefinite future, it follows that the temporality of the national allegory is the time of pure potentiality, an adolescent counternarrative of national destiny made to fit those "childish spirits," Irish artists and thinkers.[25] This picture of Ireland as a nation of great potential but unworthy political self-formation in the present mirrors, and perhaps structures, the novel's portrait of Stephen. The fundamental split in Joyce between a sardonic rejection of Irish nationalism in practice and a playful utopian interest in a renascent Ireland takes aesthetic form in *Portrait* as the plot of incomplete formation for both hero and nation.

At the pragmatic level of composition, though, the novel has to blend the uninflected temporality of mere becoming and the shaped temporality of discrete experience; the result is Joyce's epicyclical scheme of five chapters split between repetition and progress.[26] Facing such a temporal scheme, many readers have seen *Portrait* as a fairly conventional bildungsroman at bottom, propelled by the careful work Joyce does to "age" the style and diction of each chapter in apparent correspondence to Stephen's growth. Yet given the mainstream critical consensus that Stephen remains a consistent target of Joyce's irony, it makes equal interpretive sense to say that the novel's changing style marks a limit in Stephen's maturity, perhaps even that stylistic advances throw into relief the recursive elements of the plot and the persistently adolescent features of Stephen's thinking.[27] Taking the force of style, plotting, and characterization together, we might say that the novel warps and defamiliarizes the conventions of the novel of progress, but does not destroy them. Where Conrad uses embedded subnarration and ponderous description to break the flow of plot, Joyce follows Stephen's mental voice into a minute rendering of sensory and cognitive experience and, underneath that, a prismatic account of language itself. Stephen does not just recall, but reenacts, revises, and revisits events and the words used to store and distort them in the mind. Once stationed outside the lines of Goethean destiny, Stephen exhibits signs not just of arrested, but also of accelerated, development: He is by turns premature and immature, juvenile and fusty. He leapfrogs ahead of his time, then treads the temporal waters. In essence, the figure of Stephen is recalcitrant to the standard narrative sequence of youth-into-age.[28] Mixed temporal effects in Joyce—what we have described in other texts as the co-presence of over- and underdevelopmental logic—disorganize the socialization plot in several ways at once.

Few things happen once in *Portrait*. Repeated and remembered episodes (the square ditch at Clongowes, for example) offer a psychologically realist depiction of a layered mind developing its recursive path through life and give the plot its strongly patterned symmetries. Within the diegetic frame, Stephen conducts a proud and holy campaign to separate himself from the crowd, to force his socialization narrative onto a separate and privileged track. Stephen's hyperindividuation parodies self-formation as an aesthetic and social value; he exposes the epigenetic logic of the bildungsroman ideal by dwelling on the mythic act of self-creation. Stephen's ludic fascination with self-authoring continues, of course, into *Ulysses*; here it takes the form of a callow, even arrogant, mission to shrug off the burdens of identity politics and group formation. In chapter 2, a precocious Stephen has already turned rebellious moods into personal policy by rejecting the standards of middle-class Irish Catholic male identity. Asked to play the role of gifted redeemer to a series of corrupt, fallen, or dishonored institutions, he tries instead to deny the "din of all these hollowsounding voices," the voices telling him to be a gentleman, a good Catholic, a devout son to a bankrupt father, a decent mate to his fellows, and a hale, manly patriot to champion poor Ireland's "fallen language and tradition" (88). To save himself—to become himself—Stephen vows to join "the company of phantasmal comrades" (89).

Stephen's preference for phantasmal comrades over against any functional male subgroup not only marks out a key point of departure from the Goethean proto-type of the *bildungsheld*, Wilhelm Meister, but it also serves to emphasize to read-ers a particular crisis of Irish masculinity in which both rebellion and authority can, it seems, only be articulated in terms pre-scripted by the stereotype factory of the Anglo-Irish colonial encounter. Stephen's double bind in the face of patriarchal and national/imperial authority comes into sharp focus during the trip to Cork with his father in chapter 2. Stephen proudly recoils from his father's coarse bon-homie, leaky libido, profligate drinking, and masculine bravado—all of which are accentuated as father and son rejoin the father's old mates in Cork. The acid com-mentary of Stephen's interior monologue conveys familiar adolescent disgust at the foibles of the older generation, but this cliché of youth takes on greater force when Stephen refuses to be identified not just with his father but with his grandfather. Joyce embeds the drama of disfiliation within a legible array of national types and stereotypes, so that it expands into a wider story of Irish national and colonial dis-affiliation (98–101). Simon's friends hector shy Stephen throughout the scene until one unnamed Corkman asks him which of two Latin slogans is correct: "*Tempora mutantur nos et mutamur in illis* or *Tempora mutantur et nos mutamur in illis*" (100). Seamus Deane renders the line as "Circumstances change and we change with them" and suggests that the comparison of the two phrases—both grammati-cally correct—is merely academic (*Portrait* 295). But the slight variation, when viewed through the central lens of the soul-nation allegory, takes on an interesting inflection: "Times change and we change with them" or "Times change and we are changed by them." The shift from a parallelism implied by "with" to the causality implied by "by" contains in a grammatical nutshell an entire open question around which *Portrait* as a late or metabildungsroman might be said to revolve: Is the self a product of its historical circumstances or a self-producing, self-authoring entity restricted—but not wholly formed—by its circumstances?

In particular, Stephen wonders whether he can break from the traditions and values embodied by his bluff and rivalrous jackass of a father. Is rebellion—already cataloged by Arnoldian ethnology as a cliché of the Irish soul, already jocosely dismissed by his father as a toothless adolescent pose—even possible for Stephen under these conditions? How to rebel within an Irish nationalist culture of failed rebellion? Watching his father and friends drink a self-satisfied toast, Stephen imagines a crisp break between the generations:

> An abyss of fortune or of temperament sundered him from them. His mind
> seemed older than theirs: it shone coldly on their strifes and happiness and

regrets like a moon upon a younger earth. No life or youth stirred in him as it had stirred in them. He had known neither the pleasure of companionship with others nor the vigour of rude male health nor filial piety.

(101–2)

Where the youth of his father and his ilk is of the conventional, phased kind—discrete and free and pleasurable—Stephen's is an unpredictable, idiopathic style of youth, riddled with inhibitions, devoted to abstract rewards of aestheticized intellection, and elastic in its temporality. Failure to be youthful here means failure to observe a proper youth-age sequence; failed youth also provides the aegis for Stephen's sweeping rejection of male companionship and homosocial bonds. Stephen's alienation from the spectacle of youth as pre-manhood constitutes a serious falling away from the homosocial Goethean subsociety, understood as the key agent of social reconciliation for the bourgeois-bohemian apprentice. If the Goethean hero (recycled, for example, in the Dickens novel) seeks paternity everywhere, Joyce's hero seeks to *reject* paternity everywhere, claiming proud exclusion from the homosocial clique as well as the national patrimony. For Stephen, naturally, this obsessive and disfiliative plot cycle has the effect, as the passage makes perfectly clear, of scrambling both the social repertoire and the organicized timetable of youth-maturity.

Stephen, operating only semiautonomously from the indirect discourse of the narrator, casts this social fracture as a temporal break between himself and his own past:

His childhood was dead or lost and with it his soul capable of simple joys, and he was drifting amid life like the barren shell of the moon.

Art thou pale for weariness
Of climbing heaven and gazing on the earth,
Wandering companionless . . .?

He repeated to himself the lines of Shelley's fragment. Its alternation of sad human ineffectualness with vast inhuman cycles of activity chilled him, and he forgot his own human and ineffectual grieving.

(102)

Stephen's lunar self-image implicitly refutes the *Tempora mutantur* of the crony from Cork: Where that motto speaks to the integrated and reciprocal relation between the subject and his times, Stephen becomes the companionless moon, quite out of joint with his times.

Stephen's interest in the Shelley fragment centers on the *alternation*, not integration or synthesis, between human and inhuman activity, between inner experience and outer signs, a problem chilled and condensed into an impersonal verse form. Stephen articulates via Shelley a problem—am I overdetermined or self-determining?—that cannot be resolved.[29] Joyce thus positions Stephen not simply as the typical protagonist of a disillusionment plot, a rebel in the face of bourgeois compromise, but also as a belated subject who marks the breakdown of the core soul-nation allegory. In particular, Stephen's capacity for masochism allows Joyce to describe subject formation in terms of an overidentification with authority, and thereby to balance out the rebellious Luciferian streak of Stephen's "non serviam." Reading *Portrait* this way, we can understand afresh some of Stephen's self-glorification and self-mortification; they make sense not just as adolescent emotionalism but as signs of Joyce's attempt to modernize literary character. With recent colonial, semicolonial, and postcolonial Joyce criticism in mind, we might say that *Portrait* casts the struggle of Irish national emergence as a historical condition for Joyce's novelistic critique of the European novel of progress.

If Stephen's rebellious individualism and Joyce's modernist will to innovation take the form of an adolescent indifference to the narrative conventions of moralized, nationalized progress, they must then confront the temporal registers that fall outside the model of shapely progress: static and infinite time. And these are not just theoretical markers of time in *Portrait*, but take their place inside the rhetoric and ideology of the very authorities against which Stephen attempts to rebel, that is, the colonial and imperial centers of patriarchal power. Stephen's volatile self-understanding in relation to those sources of patriarchal authority accounts in part for the length and detail of Father Arnall's hell sermon—an episode during which Stephen's propensities for self-mortification and self-glorification blur into one. What makes that long passage even more germane to Stephen's place at the center of a colonial novel of arrested development is that, as Tobias Boes has aptly noted, the priest's vision of hell is "development at a standstill" ("*Portrait*" 777). Indeed, Joyce lingers on the infernal rhetoric so as to give Stephen—and readers—a foretaste of eternity itself: "ever never ever never" (143). Eternal damnation, in other words, feels like pure narrativity with no closure.

But the rhetorical reach of Father Arnall's sermon extends beyond hell to an alternative language of destiny too:

> Time has gone on and brought with it its changes. Even in the last few years what changes can most of you not remember? Many of the boys who sat in those front benches a few years ago are perhaps now in distant lands, in

the burning tropics or immersed in professional duties or in seminaries or voyaging over the vast expanse of the deep or, it may be, already called by the great God to another life.

(117)

This official and clichéd account of the boys' pathways to adulthood emphasizes service in two alien hierarchies, the Catholic church and the British empire. More to the immediate point, it describes futures—professions, priesthood, death, and imperial adventure—that are grand callings, tilted toward the romanticized extremes of adventure and of destiny. Life, it seems, is a mission and a project, and the diction ("distant ... vast ... expanse ... deep ... great") directly echoes the endless, boundless qualities the sermon associates with eternal hellfire. The future stretches to far horizons rather than attaching to fixed and stable places. The extranational authorities that dominate *Portrait* have their own versions of infinity: the empire's endless Great Game of imperial expansion and the church's boundless rhetoric of hell. Nowhere in *Portrait* is the language more clearly anatomized for the way in which it connects destiny and adventure itself to the twin imperialisms of Rome and London and to the bad infinities (spiritual, spatial, existential) that they seem to represent. The sermon is a lurid, sensually rich version of a never-ending story: precisely what a novel of arrested development threatens to become if it generates no inner checks. To get outside the soul-nation allegory of nineteenth-century convention is thus to risk confrontation with or suspension in a demoralized, nonprogressive temporality— the empty chronos that is the dark other of the bildungsroman itself.

As in the novels explored in previous chapters, Joyce must find a way in *Portrait* for Stephen, as a figure, to remain poised between the Scylla of pat and linear national *Bildung* on the one hand and the Charybdis of shapeless or empty time on the other. At the thematic level, this means giving fictional form to an alternative ideal of Irish nationality outside the prescriptive and restrictive canons of official nationalism.[30] The complexity of *Portrait* and its reception by postcolonial critics especially has always been that Stephen seems to be a nationally representative type who also rejects nationalism (if not nationality); that is, he can be read as representatively or typically Irish only in his paradoxical disavowal of the burden of Irishness. The novel thus preserves and cancels the apparatus of the soul-nation allegory, splitting the national hero between residual and emergent times, between recursive patterns and sequential narration. In making Stephen a specialized talent and a highly self-conscious historical thinker, Joyce breaks with the Lukács-Scott model of the "typical" realist or historical protagonist since, as Lukács suggests, "a biographical portrayal of a genius . . . conflicts with the means of expression peculiar to epic art" (*Historical Novel* 303). The modern epic genres of historical and realist fiction, that is, require the average or middling hero, but Stephen cannot operate like a Scott hero because he is not a historiographical innocent. He knows too much and, what is more, he takes history too personally. He cannot function as the unwitting embodiment of historical forces but must be a kind of delector of historical possibility, positioned at the far side of a century chock-full of historical fiction canonized in the wake of Scott for its ability to narrate collective destiny under the sign (however naturalized) of the nation.[31]

Even more particularly, we can think of Stephen's aesthetic individualism as a mark and symptom of a colonial intellectual's suspicion of the logic of the representative type. In a series of related essays, David Lloyd has, for example, proposed that nineteenth-century European literary cultures projected their own modernity and centrality through the logic of the representative or archetypal soul—an extension of a German-idealist concept into contact zones and peripheral regions in Europe and beyond ("Arnold, Ferguson, Schiller" 161). *Portrait* modernizes the historical novel for a new century of devolutionary and decentering social and political movements, that is, for historical forces and events that cannot be fit to Lukács's unilinear metanarrative of national emergence. One might say then that Joyce uses Stephen to update the symbolic function of the Scott hero for a heterochronic world of alternative modernities. Scott Klein, working from Stephen's apparent allusion to Scott's *Bride of Lammermoor* in chapter 5 of *Portrait*, has developed a thorough and convincing reading of Scott's relevance to Joyce. Klein notes that Scott operates in the text as a transcended double, one whose fictional mode of romantic historicism Joyce cannot and would not wish to recreate, but whose problem of national culture and national emergence within the British empire prefigures and influences Joyce's own (Scotland after 1800 anticipating Ireland after 1900) (1018–25).[32] Taking *Bride* rather than, say, *Waverley*, as an intertext for *Portrait* is significant, Klein observes, because *Bride* has a less clear, less resolute closural plot and thus conforms less readily to the Lukácsian model of the middling hero whose quest mirrors and embodies larger historical forces. It anticipates the Joycean plot, in other words, in the mode of what Klein calls "ironic historiography" (1028). What this intertextual aside reveals about *Portrait*, I think, can be framed in the terms outlined so far in this way: Joyce operates in the novel under the aegis of national allegory, but not of developmental historicism, with the result that all the buried correspondences between soul and nation are brought to the surface and exposed as semifunctional, sometimes ironized to the point of near breakdown. It is important to emphasize that, however much the would-be iconoclast Stephen imagines himself escaping or opposing nationalism as a creed, he cannot escape the force of nationality as an epistemological precondition for historical being.

If Joyce updates and dialectically transcodes the mode of Scottian historicism, the procedure unfolds at several levels, with the Irish urban novel self-consciously breaking from the gentrified codes of Victorian English fiction; the plot of sexual irresolution opposing both standardized marriage and gendered socialization; the plot of national irresolution opposing the mythic emergence of the nation as the political expression of the people; the narrative of the egoistic cosmopolitan artist breaking from the convention of the representative (national) protagonist; and the *Kunstlerroman* centered on a passive, even decadent, artist-antihero shifting away from the tale of the Political Action Hero à la Scott.[33] The national coding of these shifts is significant: Joyce sees in Scott a Celtic precursor working inside the greater British or Anglophone sphere, but he even more openly identifies with a Flaubertian (or Wildean) lineage as against the classic English brand of realism.

Such a reading certainly resonates with Joyce's stated understanding of the difference between Irish and English literature, particularly in the case of the novel. For Joyce, the signal instance of English realism is *Robinson Crusoe*, the novel of self-formation and of British colonial modernity par excellence. *Crusoe* is prophetic, Joyce states, of the centuries of British expansion and colonization that followed it. As Joyce notes in his 1912 lecture "Realism and Idealism in English Literature," *Crusoe* inaugurates the great tradition of English stories centered on an emergent self working in tandem with colonial and economic modernization:

> The true symbol of British conquest is Robinson Crusoe who, shipwrecked on a lonely island, with a knife and a pipe in his pocket, becomes an architect, carpenter, knife-grinder, astronomer, baker, shipwright, potter, saddler, farmer, tailor, umbrella-maker, and cleric. He is the true prototype of the British colonist.
>
> (*Occasional* 174)

Crusoe, the hero of modern British imperialism, is also the hero of English realism. He is the maker of his own destiny, literally and physically, and the activist archetype of what Hannah Arendt calls *homo faber* (man the maker), to which Stephen is the ironic colonial antitype. Indeed Stephen seeks both to invert and to usurp the role of *homo faber* in the antidevelopmental story of *Portrait*, first by establishing the passive antihero, then by converting that antihero into a symbolic smith, a forger of national myth, a Daedalian hero for an unheralded race.

If Joyce transvalues the concept of *homo faber* in *Portrait*, it is not just to play on the colonial dynamics of active/passive heroes but to explore the problem of the enunciated and narrated self from the point of view of minor literature or of a colonized relationship to language.[34] The inversions of *Portrait* violate developmental time; they also—as the masochistic and self-negating elements of Stephen's subject formation suggest—address a type of self-alienation endemic to the colonized position. Faced with this predicament, Stephen self-consciously assumes the mantle of the Irish artist but allocates the burden of Irish iconicity to the people around him (particularly women).[35] Both crones and cronies figure in this game, as Stephen measures his adolescent national ideals against the failings of harridanish Cathleens, secondhand *aislings*, clay-footed men, and vainglorious or politically correct fools that populate his Dublin. Stephen's oedipal/anti-oedipal anxiety about maternal and sexual plots involving women, most of which cast him as the passive or childlike object of a devouring other, are as bound up with his disaffected patriotism as are all the episodes of disavowed male homosociality.

Inspired by his mate Davin's story of a lonely Irish peasant woman on the roadside, Stephen elaborates Davin's adventure into a fantasy for his own private sense of national mission, seeing in his mind's eye the woman "as a type of her race and his own, a batlike soul waking to consciousness of itself in darkness and secrecy and loneliness." But in the next moment, Stephen quickly dispels this vision by concentrating on a real Irish girl, a flower seller of "ragged dress and damp coarse hair and hoydenish face" (198). Even so, he remains taken with the motif of the batlike soul—his and the woman's—folding into his personal mythology the idea of himself as the savior of a shrouded people. He effects a Cartesian separation of the body and mind of Ireland, assigning the former to the predictable female icon and reserving the latter as the basis for his own Parnassian intervention. In other words, Stephen projects himself beyond the logic of the hero who embodies national destiny by imagining himself as the artist who conceives it. This requires not only a kind of self-removal and spiritual exile, but a thwarting of the narrative conventions of the historical novel and the bildungsroman alike. Stephen's mode of fashioning a destiny is to imagine the awakening of an other; he routes his concepts of the future through passive fantasies of self-negation. Joyce thus estranges the Goethean project of self-formation, introducing in its place a colonial dialectic of self-possession vexed and vitiated by self-dispossession.

If profound doubts about Victorian womanhood led Woolf to look askance on the generic ideals of the bildungsroman—and to graft a colonial motif of failed self-possession into her first novel—then for Joyce we must imagine that a more direct sense of colonial history conditions the critique of male destiny as the symbolic proxy for national emergence. Joyce isolates and reorganizes that symbolic tie between and soul and nation, particularly with regard to its traditional narrative destination of self-fulfillment or self-possession. It makes strict formal sense that *Portrait* must hang fire on Stephen's coming of age rather than produce a straightforward or traditional postcolonial novel of emergence (which is what a strictly nationalist cause might see as the desideratum for the Irish novel in 1916). As a result, *Portrait*, with all its idiosyncratic elements marking it off as a creative response to particular aspects of Irish experience, also takes part in a larger modernist project, the critical dismantling of the temporal and allegorical givens of the historical bildungsroman centered in the European nation-states.

The modernizing frame of the industrial nation-state allows the ideal or classic bildungsroman to project a certain synchronization between economic and emergent modernity as the joint horizon of closure. Joyce's *Portrait*, by contrast, is an object lesson in the disjunction between Ireland's political modernity—as ratified by the march toward independent republic status—and its economic conditions—a breach mediated by the cultural and aesthetic projects of the Irish Renaissance. But as a putative "novel of development" *Portrait* has a special status within the Revival or Renaissance era; in its rewiring of the bildungsroman into a novel of pure adolescence it continually signifies the problem of Ireland's own partial or *alternative* modernity.

From *Dubliners* on, Joyce is a keen and cold observer of economic underdevelopment, and of the contradictions between debased and debasing economic conditions on the one hand and the highflying rhetoric of Irish cultural modernity on the other. As he notes in "Ireland, Island of Saints and Sages," "The economic and intellectual conditions of his homeland do not permit the individual to develop" (*Occasional* 123). Irish literary and historical studies of the last many years have centered on the various kinds of anachrony produced by the specific colonial, semicolonial, or metrocolonial conditions of Irish modernity, with special attention to the variations between Irish modernization processes and the norms or standards set by Euro-American narratives of reformation, liberalization, industrialization, secularization, and urbanization. In Attridge and Howes's *Semicolonial Joyce*, one of the best recent treatments of these questions within Joyce studies, Marjorie Howes, Luke Gibbons, and Enda Duffy all address uneven development in Ireland—what Howes defines as the "geographical expression of the contradictions of capital" (61).[36] In *Dubliners*, Joyce frames that contradiction spatially using the famous structuring motif of paralysis. In *Portrait*, he uses scenes of transit through Dublin to underscore his parodic inversion of the Goethean soulmaking narrative and its cosmopolitan-elite modes of travel. And toward the end, he emphasizes a shift in scale from the hero who leaves behind the provinces for a national capital to the hero who wishes to leave behind a provincialized nation for the metropolitan center.

But flight never quite wins out over nets in *Portrait*. From the perspective of his own expatriated status, Joyce can see that the art of the Irish genius is an art made not from what Cranly jeeringly exposes as a bogus ideal of "unfettered freedom," but from the tension between self-determination and social conditions (267). Joyce does not condescend to Stephen's ideal of a radical individuation that would save him from the burdens of the young Irish artist, but neither does he accept the idea that a workable aesthetic can emerge for Stephen from his dreams of companion-less exile. Moreover, Stephen himself offers an oblique aesthetic rationalization of paralysis as stasis, valuing the Aristotelian principle of "arrest" as against the kinesis of plot (desire/loathing).[37]

Of course, Stephen's theory of aesthesis is a tragic-dramatic one, not a narrative one: It is therefore outflanked by or subsumed within the narrative frame. This is not just a theoretical or generic fact about novels, but the topic of what appears to be some of Stephen's most scholasticist contemplation. Drawing from Aquinas, he hypothesizes that even when two people or two cultures apprehend different objects according to different scales of beauty, both are proceeding through certain universal or fixed "stages . . . of all esthetic apprehension" (227). His analysis, in other words, depends on breaking the instant of apprehension into a process of stages, so that he recaptures a narrative sequence out of what would seem to be a moment in time. Not surprisingly, Stephen's reflections on aesthetic process conjure for his friend Donovan the thought of Goethe and of Lessing's *Laocoön* (229). Donovan's allusion may be shallow, but Joyce's is not: Stephen is working at questions about the relation of temporal to nontemporal art in the line of Lessing and Goethe just as Joyce is attempting to interpolate antinarrative elements into a conventional narrative genre. If Lessing stands for the attempt to separate art into plastic and poetic (spatial and temporal) media, Goethe stands in a sense for the synthesis of the spatial and the temporal in narrative form. The ghost of Goethe presides quietly over Joyce's attempt to square developmental and antidevelop-mental time. As in the cases of Wilde, Conrad, and Schreiner, Goethean allusions signal a formal problem and a historical predicament to which the novel of unsea-sonable youth seeks to respond.

Even among the stalled-adolescent protagonists already addressed in this study, Joyce's Stephen stands for the diagrammatic clarity with which he reorga-nizes the humanist motif of Goethean destiny. His story is almost entirely built from minutely subjective responses to the call of the future: His action is its con-templation. After the spiritual retreat of chapter 3, a cross and stupefied Stephen consumes a greasy meal and feels himself a mere "beast that licks its chaps after meat." "This was the end," he thinks, and gazes out at dull Dublin:

> Forms passed this way and that through the dull light. And that was life. The letters of the name of Dublin lay heavily upon his mind, pushing one another surlily hither and thither with slow boorish insistence. His soul was fattening and congealing into a gross grease, plunging ever deeper in its dull fear into a sombre threatening dusk, while the body that was his stood, listless and dishonoured, gazing out of darkened eyes, helpless, perturbed and human for a bovine god to stare upon.
>
> (119–20)

Listless and dishonored, Stephen Dedalus stands as an anti-hero devoid of enterprise and motivation and hope—all the qualities that define the protagonist in a novel of progress.[38] His soul resonates to the world outside his window. The dullness and dusk of the city are assimilated to him as features of his own self, reflecting the shared inanition and squalor of ego and city. Disaggregated, the letters D U B L I and N go hither and thither without purpose or direction—a perfect symbol of the vectorless anachrony of Dublin, signifying moreover the lost animation of Stephen's soul and the slippage from a novel of development to a novel of antidevelopment.

Joyce's techniques for rewiring the bildungsroman are, as we have seen, inflected by a distinctive Irish experience of colonial modernity, but he also inherits many of the same historical and literary-historical conditions that shaped the work of Woolf, Wells, Wilde, Conrad, Schreiner, and Kipling. In all these cases, prolonged or lingering youth embodies an antidevelopmental logic that registers not only the moralized or eschatological time of the nation and its imperial extension (development to a fixed point of political actualization), but the open-ended and boundless time of capitalism in the age of empire. Seeking to assimilate the open yet uneven form of postnational development, Joyce must confront the same kind of closural problem that bedeviled most of these earlier writers: What kind of terminal plot makes sense in the face of a never-ending narrative of modernization, especially once the chronotope of national *Bildung* has been demystified or disqualified? More precisely, what kind of narrative maneuvers can represent both the infinity of world-historical development and the residual time-shaping power of the organicized nation (and its symbolic familiar, the biographical novel)?

In one of his visionary moments, Stephen seems to recognize the root problem in the narrative of endless becoming or pure potential; listening to the music of his soul, he seems almost to make a sly address to the formal problematic of the novel itself:

> It was an elfin prelude, endless and formless; and, as it grew wilder and faster, the flames leaping out of time, he seemed to hear from under the boughs and grasses wild creatures racing.
>
> (179)

On the surface, this music reflects Stephen's wayward instincts, but the flames and hoofbeats of an amorphous and boundless energy also describe the Joycean narrative itself, straining to manage the infinite with some token of the finite. The language of Stephen's grandiosity is the same language that records for the reader the danger of formlessness: if Stephen's horizons are ever-enlarging and ever-receding, no lines can finally be crossed, no act fully realized. His own experience stands and remains as an "elfin prelude" to some larger achievement. By this light, the novel itself comes to seem an elfin prelude not just by extratextual reference to *Ulysses*, but by its own operations, in which moments—however epiphanic—keep melting into their own failed immanence, paling before the vast potentialities that extend out of them, and beyond them. If *Portrait* devolves, from this perspective, into a long ironic prelude, it is equally true that Woolf's *Voyage Out* reads like an extended, bathetic denouement; both are novels without arcs, and the missing arc is the sign of a cancelled historicism concretized in fictions that feature both youth and death, but little progress in between.

Since a novel that never ends (and never begins) is an impossible artifact, an antidevelopmental fiction must in some sense adapt the metabildungsroman strategy of writing not beyond, but about, the contradictions of the national coming-of-age tale.[39] The antidevelopmental logic so thoroughly tested in *Portrait* situates Stephen at a modernist switchpoint where a double temporal register is needed, one that incorporates without synthesizing the moralized time of progress (soul and nation) and the empty time of pure chronos, manifested in the endless revolutions of global modernity. But if this is a logic immanent to the text, it is not a "resolution" or synthesis available to Stephen Dedalus himself. Arrested forever at the threshold of flight, Stephen is interred in his diary, not self-actualized by it or in it.[40] In this sense, even with his Promethean intellect afire, Stephen is more akin to the blinkered, ill-fated Rachel Vinrace than it may appear, closer in his frozen youth to death than to life.

6. Virgins of Empire: The Antidevelopmental Plot in Rhys and Bowen

I was thinking "I'm nineteen and I've got to go on living and living and living."

—Rhys, *Voyage in the Dark*

After every return—or awakening, even, from sleep or preoccupation—she and those home surroundings still further penetrated each other mutually in the discovery of a lack.

—Bowen, *The Last September*

Gender and Colonialism in the Modernist Semi-Periphery

From George Eliot (1860) through Olive Schreiner (1883) to Virginia Woolf (1915), this book has followed a genealogical line in which plots of truncated girlhood work to spare protagonists from the social limits of womanhood and in which—despite manifest differences of epoch and style—there seems to be a deep symbolic substrate connecting provincial girls to stalled or uneven modernization in the rural/colonial peripheries of the Anglophone world. In this chapter, we turn to two more writers—Jean Rhys and Elizabeth Bowen—who extend that lineage into interwar modernism, into a crepuscular historical phase where the emergent logic of postcolonial nationalism signals the break-up of the old European empires. That devolutionary shift features centrally in Rhys's *Voyage in the Dark* (composed mostly before 1914, but published in 1934) and in Bowen's *The Last September* (published in 1929). In both novels, autobiographical protagonists fail to achieve a stable social role ratified by adulthood, and their frozen adolescence seems to correspond to the retarded modernization of two colonial contact zones, the Anglophone Caribbean and post–World War I Ireland. The two novels feature stepdaughters of the plantocracy, Anna Morgan and Lois Farquar, girls whose fates register the anachronistic logic of colonial modernity and open up narrative space for stylistic experimentation.

Before proceeding with the cases of Rhys and Bowen, it might be worth reflecting briefly on the difference that gender makes to the analysis of the revisionary modernist bildungsroman. If we update the classic feminist accounts of the problem of the Victorian female bildungsroman (Abel, Hirsch, and Langland, Fraiman, Gilbert and Gubar, Showalter) to include the problem of the metropolitan periphery—that is, the global as well as the national provinces, it becomes quite startling to consider how many important women writers of the late Victorian and modernist periods embed the representation of patriarchal social structures within plots centered on the underdeveloped pockets of colonial modernity. With Schreiner, Woolf, Rhys, and Bowen as our key examples—and we might add Katherine Mansfield and Miles Franklin on the early side as well as Janet Frame and Doris Lessing on the late side—we find a set of Anglophone women writers working at the social and geographical edges of British modernism.[1] All of these writers conceive the history of colonial contact zones in ways that expose with renewed feminist vigor the inherited problems of the nineteenth-century coming-of-age plot. Their fiction rewrites Goethean models of male destiny, exposing as uncertain and uneven the promises of progress that were knitted into the narrative code of the (male) bildungsroman.

The antidevelopmental principles of plot construction that I have traced so far in this study tend to index a resistance to the twin teleologies of the classic bildungsroman, adulthood (understood as a fixed social form of subjectivity achieved by social reconciliation) and nationhood (understood as a fixed social form of collectivity achieved by political modernization).[2] The early novels of Schreiner and Woolf—and, as I will suggest, those of Rhys and Bowen—expose the interconnected languages of male vocational destiny and national-imperial destiny with acute precision; they expose, in the process, the ideological underpinnings of the bildungsroman as the realist genre of socialization and modernization. While the revisionary motif of arrested development installed at the center of these later modernist works cannot, in a symbolic or counterdiscursive revolution, utterly break down the symbolic value and social expectations attached to the bildungsroman, it can lay those inherited conventions bare and interrupt the progressive logic governing both personal and national evolution. It can, in other words, address the ideology of the genre from within.[3]

Working in this frame of analysis, we can identify a number of Victorian and modernist women writers who gravitate to a double critique of the bildungsroman, questioning the logic of the representative protagonist who embodies collective fate and exposing the progressivist tilt of plots organized by that logic. Skepticism toward the soul-nation allegory crops up everywhere in nineteenth-century women's fiction. This is no surprise given that women were barred from or disadvantaged within so many aspects of civil society and that traditional feminine icons of nationhood were so often presented as symbolic proxies for women's actual emancipation. For Eliot's Maggie Tulliver, as for Schreiner's Lyndall—and, as we will see, for Rhys's Anna Morgan and Bowen's Lois Farquar—the improbability and even impossibility of a fully-fledged bildungsroman plot corresponds to the problem of living between two historical chronotopes. Rather than embodying the cusp of a modernizing process, after the fashion of a Walter Scott hero in Lukács's model of historical fiction, these protagonists in their very adolescence seem to embody the futurelessness of a particular provincial or colonial class.

Rhys and Bowen both wrote with an acute awareness of a fallen, ex-British world of the settler plantation class in the West Indies and in Ireland.[4] Their experimental fictions register not just the post-Victorian vogue for achronological plotting, but a profound, sometimes tragic, sense of dispossession, one that cannot and should not be reduced to special pleading for a politically disgraced settler class. Far better, I think, to read these novelists in relation to a historical complex comprising both the residual power of the European colonial empires and emergent power of a neocolonial world-system organized into anthropologically separate cultures yoked to politically discrete nations. Despite their patent stylistic differences, and despite the important historical differences to be assayed between the postslavery Caribbean economy and the neofeudal Irish land system, Rhys and Bowen come to the historical predicament of the Anglophone plantocracy at the end of empire, and to the aesthetic problem of the novel at the end of Victorian social realism, armed with certain overlapping perspectives.

Both Rhys and Bowen often return, in their fiction, to the vulnerable social situation of the belated offspring of the colonial plantocracy—orphaned and disinherited children with a precarious foothold in a class that itself has a precarious foothold in history.[5] Their characters are the progeny of houses falling to ruin in the valedictory phase of colonial settlement—the phase of withdrawal and collapse. For both, the image of the plantocratic manor house going down in flames is iconic. In addition to this shared history, Rhys and Bowen display many affinities of biography and literary theme that invite critical comparison. Both lived from the 1890s to the 1970s, a life span that covers all the major stages of devolving British power, from the Boer War and Home Rule, through to the Suez crisis and Asian/ African decolonization. Both Rhys, the Welsh-Dominican Creole, and Bowen, the Anglo-Irish heiress, wrote in English but experienced England as a kind of alternative territory to their home islands and frequently portray characters who feel suspended in the space between metropole and colony.

Moreover, in their mature fiction, Rhys and Bowen both describe a particular interwar territory of exile: hotel rooms and boardinghouses located at the edges of various European metropoles and demimondes. Women protagonists—even those with some means—occupy the uneasy position of the lonely émigré living outside the secure territories of home, nation, and family.[6] Although the motif of the metropolitan wanderer might seem to stand at the center of most canonical/ conventional accounts of Anglo-American modernism, neither Rhys nor Bowen has enjoyed secure canonical status within modernist studies for very long. For many years, particularly before the academic rediscovery of *Wide Sargasso Sea*, Jean Rhys stood as a somewhat dated Left Bank writer who had once been Ford Madox Ford's lover and protégée, while Bowen endured a long semicanonical twilight in the shadow of Virginia Woolf. In the last twenty years, the fortunes and literary reputations of both writers have risen, and, while it is not my purpose to spread the modernist honorific far and wide as a way of conferring status on this or that writer, I do in this chapter pursue an implicit argument about the formal innovations of both Rhys and Bowen that might draw them closer to the circle of high modernists that includes Conrad, Woolf, and Joyce.

The early novels of Rhys and Bowen examined in this chapter offer a particular colonial and youth-fixated version of a larger problem of social reproduction associated with the novel of disillusionment beginning in the later nineteenth century. As Edward Said notes, the "world of high modernism" seems to highlight a pervasive crisis of reproduction so that the familiar Victorian orphan plot morphs and branches into recurrent motifs of sexual impairment, celibacy, sterility, and abortion (*The World* 17).[7] Both Rhys's Anna Morgan and Bowen's Lois Farquar are the nieces of imperial planters who represent a class that cannot—or at least does not—reproduce itself. But something more specific is afoot here in this comparison, something that links the colonial background these writers share to the familiar foregrounds of their fiction, in which domestic spaces are so often unsettled, where the home territory is always shifting, often evaporating, rarely defendable. Rhys and Bowen are writers acutely attuned to the shocking, but muffled and perhaps politically unmournable, predicament of dispossessors dispossessed. Still, they are not just chroniclers of a class or caste (the plantocracy) going down in history; they are authors of fictions in which the problem of failed modernization transforms into a pervasive critique of colonial modernity rather than remaining, at the level of political affiliation, a settler-class paean to a vanishing way of life.

To interpret these novels beyond their mixed class/nation sympathies is to try to return to the interpretive stance described from the outset as political formalism in an effort to avoid reductive or intentionalist conclusions. Rhys and Bowen, like Schreiner and Woolf, continue to attract critical interest because they are difficult to pigeonhole with ideology critique, and the complications only multiply when we try to remain attuned to gender and sexuality as well as to race and colonialism. Just as one can read Schreiner as sympathetic to Boer nationalism and Woolf as heavily implicated in British ruling-class values, it is quite possible to see both Rhys and Bowen as invested in nostalgic colonial formations. Within the recent history of Bowen reception, for example, Seamus Deane triggered a key round of debate by claiming that Bowen's fiction betrays a conservative interest in the Anglo-Irish settler world of Ireland. Many Bowen critics think Deane does poor justice to Bowen's work. Along similar lines, in a recent reconsideration of Rhys's *Wide Sargasso Sea*, George Handley summarizes an ongoing divide in Rhys criticism: On one hand, scholars such as Susan Stanford Friedman (in " 'Beyond' Gynocriticism") and Gayatri Spivak see Rhys largely as a postcolonial writer producing a counterdiscourse to the established power of British imperialism; and, on the other hand, scholars such as Peter Hulme and Handley himself see *Wide Sargasso Sea* as "fundamentally sympathetic to the planter class ruined by Emancipation" (Hulme qtd. by Handley 150).[8] Faced with Rhys's apparent vacillation between sympathetic nostalgia for the plantocratic world of the past and semiburied indictments of its racist and patriarchal politics, Handley and most critics have settled, reasonably enough, on a kind of tragic strain in Rhys that sees those two ideological poles as permanently disjunct.

In my view, the frozen adolescence of Rhys protagonists such as Anna Morgan in *Voyage in the Dark* or Antoinette Cosway in *Wide Sargasso Sea*—or of a Bowen protagonist like Lois Farquar—captures not just a tragic dichotomy of colonial politics or a stock plot of female self-renunciation, but a profound contradiction within the gender and colonial systems of modernity—one with deep-seated implications for modernist narrative form. The contradiction, fully-fledged and highly visible during the last era of high British imperialism, is between the modernizing, developmental discourses of emancipation-and-empire and the exoticizing, underdeveloping practices of patriarchy and imperialism. The formalization of this historical contradiction in modernist plots produces the metabildung-sroman, a coming-of-age tale with its inbuilt progressive time spliced to other temporalities—static, regressive, accelerated, syncopated.

In this study so far, we have explored a set of writers with widely differing aesthetic projects and ideological backgrounds, building the argument around a limited model of generic and thematic convergence in their fictions of adolescent fixation and late colonial modernity. It is especially fitting then to turn to Rhys and Bowen as semi-peripheral modernist writers, for they stand as hyphenated (Anglo-Irish) or creole (Welsh-Dominican) intermediaries between writers with more obvious points of identification as either colonizer or colonized. With Rhys and Bowen in view, we can extend the claims of the early chapters to suggest that the problem of colonial timelessness—and its inscription into models of stunted youth—presents itself as a structural condition of the age of empire rather than a ruse of either colonial or anticolonial reason. The variety of texts and writers already examined suggests, I think, that from many different geopolitical vantage points modernist fiction seems to apprehend in the language of uneven devel-opment a broad and deep crisis in the European historiography of progress. For Rhys in particular, as a transatlantic migrant writer claimed for both modernist and postcolonial canons, our interpretive models cannot themselves devolve into simple reinscriptions of terms like center and margin, or colonizer and colonized.

Nor should we, however, celebrate Rhys on the mere grounds that she is a poly-morphous border-crosser and category-breaker: Categories and borders are not in themselves bad. The point, rather, is to use powerful literary figures like Rhys to challenge ossified models of the West/non-West by trying to understand the intercultural formation of modernism within a particular phase in the rise and fall of the colonial world-system. More specifically, if we can reread Rhys in relation to a variety of Anglophone modernists (Wilde and Conrad, Bowen and Joyce), we can work against the idea of an old high modernism of the center and some new alternative modernisms of the periphery. It is not that the old high modernism was European until the "new modernisms" came along to challenge and reshape it: The old high modernism was always a formation shaped globally and by forces that included, from the start, anticolonial resistance movements. To do justice to the stark yet bristling quality of Rhys's language is to remind ourselves that modernist literature has the capacity to register in aesthetic form a complicated world situa-tion in which both European and non-European historical experience shape each other. If Rhys writes as a symbolically disinherited niece of the old West Indian plantation, she nonetheless, in the alembic of her art, produces fiction in which the reorganization of the entire system—and not just the death of a class—can be apprehended. It is indeed, only against the grinding forward motion of an unevenly developed world-system, of new nations and emergent social categories, that the forestalled maturity and postponed modernity of the Rhys-Bowen heroines, those virgins of empire, can be grasped.

Endlessly Devolving: Jean Rhys's *Voyage in the Dark*

It is not just the most immediate but also the most striking fact about Jean Rhys's *Voyage in the Dark* that it begins, and ends, on the point of beginning again: "Born again" on the first page of the novel and "starting all over again" on the last, Anna Morgan is a startling young protagonist who dwells not in the current of progressive time but in a dark perpetual present of disorientation and disintegration (7, 188). The ending of the first published version seems in a sense to parallel that of Joyce's *Portrait*, in which an urban teenager vows (to himself) to start again, to go forth for the millionth time. Although the tone of Stephen's diary differs sharply from that of Anna's delirious inner monologue, both novels seem carefully constructed to produce a recursive or circular effect, to produce rhythmic repetitions that cut against the narrative trajectory and, of course, to interrupt and retard the standard process of maturation. The perennial problem of assessing Joyce's irony at the end of *Portrait* leaves us, like generations of readers before, wondering how far Stephen has come in his voyage and whether he is abandoning or reiterating the callow flailings of a precocious teenage aesthete. About Anna Morgan, we can have little doubt: Her journey cannot be understood as one of destiny, fulfillment, or social adjustment. Of course, Rhys's original ending had Anna dying on an abortion table at age nineteen, a symbolic victim (like Woolf's Rachel Vinrace in *The Voyage Out*) of the late Victorian sex-gender system. Rhys, Joyce, and Woolf were all writing their stalled *bildungsromane* in the 1905–1914 period, though Rhys's was not published until roughly twenty years after Joyce's and Woolf's. In these three novels, the plot of frozen youth breaks the tempo of harmonic growth, and bourgeois social adjustment is not a possible, indeed barely even a plausible, narrative outcome.

In *Voyage in the Dark*, Anna Morgan feels herself to be outside the norms not just of middle-class womanhood but of Englishness. Anna's inner voice strains to reconcile places and spaces, but fails; there is, for her, no common ground or frame of reference between Western Europe and the West Indies and thus no way to compare experience transatlantically. Here is one reason that Rhys's work has gained so much traction in the last twenty years: It narrates exile as an unrepairable existential and political gap. Indeed, to focus on Anna's self-discontinuity in relation to the geography of exile and colonial displacement is to address a touchstone in Rhys criticism, particularly as it combines feminist and postcolonial approaches to the problematic selfhood of Anna Morgan and other Rhys protagonists.[9] Most readers of *Voyage in the Dark* pay close attention to Rhys's fashioning of Anna as a dispossessed "white creole" whose unfitness for national (and racial) belonging in England redoubles her sexual unfitness as a young woman without proper connections. Rhys explicitly casts Anna's crisis of identity as a geographical problem: "Sometimes it was as if I were back there and as if England were a dream. At other times England was the real thing and out there was the dream, but I could never fit them together" (8). Although passages like this can be read as establishing the basic theme of exile or cultural alienation, there is more to say here beyond observing that the split between metropole and colony frames Anna's sense of loneliness and dislocation.

First, the disorientation effect determines the fact that Anna's selfhood cannot be developed or domesticated. Living in disjointed space seems to break the accumulative model of identity-formation over time, so that Anna dwells in a kind of vortex of selfhood:

> I am hopeless, resigned, utterly happy. Is that me? I am bad, not good any longer, bad. That has no meaning, absolutely none. Just words. But something about the darkness of the streets has a meaning.
>
> (57)

This postcoital dizzy spell is a telegraphic message to readers, showing that Anna is profoundly alienated from any available moral and psychological schemes for self-formation. She attempts to stabilize meaning in the "darkness of the streets," a motif that anchors Anna, and her new urban world, not so much to meaning as to its absence.

Voyage in the Dark reinforces the recursive logic of Anna's nonprogress with relentless, one might even say compulsive, replication at every level of the text: grammatical, stylistic, imagistic, structural, psychological, and sociohistorical.[10] Consider this typical slice of syntax as Anna takes stock of her situation: "And the cold nights; and the way my collar bones stick out" (17). Dropping verbs and actions out of the narrative grammar, Rhys renders daily experience as a litany of recurrent sensations that harrow Anna and press her inside a thick, foggy medium of static time. She can gain no footholds in the accounting of her own sensation of time, but must suffer through sporadic bouts of illness and bodily collapse: "When you have a fever you are heavy and light, you are small and swollen, you climb endlessly a ladder which turns like a wheel" (33). Endless and originless, Anna's inner world—a true stream of consciousness—seems constructed to reveal how pat and shapely are the normal models of character in English fiction. In a major initiation scene, Anna, barely afloat as a chorus girl, braces herself for a first sexual encounter with Walter, whom she hopes will protect and provide: "Like when they say, 'As it was in the beginning, is now, and ever shall be, world without end.'" (41). Anna readies and steadies herself for trauma, but this trauma cannot function as a soul-shaping event, a negative rite of passage; instead it hits Anna as yet one more damaging event in a dizzying sequence without beginnings or ends. Sex is the trauma that voids the concept of destiny in the novel; in its wake, Anna cannot gather or bank her experiences into a repository of personal identity: "It's funny when you feel as if you don't want anything more in your life except to sleep . . . . That's when you can hear time sliding past you, like water running" (113).

Rhys's language of stasis and endlessness means that Anna cannot recognize herself as an integral subject developing continuously in time. The shallowness of her experience, though, is not simply the product of sexual and social trauma in England; she was already lost and alienated in post-plantation Dominica. So stringent is the novel's antiformational logic of character that even the merest colonial nostalgia is removed as source or ground of a functional expatriate identity. Anna's disorientation and her failure to mature or progress are symbolically rooted in the massive anachronisms produced by late colonial life in the West Indies, so that the uneven modernization of Anna's childhood echoes and anticipates the uneven development of her own psyche. Neither Anna nor Dominica appear to go forward in time: They are stuck at a threshold, unassimilable to the progressive time of modernity, much like the adolescent slave girl Maillote Boyd, whose frozen-in-history documents are part of Anna's thought-collage (56).[11]

In this antiromance of colonial childhood, Anna remembers a sensually rich but socially isolated past in post-emancipation Dominica. When Anna lapses, or plunges, into childhood reverie, we find ominous notes of racial antagonism and social insecurity that redouble rather than relieve her English alienation. An avatar of both a life (hers) and a way of life (that of the old plantocracy) that have no way forward, Anna is adrift in history. Like Maggie Tulliver before her (and like Lois Farquar in the section to come), Anna is a frozen youth who figures the futurelessness produced along the margins by the future-making machinery of global capitalism's rhetoric of development.

Anna's homesickness rises to the level of Lukács's transcendental homelessness; she suffers not a displacement from familiar to alien spaces, but a pervasive and chronic dislocation from any space. Worse still, she cannot even track and stabilize spatial difference as an epistemological or psychological category. The text insists on this point, showing us that Anna can only blur the boundaries of space, producing an illusion of boundarylessness to match her temporal sensations of endlessness. The plotline moves—one hesitates even to say advances—in a series of cinematic and spatial dissolves, shading from one rented room to another, measuring Anna's de-formation in terms of her incapacity to distinguish place from place. The problem is evident from the start: "The towns we went to always looked so exactly alike. You were perpetually moving to another place which was perpetually the same" (8). But it becomes more desperate:

> I kept telling myself, "You've got to think of something. You can't stay here. You've got to make a plan." But instead I started counting all the towns I had been to, the first winter I was on tour—Wigan, Blackburn, Bury, Oldham, Leeds, Halifax, Huddersfield, Southport . . . I counted up to fifteen and then slid off into thinking of all the bedrooms I had slept in and how exactly alike they were, bedrooms on tour. Always a high, dark wardrobe and something dirty red in the room. . . . And then I tried to remember the road that leads to Constance Estate.
>
> (150)

Toggling back to Dominica, Anna finds herself, again, stranded among spatial multiples with no fixed landmarks: "Everything is green, everywhere things are growing" (151). This blurring of figure and ground and lack of whole or framed spaces always underscores the parallel absence of stable temporal markers that might be used to break off one meaningful segment of time from another. Disrupting the protagonist's ability to experience finite space and discrete time, Rhys strikes with surgical precision at the heart of the Goethean model of self-formation, in which temporal progress is always legible in the form of spatial meaning.

The Goethean subject transforms himself as he crosses borders, takes account of spatial and cultural markers of difference, and contemplates the developmental processes of which he is both connoisseur and embodiment. It is hard to imagine a more thoroughgoing inversion of that model than the figure of Anna Morgan, for whom travel through Atlantic and urban spaces marks a series of dispossessions rather than a process of self-possession. Urban space swallows rather than sustains Anna's interiority; environmental determinants shape her will in a thoroughgoing naturalist plot that extends beyond the passive, disillusioned heroes of Flaubert into the downtrodden heroines of Zola.[12] Rhys tips her readers to this literary debt in the opening scenes, where Anna reads a copy of Zola's *Nana*, her anagrammatic precursor in sexual victimhood. Immediately, Anna's friend Maudie rejects the prestige of the genre, imagining all the lies entailed in the project of a "man writing a book about a tart," though literature in general is bogus to Maudie: "All books are like that—just somebody stuffing you up" (10). Anna may not be so sure, but she shares enough of Maudie's skepticism to mark herself out yet again as an anti-type of the Victorian or classical *bildungsheld*: She finds that she cannot or will not shape her mind and destiny based on the vicarious data transmitted to her through literature.[13] Unlike Conrad's Jim, who stuffs himself up on adventure tales but cannot enact a Goethean integration between heroic self-image and degraded social conditions, Anna does not even really initiate the romantic process of self-making.

Rhys refuses the literary scene of instruction so thoroughly, in fact, that Anna cannot read *Nana*: "The print was very small, and the endless procession of words gave me a curious feeling—sad, excited, and frightened. It wasn't what I was reading, it was the look of the dark, blurred words going on endlessly that gave me that feeling" (9). Here the echoing repetitions take on the stilted quality of a Gertrude Stein paragraph: "endless—words—gave me—a feeling . . . endlessly—words—gave me—that feeling." To the disorienting parade of spatiotemporal markers we must now add written language itself—yet another endless flow of signification without any discrete, finite, or meaningful order by which Anna might situate herself within a redemptive or even intelligible experience. The stasis of endless flow is replicated in Anna's psyche and sensorium, writ large across the spatial poles of her transatlantic world, and writ small in the very language of the text, and within the text.

The repetitive cadences of Anna's inner monologues keep us at the phenomenological surface of her mind, just as her way of reading Zola almost parodically avoids the depth of the text, so that Rhys chips icily away at the motif of cultivated interiority in the literate middle-class protagonist. Unlike other fallen women in the naturalist line, such as Hardy's Tess, Anna Morgan meditates very directly on her lost agency and interiority, as discrete experiences feel denuded of the magic connective threads of destiny:

> Of course, you get used to things, you get used to anything. It was as if I had always lived like that. Only sometimes, when I had got back home and was undressing to go to bed, I would think, "My God, this is a funny way to live. My God, how did this happen?"
>
> (40)

Like another antidevelopmental writer of the period, Kafka, Rhys tracks her protagonist's mental life along surfaces and from the outside, with eerie flatness, as if interior monologue were being conducted by a monitoring consciousness detached from the body in which it resides.[14] Psychological realism is reduced to a set of behaviors, perceptions, functions, and appetites without an organizing will; action is systematically stripped of the self-forming ethos enshrined in classic nineteenth-century realism. What Rhys describes here is a mind trapped in a (female) body trapped in a (dingy) room trapped in a (metropolitan) city. Mobility, the Goethean motif of managed spatial difference, and interiority, the psychological project of depth formation, are comprehensively removed from the picture just as they are remorselessly travestied in Kafka's *Metamorphosis*.

In Kafka's dark naturalist fable of unbecoming, oblique forms of sexual and economic competition drive the perverse family romance of the Samsas. Much more overtly in *Voyage in the Dark*, Rhys highlights Anna's vulnerability to a system of harsh sexual and economic competition, among women and between the sexes. As she watches her hungry and morally hysterical flatmate Ethel watching her, Anna notes: "Feelers grow where feelers are needed and claws where claws are needed" (107). Embedded in a story of cavalier male exploitation and patriarchal privilege, this kind of animal imagery does not mark Rhys as an antifeminist, but as a ruthlessly systematic feminist, for whom women as much as men are conscripted into maintaining a punishing sex-gender system. Anna's place in that system is triply determined by her status as an impoverished young creole woman, but what marks out Rhys's place in the naturalist strand of modernist writing is her attention to the biological dimensions of her economic situation. Anna's racialized and sexualized body disqualifies her from a narrative of social mobility and self-improvement, so that Rhys offers us one of the clearest examples of a biopolitically organized inversion of the novel of progress. If in the Victorian female bildungsroman girls confront a socially circumscribed destiny as they come of age, here Anna's nondevelopment is conditioned by unmovable forces wired to the body.

The interimplication of Anna's racial (national) and sexual (gender) status is made clear not just by the fact that Englishmen and Englishwomen code Anna as a creole sexpot, but by the harsh education in femininity meted out by her stepmother Hester. In both Dominican flashbacks and English present-tense scenes, Hester confronts Anna with a stark choice: She must decide to be either lady or nigger. After a girlhood of fluid relations to the colonial color line, sexual initiation brings the trauma of enforced racial identification. Here is Anna's most overt resistance to coming of age itself:

> Being white and getting like Hester, and all the things you get—old and sad and everything. I kept thinking, "No . . . No . . . No . . ." And I knew that day that I'd started to grow old and nothing could stop it.
>
> (72)

Rhys describes a common colonial situation, reminiscent of Kim's impossible choice at the end of Kipling's novel, in which the colonial child's attainment of racial and sexual adulthood requires a disavowal of cross-racial or cross-cultural intimacy. Kim maintains his innocence to the end as Anna cannot, though in both cases the narrative of arrested development captures the protagonist's symbolic refusal to commit to an adulthood based on racial exclusion and colonial respectability. Having identified and socialized with slave descendants in her girlhood, Anna nonetheless cannot maintain a sympathetic connection to nonwhites given the polarized racial politics of Dominica. Nor will Rhys indulge in a woman-native allegory of social marginalization despite the fact that Anna is repeatedly coded as un-English and subwhite.[15] Indeed, at each disarticulated stage of the novel, Anna remains outside both the Dominican caste system and the English class system, consigned to identify—sporadically to be sure—with those who do her harm (especially moralizing white women such as Hester). For Anna, the incomplete and impossible transition from "nigger" to "lady" assures her social vulnerability and perpetuates her adolescence.

Unmoored from the neofeudal gender norms of the plantocracy, and stranded within a new and viciously commodified English sexual system dusted with post-Victorian hypocrisy, Anna is a hapless ingenue, both mis- and undereducated.[16] She undergoes an instant and violent conversion from virgin to concubine. The first movement of the novel describes this cruel short circuit from sexually inexperienced to sexually devalued. Through the eyes of the upper-middle-class men who exploit her, Anna—a teenager—goes from being "only a baby" on the night of her first sexual encounter to being "hard" some few months later (51, 174). And in the shortness of the circuit, Rhys underscores the fact that a brutal sexual (and racial) system of objectification and commodification is what determines Anna's missing narrative of emergence and development. Like Gregor Samsa, Anna can wake up and find herself transformed, but she cannot participate in a plot of self-transformation. The quick switch from virgin to tart is replicated in the original novel's equally quick line from youth to death, a line that shows female socialization as a negative process of reduction and decline, from body to commodity (virgin), from commodity to declining commodity value (tart), and from there to death.

This temporalization of women's social existence according to a narrow life cycle of sexual value was not an entirely new aspect of British fiction in the interwar period, but Rhys's capacity to unmask its force and pose its devastating effects against the narrative values of autonomy and progress must have seemed strikingly modern in 1934. It still does. If Rhys details the short-circuiting of virginity, Bowen, as we will see, narrates its endless prolongation. Both describe virgin protagonists caught on the cusp of sexual adulthood in ways that are conditioned by their identification with a plantation class likewise caught on the cusp of modernity, unable to adapt to a new, postcolonial phase of its historical existence.[17] It is in this sense that I describe the Rhys and Bowen protagonists as, in the title of this chapter, virgins of empire.[18]

Rhys's girls and young women are deeply shaped by the economics of sexual value and sexual purity in ways that resonate strongly with the commodity value and virgin purity of untrafficked and exploitable economic value in the colonial world. That connection between exploitable sexual and economic value animates much of the dark critical energy in Rhys's fictions of exiled colonial women, from *Voyage in the Dark* all the way through to *Wide Sargasso Sea*. In *Voyage*, Rhys brilliantly dramatizes Anna's intuition that British export-commodities bespeak and embody a discourse of racial and sexual purity that excludes her desire, if not her body, from the start. Here advertising copy shapes her interior monologue:

> "What is Purity? For Thirty-five Years the Answer has been Bourne's Cocoa."
> Thirty-five years . . . Fancy being thirty-five years old. What is Purity? For Thirty-five Thousand Years the Answer has been.
>
> (59)

Already we can see that Anna's sense of subjective destiny has become, under the pressure of her own reification as a usable object, warped and unfulfillable; the ellipsis in the text marks out a bitter joke that need not even reach its conclusion to hit its mark.

Sexual and colonial commodification intersect even more vividly toward the end of the novel:

> I got into bed and lay there . . . thinking of that picture advertising the Biscuits Like Mother Makes, as Fresh in the Tropics as in the Motherland, Packed in Airtight Tins . . .
>   There was a little girl in a pink dress eating a large yellow biscuit studded with currants—what they call a squashed-fly biscuit—and a little boy in a sailor-suit, trundling a hoop, looking back over his shoulder at the little

girl. There was a tidy green tree and a shiny pale-blue sky, so close that if the little girl had stretched her arm up she could have touched it. (God is always near us. So cosy.) And a high dark wall behind the little girl.

Underneath the picture was written:

The past is dear,
The future clear,
And, best of all, the present.

But it was the wall that mattered.
And that used to be my idea of what England was like.
"And it is like that, too," I thought.

(148–49)

The pastoral and domestic elements of this picture of commodified innocence recapitulate all the key themes in Anna's voyage, rendering them in terms of a bright, hyperreal, hack imagery we have been trained to see always in dark and satirical terms. There's a precision to Rhys's language here that extends the meaning of the Bourne's Cocoa advertisement: The airtight tins of domestic biscuits—packed with their visual icons of gender propriety—can be transferred fresh from Motherland to Tropics (and back again). The overlapping power of commodity imperialism and maternal ideology produces for Anna an instant hollowing-out of her imagination; they block her ability to project herself into prevailing narratives of innocent Englishness.

Even more striking, given how superbly Rhys has framed Anna as trapped in an endless, indiscrete flow of unmarked time and unbounded space, is the visual capture of shapely time and moralized space in this image. The "tidy green tree" echoes in contrast with the "green green everywhere" of Anna's Dominican jungle past and with the endless procession of gray English towns in Anna's present. The cozy sense of God and the high dark wall works together to cut off the elect from the disgraced, the educated from the abandoned, underscoring Anna's utter disorientation in space and time and her vulnerability to the alternately carceral and bewilderingly open spaces of the metropole. The rhyming jingle gives a cartoon version of harmony between a dear past and a clear future, as if to suggest in ersatz miniature the devastating absence of a narrative of self-formation in Anna's life. The diagrammatic clarity of this negative encounter between subject and image registers in stark terms the anti-*Bildung* elements of *Voyage in the Dark*: stripped agency and eviscerated temporality, which write themselves into the very syntax of the sentences Anna forms as she reflects on the biscuit ad—a triple shot of flat, repetitive, subjectless statements strung together in a way that turns narrativity itself inside out: "[And] it was the wall that mattered"; and "that used to be my idea"; "and it is like that too" (149).

England, for Anna, actually embodies its own ideological self-projections, in part because its citizens seem to enforce the social divisions implied by the wall in the biscuit ad, a process of enforcement that leaves Anna frozen out and frozen between varieties of phantasmatic girlhood without social accommodation. In this plot of stunted youth, Rhys underscores her character's reduction to commodity logic in the sexual economy and to colonial difference in the nation-race matrix of the interwar metropolis. As we saw in Wells's *Tono-Bungay*, the modernist novel of untimely youth is a powerful symbolic tool for unveiling the process of reification as the humanist language of novelistic subjectivity gets rewritten into the warped and empty time of commodification. *Voyage in the Dark* gives us an even more bitter rendering of the same problem: Reification displaces self-making, and the manipulative rhetoric of mass consumerism displaces the formative power of the old high culture—now seen as "stuffing up." It is fitting then that the women against whom Anna measures herself—the nameless women who manage to keep their eyes "fixed on the future" and seize for themselves some simulacrum of a secure social destiny—are entirely inside the commodity system. Their clothes "were like caricatures of the clothes in the shop windows" (130). In a set of strikingly prescient passages set against the backdrop of urban consumerism, Rhys's Anna observes the more or less complete emptying out of narratives of self-fashioning by the power of fashion itself.

In such a context of deep economic naturalism and post-Victorian reduction of the body to signifiers of race, citizenship, and sexuality, Anna's voyage in the dark operates as a negative allegory of socialization. But even as it turns the old Goethean model of self-formation on its head, Rhys's novel cannot but reincorporate some of the temporal elements and generic conventions of the bildungsroman, or at least of the organic model of time institutionalized in that genre. As in our earlier readings, so in *Voyage in the Dark*: A novel of stunted or frozen youth must confront the problem of closure at some point, and it is at that point that a metabildungsroman has to expose the oddity of a biographical novel stripped of the aging plot. Without aging, the novel of untimely youth calls attention to its final product—either a youthful body or a youthful corpse—as the antitype of the socially reconciled adult. My guiding claim has been that both outcomes—the eternal adolescence of Kipling, Wells, or Joyce and the sudden death of Schreiner, Wilde, Conrad, and Woolf—represent a single and definable modernist project. Both sets of novels seek to explore unconventional or stylized models of emplotment, dissident or bohemian models of socialization, and nonteleological or nonlinear models of historical development (particularly as situated within a global system of colony and metropole). Rhys, for her part, produced both corpse and youth. In the original unpublished version of *Voyage in the Dark*, Anna Morgan dies in the final chapter. But Rhys's editor prevailed upon her to change the ending, with the result that the published novel concludes with Anna swooning in pain after a difficult abortion.[19]

Both endings in fact announce the novel's commitment to antidevelopmental time, linking it back to the work of Woolf and Schreiner (whose first title for *African Farm* was "a series of Abortions") and forward to the work of Elizabeth Bowen.[20] As in those cases, this novel sets the story of failed or missed maturation against a wider backdrop in which a colonial society fails to "come of age" in time with a Eurocentric narrative of global modernization. At the end of her story, Rhys's Anna, barred from any foreseeable future, dwells in a delirious and infinitely receding colonial past. Despite the manifest irony of Rhys having been directed by a (male) publisher to rewrite her novel, the closing abortion sequence nonetheless offers a satisfying artistic solution to the problem of Anna's fate. A callous male professional (one more version of Anna's faithless lovers) operates on Anna, etherized upon a table, and asserts biopolitical control over her body, excluding it from the sanctioned sexual and reproductive arena of English womanhood. Meanwhile Anna revisits her semitraumatic, post-plantation colonial past in an extended, italicized interior monologue that comprises most of part 4 of the novel. As Anna's world contracts, Rhys tracks the process with shorter and shorter narrative units that collapse more and more into the language of isolated subjectivity. The novel takes us spiraling downward and inward from the national tour of the opening, to the London cityscape, to the shared apartments, to the isolated bedchambers, to the operating room, to the inner world of Anna's mind. In this Kafkaesque winnowing of Anna's experience—rendered finally in terms of a merely phenomenological recording of sensations and shards of associative memory—Rhys inverts the worldliness and expansiveness of the Goethean novel of mobility and destiny.

In the novel's fourth part, as in earlier sections, Rhys's inner voice repeats itself, falls into gutters and trenches of the mind, and eddies backward into memory, flowing forward without proper punctuation in a last demonstration of the "endlessness" of time, language, and experience that has plagued Anna throughout. In several of Anna's reveries, Rhys includes segments of language—for example, archival excerpts drawn from slavery-era Dominica—that seem not to belong to a psychologically realist presentation of Anna's consciousness. With this mental collage-effect bleeding in and out of the proper subjectivity of Anna Morgan, Rhys modifies her presentation of a rounded Anna with a commitment to reframing Anna as a symbolic device. At such moments, Anna's allegorical function outstrips her merely characterological one. Specifically—and since so much of Anna's embodiment of nondevelopmental time is coded in relation to her West Indian background—we might say that she is at times an emblem of colonial/creole experience rather than a psychologically unified product of that experience.

Like the colonies described by Schreiner, Conrad, and Woolf, Rhys's Dominica is a virgin land stripped of resources and turning into a nonproductive space: Its dwindling contributions to the modern world-system are out of step with a model of continuous integration and capitalist development. Economic anachronism— the failed modernization of the plantation mode of production—colors Anna's family experiences and memories. Moreover, the nonaccumulation of wealth in her fallen Dominica seems to parallel her own nonaccumulation of experience. As a figure of nonfuturity, Anna symbolizes the inability of the Creole plantation class to reproduce itself in a post-emancipation, post-plantation, postcolonial world. Even in the fragmentary bits of Anna's childhood memory, we can see that the folkways of the freed slaves and the manners of the ex-slave owners are part of an anachronistic way of life ("Aunt Jane said I don't see why they should stop the Masquerade they've always had their three days Masquerade ever since I can remember why should they want to stop it some people want to stop everything" [184–85]).

Moreover, the colony in this case is not yet a postcolony, let alone a nation, so that it cannot avail itself of the language of national emergence by which political units mark their achievement of modernity in the twentieth century. West Indian postcolonies like Dominica are paradigms of colonial belatedness in that they continue up to the present to be defined by imperial relations rather than by territorialized programs of national sovereignty. Dominica's arrest, like Anna's, is a symptom of failed self-possession. Rhys's globalization of the motif of the doomed provincial woman, recoded as nationless subject, modernizes the figure of the futureless Victorian girl, extending its allegorical function from the intranational to the international system of uneven development. The plot of Rhys's novel encodes within its nondeveloping protagonist the broad contradiction of a colonial-neocolonial system in which progress and modernity are themselves almost endlessly deferred for the peripheral subject.

Reading *Voyage in the Dark* back against the history of the bildungsroman as a genre of national emergence thus highlights Rhys's particular configuration of the postnational novel of stalled development. But it also underscores a deeper connection to what I have so far called the biopolitical dimensions of Rhys's naturalism: the reframing of social marginality and social antagonism in terms of biologized categories of difference, particularly race and sex. That is, the bildungsroman plot depends on social mobility across class lines; the post- or metabildungsroman works to reveal the datedness, the impossibility of such plots of mobility and progress in a biopolitically organized society. As we have seen, beginning in the late Victorian period and extending into the epoch of interwar modernism, both colonial and metropolitan fictions with antidevelopmental plots seem to represent with special trenchancy the missing elements of class mobility, self-development, and national emergence. Such antidevelopmental plots—of which Rhys is perhaps the ultimate artist—tend to emphasize the determining role of incorrigible cultural and biological differences, for which the attenuation of the middle-class upward-mobility novel is both a sign and a symptom.

Anna's understanding of the world seems to exclude all notions of self-formation and social transformation, as in this memory of church services in Dominica: "The poor do this and the rich do that, the world is so-and-so and nothing can change it. For ever and for ever turning and nothing, nothing can change it." (43). Anna's naturalist sense of powerlessness, of social life as a "second nature," filters not only through her English experience, but through her reflections across the Atlantic world of her ken, where biopolitical categories like sex and race seem equally impervious to the language of evolution and development.[21] Rhys stands at such a central place in that history of the novel because her work makes visible the transfer of racialist and biopolitical thinking between the colonial sphere and the metropolis: Anna's experience as nondeveloping subject, in other words, gives readers the subjectively (and harrowingly) framed narrative of the end of the novel of progress, its foundering and faltering in a devolutionary epoch where racial and cultural differences become the model for social antagonism.

This broader intellectual and historical context helps explain the currency of Rhys's fiction, particularly *Wide Sargasso Sea*, among readers and teachers today. Like Rhys's earlier novels, *Wide Sargasso Sea* insists on the tragic consequences of certain intractable, inherited categories of race, gender, and sexuality. And it goes one step further in taking those tragic consequences as an occasion to revise and objectify the inherited literary conventions of self-making in the European novel. Indeed it aims squarely at the classic novel of British social mobility and female *Bildung*, Charlotte Brontë's *Jane Eyre*. Written decades after the first phase of Rhys's career, *Wide Sargasso Sea* expands the West Indian motifs of *Voyage in the Dark* into a full-blown version of plantation gothic, a genre that derives meaning and sensation precisely from the anachronistic, thrilling elements of premodernity within the plantation society of a West Indian settler colony. In writing back to *Jane Eyre*, *Wide Sargasso Sea* constitutes itself as an obvious antibildungsroman, though like all the novels under examination here, it combines elements of conventional coming-of-age tale with more recursively and atavistically organized plotlines.[22] Antoinette/Bertha Cosway, the revenant madwoman of Rhys's story, gets made and remade in the text by the historical power of racial and sexual discourses advanced by colonial modernity and its regimes of economic rationalization. But this is no simple creole-feminist revenge tale: If Rochester plays at times like a sexually panicked patriarchal villain, he also emerges as himself a victim of the class-and-property system of early capitalism in England and the colonial world. Rhys's virtuoso retelling of the burning of Thornfield Hall not only reimagines Brontë's original, but also establishes it as part of an intercolonial gothic pattern of return, where Antoinette, moving backward through her own story line, compulsively repeats the burning of Coulibri, the West Indian plantation of her childhood.

Rhys's burning-house narratives anticipate and echo the main plot of yet another antidevelopmental novel of the devolutionary era, Elizabeth Bowen's *The Last September*. Describing the conflagration of an Irish Big House, Bowen chronicles the dramatic endpoint to a long history of colonial settlement in Ireland. As in Rhys, the futurelessness of a people—the Anglo-Irish plantocracy—shapes and is shaped by a youthful protagonist who cannot come of age, a dispossessed daughter who has to embody a "vanishing way of life."

Querying Innocence: Elizabeth Bowen's *The Last September*

The Last September (1929) invokes yet cancels the generic protocols associated with two nineteenth-century novel forms, the gothic romance and the bildungsroman. These we might define briefly and respectively as the genres of regress and of progress, of female dispossession and of male self-possession.[23] Before comparing Bowen's revision of bildungsroman codes to Rhys's, I want briefly to set her text in relation to gothic conventions because, as a belated version of the Irish "Big House" novel, it must at least implicitly acknowledge the gothic devices that had filtered into that national subgenre since the publication of Maria Edgeworth's *Castle Rackrent* in 1800. One might, moreover, place the Big House novel into a wider colonial and historical frame by identifying it as an Irish variant of the plantation gothic, a characteristic genre of settler-colonialism, found in the plantocratic contact zones from Ireland to the slave economies of the New World, in the works of Faulkner and Rhys, and in the Caribbean zombie films of 1940s Hollywood.[24] In plantation gothic, colonial violence is generally displaced into domestic battle, sexual sensation, or hysterical psychomachia. *The Last September* does traffic in a set of familiar gothic tropes (burning house, trapped daughter, locked rooms, mysterious visitors) but desensationalizes all of them, telling its story in the intricate, indirect language of a novel of manners.

In this sense, the more apt *stylistic* comparison for Bowen's text would be Forster's *A Passage to India*, perhaps the best-known example of the colonial novel of manners. Published just five years earlier, it too depicts the drama of devolution played out at the edges of a moldy-chivalric British garrison. In both novels, polite exchanges within an immured society take on the symbolic weight of the colonial encounter, with various kinds of settlers and visitors mediating between imperial and local values while screening out the most alienating forms of "native" presence. In *The Last September*, the double displacement of violence—first privatized and sexualized in gothic terms, then shunted into a set of muffled offstage events— produces a certain effect of plot syncopation and distention, slowing the pace and loosening the fabric of the narrative to allow for Bowen's style to emerge in the form of proliferating anticlimaxes, close psychological portraiture, oblique descriptions, and elliptical swoops in and out of free indirect discourse.[25] In these stylistic features, Bowen's novel resonates with Woolf's novel of tropical manners, *The Voyage Out*. In both, highly mediated colonial encounters provide a temporary basis and thematic springboard for the development of a distinctive modernist style. Bowen (in her second novel) and Woolf (in her first) seem to have found anachronistic colonial history useful for deforming the biographical plot and for testing middle-class English mores.

One should not, in a reconsideration of Bowen, invoke the predictable Woolf comparison without good reason. In this case, I think, we can gain some insight into the formal principles of *The Last September* by observing that its protagonist, Lois Farquar, like Woolf's Rachel Vinrace in *The Voyage Out*, acts as a frozen-adolescent figure whose own uneven development seems to correspond to the temporal oddities of the surrounding colonial history. This symbolic exchange between youthful protagonist and colonial setting situates Bowen within a wider literary network reaching beyond Woolf to Kipling, Conrad, and Wells—writers not often compared to Bowen. Moreover, it is surely no coincidence that the great Irish novels of the two generations preceding Bowen's—Joyce's *Portrait of the Artist* in 1916 and Wilde's *Picture of Dorian Gray* in 1891—both organized their plots around the problematic of a youth that cannot come of age in the proper temporal order.[26] Like those novels, *The Last September* generates both historical meaning and stylistic originality by taking apart the basic progressive structure of the bildungsroman.

To read *The Last September* in this broader modernist and comparative-colonial frame is already to move away from the terms generally set by the debate over Bowen's political and affective relations to the world of the Anglo-Irish Big House. In the last fifteen years, that debate has centered on the claim—influentially made by Seamus Deane in *Celtic Revivals*—that one cannot really avoid seeing Bowen's work as a conservative and nostalgic investment in a dying class. Many Bowen critics, including Vera Kreilkamp, have riposted by arguing that Bowen is not so much a nostalgic apologist for the Anglo-Irish (here taken narrowly to designate the residual landholding class of the Protestant Ascendancy) as a cold-eyed chronicler of their historical doom.[27] We can perhaps shift the terms of debate now by attending more to the novel's formal principles than to Bowen's emotional affiliations and apparent political intentions. While Bowen may have imbued the novel's autumnal scene with a certain wistful appreciation for the civilization of the Anglo-Irish, the novel's plot, language, and characterization in fact tend to encode a deeper and more systematic narrative meaning in which the frozen, virginal fate of Lois Farquar indexes the structural contradictions of settler colonialism and the larger inevitabilities of postcolonial nationalism.

Lois's dilated, inverted bildungsroman plot captures, in other words, the historically fixed, politically vexed, permanently adolescent status of the Ascendancy itself, the anachronistic class described by this novel. Bowen uses a Proustian epigraph to set the terms by which she will condense historical experience into characterization: "They had the regrets of virgins and lazy men."[28] Lois and her equally virginal cousin, the world-weary Laurence, represent the historical dead end of a class that can neither reproduce nor transform itself. In this way, the language of the book encodes the broken and jagged time of a dying colonial modernity into the trope of adolescence, destabilizing the allegory of individual and social progress endemic to the classic bildungsroman.

The Last September takes place at Danielstown, a prototypical Anglo-Irish Big House, during the 1920 War. The inhabitants of this fragile oasis of settler privilege are surrounded by and torn between Irish republicans (who elicit their feudal and territorial sympathies) and the British army (who are their nominal allies and social intimates). The central plot concerns an abortive courtship between Lois, a slightly *déclassé* Anglo-Irish orphan, and Gerald Lesworth, a dim, earnest English officer. The other Irish—the "real" Irish (rural, Catholic, Republican)—lurk at the margins of the text. The English (mostly bluff army men and vulgar wives), meanwhile, represent rank middle-class materialism. Floating above and trapped between these two forces lie the Anglo-Irish landowners, subsisting almost entirely on genteel traditions, autumnal sighs, and tennis parties. The Anglo-Irish characters frame their relation to the English military occupation in the terms of a hostess eager to ensure a ready supply of gallant dancing partners: "It would be the greatest pity if we were to become a republic and all these lovely troops were taken away" (30–31).

Lois's cousin Laurence, who utters the line, in fact maintains an ironic distance of half-affection toward both the Irish and English forces. It is this kind of language, however bathed in irony, that has made Bowen vulnerable to readings that place her, with her characters, inside the bubble of Anglo-Irish privilege and willed innocence. But Bowen has always been a writer given to the scrupulous exploration of innocence as an historical and social theme, not to its willful performance. In her essay "The Roving Eye," she suggests that at the center of any writer's work, underneath all outward complexity, there is "a core of naivety." "Somewhere within the pattern," Bowen writes, "somewhere behind the words, a responsive, querying innocence stays intact" (qtd. in Lee 2). Hermione Lee has shrewdly observed, in fact, that Bowen's novels are "full of retarded overgrown juveniles . . . , reckless innocents, characters who haven't found ways of compromising with adult society" (3).[29]

The motif of the retarded juvenile provides *The Last September* with its opening note and its governing temporal logic. From the first, the figurative and descriptive language describes a lyrical interlude in the onrush of historical and biographical time, an interlude whose narrative correlate is the plot of arrested development. Thus Lois emerges in the opening scene suspended in a gentle puff of late-summer evening air, wrapped in a phrase that marks her off as part of a delectable past: "in those days . . . " (3). The motif of frozen time almost immediately takes psychological form in Lois's own will to youth: "She knew how fresh she must look, like other young girls"; she "wished she could freeze the moment and keep it always" (3–4). The novel thus quickly assimilates the characteristic temporality of Danielstown itself, a "cancelled time" that encapsulates itself rather than rolling out into the future (28). In love with indefinition and locationlessness, Lois loiters in the thresholds and anterooms of the house, and of the text, dodging every sociological category or spatial commitment that might attach her to an identity or a destiny.[30]

Like the protagonist of *The Voyage Out* or, for that matter, of *Lord Jim*, Lois will remain a nebulous figure at the center of the plot, one whose youth never takes on the sharp edges of maturity. As Mrs. Vermont, an English officer's wife, puts it: "Lois is so—I mean, well, you know—vague, isn't she?" (46). Where the young hero of a classic bildungsroman cultivates himself as an object of destiny, a product to be rounded into shape, Lois—with equal deliberation—cultivates her youth as pure potentiality with no actuality, a state of suspended animation. Indeed, she revolts not just against the expectations of adults (what adolescent heroine does not?), but against the expectation of adulthood. In one typical scene, Lois eavesdrops on her aunt and a visitor, then realizes with horror that the conversation is about to pin her to her own essence: "But when Mrs. Montmorency came to: 'Lois is very—' she was afraid suddenly. She had a panic. She didn't want to know what she was, she couldn't bear it: knowledge of this would stop, seal, finish one" (83). To keep the ellipsis of her identity elliptical, Lois interrupts the conversation by shattering a water basin and salvaging her formless youth. Even after the basin is glued together, the resulting cracks mark the fault line between herself and her destiny: "Every time [she saw them] she would wonder—what Lois *was*. She would never know" (83). The last four words in the passage are, from a dramatic point of view, gratuitous. The word "never" suggests the permanence of Lois's un-self-aware state even though Bowen, in a gesture of throwaway realism, gives us to understand that Lois ends up living (and presumably maturing) in France after Danielstown burns to the ground.

Bowen uses the technique of anticlimax and the motif of inhibited action to render the historical problematic of Ascendancy decline into the idiom of plot and character. In *The Last September*, these devices work together to produce an atmospheric novel of place in which character is always forming rather than formed, plot always dissolving rather than resolving. Danielstown, Lois reflects, is a place where "being grown up seems trivial, somehow" (140). And when Marda Norton observes that, at Danielstown, "there seems a kind of fatality," Lois shoots back: "I *know*" (110). Her emphasis—both urgent and resigned—indicates that she already understands that the inevitable flipside of her own cultivated (though not at all coquettish) ingenue status is the utter lack of a future (110). With gestures like this, the novel reminds us that it is not imposed authorial sentiment that shapes the Anglo-Irish into the blinkered virgins of history, but a kind of compositional and characterological fidelity to the experience of a settler class still posing as landholders even after history has laid siege to their land.

The belabored effort to sustain Lois's innocence, an effort undertaken both in and by the novel, corresponds to the belabored effort of the Ascendancy to enshrine their way of life as a permanent aspect of the Irish landscape. But if we restrict our analysis to this point, we will have ignored an even more subtle element of the novel's construction, since it is in fact not only a story of freeze-dried virginity, but of the unsteady, uneven temporal mix that both retards Lois and then hurtles her into the future. After all, no way of life is timeless; no adolescence remains static.

The Last September reveals the impossible future (and present) of the Anglo-Irish in 1920 by narrating the impossibility of a youth with no end. Since youth's essence is its temporariness—it is by definition a stage or prelude—a novel that fixates on youth must always draw attention to its own effort, its own estrangement from the inherited techniques of the coming-of-age tale. For Lois, youth becomes a spent quantity, which is to say, an absent signifier marked precisely by its inability to be fulfilled through transformation, through self-possession: "She thought she need not worry about her youth; it wasted itself spontaneously, like sunshine elsewhere or firelight in an empty room" (214). Rather than simply dispense with the progressive conventions of the genre, the novel at once invokes and inverts them, objectifying the bildungsroman tradition without imagining a facile escape from its influence.

Indeed, the real temporal essence of *The Last September* as both a historical and a psychological novel is the combination of dilation and compression. Lois, though she seems fixed in her hazy girlhood nimbus, is also moving rapidly into the future and growing up "very fast" (25). As Marda Norton observes: "She is in such a hurry, so concentrated upon her hurry, so helpless. She is like someone being driven against time in a taxi to catch a train, jerking and jerking to help the taxi along and looking wildly out the window at things going slowly past" (118). This quick sketch of Lois "driven against time" combines impatience with retrospect, passive immurement with futile action, perfectly capturing the problem of Lois's youth. What might seem at first glance a familiar, possibly even banal, description of adolescence as an oscillation between childhood and adulthood gains a kind of historical depth because of its programmatic association with the colonial legacy of uneven development in Ireland; that is, with the anachronistic existence of the plantocracy itself.

Strictly speaking, then, *The Last September* is neither a bildungsroman nor an antibildungsroman, but a novel that deliberately splices together the antiprogressive time of Anglo-Irish history and the progressive conventions of the coming-of-age novel. It stylizes youth, but finally exposes and concedes the necessity of the most basic temporal imperatives in the construction of novelistic plot, of personal identity, of national history. Bowen herself provides a clue to her own method in "Notes on Writing a Novel": "Plot must not cease to move forward. . . . The actual speed of the movement must be even. Apparent variations in speed are good, necessary, but there must be no actual variations in speed" (*Pictures and Conversations* 171). Later in the same essay: "For the sake of emphasis, time must be falsified. . . . Against this falsification—in fact, increasing the force of its effect by contrast—a clock should be heard always impassively ticking away at the same speed" (188). It is precisely this combination of "falsified" time and clock time—especially when laid bare rather than naturalized—that defines what we take to be the virtuoso Bergsonian innovation of modernist fiction. The interplay between impassive, linear time and its "falsifications"—dilation, compression, acceleration—in Bowen's text syncopates the joint allegory of Lois's deferred maturity and the Anglo-Irish gentry's deferred modernization.

Dilation and acceleration, despite their superficial opposition as slow and fast time, work together to capture the novel's central historical problem, which is the anachronistic persistence of a futureless and suddenly "foreign" planter class in nationalizing Ireland. In my view, the book's success can be defined in terms of how well Lois's persistent youth and voided destiny encode that colonial problematic of development. Lois's story, her life plotted as a "way of life," almost explicitly negates the classic bildungsroman plot of progress and fulfillment. Lois remains stubbornly "intransitive" and "virginal" from start to finish. She almost recognizes, and certainly experiences, the burden of embodying a negative allegory of acculturation:

> She could not try to explain the magnetism they all exercised by their being static. Or how, after every return—or awakening, even, from sleep or preoccupation—she and those home surroundings still further penetrated each other mutually in the discovery of a lack.
>
> (244)

This passage, probably the most cited in critical readings of *The Last September*, resonates with my analysis by confirming the reciprocal (and magnetic) symbolic relationship between an unaging youth and an anachronistic colonial setting.

The two resident late-adolescents at Danielstown, Lois and her cousin Laurence, seem self-consciously to defer and ironize their own impossible adulthood, a problem they charge to the "positive futurelessness" of their people (153). Bowen makes their shared state of mind clear:

> But to Laurence and Lois this all had already a ring of the past. They both had a sense of detention, of a prologue being played out too lengthily, with unnecessary stresses, a wasteful attention to detail. Apart, but not quite unaware of each other, queerly linked by antagonism, they both sat eating tea with dissatisfaction, resentful at giving so much of themselves to what was to be forgotten.
>
> (170)

Bowen's rewriting of the bildungsroman dynamic of progress follows from her exacting portrait of a colonial settler class that cannot reproduce itself. Such a portrait has a venerable place in the tradition of Anglo-Irish gothic, of course; as Victor Sage notes, the gothic has often served as a kind of tacit (and premature) obituary, an account of "the sterile genealogy of a landowning class": "The whole blood-line has committed suicide, and stolen its own future. It is a conspiracy to substitute repetition for development" (198). Repetition over development: It is this formula that Bowen elaborates in *The Last September*, desensationalizing the gothic while knitting a recursive and regressive temporal logic into the somewhat etiolated generic frame of a late bildungsroman. Both the prevailing "sense of detention" and the queer antagonisms of the previous passage establish a clear resonance with an earlier moment of Irish gothic, the Wilde/Stoker phase in which figures of a decayed bohemia (Dorian Gray) or a dying aristocracy (Dracula) distort the realist chronology of youth/age/death. In keeping with her fine sense of Flaubertian bathos, Bowen rings a subtler, less lurid change on that realist chronology, compressing progress and regress into a novelistic form whose sense of time is both recognizably modernist and wholly idiosyncratic.

The novel links the temporal problem of nonfuturity to the spatial predicament of the Anglo-Irish, whose disappearing territorial base makes them the quintessential dispossessors on the eve of their own dispossession. Lois embodies their stranding in time and in space:

> She was lonely and saw there was no future. She shut her eyes and tried—as sometimes when she was seasick, locked in misery between Holyhead and Kingstown—to be enclosed in nonentity, in some ideal no-place perfect and clear as a bubble.
>
> (127)

Suspended in the wide and watery gap between Britain (Holyhead, Wales) and Ireland (Kingstown, County Dublin), Lois almost explicitly decodes the political history of her own liminal or negative relation to the land. The classic gothic plot of female dispossession here takes the form of a bittersweet and personal—but no less historically severe—crisis. There simply is no space for Lois; her temporal status as a stalled protagonist finds a perfect spatial equivalent when she feels herself cradled in a bubble, an ideal no-place.

Although Lois and Laurence, the nonheirs of Danielstown, both inhabit the problem of their class's eternalized naïveté, Lois's experience of isolation is exacerbated by virtue of her gender. She has no access to the real struggles of Irish nationalism, a fact that undergirds her inability to achieve any kind of social role or personal destiny. Like Rachel Vinrace of Woolf's *Voyage Out*, Lois combines vague talent (can she paint?), dissident sexuality, sporadic self-knowledge, and a listless will. She is a protected girl inside a protected ruling class, continually juxtaposed to, but only half exposed to, the social contradictions of colonial modernity. Her story gives a colonial inflection to the broader generic principles of the (Victorian) female bildungsroman, wherein the heroine's blocked access to education, culture, and politics produces a vivid contrast to the Goethean ideal of self-fulfillment in the public sphere.

When Lois becomes the protected object of Gerald Lesworth, the English army officer, she recedes further into multiple layers of enforced inanition. Uneasy in her role as fiancée—though not rebellious in any simple or especially fierce way— Lois cannot quite avoid the sexual and social trappings of womanhood in a patriarchal ruling class that is ironically feminized in relation to the British occupiers.[31] Upon declaring that she has "no future," Lois immediately and tellingly follows with this report: "I have promised to marry Gerald" (258). Gerald, for his part, fully subscribes to the view that Ireland, and women, and, *a fortiori*, Lois (both Irish and a woman) exude a not entirely unpleasant mystique and require his kind of protection (125). Nothing irritates Lois more than the fact that Ireland (by which she, and Gerald, mean the Anglo-Irish landed class) is treated by the English much as a frail woman is treated by a chivalrous gentleman (66).

The novel makes it clear that Gerald's libido and elevated sense of mission are both wrapped up in an English pastoral dream, a kind of willful innocence that neatly matches his projection of ingenuousness onto Lois. But when Gerald seeks to actualize his fantasy of possession by kissing Lois, she rebuffs him with a brutally apt scolding: "I do wish you wouldn't, Gerald,—I mean, be so *actual*" (126). Once again, the scene resonates very strongly with a key moment in *The Voyage Out*, wherein Woolf's arch-imperialist and paragon of English manhood, Richard Dalloway, imposes a kiss on Rachel Vinrace. In both cases, the formless heroine, fearing the impress of a specifically Anglo-imperialist man, seeks to reclaim the open potential of her youth, an act that foreshadows her later attempts to forestall adulthood in general and marriage in particular.

Lois's historical virginity is sustained through a set of missed encounters with the troubles of 1920. "How is it," Lois wonders, "that in this country that ought to be full of such violent realness, there seems to be nothing for me but clothes and what people say? I might as well be in some kind of cocoon" (66). And when, in an epilogue deliberately set off from the main timeframe of the novel, the conflagration finally does come to Danielstown, Lois has already been removed to France. Along the way, as most critics have noted, Lois remains literally blanketed on the estate, as gun-runners, peasant spies, and armed fugitives pass her by. At one point, Lois and Marda Norton run into an armed rebel who has taken refuge in an abandoned mill. In a moment that is never directly narrated, and is only recounted in bare fragments, the rebel's gun appears to have gone off, grazing Marda's hands. The whole episode ends abruptly with a hushing-up, and no one—neither characters nor readers—can be quite sure what has in fact happened in the echo chamber of the old mill (180–83). Here, as in the Marabar Caves of Forster's *Passage to India*, colonial antagonists encounter each other with an obliquity that is unmistakable; colonial violence is temporarily broached, obscurely sexualized, narratively displaced, and finally just dispersed into murmuring anticlimaxes until the two sides retreat behind the *cordons sanitaires* of a dying imperialism.

Lois, for her part, knows that she has no place in the historical struggle for Ireland. She "could not conceive of her country emotionally: it was a way of living, abstract of several countrysides, or an oblique, frayed island moored at the north but with an air of being detached and drawn out west from the British coast" (42). What Lois cannot conceive of—"her country"—is of course really not the same collective that she embodies (her class). She can only think of Ireland from an Anglocentric point of view as "a way of living" off the British coast. Standing at equal and hyphenated distance from both Anglo and Irish, Lois reveals the impossibility of national allegory or national emergence for the Anglo-Irish. The slippery symbolic relationship between the characters and their collective destiny is, of course, not just a submerged technical matter, but an open topic of discussion. Consider Hugo Montmorency, another representative figure of the settler class who bears the signs of frozen youth (though middle-aged, he has both the "churlishness of a schoolboy" and an "unfortunate ability to be young at any time" [177]). In one scene, Hugo, posturing a bit, observes the following: "What's the matter with this country is the matter with the lot of us individually—our sense of personality is a sense of outrage and we'll never get outside of it."[32] To this self-fulfilling prophecy, Marda Norton has the following unspoken response: "But the hold of the country *was* that, she considered; it could be thought of in terms of oneself, so interpreted. Or seemed so . . ." (117). When Marda trails off, we are forced by Bowen to stay alert to the fact that the central pretense of modern national identity (thinking of one's country in terms of oneself and vice versa) can no longer be counted on to work for this tribalized class residue ("or seemed so . . .").

At this point we can begin to see the novel laying bare its own principle of composition—the idea that Lois and her "people" are in a reciprocal allegory staged as a story of historical anachronism and prolonged adolescence rather than of joint progress. As I have suggested, the antidevelopmental plot coexists with a more traditional and mechanical concept of "clock time"; it is not that the traditional bildungsroman allegory of national and personal formation is fully abandoned, but that it is present in an objectified or estranged form. *The Last September*, in other words, captures a way of life that cannot survive in a brave new post–British Empire world of separated and relativized national units. The Anglo-Irish themselves recognize, with varying degrees of acuity, that their mannered and manorial existence is a relic of British imperialism. This is not just a buried framework, but part of a continual and bad conversation between the occupying English and the resident Anglo-Irish. The displacement of colonial encounter (and its real violence or violent realness) into bad conversation is a technique that Bowen here elevates into art, tracking miscues, dropping ellipses, punctuating talk with mutter. This is civil strife and national devolution as the stuff of a thousand awkward cocktail parties, perhaps the most politely apt description of postcolonial fragmentation since Forster's "drab sisterhood of nations."

To turn the analysis in that direction, let us return to a crucial scene not often probed in depth by Bowen critics. In it, Gerald Lesworth seeks to explain his role as imperial policeman to Laurence, who turns his waspish intellect to the task of baiting Gerald into a naked and fatuous expression of Anglo superiority:

> "Well the situation's rotten, but right *is* right."
>
> "Why?" [asks Laurence]
>
> "Well . . . from the point of view of civilisation. Also you see they [the Irish republicans] don't fight clean."
>
> "Oh there's no public school spirit in Ireland. But do tell me—what do you mean by the point of view of civilisation?"
>
> "Oh—ours. . . . If you come to think," he explained, "I mean, looking back on history—not that I'm an intellectual—we *do* seem to be the only people."
>
> "Difficulty being to make them see it?"
>
> "—And that we are giving them what they really want. Though of course the more one thinks of it all, the smaller, personally, it makes one feel."
>
> "I don't feel small in that way. But I'm not English—"
>
> "Oh, no—I beg your pardon."
>
> "—Thank God!"
>
> "Don't understand?"
>
> "God may. Shall we look for the others?"
>
> (132)

Laurence mutters his relief at not being English himself—an ostensible insult to Gerald's national pride that he only half hears. The whole exchange unfolds as a set of unfinished lines, miscues, and interruptions, all mixed with interior monologues that confuse more than clarify the dialogue. This method is typical of Bowen's emerging style and takes on exemplary significance in the colonial field of contact. She narrates:

> Their conversation, torn off rough at this edge, seemed doomed from its very nature to incompletion. Gerald would have wished to explain that no one could have a sounder respect than himself and his country for the whole principle of nationality, and that it was with some awareness of misdirection, even of paradox, that he was out here to hunt and shoot the Irish. . . . Laurence had not hoped to explain, but had wished that Gerald could infer, that there was a contrariety in the notions they each had of this thing civilization. As a rather perplexing system of niceties, Laurence saw it; an exact and delicate interrelation of stresses between being and being, like crossing arches; an unemotioned kindness withering to assertion selfish or racial; silence cold with a comprehension in which the explaining clamour died away. He foresaw in it the end of art, of desire, as it would be the end of battle, but it was to this end, this faceless but beautiful negation that he had lifted a glass inwardly while he had said, "Thank God!"
>
> (133–34)

I quote at length because this scene beautifully enacts and anatomizes the fumbling of meaning across cultural lines. It highlights miscommunication between someone who believes that civilization occurs in the effort to communicate cross-culturally, albeit from a position of moral authority secured by dint of colonial force (Gerald) and someone who believes that civilization occurs only when such communication is acknowledged as limited and partial, tending ultimately toward silence and negation (Laurence). Explanation is the key term of this passage. Gerald would have liked to explain himself; Laurence hopes not to have to; in a crucial earlier passage, Lois cannot hope to explain herself. All this thwarted expression seems to signal precisely the end of the "explaining clamour," the incipient silence and negation of Laurence's civilization.[33]

Gerald's thirst for explanation is a familiar quest to transcend cultural difference; it indexes a normative, universalist, and integrative imperative that must be advanced in the colonial contact zones, in the endless and endlessly discursive Great Game that blows hot and cold across the planet. He labors under the White Man's Burden and faces down other (Irish) white men, though he is perplexed, understandably, by the contradictions of imperial power according to which the British forces of civilization must prevail over any merely national claim in order to guarantee the principle of national self-determination. Laurence's contrary notion of civilization is not the integration, but the disintegration of difference. He assumes an impersonal ethical posture that is also a tacit historical observation: The clamor of empire wears away into the cold comprehension of difference. This, I take it, is the buried keynote of the novel's political history. Against Gerald's notion of a permanent (Anglocentric) civilizing mission, Laurence offers a glimpse of national devolution, a strictly *post*colonial gesture in that is neither pro- nor anticolonial. His beautiful negation is, in a sense, what others have called the end of history: Someday, soon perhaps, the wars, the political passions, and the cultural projects that are dedicated to cross-cultural "explanation," and integration, will all come to an end.

What Laurence glimpses or imagines is a burdenless, plotless future of pure coexistence, with difference neither annihilated nor integrated (the twin and contradictory goals of empire), but neutralized into a world map of territorial and identitarian divides. His vision of civilization—a mannerly system of intersubjective checks and balances—does not so much manage the clamorous encounter of difference as defuse it into a bloodless and static silence. He imagines a cellular structure—made *spatial* in the "crossing arches" image—that negates difference and removes the dynamic, libidinal friction of historical encounter. Laurence's tacit "never again" echoes the "not yet" that marks the closing note of *A Passage to India*: Like Forster's Fielding, though in a less elegiac mode, Laurence sees in empire's wake not just national freedom (and not a perpetual round of neocolonial skirmishing), but the broken conversation where colonial contact (and associated forms of conflict or desire) once stood. His vision finds fulfillment in what we might call the devolutionary and anthropological logic of the postcolonial era. Viewed from this perspective, modernist texts like *The Last September* can be seen to chart the emergence of a planetary system of crossed arches, that is, of ethnically and territorially defined cultures devolving into nation-states out of multiracial and multinational empires (and, of course, evolving *into* nation-states out of smaller, differently organized regional units).[34]

Laurence's enervated, proleptically postcolonial viewpoint seems at first to express but ultimately to transform Bowen's nostalgia for the Anglo-Irish past. The knotty and rather abstract figurative language used to capture Laurence's concept of civilization suggests a complex historical attitude that cannot be equated to nostalgia (nor, for that matter, to the callow nihilism often ascribed to Laurence).[35] The text should not be reduced to Bowen's sympathetic recuperation of Anglo-Irish life nor to some kind of moralizing fish-in-a-barrel critique of Ascendancy privilege. Instead, the odd, even strained metaphors of Laurence's meditation can point us to a reading of the novel in which the rich peculiarity of both the figurative language and the antidevelopmental plot reveal not narrow political poses, but a deep-structural view of history. What we see in that view is not just the doom of the Anglo-Irish, but the larger devolutionary shift in which the historically volatile arena of the Anglo-Irish colonial encounter is being reorganized, first, into a battleground, and, eventually, into a no-fly zone of separation and relativism, of artificially bounded national units with territorial claims. Indeed, the futurelessness of the Ascendancy can be charged to the fact that their *class status*—with all the contingencies and mixed loyalties of an intermarried, semimodernized, neofeudal, intercultural existence—has been nationalized, even racialized to some degree, into a fixed *cultural identity*.

This frame of reference for Bowen's project suggests a somewhat unfamiliar and refracted point of comparison to another semi-peripheral site of modernist fiction of the late 1920s and 1930s, a place that, like Bowen's Ireland, is semi-gothically haunted by a planter class in its dying throes: Faulkner's Yoknapatawpha. Here, as Walter Benn Michaels has observed, the novels (his example is *Absalom, Absalom*) shed light on a *soi-disant* civilization that morbidly adheres to its own vanishing way of life ("Absalom, Absalom!" 140–41). If Faulkner, as Michaels would have it, "defeats Sutpen's class ambitions by racializing them" (147), then Bowen too narrates the historical end of the Anglo-Irish in part by indicating the fatefulness of their own self-understanding as a "people" rather than the heirs to certain economic interests definitive of a class. In other words, Faulkner's planters, like Bowen's, have assimilated a justificatory rhetoric of identity by acceding to the dignified—but ultimately fatal—concept of a "way of life." Only this, I think, can explain the finality of Bowen's title and of Danielstown's burning as a horizon beyond which Lois and Laurence's destinies are quite unnarratable.

One thing Bowen's novel does, then, is measure the consequences of an inappropriate, but probably inevitable, extension of the totalizing language of culture to a class. Of course, the accretion of cultural meaning to the category Anglo-Irish is gradual and deep; it is neither existentially superficial nor merely epiphenomenal to the class formation in question. Still, it is possible to say that the Anglo-Irish continually misrecognize themselves as a twentieth-century "people" rather than a social fraction because they are unable to resist the blandishments of national identity, of the dignified but deadly claim to a "vanishing way of life." A pseudoculture without a territorial or political base, they are, in effect, an extinction waiting to happen. It is that odd temporality of anticipated doom in the novel's 1920 setting—combined with the retrospective foreclosure of its 1928–1929 date of composition—that Bowen so compellingly encodes into the fabric of its characterization. Lois, in other words, is the living figure of a cultural death.

The plantocratic end of history adumbrated in Laurence's cold fantasy of devolution points precisely to his own and Lois's symbolic place inside a larger transformation of national culture along lines that provide no mobility, no exit from the prisonhouse of identity. The antidevelopmental plot, crystallized in Lois's arrested adolescence, highlights the utter absence of an undergirding concept of historical progress and social mobility. *The Last September* offers a specifically Anglo-Irish instance of the fundamental shift in the history of the novel that I have been describing in terms of modernist antidevelopmental plots. Modernist novels of youth are generally not novels of social or civilizational progress in any simple way; the older plots of class mobility give way to more clotted and uneven plots pegged to socially fixed identity categories, as in the biopolitical fictions of Jean Rhys.

To put this compressed hypothesis about changing literary forms and devolutionary history into schematic terms, I am taking the antidevelopmental plot in general, and Rhys's and Bowen's versions of it in particular, as signs of modernist fiction's recoding of social antagonism into cultural difference. The colonial setting may provide a particularly clear sense of the historical pressures behind this process—and the trope of frozen youth a particularly visible sign of its narrative entailments—but there are many kinds of modernist texts that encode this broader translation of difference into the increasingly rigid race-culture-nationalism language of twentieth-century devolution. Such an approach to Bowen's work places her at the center of a revisionary model of modernist fiction, understood in terms of the partial displacement of nineteenth-century historical concepts of progress by twentieth-century anthropological concepts of difference as the major frame of reference for novels. Lois Farquar's balky nonprogress to adulthood thus allows us to apprehend modernism's assimilation of the temporally static concept of cultural difference into the novel of social realism.

Once subjectivity bears within itself the devolutionary logic of modern cultural nationalism, the old plotlines of social accommodation and functional intersubjectivity appear to falter on separate tracks. Such a conclusion need not insist on some historically determined law of genre, nor on the absence of metahistorical narratives and civilizational allegories—much less the absence of "history" or "politics" *tout court*—in modernist fiction, but rather on their complicated replotting within a more static, if more globally democratic, map of cultural zones. The formal effects or stylistic correlates of the problem I have described—of social antagonism recoded as cultural difference in general, the devolutionary logic of *The Last September* in particular—are both legible in the reorganization of progressive time signaled by the motif of adolescence. Frozen in her youth, stuck between cultures, hopelessly virginal, Lois can be read as a brilliantly condensed figure for the broader postcolonial process: the widening gap between an imperial and enlightenment narrative of progress and an actual colonial history of broken or uneven development, of civilization splintering into incommensurable cultures. In foregrounding the culture death or historical stalemate of the Anglo-Irish, Bowen's text registers the assimilation of structuralist-functionalist thinking into modernist form, where cultural equilibria—the "crossing arches" of Laurence's new civilization—obscure any universal narratives of historical evolution. Or, rather, the historical change that they chronicle is precisely the twentieth-century story in which the old notion of world-historical progress gives way to innumerable alternative modernities.

7. Conclusion

Alternative Modernity and Autonomous Youth after 1945

Life in the late capitalist era is a constant initiation rite.

—Adorno and Horkheimer, *The Dialectic of Enlightenment*

Yes—"maturity" is hardly compatible with "modernity." And contrariwise. Modern Western society has "invented" youth, mirrored itself in it, chosen it as its most emblematic value—and for these very reasons has become less and less able to form a clear notion of "maturity." The richer the image of youth grew, the more inexorably that of adulthood was drained. The more engaging, we may add, the "novel" of life promised to be—the harder it became to accept its conclusion.

—Franco Moretti, *The Way of the World*

In chapter 6, I located in the fiction of Jean Rhys and Elizabeth Bowen a devolutionary cultural logic that charts the waning power of the old European empires and points to an emerging world-system of ostensibly self-determining national-cultural units. Writing at some insecure remove from the category of citizen, Rhys and Bowen both serve as telling figures in this transition: Their careers carry over from the interwar period into the postcolonial and postmodern era, where the bildungsroman lives on, not only via ongoing experiments with the modernist plot of unseasonable youth but also in the form of more traditional, linear novels of formation. In both of these generic variations, the biographical novel of youth retains a central place in the literary marketplaces of the world. The heterogeneity of the *bildungsromane* in post-1945 canons of Anglophone and world literature should come as no surprise to us: Writers and readers are always free to ignore even influential period-styles attached to self-conscious literary vanguards of the past; more to the point, modernism's attack on linear plots was itself a contradictory project, both developmental and antidevelopmental in the end.

Thus despite the modernist vogue for wayward story lines and extended adolescence, and despite the modernist-era critique of the historicist logic underpinning the bildungsroman, both the coming-of-age novel *and* its developmental imperatives persist alongside of, and after, any modernist revolution of form. In this brief and synoptic conclusion, I try to assess the conceptual and historical limits of this book's claims by considering the afterlife of the unseasonable youth plot, first in relation to challenges posed to developmental discourse by cultural theories of (colonial) difference, then in relation to the Anglophone novel of youth after World War II.

At the start, I proposed that one useful way to define the historical specificity of the modernist era is to locate it at the dialectical switchpoint between residual nineteenth-century narratives of global development and emergent twentieth-century suspicion of such narratives as universalist and Eurocentric. The antidevelopmental bildungsroman reached a peak of symbolic currency in the modernist period perhaps because it mediated—in a recognizable aesthetic form—and staged—in visibly global terms—this deeper struggle between Hegelian historicism and post-Hegelian critiques of historicism. This may also be why modernist fiction still resonates for twenty-first-century readers confronting a theoretical and political divide between worldwide development and a world of differences—that is, between a singular-modernity model that projects a global narrative of modernization and an alternative-modernities model that describes a detemporalized map of raw cultural difference.[1] In the face of these somewhat entrenched positions, the modernist novel of youth, which assimilates into form the dialectic of a developmental time-concept that is undoing itself, may serve as a vital conceptual resource.

The idea of alternative modernities has gained wide currency in the social sciences and the humanities over the last fifteen years. Its force depends largely on the pressure that postcolonial and subaltern studies (and scholarship based on the new social movements) have put on both Hegelian/Marxist and liberal/neoliberal discourses of globalization and on various versions of modernization theory that were dominant in academic and policy circles during the Cold War.[2] The literature of alternative modernities challenges unifying or universal models of world history—what Gayatri Spivak succinctly identifies as "yesterday's imperialism, today's 'Development'" (124)—and particularly resists a modernization model that insists on linking economic and cultural processes in lockstep (so that, for example, a certain degree of capitalization implies a certain kind of secularization). Even modernization theories that try to do justice to historical differences and diverse geographies by invoking the concept of uneven development have been rejected. In the work of Dipesh Chakrabarty, for instance, the ongoing influence of a falsely universal narrative issuing from Enlightenment thought challenges today's historians to shed all forms of stagist thinking as inherently, balefully Eurocentric (9). For Chakrabarty, any totalizing narrative of modernity, "*howsoever* internally differentiated," conjures up that bad metahistorical mantra: "first in the west, then elsewhere" (47; emphasis mine).[3]

Much of the most influential recent work in postcolonial and transnational studies has attempted to work its way outside the Hegelian and Marxist historiographical traditions, often using theoretical resources derived from Nietzsche, Benjamin, Heidegger, and/or Derrida. Alternative modernities positions tend to be staked more or less explicitly to New Social Movements (sex, gender, indigeneity, locality, religious or environmental interest). The rethinking of modernity has come in the form of disciplinary critique (Appadurai in sociology, Chakrabarty in history, Fabian in anthropology, Taylor in philosophy) and from newer academic formations such as Black Atlantic studies (Baucom, Gilroy). It also comes from direct efforts to "unthink Eurocentrism" (Shohat and Stam), to rehistoricize or reorient the global vectors of modernization (Abu-Lughod, Frank), and to understand modernity's complex emplotment and translation in various semi-peripheries (Bhabha, Cheah, Krishnan, Mignolo, Mitchell, Ramos, Saldaña-Portillo, Schwarz, Scott). These varied projects—only some of which proceed under the open banner of "Alternative Modernities"—all in one way or another attempt, in the words of Dilip Gaonkar, to "think with a difference" in order to "destabilize the universalist idioms" of the disciplines (15).

Within literary studies, David Lloyd stands out as a voice that aligns closely with the critical project outlined by Gaonkar and advanced by Chakrabarty, proposing "at once the critique of a singular developmental model and the rethinking of historical time in terms of its possibilities rather than its determinations" (*Irish Times* 100). In a recent rereading of the "medieval sill" in *Stephen Hero* and *Portrait of the Artist as a Young Man*, Lloyd argues that the "assumption of modernity, that its unidirectional flow into the future furnishes the model for all cultures and societies, stumbles and halts at such a threshold." As I have noted in earlier chapters, Lloyd's critical resistance to the "iron temporal logic of developmental historicism" resonates strongly with the figure of extended adolescence in modernism, quite beyond the immediate case of Stephen Dedalus (*Irish Times* 75). Unseasonable youth novels tend to unsettle the assumptions targeted by Lloyd, and—more to my own immediate point—they do so by revealing on every page the overdetermined role of the nation-state form in securing and shaping the narratable destinies of individual and collective subjects (whose modern lives are, of course, never as shapely as the generic coming-of-age plot suggests).

Lloyd's literary criticism locates in symbolic form what Chakrabarty sees in the texture of posthistoricist inquiry, that is, a resistant content or remainder not already modern, nor simply premodern, but legible as a discordant element "internal to the very being (that is, logic) of capital" (65).[4] The rhetoric of recalcitrant or discordant elements quickly assumes the form of a spatial logic within the critical discourse of alternative modernity, and that discourse is intellectually symbiotic with a larger "spatial turn" across the humanities and interpretive social sciences. Within the more delimited field of modernist literary studies, spatial and geographical models have taken hold and illuminated much new territory, contributing to an anti-Eurocentric renovation of the prevailing methodologies.[5]

The spatial turn, with its ongoing call for methods that recognize cultural difference and alternative modernity by the hygiene of geographical rather than historiographical inquiry does, however, carry its own specific intellectual risks: it risks turning comparative analysis into an exotic catalogue of pure differences and it risks an inadequate historical reckoning with the facts and legacies of European/Western power. That is, if a thick description of a frankly Western modernity had once seemed to recapitulate the uncritical self-narration of the rising European bourgeoisie, it has now become clear that a culturally denuded and thin description—or a radically anti-Eurocentric one—can omit the living history of Europe's impositions on non-Western societies.[6] To place many varied artistic and intellectual projects into a drastically foreshortened narrative, one might observe that some of the most challenging attempts to build models of alternative modernity continue to draw on French poststructuralism, a midcentury theoretical avant-garde that staged (via Nietzsche and Heidegger) its own confrontation with Hegelian-Marxist conceptions of historical time and that emerged from the fading power of a historical avant-garde (surrealism in particular) that also tried to storm the Hegelian tower and upend the predominantly narrative forms of nineteenth-century literature and historiography.[7] Aesthetic or cultural anti-Hegelianism, attempting to eschew or escape from unilinear historical time, seems often to court the kind of failure that worried Walter Benjamin, that of heroic philosophical gestures of interruption becoming, in a flash, evanescent motes in a commodified marketplace already glittering with mere sensations and bits of banal information.[8] This could describe the panoply of interwar avant-garde techniques based on shock, interruption, juxtaposition, spatial form, abstraction, frozen dialectics, messianic time—all heroic measures taken against the combined forces of the Hegelian and Whig historiographical imagination and all vulnerable in our own moment to what Fredric Jameson has called the "reduction to the present" ("End of Temporality" 709).[9]

I am suggesting a provisional connection between the politics of time in avant-garde aesthetics and postcolonial theory, and identifying the risk of a temporal or narrative repression in the more obviously spatial or antidevelopmental forms of both. The problem for avant-garde art and radical philosophy then reemerges as a problem for postcolonial and alternative-modernities theory now: how to oppose Hegelian historical destiny without collapsing into an ahistorical vacuum.[10] What was a vital and forceful corrective to universalist metanarratives of modernization, including the Marxian analysis of capitalist modernity, and to Eurocentric accounts of literary history, including old-school glorification of Anglo-American modernism, has perhaps now come to need its own modest corrective in the form of some dialectical pressure on the assumed critical value of proliferating alternative modernities and modernisms.

And there has already been a recent turn, perhaps even a backlash in some quarters, against spatial theory and against the critical veneration of pure difference. In a somewhat dismissive broadside against alternative modernities work, Fredric Jameson has argued for a singular modernity, a unifying narrative that he proposes not so much as desirable, but as inevitable.[11] For Jameson, narrative itself is irrepressible and seeks the highest level of general historical explanation, so that a spatialized and ruptural model of alternative modernities has, at some point, to be set into an overarching temporal frame. To make that narrative productive and accurate, though, Jameson pushes for a vigorous reconceptualization of uneven development, which must be understood as something other than a catalog of way-stations and waiting-rooms on the way to some preordained Hegelian rendezvous with the end of history (*Singular* 144). In a somewhat different register, the anthropologist James Ferguson worries that alternative modernity talk seems to celebrate cultural diversity while ignoring the problems still posed by underdevelopment in the global South. Ferguson suggests that the critique of development has become perhaps only too successful at promoting a model of "alternative" rather than "less" modernity, leaving scholars (and policymakers) without a proper language to address the failures of modernization in places like Zambia. The result, Ferguson proposes, is a detemporalized graph of cultural difference, with weak geopolitical vision, no overarching concept of economic justice, and

little grip on the basic forces that shape cultural production. By banishing development, anthropology may have, paradoxically, hypostasized rather than traversed
the core-and-periphery model it aimed to displace.[12]

Along quite similar lines, Xudong Zhang offers a critical take on Chakrabarty's
Provincializing Europe: "Despite the effectiveness of Chakrabarty's discontent,
many contemporary Chinese intellectuals probably would be hesitant to wage a
theoretical critique of the universal from the self-assumed positionality of the particular. Rather . . . [they] would tend to continue to explore the dialectic of the
universal, which not only sees universality as a political and strategic rhetoric of
the particular (i.e., modern Europe), but, more importantly, allows the reinvention
and redefinition of the universal as a historical totality" ("Modernity" 171).[13] In
The Politics of Time, Peter Osborne helpfully separates the case against the Hegelian "stagist" mode from the case against historical totalization per se, arguing
that the critique of false universalism, while essential, does not necessitate forsak-
ing the concept of totalization. Like Jameson, Ferguson, and Zhang, though in a
more philosophical register, Osborne asks: "What future is there for an emphatic
conception of historical experience after the critique of Hegelianism?" (x)[14] Cultural critics who insist on the theoretical necessity of grasping global historical
processes in their totality have proposed limits on the model of wall-to-wall cultural difference or tried to declare, as Alberto Moreiras has it, the "exhaustion of
difference."[15] For Osborne the question is not *whether* totalization but *which*, for
"we cannot avoid the totalization of history because of the *existential* structure of
temporalization" (x).

The theoretical struggle between difference and development has begun to
seem like an impasse, with one camp championing alternative modernities while
trying to avoid cultural exoticism and the other championing a singular modernity while trying to avoid ethnocentric stagism. Is there a way to recoup the analytical and political value of a cross-cultural and global narrative of modernization
without rebuilding the Procrustean bed of evolutionary world history? What
methods might allow us to navigate between Chakrabarty's claim that a singular
modernity imposes a false, unilinear narrative of transition and Jameson's claim
that alternative modernity makes it impossible to describe transition at all? The
methodological formula of "one world-system, many modernities" may serve as a
working compromise that preserves our ability to think systematically and globally without positing a final or future convergence of modernization processes that
are so obviously discrepant, unequal, and out of sync.[16] In a more modest critical
project within twentieth- and twenty-first-century literary studies, such a formula
may allow us to appreciate the formal operations of novels that manage to capture

the contradictions of modernization ideologies without producing a facile utopian sense that those ideologies can be escaped by force of artistic or intellectual will.

To suggest that novels escape or outflank a theoretical impasse is to make an unapologetic case for the power of literary form as against propositional discourse, and for the residual realism of high modernism as against the more radical anti-developmental and counter-Hegelian modes of avant-gardist writing. Mainstream Anglo-American modernism has always been understood as invested in alternative historical models outside linear or teleological time. Joyce's Viconian cycles, Woolf's cultural Bergsonism, Yeats's occult repetitions, and Lawrence's apocalyptic endings, not to mention the various non-narrative effects implied by modernist totems like Epiphany, Vortex, and Montage: All of these oppose a certain progressive historical consciousness associated with nineteenth-century European thought and with the implied temporality of narrative realism. But the novels examined in the present study tend to splice these alternative or antiprogressive models into the redoubtable existential givens of the biographical novel. The resulting forms are flexible, even motley creations that both reflect and reflect upon the inherited Hegelian time-concepts of modernity—literary objects that resist *and* recapitulate developmental historicism in the verbal tissue of plot, characterization, and imagery.

Many of the antidevelopmental plots that I have identified in modernist fiction coordinate endless youth with arbitrary closure to produce an ironic form. In this way, they can encode a simultaneous rejection of and subjection to existential, bottom-line temporality—the global time of Hegel's world history in one sense (modernization), and the organismic inevitabilities of life span in the biographical novel on the other (maturity, death).[17] With their heterochronic and dilated time-schemes, modernist novels offer, I think, a more critical and more dialectical rejoinder to the Hegelian developmental imperative than did the experimental modes of the historical avant-garde, whose counterdiscursive strikes against the ideology of progress have been, in the long run, more easily assimilated and commodified or dismissed as an encapsulated radical outburst. Modernist fictions of endless youth, even when they make stylistic and aesthetic value out of a detemporalized plot, also reveal the contradictions and vulnerabilities attached to non-modern subjects in a world still organized by modernization theory (despite its disfavor in academic circles).[18]

My reading of modernist fiction has attempted to disclose not just the condensation of historicist and antihistoricist logic into the trope of unseasonable youth, but also to suggest a kind of functional alignment between Anglophone modernism's suspicion of linear time and an anticolonial intellectual project that casts doubt on Western or Eurocentric models of development. It would be easy perhaps to overstate or overvalue this alignment between, on the one hand, the larger decolonizing project with its ideological challenge to developmental historicism (taken, à la Spivak, Chakrabarty, and Lloyd, as a rhetorical technique of Western hegemony, a fusion of Hegelian logic and imperial practice) and, on the other hand, Western aesthetic challenges to developmental or rationalized time both as a "philosophy of history" and as a convention of progressive-biographical fiction. Still, though my textual analysis leans heavily on Western(ized) subjects and their representation, the methodology depends on understanding that even the most intimate modernist interiors open out to a world of political and historical effects shaped in and by colonial as well as metropolitan subjects.

I have to this point finessed the pressing methodological question of whether the changing world-system is a material predicate for the antidevelopmental novel of youth in modernism, or whether there is instead simply a convenient symbolic affinity (a "neat fit") between uneven development in the geopolitical sphere and arrested development in the modernist novel. Having now adduced the literary evidence, I would venture to say that the intellectual crisis of progress in the late nineteenth century (and its associated historiographies of decline, its new human sciences of biopolitical difference) does strongly, if not deterministically, mediate between the material collapse of the Western empires and the artistic power of modernist form. The texts examined here, in all their variety, cut the process of aging from between the twin plot points of youth/exposition and death/closure, removing the connective tissue definitive of historicism itself. The resulting form establishes a dialectical rather than an antinomial relation between world-historical development aimed at a shared destiny and a world of static, anthropologized differences splayed on a planetary grid.

Such a dialectical relation, I have claimed, can be rendered in narrative form more powerfully and more subtly than it can be established in direct or propositional discourse.[19] The novels at the center of this study give vivid narrative form to the central contradiction of modernity, a contradiction made most conspicuous in the colonial contact zones of the last hundred years: Modernity is a state of permanent transition. Its most trenchant literary incarnation is, then, the story of endless youth. The trope of adolescence, once conceived as but a prelude to age, as referring to the inexorably organic process of maturation, and—by allegorical extension—to some particular script of full modernization, can and does change its meaning and function over time. A sedimented logic of organic development lingers on necessarily in the bildungsroman's "ideology of form," but modernist practitioners are able to take account of the genre's own aging and transformation (its own historicity), and thus to objectify and expose (without eliminating altogether) its progressive conventions. In certain fictions, indeed, youth seems to refer simultaneously to the developmental process (maturation, modernization) *and* to its arrest or undoing in the form of adolescence-without-adulthood. If fictions of pure youth invert the classic plot of formation and assimilate the differential temporality of uneven development, they also reveal the ideological romance of permanent adolescence by insisting, with clear-eyed political realism, that modernization, like human aging, cannot be forever forestalled. They peel away the residua of romantic nationalism from the bildungsroman plot, compromising its ability to turn the *chronos* of open-jawed modernity into the *kairos* of national destiny; in this sense, they present the trope of youth in its essence as endless mutability, confessing in its refusal of fixed adulthood to the permanence of our revolutions, to the evergreen and ruthless vitality of capitalism's creative destruction. In this precise sense, too, the fiction of unseasonable youth stays relevant because it gives aesthetic form to what Edward Said called "the unresolved (and unresolvable) dialectic of colonialism" (*Reflections* 263).

Unseasonable youth, in short, activates two reality principles within the modernist novel: 1) that capitalist transformation has been a constant revolutionary force in modernity not to be harnessed or naturalized by an organic rhetoric of subjectivity or statehood; and 2) that the force of historicist or teleological thinking animates colonial and neocolonial projects even after its universalist substrata have been exposed, challenged, and discredited. To imagine a purely intellectual or philosophical or aesthetic redress to the force of developmental historicism—to conjure a space fully outside of its effects—is to lose a critical grip on the need for actual social transformation to accompany any revolution of ideas or values. My own investment in modernism's dialectical relationship to the contradictions of progress discourse translates into an interpretive method via this Adornean principle: "A successful work . . . is not one which resolves objective contradictions in a spurious harmony, but one which expresses the idea of harmony negatively by *embodying* the contradictions, pure and uncompromised, in its innermost structure" (*Prisms* 32; emphasis added). I have staked this book's argument to works that only partially and only dialectically exert their force against the progressive logic of developmental historicism enshrined in classic *Bildung*. Modernist narratives that mix frozen youth and sudden death, that graft regressive, decadent, and static temporal sequences onto otherwise linear plots—these texts continue to engage readers now because we are still in doubt about the outcome of an ongoing globalization process. Whether modernity's future is discrepant and divergent, or singular and unilinear, remains an open question in 2011 much as it was in 1911.

Narratives of autonomous or endless or stunted youth thus offer back to Western and non-Western readers a deeply layered and embedded allegory of uneven development, an encoding of the contradiction between an always underdeveloped or immature economic periphery and an ultimately false but still influential narrative of planetary progress and socioeconomic convergence. It makes sense, therefore, that even long after 1945 and the supposed end of modernism, the arrested-development plot remains valuable and resonant as a narrative device, a running dialectical rejoinder to the most rigid or incoherent forms of developmental historicism, alive at once to the risks of stories with false endings and stories with no endings.

. . .

Having left off my literary history in chapter 6 with Elizabeth Bowen and interwar Ireland, it is perhaps fitting to pick up this brief genealogy of late and broken *bildungsromane* with Samuel Beckett and Flann O'Brien, two Irish novelists committed to the plot of the arrested protagonist. Beckett's *Murphy* and O'Brien's *At Swim-Two-Birds*, both published in 1938, define a parodic line of Irish modernism by warping—more deeply than did Joyce—the generic ideal of a self-possessed hero coming of age in sync with his society. In *At Swim*, the plot simply opens up and self-divides rather than moving forward while the protagonist-narrator remains in a languid adolescent funk. In *Murphy*, the titular hero takes failed development and moral stasis to even more hilariously and scabrous parodic extremes, travestying the modernist novel of consciousness, the naturalist novel of downward mobility, and the realist novel of vocation and courtship alike. Murphy turns the Goethean formula of "mobility and interiority" on its head, seeking nothing less than pure immobility (for which he will bind himself to a chair or a padded cell) and pure (if blank) ideation.[20] In his seedy intellectualism and mania for passive, indolent self-contemplation, Murphy perfectly mocks the notion of the active national hero (as in Lukácsian historical realism), flouting and fulfilling Irish stereotypes as he goes. In the end, Murphy is unmade and literally exploded; the novel concludes with a mock-tragic scattering of the hero's remains in the shrine of Irish literary tradition, the Abbey Theater. Like Rhys and Bowen (though with a more satiric tone), and indeed like Joyce and O'Brien, Beckett invites his readers first to recognize the residual signs of a soul-nation allegory, then to delight in their comic devastation as ideological or narrative points of organization for the modern novel.[21]

These colonial writers fit into what we now see as a global Anglophone canon of twentieth-century writing. To take up one further 1930s example, we might cite Mulk Raj Anand's *Coolie* (1936), which also casts doubt on the notion of the heroic protagonist, the representative youth, and the entire mode of biographical closure. As Jessica Berman notes in a recent examination of *Coolie* within the networks of transnational modernism, and particularly in relation to the influential model of Joyce's *Portrait of the Artist* as a story of unfulfilled destiny: "The imbrication of nation and biography within a bildungsroman set in a colony struggling for its independence ensures that the biography cannot go far" (476). Another early landmark in the Anglophone colonial/postcolonial canon of revisionary novels of youth is G. V. Desani's *All About H. Hatterr* (1948), which operates in the expansive, comic, and dilatory mode of *Tristram Shandy*.

In the period immediately following World War II, plots of frozen youth and compromised closure continue, as in the modernist period, to signify in two directions at once, marking the overlapping territories of failed or stalled modernization and of incessant or hypermodernization. Among the landmark novels of arrested/accelerated development in the 1950s, perhaps the most scandalous is Nabokov's *Lolita* (1955). In it, the exiled aesthete Humbert Humbert, adrift in consumerist America, fixates on Lolita's adolescence as a token of timeless desire and discovers that he is himself an arrested naïf. With obliquity equaling Beckett's, Nabokov's playful work refracts and transcodes the historical traumas of Europe (revolution, world war, holocaust, totalitarianism, and the dawn of the nuclear age) into a plot of stalled subject formation. So too does Günter Grass's *The Tin Drum* (1959), the book that most crystallizes the trope of frozen youth as an indispensable and flexible literary device for the post-1945 novel of traumatic historicism. At roughly the same time, William Golding's nuclear-age parable of decivilization, *Lord of the Flies* (1954), captures even more directly the extended logic of generational rupture and autonomous youth; in the process, the novel has become a Cold War classic of and for young adults. As Franco Moretti notes, Golding's text encodes the dark myth of childhood cut loose from adult authority, elaborating a modernist tradition of the "counter-*Bildungsroman*" (232). Golding's metaphysical and parabolic novel seems also to pick up the energies of anarchic-dystopian youth plots from Graham Greene's early moral realism, as evident in *Brighton Rock* (1938) and as revived, brilliantly, in "The Destructors" (1954). *Lord of the Flies* literalizes and modernizes the mixed, ironic potential of *Lord Jim*, evacuating the twin conceits of the "boys' island" plot and the imperial quest-romance to the point of a full demystification of progressive European values.

By the 1960s, the most important challenges to the conventional novel of progress, and to "Eurochronology" itself, were said to come from the ex-colonial peripheries and semi-peripheries, particularly Latin America. Boom novelists such as Gabriel García Márquez established a house style for international magical realism that organized itself against the standard tropes of biographical and developmental fiction. Quite soon after this, the Anglophone novel of the global South had its own practitioners of fabulist and experimental historical fiction, most notably the hypercanonical Salman Rushdie, whose *Midnight's Children* (1981) stands out as an influential novel of youth for the post-1945 period. Rushdie's exorbitant and dilatory narrative conceits draw from many Western and non-Western sources, ranging from *Tristram Shandy* to the *Arabian Nights*; he also cites Günter Grass as a formative influence on his early work. No surprise then, that Saleem Sinai, the protagonist of *Midnight's Children*, comes of age in a most unusual way, shaped overtly by the problem of national allegory, which Rushdie presents as a convention overcoded and overdetermined by new nationhood on the one hand and by English and Indian literary traditions on the other. Saleem opens the novel in direct first-person address to his allegorical predicament: "I had been mysteriously handcuffed to history, my destinies indissolubly chained to those of my country" (3). Later, Saleem tells readers what we already know: "You will perceive the unavoidable connection between the infant state's attempts at rushing towards full-sized adulthood and my own early, explosive efforts at growth" (286). Saleem's body bears the telepathic and representative burden of nationhood so spectacularly that he estranges the conventions of the soul-nation allegory all the way back to Goethe.[22]

Rushdie's conceits reveal the inherent contradictions of national allegory, underscoring the limits of the organicist and idealist logic attached to soul-nation stories of harmonized growth. In the end, Saleem (like Beckett's Murphy) falls prey to a mock-tragic *sparagmos*, the dismemberment of the nation. The hero falls to pieces: "I am literally disintegrating, slowly for the moment, although there are signs of an acceleration. I ask you only to accept (as I have accepted) that I shall eventually crumble into (approximately) six hundred and thirty million particles of anonymous, and necessarily oblivious dust" (37).[23] Later, in *The Moor's Last Sigh* (1995), Rushdie revisits the trope of the unseasonable hero, reversing Saleem Sinai's urge to "grow illogically backwards in time" by imagining a hero, Moraes Zogoiby, who grows forward in time, but "double quick" (*Midnight's* 101; *Moor's* 143). Zogoiby's half-Christian, half-Jewish, half-European, half-Asian life seems like a retroping of Saleem's merely national crisis of allegorization; now the body and fate of the ill-clocked protagonist take on the full sweep of planetary violence, displacement, and identitarian struggle, from the Crusades to the ethnic clashes of the present. History, for Moraes "the Moor" Zogoiby, as for those other unseasonable youths, Joyce's Stephen Dedalus and Grass's Oskar Matzerath, is a nightmare from which it is not possible to awake. If *Midnight's Children* is an allegory of national youthfulness and traumatic disintegration, then *The Moor's Last Sigh* is a weary saga of cosmopolitan ennui. The national youth of the one and the international senescence of the other both index a painful vulnerability to the more or less constant fallout of political history.

If we think of writers like Grass and Rushdie in the framework of unseasonable youth, we can see their point of thematic convergence on the failure of organic *Bildung* as crucial to the articulation of what has become, I think, the dominant style of belated and dispersed modernisms all over the Western-mediated literary canons of the global South: that is, a magical realist or fabulist style attached to melancholic historicism (which often entails a tonally comic explosion of the truth-value of historical records). The route from Grass to Rushdie covers the two paradigmatic forms of historical trauma in the post-1945 world—the aftermaths of European totalitarianism and imperialism. Both post-Holocaust and postcolonial legacies are indeed global phenomena in which the notion of a Western modernity leading to worldwide progress was comprehensively undone. The renarrativization of those forms of civilizational crisis must therefore be analytically central to any account of the novel of (arrested) development as a world genre in the contemporary period.

And in fact we find telling instances of the coming-of-age tale, bent and inflected by nonlinear temporalities, set as the generic pretext for experimental and fabulist distortions of developmental history. In Tahar Ben Jelloun's *The Sand Child* (1985), dizzying metafictional play underscores the unknown and truncated destiny of the transgendered protagonist, a Moroccan girl whose stunting is both literal and figurative. In Ben Okri's *The Famished Road* (1991), another postcolonial instant classic of magical realism, the protagonist is a "spirit child" who can never, in a strict sense, reach adulthood. Of course there are also dozens of significant post-1945 novels that unfold in an essentially realist idiom, complicating the coming-of-age plot more at the level of theme than in the form of an obvious stylistic experiment. In such texts, youthful avatars reveal the general failure of socialization and education in their countries, representing not the promise of the decolonization era, but the disillusionment and breakdown of postcolonial states and subjects in the late 1960s and after. Consider, for example, these novels of thwarted selfhood and often violent dispossession: Tayeb Salih's *Season of Migration to the North* (1966), Thomas Keneally's *The Chant of Jimmie Blacksmith* (1972), or Bessie Head's *The Question of Power* (1973). Many postcolonial novels anticipate or echo *Midnight's Children* (not to mention Woolf's *Voyage Out* or Mann's *Magic Mountain*) by describing a central character whose body bears symptoms of a social breakdown, a self more unmade than made. In *Nervous Conditions* (1988), Tsitsi Dangarembga describes a protagonist with an eating disorder who in a quite literal sense refuses to grow; likewise, in Albert Wendt's *Flying-Fox in a Freedom Tree* (1989), the protagonist's wasting disease seems to literalize his refusal of modernization in Samoa, rejecting growth in both organic and neocolonial terms.

Rapidly modernizing societies produce novels of troubled growth and failed *Bildung*; this fairly obvious critical observation seems to be as true of post-1945 postcolonial literary history as of the late nineteenth-century European canon. When we use a genre like the bildungsroman to track formal variation across time and space, from Hardy's Wessex, say, to Achebe's Igboland, we do not need to present the later, so-called peripheral texts as belated echoes of an original European or Western problematic. Pheng Cheah makes the point well: "The fact that these ideas received their first elaborate formalization in German philosophy does not make decolonizing and postcolonial nationalisms derivative of a European model. They are comparable responses to a common experience of intense structural transformation—whether this takes the form of Napoleonic invasion, nineteenth-century territorial imperialism, or uneven globalization" (6). What we call Goethean motifs of the bildungsroman—mobility, interiority, self-cultivation, self-possession, bourgeois-bohemian compromise, integrative realism, soul-nation allegory—are themselves already iterative and self-conscious from their inception, as critics such as Redfield and Sammons have thoroughly established. In other words, to read the bildungsroman in a cross-cultural or transhistorical way serves not so much to enshrine a genre's European origins but to underscore the iterative, belated quality of its conventions even in their supposedly original form.[24]

Even so, there are real and determinate historical changes that mark the long transnational life of genres, and while it is certainly the case that novels of integrative or "classic" *Bildung* continue to be written, published, and read across the world today, few self-consciously literary writers produce realist coming-of-age tales that sustain an unproblematic national allegory of progress without some reference to the modernist scrambling of developmental time or some recourse to the acknowledged failures of "development" as both Western ideology and global policy mantra. These factors, naturally, impinge on the postcolonial bildungsroman in ways that distinguish it from the coming-of-age novel in industrial-age Western Europe.[25] Most postcolonial fiction read in North America, whether of the magical-realist/late-modernist kind or of the more conventionally realist kind, would resist reduction to Bakhtin's concept of "national-historical time" as the mark of emergence into modernity. As Peter Hitchcock aptly notes in his recent study of the serial novel as a contemporary global form, "even when they explicitly address the critical form of nationhood," such novels tend to establish a "primary axis of narration [that] favors a chronotope irreconcilable with the nation that is its putative object" (30). What Hitchcock observes in the postcolonial tetralogies and trilogies of writers like Pramoedya Ananta Toer and Assia Djebar can also be noted in Doris Lessing's 1950s "Children of Violence" novel sequence, in which the halting progress of the youthful protagonist of *Martha Quest* throws into relief a) the failures of late colonial development in southern Africa; b) the adolescent stultification of the provincial white settler class; and c) the growing autonomization of youth subcultures from the generational power of their predecessors.[26]

Even if the national frame of development is a discredited allegorical partner for the subject growing up in the postcolonial novel, the bildungsroman as a genre of socialization and self-formation continues to operate as a vital cultural and artistic force in post-1945 literature. Bruce Robbins has made this point vividly in his readings of contemporary fiction, both metropolitan and nonmetropolitan, observing that narratives of upward mobility play a crucial role in framing, defining, channeling, and even producing the political hopes and desires of their makers and consumers.[27] We find the narrative of self-cultivation and of what Gregory Castle calls "socially pragmatic" coming of age all over the "world literature" curriculum now taught (at least in North America); here one might mention an early generation of postcolonial texts such as George Lamming's *In the Castle of My Skin* (1953), Naguib Mahfouz's *Palace of Desire* (1957), V. S. Naipaul's *Miguel Street* (1959), Chinua Achebe's *No Longer at Ease* (1960), as well as more recent novels such as Zee Edgell's *Beka Lamb* (1982), Jamaica Kincaid's *Annie John* (1985), Arundhati Roy's *God of Small Things* (1997), Jhumpa Lahiri's *The Namesake* (2003), or Khaled Hosseini's *The Kite Runner* (2003).[28]

In many of these texts, the frame of social reference for the narrative of emergence (however troubled or baffled) is not always, or not exclusively, the nation-state. For example, Rita Felski sees the possible rejuvenation of the bildungsroman in the post-1945 period in relation to women's communities. Other social movements, based on regional, religious, sexual, gender, indigenous, or ecological concepts, can and do provide a logic of emergence and development, even of potential liberation, to novels of youth. On the other hand, as Joseph Slaughter has amply demonstrated, the postcolonial bildungsroman often establishes its primary contextual relation to universalist or humanist concepts of the individual as a rights-bearing entity, and thereby deemphasizes the mediating social categories of nationality, religion, class, and gender. Slaughter's argument is crucial and timely, especially insofar as it identifies the preserved idealist core of the original bildungsroman concept, that is, the concept of free self-development that persists in the genre's postcolonial iterations and has now become "part of the freight of globalization as the West has prosecuted it through colonialism, (neo)imperialisms, international humanitarianism, and multinational consumer capitalism" (123). What Slaughter observes here is the ideological force of the biographical novel to enshrine and naturalize a flawed faith in human rights as the engine or locus of social justice in our time; moreover, his work charts a continuity from the consent-seeking function of the bildungsroman as a genre of universal development in the eighteenth century all the way through to the consent-seeking function of the genre as a specialized aesthetic commodity in the current world-system of literature.

It is however also true that in many cases the bildungsroman, particularly in its late modernist guise as a novel of frozen youth, resists this culturally affirmative role in order to incarnate and expose the negative logic of permanent capitalist transition, a task made all the more urgent in the era of global structural adjustments and internationalized finance. That is, by using the organismic logic of the bildungsroman against itself, by autonomizing youth into a trope with no fixed destination, the novel can continue to bring the force of modernist critique to bear on the *mythos* of development, exposing it as a more or less eternal logic of deferral. The contemporary bildungsroman often links the realist representation of autonomized youth cultures and subcultures to a more coded deployment of pure youthfulness taken as a running symbol of capitalism's endless transition, and stripped of the moralizing and dignifying rhetoric of national progress, civilizing mission, or even human rights.

This encapsulated thesis about the meaning of autonomous youth in a consumerist, late capitalist, and global context points us back to Britain, which, by virtue of specific histories and institutions of education, seems to occupy a privileged place in any analysis of youth culture as an economically and socially distinct segment of modern market society. Autonomous youth indeed provides a thumbnail description of much post-World War II fiction in the British tradition, works that we might ordinarily approach through the sociological category of juvenile delinquency in a permissive society, the psychological concept of extended adolescence in an affluent society, the existentialist description of anomie and alienation in a post-traditional society, the economic analysis of underemployment in a service- and information-based welfare state, or, finally, the moral notion of innate depravity in the neorealist or metaphysical idiom of post-1945 literary fiction.

Within the British literary sphere, the moral realism of Golding and Greene, cited earlier, and the alienation of the so-called Angry Young Men writers of the 1950s often manifested themselves in plots of moody, frozen adolescence. Both strands carry over into the 1960s in such darkly satirical and youth-centric novels as Muriel Spark's *The Prime of Miss Jean Brodie* (1961) and Anthony Burgess's *A Clockwork Orange* (1966). Spark's Brodie, perpetually in her prime, always in "a state of fluctuating development," embodies the novel's own ambivalence about the struggle between adult authority and youthful rebellion (and, at another level, between theological destiny and individual moral agency) (45). In the 1960s, and long after, novels invested in the problem of unaccommodated or stylized youthfulness continue to resonate, and to speak to a paradoxical situation in which an ever-transforming variety of consumer freedoms and technological innovations coexist with deeply limited and limiting brands of social and economic mobility.

In the Thatcher and post-Thatcher eras, British-sphere novels of youth often function as stories of alienation and of impossible social reconciliation, whether because of values conflict and identity crises (as in a text like Jeanette Winterson's *Oranges Are Not the Only Fruit* [1985]) or other forms of unemployment and economic marginalization that produce arrested adolescence (as in Irvine Welsh's *Trainspotting* [1993]), or both. Two writers whose names now crop up as representatives of the English novel—Ian McEwan and Kazuo Ishiguro—are also galvanized by the figure of uncanny and parentless youth. Rarely has the problem of mismade children—of subjects developing toward an utter absence of a social future—received a more perfectly chilled dystopian treatment as it has in Ishiguro's cloning-and-harvesting science fiction *Never Let Me Go* (2005). McEwan, for his part, picks up the threads of Greene's "The Destructors," Burgess's *Clockwork Orange*, and Golding's *Lord of the Flies* and weaves them across his career, beginning luridly with *The Cement Garden* (1978)—in which the anarchic (and incestuous) plot of children-without-grownups comes home to roost in the suburbs. More recently, in *Saturday*, terror visits the genteel domestic space of Henry Perowne in the form of another parentless and futureless figure, a stunted and diseased invader. Even before the more sensational violence of the midplot, McEwan transmits his thematic preoccupations in a scene where Perowne reflects on his own son's chaotic bedroom:

> A race of extra-terrestrial grownups is needed to set right the general disorder, then put everyone to bed for an early night. God was supposed to be a grown-up, but in disputes He childishly took sides. Then sending us an

actual child, one of His own—the last thing we needed. A spinning rock
already swarming with orphans.

(122)

The orphan swarm of British fiction rises out of the Victorian realist novel—in
which found parents, or new homes and relationships, often reattach the youthful protagonist to a social role; it then spreads much more dangerously into the
contemporary canon, where rootless, endless adolescence is rarely resolved by
novelistic closure.

Of course, there is a much lighter-hearted lineage of coming-of-age novels in
the post-1945 English scene, a set of comic or satirical youthful-alienation plots,
ranging from Kingsley Amis's *Lucky Jim* (1954) and, in a different vein, Colin
MacInnes's *Absolute Beginners* (1959) through to the work of more contemporary
"Lad Lit" writers such as Martin Amis, Jonathan Coe, Nick Hornby, and Will Self.
In 2003, Self published *Dorian*, a novel of dilated adolescence that brings my own
critical narrative full circle by announcing itself as the latest reworking of Wilde's,
and modernism's, most durably sensational plot. Tracking the century's lag from
Dorian Gray to *Dorian*, the plot of autonomous youth (that is, youth separated
from the narrative and social imperatives of maturity and social reconciliation),
once understood in the modernist canon according to the motif of the socially
marginal aesthete, seems to have taken on a more dispersed form via the sociological or commercial concept of "youth culture" as the main signifier of a generation gap. Lad Lit novels are frankly invested in the world of commodities and
subcultural styles even when maintaining a satiric distance on consumer excesses.
Calling youth culture "a genuine creation of capitalism," Francis Mulhern sees the
novel of adolescence in post-1945 Britain and Ireland as an uncritical genre reflective of a quietist and baffled form of social rebellion: "The cultural foregrounding of youthfulness idealizes an achieved process of economic and social change,
while mystifying its character and further possibilities" (*Present* 26). The novel of
youth and self-formation thus carries into the post-1945 era, in Western and non-
Western contexts, both its capacity to index the desire for liberation and self-fulfillment and a more or less continuous ironization and foreclosure of that desire.
The latter impulse finds its most vivid expression in the missing narrative station
of adulthood.

As we have seen, developmental and antidevelopmental plots always coexisted
in the bildungsroman going back to its Goethean incarnation, but the modernist
foregrounding of the antilinear and nonteleological elements of the genre left a
legacy to contemporary literature in which the range of structural and stylistic

options widened for the novel of youth and socialization. Whether in a more or less linear form, however self-consciously modernist or realist, the contemporary bildungsroman continues to be a crucial symbolic form for placing the project of individual development in relation to local, national, and global concepts of progress. As Douglas Mao notes, and as continues to be true of the novel as a world form even in so-called post-literate societies, "one of the main things literature does is tell of the growth of an individual human being in a social context" (6). Coming-of-age tales, or novels of formation and development, grow thick on the ground in almost every language and national tradition. The classic bildungsroman—a conventionally linear narrative of cultural adjustment, moral uplift, and social mobility—continues to flourish all through the twentieth century and into the twenty-first, a de rigueur model for apprentice novelists entering newer as well as older literary marketplaces across the globe. Of course, a subset of youth novels, the stories of *failed* maturity, tends to be canonized by elite literary institutions attuned to the tragedies of modernization. In those latter novels, unseasonable youth points readers away from the eschatologies of identity formation, and toward a never-ending story of social transformation within the capitalist world-system.

Those now-classic texts of frozen youth, *Dorian Gray, Lord Jim, The Voyage Out, Portrait of the Artist*—and all the others examined in this study—reveal that the bildungsroman (and critical reflections on it) always serves as a laboratory for reflection about the place of the individual self in larger histories. The novels of Wilde, Conrad, Woolf, and Joyce constitute a somewhat domesticated modernism of the North American curriculum—the books many of us continue, rather unexperimentally, to read, love, and teach. But they are, however familiar now, still stunning narrative experiments that break up and reorganize—without seeking fully to banish or destroy—linear, historicist time as the organizing principle of form, biography, and history itself. To my view, that is the source of their ongoing relevance and resonance as historical artifacts marked by a certain moment in the history of forms and social formations, but also as irreducible narrative works in their own right, unexhausted by analysis and allegorization. As densely compacted as modernism's unseasonable youth is, working so intensively to trope the impossible historicism of a postnational age of empires and global markets, the figure of unseasonable youth cannot be exhausted by the analytical category of uneven development. Outside any critical reading of this polyvalent figure, beyond its refraction of the past and its implication in the present, lies its ability to direct meaning to the future. Bakhtin on the semantic limits, and potential, of biographical form:

An individual cannot be completely incarnated into the flesh of existing sociohistorical categories. There is no mere form that would be able to incarnate once and forever all of his human possibilities and needs, no form in which he could exhaust himself down to the last word, like the tragic or epic hero; no form that he could fill to the very brim, and yet at the same time not splash over the brim. There always remains an unrealized surplus of humanness; there always remains a need for the future, and a place for this future must be found. . . . Reality as we have it in the novel, is only one of many possible realities; it is not inevitable, not arbitrary, it bears within itself other possibilities.

(*Dialogic* 37)

So it is that the modernist novel of unseasonable youth—far from remaining a fixed allegory, frozen in its own time or yoked to a receding legend of sepia-tinted crisis in the West—continues instead to tell us stories of a yet unrealized humanity, opening up new possibilities for other seasons, and in the minds of other readers.

Notes

Chapter One: Introduction

1. While the experimental motifs of reverse aging and frozen youth are not restricted to Euro-American modernisms of the 1880–1940 period, there is a notable concentration of key novels within that frame. One might, for example, describe *The Great Gatsby* (1925) as a hypercanonical novel of arrested development; just a few years before *Gatsby*, Fitzgerald published "The Curious Case of Benjamin Button" (1921), in which the protagonist ages backward. From the semiperiphery of the Atlantic world, Machado de Assis's stunning 1881 masterpiece *The Posthumous Memoirs of Brás Cubas* reinvents the coming-of-age tale by describing the "decomposition" of its shabby-aristocratic Brazilian protagonist (*Brás Cubas* 18). Viewing the same problem from the decaying center of the old European empires (in this case, the Hapsburg empire), Stefan Jonsson cites Musil's work as another endpoint for the norm of socially integrated character formation, arguing that *The Man without Qualities* "orchestrates a historical moment in which development has reached a halt and nobody knows how to move forward." More to the point, Jonsson notes that "the multiplication of narrative lines reflects a social situation in which no normative national and imperial identity exists" (240). On twentieth-century *antibildungsromane* in the German tradition, see Barney and Boes ("Apprenticeship").

2. The modernists themselves, of course, declared their intentions to reorganize character and plot in ways that would challenge linear or progressive assumptions about both subject formation and novelistic form—assumptions that they attributed, however tendentiously and oedipally, to the Victorians. Since then, most critical studies identify nonlinear development as fundamental to modernist expression in prose fiction. Representative critics would include Irving Howe, who wrote in the 1960s that modernism tends to see character, "not as a coherent, definable, and well-structured entity, but as a psychic battlefield, or an insoluble puzzle, or the occasion for a flow of perceptions and sensations" (qtd. in Lunn 37). Astradur Eysteinsson, some twenty-five years later, notes that "the aesthetic proclivities of modernism seem bound to go against the very notion of narrativity, narrative progression, or storytelling in any traditional sense" (187). In *Chronoschisms*, Ursula Heise proposes that the generative and generational time schemes attached to the

human life span or family saga in nineteenth-century fiction become compressed and syncopated in modernism (52).

3. Patricia Spacks's *Adolescent Idea* takes an extended view of literary history, resisting any periodizing that is cut too fine and describing childhood and adolescence as focal points for literary nostalgia over a long period beginning in the late eighteenth century. But she does assign a particular salience to modernist adolescence: "Tension between generations, adult fear of youthful sexuality and aggression, anxiety about the loss of passional energy in moving from youth to maturity—these issues recur from *Pamela* to *The Bertrams*: and after. As the nineteenth century drew to a close, however, England had partly lost the context of social and moral assumptions that once contained and controlled such tension, fear, and anxiety. Valuing innocence over experience, yet understanding the distortions implicit in efforts to preserve innocence, thinkers about youth had reached a logical impasse" (226). Ever attuned to the intellectual foibles of his fellow modernists, Wyndham Lewis had already begun to identify and deride the cult of youth in the 1920s and 1930s, blasting it comprehensively in his 1932 *Doom of Youth*.

4. *Peter Pan* is a signature text of the Edwardian period and, like so many of the novels analyzed in this study, seems to have its figuration of youth strongly modulated and inflected by the politics of empire. In her authoritative study of *Peter Pan*'s cultural profile, Jacqueline Rose observes that "racism has indeed always been one of the subtexts of *Peter Pan—Peter Pan* can also be read as one of the great myths of an empire in decline" (xii). On the formal level too, Rose's study proves relevant to the modernism of stalled adolescence. One of Rose's points in reviewing the publication history of *Peter Pan* is that Barrie had a difficult time turning the dramatic situation of *Peter Pan* into a *narrative*, particularly insofar as it was built around that famous and sprightly paradox: "all children, except one, grow up" (Rose 67).

5. Simon Gikandi has suggested a similar reconsideration of modernism in relation to empire: "We have forgotten how often modernist art forms derive their energy from their diagnosis of the failure of the imperial enterprise, and how modernism produces its narrative authority by becoming enmeshed—against its overt intentions, perhaps—in the politics of empire and in the conflict between colonial culture and a changing global economic and cultural system" (161).

6. I use the terms "underdevelopment" and "underdeveloped" in this book to describe what, from a Western perspective, appears as the uneven economic and technological development of the colonial periphery. Seeking to analyze rather than to replicate a progressivist and Eurocentric logic, I do not attach specific cultural value to the terms "developed" and "underdeveloped."

7. This claim builds on Raymond Williams's basic insight that the "real historical development" of the twentieth century was the "extension to the whole world of that division of functions which in the nineteenth century was a division of functions within a single state" (*The Country and the City* 279). For a parallel argument that follows the division of labor in particular from intranational to international forms, see Robbins, *Upward Mobility* 232–43.

8. Edmund Wilson's "The Kipling That Nobody Read" (1941) argued that Kipling fails to resolve the dualism implied in the tug-of-war between East and West. Irving Howe's rejoinder—subsequently endorsed in the main by Noel Annan and Edward Said—is that there is no conflict, in fact, since neither Kipling nor Kim sees the interests of colonizer and

colonized as fundamentally opposed (Howe 154; Annan 342–43; Said, Introduction 23). Of course, the absence of ideological conflict from the consciousness of characters or author does not imply its absence from the text; as Benita Parry observes: "If Kipling was serenely unaware" of rising Indian nationalism, "his writings were not" (128).

9. As Kim himself notes, he seems to embody a principle of pure narrativity: "I go from one place to another as it might be a kick-ball. It is my *Kismet*" (101). Kipling later observed in *Something of Myself* that, "*Kim*, of course, was nakedly picaresque and plotless—a thing imposed from without" (*Kim* 277). The odd temporality of the text means that it both is and is not a tale of arrested development; Suvir Kaul observes that Kim "remains a boy" yet has experiences that are "adult in their form and significance" (427).

10. Irving Howe notes, somewhat in passing, that Kim is Huck Finn's "distant cousin" (148).

11. The quoted phrase is Francis Huchins's indelible description of British rule in India.

12. Likewise John McClure notes that, in *Kim*, "what Kipling excludes, ultimately, is history, the vital forces changing Indian society" (80). Many critics past and present have seen *Kim* as a projection of its author's blinkered and even puerile political views. George Orwell once described Kipling as a "sulking" adolescent who "never had any grasp of the economic forces underlying imperial expansion" (273). Howe too describes Kipling's sensibility as having an "adolescent and stunted" dimension (148).

13. Kipling was aware of his limits as an architect of narrative form: "As to its form there was but one possible to the author, who said that what was good enough for Cervantes was good enough for him," to which his mother replied, "Don't you stand in your wool-boots hiding behind Cervantes with *me*! You *know* you couldn't make a plot to save your soul" (*Something of Myself*, qtd. in *Kim* 275).

14. It little needs repeating that there are imperialist and racialist fantasies at work in the conceit of the white Irish foundling who passes in India as the Little Friend of all the World. Kipling's bedrock commitment to the curatorial idea that the British imperial state is adequate to the protection and sponsorship of native culture and religion means that there is no felt need in his work to imagine a local nationalism whose goal would be Indian self-rule. In a curious twist of cross-cultural allegorization, Kim's willingness to act as permanent disciple and apprentice (as spy or *chela*) seems to support the text's fantasy of an India willing to defer its own self-possession. In this reading, the blocked autonomy of the Indian people as a national subject is curiously screened by and yet embodied in the stunted or incomplete subjectivity of the hero.

15. Both intra- and extra-diegetically, youth as such must be preserved, even if its essence as a temporary phase threatens to congeal into an eternal state. Kipling and his textual surrogates (the various father figures) manage Kim's education in order to keep him adolescent. Toward this end, Kipling deploys a somewhat predictable colonial stereotype, casting the tropics as a temporal hothouse in which the punctual and linear codes of European industrial society are violated willy-nilly: "At St. Xavier's they know the first rush of minds developed by sun and surroundings, as they know the half-collapse that sets in at twenty-two or twenty-three" (107). Kipling also presents Kim's Irish heritage as part of his "natural" resistance to the orderly accumulations of character, education, vocation, and fortune. As the narrator would have it, the "Hibernian" and "Asiatic" elements of Kim keep him boyish.

16. One element of the Goethean plot that persists in Kipling (and Conrad) is the role of the secret sub-society as a mediating device. Like Wilhelm Meister's Tower Society, Kim's homosocial spy ring allows him to forge a compromise between the free cultivation of his desires and the apparent unfreedom of social conventions. In Kim's case, the elite subsociety dignifies his preferred activities (adventure, disguise, game-playing, thievery) with adult pay, apprenticeship status, and political significance. Kipling's Indian fiction is, of course, everywhere full of reference to the Masonic order—another example of a secret masculine society that preserves a romantic conception of the cadre in the face of a heavily institution- alized and bureaucratized apparatus for forming adult professional men in late Victorian society.

17. Walter Michaels describes the racial limits of social mobility in the novel: "It's because he's an O'Hara and not a 'nigger' that Kim can hope to become a Creighton; it's because he speaks like a 'nigger' and not like an O'Hara that Kim can succeed in becoming a Creighton" ("Local Colors" 752). John Kucich has also recently reexamined *Kim* in terms of class structure rather than race-and-hybridity thematics. Kucich's approach emphasizes the implicit politics of "sadomasochistic groups" and middle-class authority in Kipling's fiction set in both England and Anglo-India ("Sadomasochism" 34).

18. As S. P. Mohanty notes, along similar lines, Kipling's fantasy is of "imperial subjec- tivity as abstract . . . floating above desire and ideology" (36).

19. When the original antinomies of the bildungsroman (story/closure; becoming/ being; modernization/nationhood) are exposed and exacerbated, yet preserved within the narrative, the result is more a metabildungsroman than an antibildungsroman. My thanks to Amanda Anderson for this clarification of terms. In a metabildungsroman, the generic conventions survive albeit in ironic, partial, and belated form; the genre thus in effect discloses *its own aging process*.

20. Phillip Wegner argues that Kim includes by negation the idea of real conflict or real challenge to British power in India (153). Toward that end, Kipling has to freeze his protagonist in time, a conspicuous act of narrative (or antinarrative) legerdemain that allows us to measure the distance between *Kim* and the classic bildungsroman of social- ized maturity. Wegner further proposes that Kim is "the decentered subject that moves through the materiality of the imperial territory," and, "will finally be 'reattached' on the abstract level of the global state" (150). When Kim is "reattached," the text reveals rather than conceals the fact that the paradox of endless youth is unresolvable in narrative terms. Whereas a traditional novel of development can mediate between youth and adulthood using national allegory to give shape to modernization/maturation processes that are otherwise too abstract, too continuous, and too messy to represent, a novel of endless development (i.e., permanent youth) cannot use a "world-systems allegory" to achieve the same kind of epistemological or aesthetic feat. If Kim is "attached" to some kind of global or imperial state (rather than to a territorially bounded national culture), he is thereby—or so my argument runs—also detached from the closural plot of adulthood, that is, from the coming-of-age format itself.

21. Salman Rushdie, who adapted much of *Kim*'s plot for his own groundbreaking novel of national youth, *Midnight's Children*, has characterized Kipling as a split personality, "part- bazaar boy, part sahib" (Introduction to *Soldiers Three* ix). Zohreh Sullivan calls Kipling "the quintessentially divided imperial subject" (6). The self-division is amplified in the creation of Kim, whom Kipling invented as an agent and subject of empire, an Irish-Indian emblem

of marginalized sub-Britishness yet a marvelously endowed figure of strategic power. In a more recent version of the claim about Kim as hybrid figure, Don Randall argues at length that Kipling's imperial boys are figures standing "in between formations of the subject encoded as 'European, imperial' and 'non-European, colonial'" (3).

22. For an account of youth's meaning that emphasizes the essential difference between colonizer and colonized experience, see Benedict Anderson (119). I adapt the term "contact zone" from Mary Louise Pratt in part to establish the point that my governing trope seems to operate in colonial *situations* rather than to emanate in some exclusive way from either the colonized or colonizer perspective. Pratt uses the term *contact zone* to emphasize "interlocking understandings and practices" that run across the colonial divide even as they are conditioned by "radically asymmetrical relations of power" (7).

23. Fanon's diagnosis of the retarding effects of colonialism on the social and intellectual development of colonized peoples is matched and to some extent anticipated by Albert Memmi, who writes in 1957: "The colony's life is frozen; its structure is both corseted and hardened. No new role is open to the young man, no invention is possible" (98). Throughout *The Colonizer and the Colonized*, Memmi emphasizes figures of petrifaction, mummification, calcification, catalepsis. Such conditions of stasis are charged to colonial contact: "After having shut the colonized out of history and having forbidden him all development, the colonizer asserts his fundamental and complete immobility" (113).

24. The rationale for critical abstraction is that it keeps open the delicate, diverse meanings of and within novels while allowing us to try to discover interpretive patterns of sufficiently general interest. In order to isolate the connection between formal innovation and historical situation with some subtlety, I have attempted to subordinate (though not ignore) the political intentions of novelists. My methodological guide is Lukács, who, in his readings of Scott and Balzac, insists that a novel's capacity to render in art the deep forces of history does not depend on a certain political orientation or sympathy on the part of the novelist—and indeed that novelists can, and often do, write against what one might assume to be the political interest of the social groups to which they are consciously affiliated.

25. Sammons identifies the main elements of the original genre: its basis in Enlightenment notions of progress; its emphasis on "the morphological development and enhancement of the self"; and its thematic attention to the story of a "young person entering upon life and the world" (232–33). Sammons is working partly within (and against) the critical context in which the term *bildungsroman* was extended from its relation to "peculiar German social conditions" into other, particularly English and French, contexts and novel histories. Susanne Howe long ago opened up the adaptation of the term to the English tradition; her work was extended by Jerome Buckley in a positive and descriptive history of the genre that goes well into the twentieth century. Since Buckley, most critics of both Anglophone and continental literature have tended to dematerialize the genre or delimit its reach. See, for example, Boes, "Apprenticeship"; Felski, *Beyond Feminist Aesthetics*; Fraiman; Kontje; and Pfau.

26. There are two main theoretical schools here: 1) the more empirical and materialist tradition exemplified by Lukács, Bakhtin, and Moretti; and 2) the poststructuralist approach exemplified by Redfield (following Lacoue-Labarthe and Nancy). The two sides are separated more by shades of emphasis than absolute methodological difference, but in a sense the former tends toward a positivist and normative account of an actual generic history of the bildungsroman where the latter tends to insist that the genre only ever really exists as

a kind of heuristic construct of literary history. Among Germanists, Kontje is clearest in seeking to abandon the positivist and progressivist connotation of the term (141–42). For a thorough and skilled summary of the field of the "missing bildungsroman" from an English studies point of view, see Castle 8–15.

27. For useful methodological formulations of this point, see Adorno ("The existence and teleology of objective genres and types are as true as the fact that they must be attacked," *Aesthetic Theory* 201); Jameson ("*all* generic categories, even the most time-hallowed and traditional, are ultimately to be understood (or 'estranged') as mere *ad hoc*, experimental constructs, devised for a specific textual occasion and abandoned like so much scaffolding when the analysis has done its work," *Political Unconscious* 145); and Dimock ("Genres are thus weakly designative and weakly determinative" and "are subject to large-scale transformation over time," 91).

28. As Jesse Matz reminds us, Bergsonian flux means that even the adult psyche is in a continuous state of becoming—a modernist philosophical challenge to the bildungsroman conceit of the spiritually finalized and static adult mind ("T. E. Hulme" 342–43).

29. In addition to the work already cited in the main text, I might point to a number of recent articles in modernist and postcolonial studies; see, for example, Barnard, Jessica Berman, Chalk, Cheah, Jeffers, Lima, Seshagiri, and Slaughter.

30. Spacks describes *Adolescence* as a book that "inaugurated a period, still continuing, in which the adolescent assumed a place of pivotal importance in sociological, psychological, and literary thought, and in the popular imagination as well" (228). "'Adolescence,'" she goes on to say, "means possibility: so writers in all centuries have felt. Not until G. Stanley Hall's century have novelists sustained a fantasy of preserving its values and its indeterminacy. Dickens's narrators convey regret for the loss of youth, but they do not imagine an alternative" (250). On the wider cultural horizons of a late Victorian "culture of adolescence," see Neubauer.

31. Castle's general approach to the problem of the modernist bildungsroman, and in particular his readings of Wilde and Joyce, have influenced my approach to these writers, though there are also important differences of emphasis. For example, his reading of Joyce's *Portrait* focuses on the frame of colonial provincialism as inadequate ground for the humanist ideals of *Bildung* (127); by contrast, I focus on the question of developmental allegory as revised and ironized in the novel of frozen youth. Castle argues that modernism revitalizes the bildungsroman at the end of an instrumentalized nineteenth century, rejecting by and large the claim that the genre is dead on arrival in the twentieth century. My own approach emphasizes less the revitalization of the genre's ideals of self-formation (even in the vitiated bohemian form of the artist-as-outsider) and more the dialectical shape of a genre revised in the modernist era in response to a postnational framework for imagining progress or destiny.

32. Mandatory public schooling in Britain after 1870 signals one major shift in the direction of a bureaucratized, institutionalized youth that, in Moretti's account, increasingly threatens not just the neo-aristocratic dimensions of aesthetic education but the more thoroughly middle-class elements of self-cultivation. The increasing force of institutional and professional forms of education means that the old Schillerian ideals (which bear an intrinsically anti-institutional romanticism within them) become marginal and, in the British idiom of residual class coding, take refuge in the ideal of amateurism. Nowhere is the split

more clear than in the imperial zone, where gentlemanly and amateur values propagated in the public school model are kept alive precisely by absorption into the professional ranks (army, civil service). Thus the contradictions of the Goethean model of subject formation are obvious and the notion of the perpetually laddish and naive/sentimental imperial type becomes a colonial British stereotype. For more on the rise of professionalism in the imperial arena, see John Marx (121).

33. In Moretti's account, "Objective culture, congealed in conventions and institutions, no longer helps to construct individual subjects, but wounds and disintegrates them" (*Modern Epic* 195). The democratization of Schillerian ideals also means their dilution into less recognizable forms of bourgeois compromise. On this point, see Giddens's view that the "reflexively organised endeavour" of self-formation broadens its franchise from being an aristocratic notion to a relatively democratic concept of destiny for most modern subjects (5). Janet Lyon offers an elegant summary of another facet of the problem for idealized and autonomous subject-formation in the modernist era: "The accelerated diversification of modern social structures ensures that there can be no fit between an individual and any one community. Identity is striated across a series of function groups (economic, social, sexual, national, and so forth), and this process reveals retroactively the absence of organic or originary communities through which the I of the artist secures value and ground in modernity" (190). Lyon's point is as true for protagonists in novels as it is for the artist writing them.

34. Although important recent work such as Ian Baucom's *Spectres of the Atlantic* (building on Arrighi) pushes finance capitalism's colonial roots back further, into the eighteenth century, Edward Soja and other geographers of empire and globalization (David Harvey, Neil Smith) still tend to emphasize the significance of the shift in the late nineteenth century: "Capitalism did not suddenly internationalize. Mercantile capital had been operating to extract superprofits throughout the world for centuries through commodity trade. Imperialism, however, internationalized another circuit of capital, involved in finance, money, and investment transactions, which more efficiently organized the international economy for larger scale geographical transfers of value than had ever before been possible" (Soja 165; thanks to Scott Cohen for this reference).

35. Said's version of the periodizing claim is the suggestion that, by the 1880s, "European and Western control over the non-Western world was taken as fact, as inevitable" (*Culture and Imperialism* 186). For another strong model of this periodization, in which the moment of high imperialism is set off against the longer waves of European colonialism, consider Benita Parry: "Not until the late nineteenth century and the massive land expropriations in Africa, intensified capitalist interventions in Asia, and the incorporation of Latin American republics as economic dependencies of western capital, did imperialism's spokespersons and propagandists invent an exorbitant and anomalous idiom of messianic utilitarianism and bellicose mysticism; here the positivist and aggressive phraseology of national self-interest, territorial acquisition, the aggressive appropriation of the material and labour resources of other continents and compulsory universal modernization are combined with the anachronistic and chimerical lexicon of chivalry, 'a mandate of destiny' and 'a high and holy mission' serving as ideological pillars of imperial ambitions" (114). David Scott's *Conscripts of Modernity* also argues for the analytical value of separating the intense burst of imperialist activity in the late nineteenth and early twentieth centuries and, moreover, sees

this periodizing model as relevant to both colonizer and colonized histories (110–17). On this point, see also Begam and Moses, Chrisman, and McClintock.

36. Lukács suggests that after the failed 1848 revolutions, and with the widespread discrediting of Hegelian thought, "the idea of progress undergoes a regression." In other words, the proper concept of continual but uneven and contradictory social evolution gives way to twin and opposing concepts of history, both groundless and nondialectical: 1) the bourgeois hypostasy of progress, a cartoon teleology in which "history is conceived as a smooth straightforward evolution"; and 2) the doctrines of stasis and decline in the West, an increasingly popular "tendency to modernize, and . . . mystify history, which in the age of imperialism reached its apex in conceptions like those of Spengler" (*Historical Novel* 174–77). These are the twin ideologies of history—the simple-progressive and the static-regressive—that can be mapped onto the narrative categories of romance and tragedy, the torn halves of the realist novel. Thomas Pfau, reading Spengler, offers the complementary claim that the shifting nature of capitalism (from national-industrial to financial-imperial) in the later nineteenth century is crucial in understanding the fate of the bildungsroman in the modernist period. Like Lukács, Pfau reads Spengler as "presaging the defeat of the nineteenth-century ideal of *Bildung* by a technology- and capital-driven process of globalization" (160).

37. Armand Mattelart's *Networking the World* provides a more technologically inflected account of the 1880–1920 period as the key phase in a long globalizing and colonial process, noting that the late Victorian period marks the standardization of many different measurements across the world as well as key advances in transportation and communication (11–13).

38. Svetlana Boym observes in *The Future of Nostalgia* that "progress was not only a narrative of temporal progression, but also of spatial expansion" (10). For more on the ways that imperial expansion was represented as the spatial base for, and index of, rational progress, see Benita Parry (114). For research on the "fin du globe," see Stokes.

39. Heather Love has developed at large the important claim that "sexual and gender deviants," like nonwhite and colonized peoples (among others), were "marked as inferior by means of the allegation of backwardness" (5–6).

40. For more on the relationship of queer and colonial discourse, see Castle, Lane, and Valente, *James Joyce*.

41. In both queer and colonial (anti)*bildungsromane*, the shared theme is one that Edward Said has identified as essential to the literature of the 1880–1920 period, that is, a dramatic "failure of the generative impulse" that breaks the "natural continuity between one generation and the next" (*The World* 16).

42. Hirsch emphasizes the inward turn within a woman-centered lineage of coming-of-age novels, calling "inner development" the "only area of development open to women in the nineteenth-century novel" (26). John H. Smith holds that "female Bildung" is "a contradiction in terms," but that there are great female-centered novels that "shatter the Bildungsroman genre by shattering its underlying conceptual and ideological frame" (220–21). The secondary literature is generally stronger on pre-1880 and post-1945 fiction than on modernist fiction. Felski's admirable account of the female bildungsroman, for example, tends to skip over the modernist era, preferring to describe both the oppositional-marginal practice of the Victorian era and the emergent feminist novel of the contemporary period (in

which more powerful stories of women's self-formation can be set against the emergence of a genuine "female community") (*Beyond* 133–34). One might read the modernist bildungsroman, then, as a mixed or transitional mode in this gendered literary history, working to combine both oppositional and emancipatory values within a single narrative frame.

43. In canonical Victorian novels of development, such as Eliot's *Mill* or Hardy's *Tess*, we often encounter female protagonists tied fatefully to some kind of modernizing landscape in which they can neither thrive nor survive. The motif of the marginalized and trapped provincial woman runs through this study as it runs through the history of the realist, naturalist, and modernist novel. In the latter stages, the scale of peripherality shifts in the direction of a colonial logic of backwardness, whether in the late Victorian generation of Schreiner, or in the modernist era of Rhys, Bowen, Katherine Mansfield, and Miles Franklin, or in the midcentury of Doris Lessing and Janet Frame, or in the post-1945 work of, say, Ama Ata Aidoo, Jamaica Kincaid, Michelle Cliff, and Tsitsi Dangarembga.

44. At a more pragmatic level of international law, Slaughter notes that the nexus of the bildungsroman and human rights gets disrupted as it moves outside the nation. The contradictions endemic to the rights-discourse that Slaughter so keenly anatomizes seem to emerge most saliently when "the nationalizing Bildungsroman" is pressed "into the service of an international order that is without the formal administrative and social structures comparable to those of the nation-state" (30).

45. For a recent discussion of these points in detail, see Martin.

46. See Ed Comentale on "the formalization of constant change," a theme Comentale traces on its way from the avant-gardes into mainstream Anglophone modernism (30).

47. On the significance of both Alexander Kojève's and Francis Fukuyama's elaboration of the Hegelian "end of history" for the study of the modern Anglophone novel, see Moses, *Novel and the Globalization of Culture*, 3–10.

48. Nietzsche's lines are taken from his 1874 essay "On the Uses and Disadvantages of History for Life," which argues that a surfeit of historical thinking has saturated and crippled European society: "We know, indeed, what history can do when it gains a certain ascendancy, we know it only too well: it can cut off the strongest instincts of youth, its fire, defiance, unselfishness and love, at the roots . . . suppress or regress its desire to mature slowly with the counter-desire to be ready, useful, fruitful as quickly as possible" (115). For Nietzsche, the crisis of historicism is a crisis of youth and for youth; the young are in danger, he writes, of "being overwhelmed by what was past and foreign" (122). In absorbing knowledge of the "past" and the "foreign," the European subject becomes a kind of adolescent hero, overripe and homeless, just in the manner dramatized by *Lord Jim*.

49. Because colonial time is out of joint with national-historical time, it provides the ground for the fission of classic realism into the hyper-objective or hyper-subjective forms that Lukács took as coextensive with modernism itself. But this is not, as Lukács would have it, a sign of bourgeois decadence or ahistorical aesthetics. The overdevelopment of both inner and outer conditions of subject-formation—the oedipalized mind and the bureaucratized world—is not the problem *of* modernism, it is rather the problem described *by* modernism. On this point, see Adorno: "The stronger the subject becomes and, complementarily, the more the social categories of order and the spiritual categories derived from these social categories weaken, the less it is possible to reconcile the subject and conventions" (*Aesthetic Theory* 204).

50. In the standard narrative, Wilde acts as a mediating figure between French decadence and Anglo-American modernism with *Dorian Gray* in particular as the early landmark for a set of modernist bohemian novels and *Kunstlerromane* (despite the fact that Dorian is more artwork or art-consumer than artist). The modernist *Kunstlerroman* works as a rarefied endgame for the novel of youth, with its artist-protagonist committed to ceaseless change outside the normalizing routines of family, courtship, and vocation.

51. Working from the lineage of Rousseau rather than Goethe, Nancy Armstrong proposes that the realist novel—emergent in the eighteenth century, dominant in the nineteenth, residual in the twentieth—generally tends toward the legitimization of the social order through narratives of "personal growth and development" (*Desire* 32–37). Likewise Moretti argues that the novel in its golden age "exists not as a critique, but as a *culture of everyday life*" (*Way* 35). The point here is not to set up a crude contrast between edgy, critical modernist novels and conformist or complicit Victorian ones, but to suggest that the specific formulae used by the classic bildungsroman to narrate consent—in particular the soul-nation allegory—gradually lose their symbolic and social power over time and require aesthetic renovation. Such renovation does not imply absolute improvement on a transhistorical scale of literary value, but should perhaps be considered as a relative shift in realism's frame of reference from national to global dimensions.

52. Two of these writers, Ford and Lawrence, are not examined here, though they produced memorable figures of arrested development: Edward Ashburnham, John Dowell, and Paul Morel. Working within thoroughly English or metropolitan contexts, Ford and Lawrence more or less corroborate my hypothesis about the effects of lost "national closure," though perhaps not as obviously as does a colonial writer such as James Joyce or Jean Rhys. In his deftly cross-referenced study of the year 1913, Jean-Michel Rabaté proposes that this is indeed the twilight moment of Eurocentrism itself and the beginning of a new and more obvious kind of globalization in the cultural sphere (5). Rabaté also notes the conjunction of Joyce's *Portrait* and Lawrence's *Sons and Lovers*, in which immaturity unfurls à la Flaubert, persistently and stubbornly in the foreground. At the same time, Rabaté rightly observes a common modernist theme of "accelerated aging processes" (99). Indeed Lawrence himself found the modernist novel of Joyce and Proust to be hobbled by its "senile precocity." In his 1923 essay on the "future of the novel," Lawrence further deprecated the artistic merits of literature based on an "adolescence which can't grow up" (144). My thanks to Bridget Chalk for these Lawrence references.

53. One might indeed read *The Theory of the Novel* as another instance of the modernist metabildungsroman, particularly in view of the fact that its 1962 preface features the old Marxist lion Lukács rebuking his idealistic younger self for romantic Hegelianism much in the manner of a classic mature narrator/immature protagonist fiction.

54. Like the first novels of Joyce, Woolf, and Lawrence, Rhys's *Voyage in the Dark* was written on the historical eve of World War I (though not published until after the war). As Mary Lou Emery suggests, Rhys's brand of modernist irony can be contextualized in terms of a World War I–era collapse in "the Idea of Progress" (Emery 68–70). Ford's *The Good Soldier*, which also invokes and undoes the beau ideal of the fair-haired, eternally youthful Englishman, is a subtle retelling in its way of *Lord Jim*. For a useful recent comparison of Ford and Conrad, see Nicholas Brown, who identifies a set of stylistic effects, such as "super-foreshadowing" and "hypertrophied digression," that seem to index a collapsed

developmental logic in the plot structure of the realist novel (90). On the question of the English soldier as a kind of stalled or failed subject, one could also invoke Woolf's *Jacob's Room* or, as Janet Lyon has suggested to me, Rebecca West's *Return of the Soldier* (1918), where Chris Baldry seems to represent an interesting variation on the plot of arrested development, entangled with both European and extra-European imperialisms.

55. As Declan Kiberd notes, in the early twentieth century, the generation gap—long a staple of the Goethean bildungsroman based on the "revolt of an artistic son against an unsatisfactory father"—became "so wide as to suggest that the young and old inhabited totally different countries"; Kiberd proposes that a certain cluster of modernist writers—Mann, Lawrence, Fitzgerald—understood themselves as writing to their own generation in an unprecedented sense. Even more to the point, Kiberd suggests that a colonial situation such as Ireland's adds urgency to the rebellious youth plot as an allegory of provincial insurgency against historical and political authority at the center (383–85).

56. Consider, in this connection, Pound's remark about Joyce: "He was presented Ireland under British domination. . . . By extension he was presented the whole occident under the domination of capital" (qtd. in Deane, *Celtic Revivals* 105).

57. For a theoretical account of this problem of *Bildung* in a global, colonial, or postnational frame, see David Lloyd's reading of James Clarence Mangan. Lloyd suggests that the harmonizing function of the national-individual allegory is to overcome social antagonism or class difference via the organic narrative of national emergence that centers on an integrative and representative soul (*Nationalism* 71). It makes sense, then, that novels committed to revealing the ossified status of the motif of the nationally representative soul would also be novels in which the integrative and conciliatory functions of national allegory are displaced by an emphasis on these new axes of difference—sexual, racial, biological—that cannot be reconciled through narratives of upward mobility or national unity.

58. The social determinants of identity—biological, racial, sexual, cultural—in Rhys's fiction recall another émigré modernist, Nella Larsen. Larsen's *Quicksand* (1928) features a mixed-race heroine who refuses the standard arrangements of bourgeois sexuality and property, then plunges headlong and disastrously into the heterosexual family. Helga Crane's lack of means to protest the instrumentalization of her (exoticized, primitivized) sexuality results, as in Rhys's *Voyage*, in a well-orchestrated failed-bildungsroman plot.

59. Nineteenth-century historical consciousness here refers not just to a German philosophical tradition denoted (for the sake of economy) by the name Hegel, but to a widespread and influential practice of historiography associated with others such as Ranke, Michelet, Tocqueville, Marx, and Burckhardt—all of whom, as Benedict Anderson notes, generated their concepts of historical practice during the age of emergent European nationalisms (197).

60. Susan Hegeman drew my attention to the aptness of Clifford's observation. For a similar overview coming from the vantage point not of anthropological theory, but of intellectual history, consider Carl Schorske in *Thinking with History*: "If we turn our gaze from the high culture of the mid-nineteenth to the mid-twentieth century, we realize how drastic has been the break from the historical consciousness" (4). From the viewpoint of literary studies, Rita Felski likewise describes the modernist era as "caught between the still-powerful evolutionary and historicist models of the nineteenth century and the emergent crises of language and subjectivity which would shape the experimental art of the twentieth" (*Gender* 30).

61. Frank Kermode defines *chronos* as the blank unfolding of time or "mere successive-ness" and *kairos* as meaningful or shaped or end-directed time, time that integrates past, present, and future (47).

62. To establish modernism's global rather than European provenance, one can begin with the case of Latin American *modernismo*. Along these lines, George Yudice has made the case that European avant-garde culture already includes the peripheries: "The context for this relation between 'center' and 'periphery' is the accelerated imperialism (and the resistance to it) in the late nineteenth and early twentieth centuries, with all its concomi-tants in technology, exploration, and the emergence of new sciences like anthropology" (54). As I have already suggested, the contours of my thesis might well follow this extension of the modernist turn outside Europe and outside the Anglophone canon to take in a novel like Machado's *Brás Cubas*. This 1881 text from the Brazilian semiperiphery, like so many other modernist novels that follow, undoes the biographical plot with great stylistic brio. In Roberto Schwarz's authoritative reading of *Brás Cubas*, Machado's emphasis on an episodic plot yields not a narrative of emergence, but a staccato story about a society both fated and belated: "The form of the Romantic novel, linked to the self-realization of the young man and the vicissitudes in his way, is present, but emptied out"; the result, according to Schwarz, is a "wandering, tensionless plot" unmoored from the figure of the "energetic, enterprising central character" (41).

63. In other words, I understand arrested/uneven development as a political problem and literary trope that is "*viewed from* but not *determined at* the center" (Cooper and Stoler 617; emphasis mine).

64. For initial points of reference, see Jameson (*Singular*) and Gaonkar.

65. To read these texts as encoding complex ideological and conceptual contradictions in the discourse of colonial development is, of course, to credit them with a certain kind of political insight or agency that seems to outstrip the intentions of the artists and authors who wrote them. Such a sympathetic account of these texts risks transferring political agency from author to form without fully considering the limits (in either critical mode, intentionalist or formalist) of their capacity to mount an ideology critique of imperial time. It is for this reason that I emphasize in the readings that follow the ways in which novels of frozen youth lay the myth of progress open to its own contradictions without claiming a position of ideological transcendence, without insisting, for example, on an Archimedean critique of empire. I thank Doug Mao and Bruce Robbins for inviting me to consider this point.

66. Unlike the ideal or classic bildungsroman, which would, in the Lukácsian view, nat-uralize the contradiction between the endless time of becoming and the bounded time of being, the late bildungsroman brings the contradiction itself closer to the surface and bears its narrative consequences in the trope of frozen youth. If such forms do not mount a thor-oughgoing critique of the organicist, Eurocentric predicates stored in the memory of the bildungsroman genre itself, it is perhaps because of their commitment to reckoning with the power of developmental historicism. Taking an interpretive cue from Adorno's *Aesthetic Theory*, we might simply say that such works need to coordinate their utopian content with the representation and replication of determinate, objective social conditions. To imagine a sudden or facile overthrow of the ideology of progress—rather than a subtle rejoinder based on its own contradictions—is to imagine a purely idealist or aesthetic solution to a problem

that continues to have both an epistemological-discursive and a material-political basis. In other words, one cannot finally dispense with the bourgeois novel of progress, or even claim that its day has passed, so long as what we might still call the bourgeois revolution is unfolding across the worldwide system of global capitalism. In the meantime, novels that question the teleologies of maturity and modernity represent, in my view, the most aesthetically complex and critically vital traditions of literary culture.

67. This way of approaching the relationship of modernism and realism accords with Fredric Jameson's recent observation that "each successive realism can also be said, in this sense, to have been a modernism in its own right" (*Singular* 123). It remains possible to theorize the bourgeois novel as a realist or historical genre well into the twentieth century unless one believes, as Lukács did beginning with *History and Class Consciousness*, that the middle classes could and can no longer grasp the shape of modern historical forces. We can perhaps dialecticize Lukácsian theory beyond Lukács's own Leninist politics by taking modernism as a new and realist phase of literary production in which biographical or otherwise "private" novels represent combined and uneven development in the global frame (rather than in the national frame where uneven development is generally modulated and mediated by the tacit understanding of the collective destiny of a single people).

68. Reading *Lord Jim* this way, for example, means believing that the involuted languages of modernist subjectivity and impressionist style are not, themselves, aesthetic evasions of the historical world, but deeply realist methods for describing the ideological evasion of history implied by imperialism (as a neofeudalist character factory preserving "honor," as a site of global capitalism's "development of under-development"). Conrad uses tales of interiority to represent objective social conditions, but those conditions include an advanced stage of capitalist modernization in which neither the material signs nor the intellectual prestige of progress as a metahistorical motif could be guaranteed. John Marx reads *Lord Jim* as continuous with the tradition of the industrial-era "condition of England" novel, insisting—I think persuasively—that it does not disguise or stylize labor/production into a modernist dazzle of absences, but shows them, as they are being transformed, by the objective processes of high imperialism (15). *Lord Jim* is a realist novel that does not so much occlude the global division of labor as draw attention to the standard languages and story lines by which that division of labor had generally been hidden from Western eyes.

Chapter 2: "National-Historical Time" from Goethe to George Eliot

1. Paul Gilroy, among others, links the eighteenth-century phase of colonial modernity to the production of a system of national cultures. Not incidentally, Gilroy identifies *Robinson Crusoe* (1725) as a "founding myth" that helps us grasp the relation between "the history of capitalist commerce" and "the geopolitical projection of states as discrete cultures arranged in antagonistic national units" (55). To call Defoe's novel a myth has a certain logic: In a sense, the concept of a permanent national essence is antinarrative in that it emphasizes continuity over change. Most modern nationalisms project a historical narrative in which, after some dark period of change and flux, the social identity of a people and place becomes consolidated into nationhood. At this originary moment (which may be, for example, a revolution, constitutional adoption, or independence movement), the national identity is both born and fixed. In nationalist narratives, then, the story of formation (or *Bildung*) reaches a point of closure after which there are no major social transformations, only minor

adjustments. On the ability of Victorian property to signify both national particularity and the "potentially limitless fluidity of the marketplace," see Plotz 23. On the nature of the nation-market compromise first in the era of industrial capitalism and, subsequently, in the era of high imperialism, see Benedict Anderson, *Imagined Communities* 3–40 and 87–93, respectively.

2. In chapter 1, I hypothesized that the metabildungsroman—or novel of endless youth—stages a confrontation with the bad infinities of imperialism and capitalism by removing the fictional ruses of symbolic adulthood that are usually deployed to contain such infinities at the allegorical level. The trope of youth-without-age is a marking device that acknowledges—and indeed conjoins—the abstract or formal infinities faced by Lukács in *Theory of the Novel* and the more existential- epistemological infinities associated with empire in Jameson's "Modernism and Imperialism."

3. Thomas Pfau states this even more clearly: "The theoretical paradigm of *Bildung* or *Kultur* would itself have a limited life-expectancy, would prove but an epoch that—like the bourgeois, liberal-democratic nation state whose emergence and consolidation it had facilitated and sustained—must eventually decline and pass away" (153).

4. For Lukács, Goethe's *Faust* and Hegel's *Phenomenology of Mind* "belong together as the greatest artistic and intellectual achievements of the classical period in Germany" (*Goethe* 176).

5. Bakhtin sees Goethe's major works as representative of the first fully scientific and geographically realistic vision of the world, of what Mary Louise Pratt would later call "planetary consciousness" (Bakhtin, "*Bildungsroman*" 44; Pratt 29–36). Marshall Berman reads Goethe's *Faust* as the signal "tragedy of development" for Western modernity: in it, self-development and economic development converge and mirror each other, producing the diabolical problem of endless life (40).

6. In *Poetry and Experience*, Dilthey authoritatively defines the bildungsroman (as against "all previous biographical compositions") in the following terms: "Lawlike development is discerned in the individual's life. . . . Life's dissonances and conflicts appear as necessary transitions to be withstood by the individual on his way towards maturity and harmony" (qtd. in Barney 359). Dilthey's formulation is the standard critical reference point, and, as Todd Kontje notes, Dilthey's ideal of "self-integration and integration into society" makes the bildungsroman into a "fundamentally affirmative, conservative genre" (140).

7. Martin Jay notes that, for Schiller, art is "a contrivance for the suspension of time, a way to avoid the open-ended boundlessness of the infinite" (51).

8. For more on the European allegorical genres that formed the basis and immediate precursor for national narrative, see Alryyes 20–25. In particular, Alryyes recounts the shift from the Romantic genre of the *Universalgeschichte* to more nationally specific genres in which "the life of one man comes to stand for the history of the nation" (21).

9. Humboldt distinguishes between *Kultur* and *Bildung* in this way: "When in our language we say Bildung, we mean something both higher and more inward, namely the disposition of mind which, from the knowledge and the feeling of the total intellectual and moral endeavor, flows harmoniously into sensibility and character'" (*Theory and Practice of Self-Formation*, qtd. in Gadamer 9). Tobias Boes has recently reminded us of the importance of Humboldt to the theory and practice of the bildungsroman, noting that Humboldt sees the "soul of a nation" as a guarantor of both narrative authority and of

a "phantasmal continuity that transcends individual perspectives" ("Apprenticeship" 284). For useful discussions of Humboldt's influence on concepts of *Bildung* (and bildungsroman), see Bruford (1–28) and Slaughter (112–22).

10. In a useful overview of national variations and translations of the bildungsroman, Castle associates the original German form with "spiritual apprenticeship"; the English version with a more pragmatic brand of "social conformity"; and the French with the narrative telos of "artistic success" (8).

11. Cheah notes that "the same concepts of freedom, culture, and organism" associated by Kant with "global community" are tied to the nation-state by Fichte and Hegel (100). Kant sees the cultivating/acculturating process as ideally cosmopolitan, thus anathematic to the frame of a restrictive or particularist nationalism, even if it is sponsored by a given "territorial state" (98).

12. Cheah's thesis is that the gift or theft of time from nature to political rationality, via the logic of organismic or incarnational theory (i.e., the state or polis naturalized to the status of a living being or fleshly body), is not an evitable error. It cannot be separated from the foundations of modern political philosophy in German idealism. But it nonetheless leaves a problematic inheritance to modern thought and culture. Of course, the bildungsroman does not merely repeat anywhere and everywhere the original organismic conceit of the genre. It has its own history of changes and, within that history, under the pressure of different contexts, generates new kinds of generic or metageneric knowledge. Thus the novel's incarnation of national *Bildung* can activate the contradictions of the organismic conceit rather than simply naturalize them afresh—and indeed this is, in essence, what the trope of unseasonable youth does.

13. Gikandi's thesis—that nineteenth-century novels gain temporal coherence via national reference—has its counterparts outside the English and European traditions. George Yudice, for example, offers more or less the same kind of periodizing overview of Latin American fiction: "If the relative coherence of nineteenth-century narrative modes were [*sic*] premised on the intelligibility and stability provided by the national frame of reference, the imminence of international political upheaval and global conflict is registered in the fragmentation of narrative representation and its lyric subject" in later novels (58).

14. Tobias Boes has recently remarked on this aspect of the history of the bildungsroman: "The genre also strives to find absolution from the narrative demands of modernity in the timeless absolute of the national community" ("Apprenticeship" 284).

15. To be precise: The bildungsroman, taken strictly as a novel of self-cultivation, operates as a subset of the novel of youth (a category including other subgeneric forms such as the *erziehungsroman*, or novel of schooling), which is itself a subset of the biographical novel centered on a key individual narrated over significant spans of his/her life, which is in turn a subset of the realist novel (already a quite strongly delimited subset within the broad history of modern prose fiction). Lukács's establishment of the classic historical novel (Scott, Manzoni, Stendhal, Tolstoy) as a nation-based form has become more or less accepted as a tenet of novel history. Here I have been arguing that novels of youth also, and quite generally, entail and imply national frames in a reciprocal allegory of bounded progress. To be clear, my claim is that nineteenth-century national chronotopes bear a special explanatory relationship to the generic code of the bildungsroman; it is *not* that the bildungsroman, among novelistic genres, bears an exclusive or special relationship to the representation

of nation-state formation. Indeed, as Katie Trumpener has amply demonstrated, there are any number of national fictional genres alive in the key period (1790–1860), including the historical novel, the national tale, the gothic romance, the panoramic novel, the family saga, and what Trumpener calls the "annalistic" novel (xii–xiii).

16. These influential discussions of national tradition and national temporality in relation to modern fiction have to some extent been eclipsed recently by closer attention to the institutions and infrastructure (both real and conceptual) of the state itself. For examples of this shift in emphasis from national culture to state apparatuses, see especially Chu, Goodlad, Hart and Hansen, Robbins (*Upward*), Rubenstein, and Szalay.

17. We might further observe that Defoe's relatively more open forms—both *Crusoe* and *Moll Flanders*—involve the free export of protagonists to colonial spaces (tropical, American) and relatively weak closural plots. In later novels by, say, Dickens, Thackeray, or Hardy, the export of characters to colonial space tends to be either merely incidental or temporary, driven by economic necessity, and often preliminary to some other mode of national closure.

18. See, for example, Suleri's account of Burke's "horror at the adolescence of the colonial enterprise" (35–36).

19. For a specific example of this conservative streak, see Sarah Rose Cole's reading of Thackeray's bildungsroman *History of Pendennis* (1848–1850); Cole argues that Thackeray converts "Balzac's narrative of revolutionary dislocation into a self-consciously British narrative of peaceful change" (3). For more on Burke's own distrust of the French revolutionary spirit, see *Letters on a Regicide Peace*, where he worries about the fading of "that narrow scheme of relations called our country, with all its pride, its prejudices, and its partial affections. All the quiet little rivulets, that watered an humble, a contracted, but not an unfruitful field, are to be lost in the waste expanses and boundless, barren ocean of the homicide philanthropy of France" (qtd. in Deane, *Short History* 127). From this point of view, one can pose Burke against Rousseau as alternative points of reference in the British and French philosophical traditions (just as one might cast Rousseau's *Emile* against *Wilhelm Meister's Apprenticeship* in the novel tradition).

20. Citing the facts of an incomplete and premature national revolution, a persistent bourgeois-gentry class compromise, and the retarding sociopolitical effects of overseas imperialism, Tom Nairn describes Britain as a "relatively immobile social order—the one world society which faced practically *no* developmental problem until well into the twentieth century" (31).

21. Christopher GoGwilt describes a "German idealist notion of 'Bildung' as a process of individual development, aesthetic education, and national culture" that became central to dispersed European accounts of culture, including Britain's (19). For a more detailed account of Humboldt's influence on J. S. Mill and English Victorian concepts of freedom and self-development, see Nordenbo. Along similar lines, Castle argues that Mill follows the modernizing line of Humboldt, attempting to forge a pragmatic concept of individual freedom in an industrializing Victorian society, as against Carlyle and Arnold, who remain more faithful to the original Goethe/Schiller concept of aesthetic and spiritual self-cultivation (48). For more on the transfer of Schillerian concepts of aesthetic education into Britain via Carlyle and Ruskin, see Mao (59).

22. As Ian Duncan notes, Scott's historical novels operate "as a form of national Bildungsroman, combining the private crisis of psychosexual formation with the public matter of

vocation and rank" (232). Along similar lines, Ala Alryyes observes, "Scott's historical novel narrates the involvement of the child-hero in the nation's historicity through the superior vision of a 'national' narrator" (202). Buzard calls *Waverley* a "forceful metafiction on the politics of cultural representation in the context of British internal colonialism" (67). For a detailed historical exploration of national tales in the "age of Waverley," see Trumpener, 128–57. Finally, Alexander Welsh's study of Hamlet narratives offers an interesting perspective on Scott's place in the Goethean tradition: "Even those who, like Karl Marx, envisioned a further revolution to come were fortified by their belief that history would then arrive at a suitable resting place. Scott's novels spoke to this faith in history; it is entirely understandable that the Marxist Lukács should champion them" (100). Indeed this "suitable resting place" goes to the heart of the matter, the fact that national discourses allowed the novel of youth to resolve itself rather than spin on endlessly in the allegorical narrative of transformation.

23. As James Buzard demonstrates so convincingly in *Anywhere's Nowhere*, for Victorian texts like these, national identity is still "a condition of bounded heterogeneity" (166). For another good instance of a mid-Victorian novel in which the central conflicts are resolved into a plot that implicitly depends on the concept of national development, see Disraeli's 1844 *Coningsby* (Alryyes 212). By the early Victorian period, Nancy Armstrong suggests, "the British novel could no longer tell the story of subject formation without telling the story of nation formation as well" (*How Novels Think* 59). For the French nineteenth-century realists, too, this seems to be understood as a basic principle of novel construction; in Balzac, for example, as Pericles Lewis notes, "the nation functioned as a limit of individual experience" (47).

24. Buzard usefully marks the epistemological limit of nineteenth-century fiction and its Faustian fantasy of complete cultural (self) knowledge; the novel, he writes, "sets processes of knowing and desiring in motion in order to contain them within the national frame" (45). He elaborates this point in terms of moral sympathy in Dickens and Eliot as held together by social webs that are finally domestic in the national sense (51).

25. Fraiman, Mao, Moretti, Redfield, and Spacks all seem to view the genre of the bildungsroman as undergoing a decline or denouement after 1860; see, for example, Mao 94–96 and Spacks 236. Another contemporaneous text already testing the genre conventions rather programmatically is Meredith's *Ordeal of Richard Feverel* (1859), which ironizes in the systems of Austin Feverel (blooming season, magnetic age) the very idea of a systematic, paradigmatic, or generic coming-of-age formula.

26. Alex Woloch notes that Magwitch's social marginalization entails or is entailed by his assimilation (symbolically) into the center of Pip's "character space" (198). This offers a classic instance of the division of narrative labor in the "one vs. many" dialectic ably captured by Woloch (14–19); the bildungsroman requires an even more asymmetrical loading of significance into the protagonist than the Victorian social novel in general. One way to conceive of later, modernist novels of youth is to see them as a transitional and residual expression of the characterological economy of nineteenth-century realism, at once loading the hero with special historical significance and exposing the contradictions of that allegorical procedure.

27. Mao notes that Lewes and Herbert Spencer were both influential in the development of an authoritative discourse of environmental conditioning as the key factor informing human character and behavior (35–37).

28. Margaret Homans suggests that *Mill* projects high Victorian elements onto a pre-Victorian setting (169). Homans's argument looks at many of the same modernization processes as mine, but sees them in the service of a historical conflation that universalizes middle-class experience. In my view, Eliot is more committed to making historical distinctions than anachronistic fusions, though the novel's complexity depends on the use of both devices. Eliot's challenge to a nationalist rhetoric of continuity, in other words, demands that she also make that rhetoric available and plausible in the text. Similarly, Eliot's revision of the classic bildungsroman requires her to reproduce some of the genre's basic structural elements.

29. Taking the latter half of this formulation to heart, Leavis influentially recruited Eliot's fiction into the service of an abiding national myth—the yeoman farmer as quintessential Englishman. In *The Great Tradition*, he recognizes historical change and in fact seems to lament the loss of organic rural communities, but his criticism emphasizes certain essential continuities in what becomes a normative discourse of Englishness. Leavis's reading of Eliot in some ways secures the imprimatur of the English yeoman ideal for what Francis Mulhern identifies as Leavis's own up-by-the-bootstraps, white, heterosexual middle class ("English Reading" 259). As noted, though, Leavis's general admiration for Eliot did not extend to *Mill*, which he perhaps intuitively understood as a challenge to recuperative national history.

30. Eliot's awareness of these issues draws on the cultural context described by Nancy Armstrong in her reading of *Wuthering Heights*. Armstrong locates that novel within an early Victorian cultural system in which "modern literate urban" Britons expressed a folkloric interest in their rural compatriots whose life was thought to constitute "the idyllic childhood of the modern nation." Armstrong points out that Victorian literary and photographic representations of a putatively authentic English past often contributed to its destruction ("Emily's Ghost" 245–53). Likewise, Eliot's ethnographic wistfulness derives from the recognition that her attempts to describe the life of St. Ogg's only widen the gap between nostalgic modern readers and the vanishing past.

31. As James Buzard observes, Eliot shares with Dickens and Brontë the "tendency to raise visions of a boundless commercial or imperial domain in order to stimulate a return of the gaze to local and national contexts" (284). Although, as Nancy Henry points out, it can be clumsy and anachronistic to reread Eliot's Victorian novels through the lens of a later and more dominant cultural presence of high imperialism, it is nonetheless true, as Henry also notes, that Eliot knew quite a good deal about the British Empire. Her partner Lewes, for example, had two sons in South Africa, and she herself had invested in the African colonial railways (Henry 95–97). Henry goes on to interpret, as I do, a number of recurrent images of virgin land and virgin waterways in *Mill* as imagistic and symbolic reflections of Maggie's own underdevelopment, and to place that reading within Eliot's widening horizons of national and global economic development. Henry also suggests, rightly I think, that Eliot's relative level of detachment from the "economic sphere of her male contemporaries" may have given her a certain kind of clarity about the costs and benefits of economic development and national progress (116).

32. These observations are indebted to Eve Kosofsky Sedgwick's discussion of "sphere ideology" in Eliot's *Adam Bede* (138–46). Following Mary Poovey in placing the domestic sequestration of women within the context of economic histories, Sedgwick argues that

Adam Bede creates a foundation for restrictive class and gender relations in the Victorian period.

33. Christina Crosby finds in Eliot a general pattern of subordinating the specific claims of woman characters to the unfolding of a Hegelian historical totality, but goes on to note that *The Mill on the Floss* presents an anomalous—and much debated—case (161–63). Even more suggestively, Crosby claims Eliot's *Daniel Deronda* as a participant in the Victorian historical industry that provided a "secular guarantee" of "origins and ends" (5). I am arguing that *Mill* departs from Eliot's normal historical commitments by challenging "origins and ends" with a historicist vision of *continual* change.

34. Marx and Engels observed as early as 1848 that the force of capitalist and bourgeois enterprise was tearing down not merely local or regional boundaries, but national ones: "All old-established national industries have been destroyed or are daily being destroyed. They are dislodged by new industries, whose introduction becomes a life and death question for all civilized nations, by industries that no longer work up indigenous raw material but raw material drawn from the remotest zones, industries whose products are consumed, not only at home, but in every quarter of the globe. . . . In place of the old local and national seclusion and self-sufficiency, we have intercourse in every direction, universal interdependence of nations" (39).

35. Elaine Showalter reads Maggie's drowning as an almost punitive foreclosure on Eliot's part, noting that if Maggie's nonadjustment to society exposes and resists the conventions of *Bildung*, it also works as a formal sentence to death. Maggie's exit from bildungsroman conventions is in this sense only a Pyrrhic victory over the constraints of gender. Some feminists read Maggie's death as an immersion in a specifically feminine (and potentially redemptive) principle such as Freud's "oceanic" or Irigaray's "liquidity." I concur with Mary Jacobus, who sees Eliot's flood as a sign of the near-impossibility of fully resisting male-oriented conventions, even if it also entails a moment of symbolic access to unmediated female desire (221-22). For a recent and persuasive rereading of the economic logic of the river and the flood, see Kreisel.

36. In a still trenchant study of death and closure in the work of modern women novelists, Rachel Blau DuPlessis zeroes in on texts that attempt to challenge the drastically limited options for women's plots in the classic realist novel, that is, death or "social failure" on the one hand, and social compromise rooted in marriage on the other (1). DuPlessis's attention to the rupturing of both plot and grammar in this lineage of writers (including Schreiner, Woolf, and Lessing) anticipates my own approach to their revision of bildungsroman conventions.

37. The last quarter of the nineteenth century was filled with narratives of provincial womanhood (regionalist, sentimental, and naturalist) in both national and international frames. One particularly apt example from 1878 is Henry James's *Daisy Miller*, in which a stubbornly innocent and provincialized protagonist never ages, but dies. James emphasizes, via the perspective of Winterbourne, the fact that Daisy is "completely uncultivated" (63, but see also 94, 106). The theme of the unsophisticated American youth—to be amplified and elaborated across James's career—takes the form of a kind of arrested development plot here in this early fiction: "Daisy and her mamma have not yet risen to that stage of—what shall I call it?—of culture, at which the idea of catching a count or a *marchese* begins" (104). The failure of culture and cultivation is, as always in James, interwoven between the personal

and national registers; Winterbourne, for example, remains "vexed at his want of instinctive certainty as to how far her eccentricities were generic, national, and how far they were personal" (107). Beyond these thematic resonances with provincialized girls barred from Goethean self-cultivation lies the fact that James engages the theme of stubborn (national) immaturity in the novella form (as in the case of Melville's *Billy Budd*, another Anglo-American drama of fatal innocence). Moreover, James's narrative organization (again like Melville's) seems to be straining at a stylized and dilatory form, so that plot momentum is displaced by what James himself called the "free play of the whirligig of time" (preface to the New York edition of *Daisy Miller*, 42). As in the rest of this study, failed progress in subject formation stands as a pretext for open stylistic experimentation.

38. Felski follows the influential Kristevan paradigm of "women's time," paraphrased concisely in this way: "First, the insertion of women into history . . . and second, a refusal of linear temporality" (*Beyond* 150).

39. Naturalist fate operates as an immediate antithesis to the Goethean ideals of self-formation and historical emergence enshrined in the bildungsroman. The high naturalist moment, 1880–1910, has been powerfully recontextualized in terms of both gender history and colonial history by recent scholarship. For an example of the former, see Fleissner; for an example of the latter, see Cleary. Along lines that resonate with the present analysis of the problem of the postnational bildungsroman, Cleary writes: "The inability to attain some satisfying integration of character and action into a satisfying totality of vision has a number of different causes. The late nineteenth-century expansion of capitalism via imperialism onto a more fully global scale may have meant that neither individual nation-states nor even continental Europe as a whole could any longer be properly comprehended as discrete, knowable spaces" (122). For Lukács, too, the crisis of bourgeois realism was indexed by the naturalist turn and exacerbated by imperialism. This inference aligns with Lukács's own anatomy of the ideological and philosophical coordinates of the later nineteenth century as an age of irrationalism and imperialism (the full version of which we find in his late, mammoth anti-Nietzschean book *The Destruction of Reason*). But already in *The Historical Novel*, Lukács's account of the sclerosis of bourgeois dynamism turns on several factors directly related to the rising importance of colonial modes of production and imperialist thought, especially the burgeoning power of Darwinian racial science as a way of understanding social struggle. Imperial expansion is, on the one hand, a sign of bourgeois decay (the economic limits of industrial capitalism having been reached in a series of financial crises) and, on the other hand, an occasion for the European middle classes to sacrifice their productivity of spirit still further by indulging in colonial wealth-extraction accompanied by neofeudal and racist social attitudes. For Lukács, a socially regressive bourgeoisie occasions quite directly the decay of the novel into naturalist ideology.

40. What makes Gagnier's discussion of emergent consumer society so germane here is the fact that the hypostasis of endless choice in that society proves to be a rich economic analogue for the hypostasis of endless youth in novels without closure. See *The Insatiability of Human Wants* 20. My thanks to Lauren Goodlad for noting this connection.

41. Along different, though parallel, lines, see Peter Bürger: "The crisis of the bourgeois individual at the end of the nineteenth century seems to produce structures of behavior that, though one cannot speak of an immediate economic causality, show a surprising analogy with imperialism" (qtd. in Schwarz 176).

42. The relevant dimensions of this wider crisis of progress as a European idea are outlined in chapter 1, but see also Eugene Lunn, who gives a useful overview of modernism as a decisive confrontation with doctrines or ideologies of progress. He cites, first of all, the movement's characteristic challenge to "positivist science and secular optimism" at the end of the nineteenth century and, second, its formation within a pervasive deflation of liberal expectations triggered by the economic depressions of 1873–1896 (38). Lunn summarizes the key point by way of a general characterization of modernist culture: "Stress upon simultaneity and a heightened 'present consciousness,' as opposed to temporal unfolding, resulted, in part, from a loss of belief in the beneficent course of linear historical development" (39).

43. Fredric Jameson reads another kind of modernist form, the national allegory of Wyndham Lewis's *Tarr*, as addressing the "increasing gap between the existential data of everyday life within a given nation-state and the structural tendency of monopoly capital to develop on a worldwide, essentially transnational scale" (*Fables* 94).

44. Pericles Lewis tracks the results in the modern novel of the growing redefinition of society in terms of groups—particularly ethnic, racial, and religious—as opposed to individuals (individuals who defined the liberal frame for nineteenth-century nations or societies) (10). For more on the waning of liberalism in relation to changing modernist forms, see Peppis, Sherry, and Tratner.

Chapter 3: Youth/Death: Schreiner and Conrad in the Contact Zone

1. This way of framing the postcolonial/feminist intersection in Schreiner is different in emphasis but complementary to the position outlined, for example, by Anne McClintock: "The radical significance of [*African Farm*] lies in Schreiner's conviction that a critique of the violence of colonialism also entails a critique of domesticity and the institution of marriage" (278).

2. For a brief consideration of *The Mill on the Floss* as a "compelling precedent" for the determinations of gender in Schreiner's *African Farm*, see Lane 99; for the lineage forward from Schreiner to Woolf and then to Doris Lessing, see Showalter 198.

3. Kucich reads the novel's structure of masochism as the key to its elusive politics. He usefully summarizes feminist approaches that have, since Elaine Showalter, centered on the fact that Schreiner's appealing female heroes are nonetheless forced to confront failure, death, and self-renunciation ("Masochism" 81). McClintock nicely captures the paradoxical and shifting views of Schreiner on race and empire (258–60); for more on Schreiner's complex, ambivalent, and shifting attitude toward European colonialism, see also Burdett and McCracken (156).

4. Kucich's recent reading of Schreiner discusses the missing elements of class society and mobility in colonial South Africa as crucial to her work and its peculiarity in the British canon.

5. As Christopher GoGwilt has suggested, it makes sense to read Schreiner's novel as a kind of limit-text for Victorian realism and for its regnant concepts of education and culture. *African Farm* signals, in his view, the "simultaneous globalization and disappearance of European cultural ideals" (5). GoGwilt rightly emphasizes the fact that imperialism seems to unsettle some of the tenets of European *Bildung*, but he argues that Schreiner's writing reveals the concept of culture—associated in the English tradition with both Arnold and

Mill—as "in its origins, nihilist" (5). Here he pursues a kind of Nietzschean transvaluation or even deconstruction of the culture concept as nihilist to its core and from its inception, recruiting Schreiner into a broad-gauge critique of Enlightenment values. By contrast, I read the text as revealing not the culture concept's *essential* corruption but its transformation and attenuation in the colonial setting of South Africa and in the historical era of the fin de siècle.

6. Of course Waldo and Lyndall's intellectual formation has other than German roots, the two most frequently noted being Spencer and Emerson. For a good discussion of the novel's steeping in various nineteenth-century discourses of progress, see Burdett 24–30.

7. For more on the general question of the female bildungsroman, see Abel, Hirsch, and Langland; Felski; Fraiman; and Showalter. For influential feminist readings of Lyndall's thwarted *Bildung*, see Gilbert and Gubar as well as DuPlessis. And for a more recent reading of the problem of women's access to education or culture in *African Farm*, see Sanders.

8. It is worth noting in this connection that, while composing *African Farm* in 1881, Schreiner was learning German in order to read Goethe (GoGwilt 107). Looking back on that phase in a 1907 letter, Schreiner describes herself as a "passionate lover of Goethe's" (*My Other Self* 482). To explore the connection further, one might consider Lyndall's interest in roles, masks, and performance as a quite direct revision of Wilhelm Meister's interest in a theatrical vocation. Schreiner was fully cognizant of the fact that women's acting, unlike men's, could be quickly assimilated to a sexualized and commodified status tantamount to prostitution.

9. The life of a sailor in the modern merchant marine is, Marlow insists, "barren of adventure," and can be redeemed only by "perfect love of the work" (50).

10. In *Nostromo*, another quintessential though expatriated Englishman, Charles Gould, embodies the ideas of stiff-lipped integrity and self-possession: "It is your character that is the inexhaustible treasure which may save us all yet, your character, Carlos, not your wealth" (309).

11. Marlow acknowledges (as does Conrad in the Author's Note) the improbable tempo and depth of his tale: "All this happened in much less time than it takes to tell, since I am trying to interpret for you into slow speech the instantaneous effects of visual impressions" (78).

12. Cedric Watts offers a nice overview of the novel's early reception, particularly noting how many readers deprecated the book as digressive and meandering; "events are almost contemptuously forestalled," wrote one reviewer in *The Speaker* (Watts 19).

13. Taking a note from Henry James, Michael Levenson offers an excellent discussion of the relative importance of "experience" to "adventure" in modernist fiction (*Modernism* 22). Marlow's mature retrospective point of view means, of course, that Conrad's technique continually displaces the time of emergence from the plot.

14. Michael Valdez Moses discusses a number of these moments in his suggestive account of Conrad's method for dramatizing the crumbling epistemological confidence of Europeans out on the colonial frontier ("Disorientalism" 44).

15. For more on the uneven geographical scheme of the novel—migration and mobility across vast stretches of the map combined with obvious spatial compression and containment in Patusan, see Scott Cohen.

16. For a recent and probing treatment of Conrad's impressionism in relation both to technical aesthetics and imperial politics, see Matz (*Literary* 138–54); for a persuasive reconsideration of the same topic more inflected by the problem of masculinity, see Katz (80–107).

17. In one of the more hackneyed portions of the text, Conrad, via Marlow, frames the geography of Patusan in terms that recall a woman's body, and he does so with as little subtlety as, say, H. Rider Haggard in *King Solomon's Mines* (205–11).

18. Michael Moses gives an excellent account of the problem of failed nationalism in Patusan and of denationalized life on the *Patna* (*Novel and Globalization* 84–92). Peter Mallios offers a useful overview of recent critical positions on Conrad's relation to nationalism, concluding that Conrad develops a "meta-national form" that allows him to stabilize his ambivalence about nationalism (pro or con) by examining the imaginative techniques and genres that tend to support fantasies of national character and national history (359).

19. Peter Mallios has directed critical attention to a very suggestive passage from *The Mirror of the Sea* (1906) that resonates with Marlow's speech; in it, Conrad writes that crisis means that "we must turn to the national spirit, which, superior in its force and continuity to good and evil fortune, can alone give us the feeling of an enduring existence and of an invincible air of power against the fates" (qtd. in Mallios 377). This version of the idea explicitly charges national spirit with the ability to impart a sense of "enduring existence" as contrasted with the vicissitudes of fate and fortune—nationalized historical being in other words, as against the sense of being adrift or homeless in a history of good and evil fortune.

20. For a thorough treatment of the sheltering conception as a motif pitched against pervasive and corrosive skepticism in *Lord Jim* and in Conrad more generally, see Wollaeger, *Joseph Conrad* esp. pp. 2–7 and 96–114.

21. For more on the novel's investment in Jim's intimacy with the native Bugis (Doramin and Dain Waris) as well as his Malay servant Tamb'Itam, see Moses, *Novel* 81–82.

22. Jim feels that his benevolent presence has liberated the local fishermen from the Rajah's exploitation: "I've changed all that" (289). But both Jim and Marlow realize that his changes cannot take on the weight of history, of political or institutional transformation, since they are temporary effects of his charismatic (white) prestige and authority.

23. A different kind of postcolonial reading of *Lord Jim* would emphasize the natives' backwardness as part of a colonial ideology that Conrad seems both to debunk and to recirculate. Here the operative questions turn more on how Conrad explores the narrative and characterological entailments of the decision to represent Patusan as resistant to the imperial discourse of progress. As Krishnan notes with great insight, the goal of assaying the ideology-content of Conrad's opinions—his complicity, say, with European imperialism—is not as important or difficult perhaps as the goal of tracing the entwined genealogy of novel forms and metahistorical narratives: "The link between interiority (in narrative) and progress (in history) as it informs representation is not as easily loosened as the empirical oppressor can be denounced" (333). For more on the place of the concept of *Bildung* in the development of a Eurocentric standard of modernity centered on interiority and subjectivity, see Lloyd, "Arnold, Ferguson."

24. Here I anticipate chapter 7 by way of a clarification that pertains directly to Conrad and to the Krishnan reading cited earlier. Krishnan's approach, I think, builds on the

conceptual bases of Gayatri Spivak and Dipesh Chakrabarty (and David Lloyd, as noted). For this group of critics, the concept of development itself more or less entails a Eurocentric view of modernity that cannot countenance colonial difference but must absorb the latter into what Krishnan calls "a tendentious discourse of 'transition.'" Krishnan asks: Can "the protocols governing literary analysis and historical evaluation . . . move beyond Europe, where 'Europe' is no longer the sign of a geographical space but an exclusive mode of temporalization?" (342). Krishnan identifies an outside to European-Hegelian metahistorical thought, a "creative space" at "the periphery of empire," generated as "an effect of the West, but whose lines of formation remain heteronomous to it" (344). Likewise for Chakrabarty, the challenge of anti-Eurocentric research is to move outside classic historicism into another mode of temporalization, an alternative modernity articulated from outside the Hegelian philosophy of history. However, it seems to me that the mode of temporalization associated with European enlightenment and empire can be exposed to a dialectical critique, based on its own contradictions, more effectively than it can be opposed by a counterdiscourse of alternative modernity. *Lord Jim* would be an example of that kind of critique in that it disenchants the narrative of European subject-formation, revealing it to be split into noncompatible temporal modes of moralized (national) progress and endless (capitalist, global) revolution. Moreover, this ironic renarrativization of the European subject (what I have called the metabildungsroman) manages to estrange the relation between Westernization and modernization without imagining a discursive revolution that ends imperialist and neocolonial projections of "progress" from Europe to the periphery. In other words, straddling a romance of colonial anachronism and a critique of European progressivism, Conrad manages to expose the latter to its own contradictions without generating a counter-romance of ideological escape from the long-term effects of Westernization.

25. In other words, the metageneric elements of the text allow us to modify and perhaps revise the following influential claim from Fredric Jameson's *The Political Unconscious*: "*Nostromo* is a meditation on History. That of *Lord Jim* remains stubbornly deflected onto the problematic of the individual act" (264). For timely reconsiderations of the novel in terms of the problem of incipient globalization and not simply the late Victorian politics of imperialism, see Ross; Harpham 31–33.

26. Such a reading is in keeping with the tragic reading of Conrad's politics, developed for example in Avrom Fleishman's influential study. Even more specifically, it follows from Michael Moses's comprehensive reading of *Lord Jim*, in which Moses writes, "If for Conrad the triumph of Western modernity is a historical certainty, it is no less the consequence of a tragic collision of cultures" (*Novel* 68). Moses rightly locates *Lord Jim* at an "impasse of modernity" in which the fate of Patusan is not utterly foreclosed or foreordained, but from which it has become impossible to project world-historical progress in the realist frame of the novel of progress: "The achronicity of the narrative suits a posthistorical consciousness that can no longer conceive of further linear movement in history" (96). For further consideration of the tragic dimensions of *Lord Jim*, see Watt 346–56 and Bongie 178–82.

27. For an excellent discussion of the importance of bureaucratic authority to *Heart of Darkness*, see Levenson, *Modernism* 44–48. Borrowing from Max Weber's discussion of styles of authority, Levenson observes that Kurtz, as a figure of charismatic authority, "accumulates too much" character. In a sense, the drama of Jim and Marlow offers a

similar study in the polarization of character and function within the overseas imperial bureaucracy.

28. In fact Conrad further attenuates the authority of Marlow, and Stein for that matter, via the offices of Jewel who, as Natalie Melas observes, comes to assume the "skeptical magnitude normally reserved for disillusioned white male colonists" (62–63).

Chapter 4: Souls of Men under Capitalism: Wilde, Wells, and the Anti-Novel

1. In "The Decay of Lying," Wilde further anticipates Lukács by implicitly favoring Balzacian realism over Zolaesque naturalism.

2. This story runs fairly consistently from Lukács's early work in *Soul and Form* and *Theory of the Novel* through famous essays such as "Marx and the Problem of Ideological Decay" and "Narrate or Describe," and into the 1930s works on the historical novel and European realism.

3. Maureen O'Connor sees the Irish myth of *Tir na nOg* as an Irish source text for *Dorian Gray*, one that already presupposes that the "land of youth" is an impossible, potentially dangerous fantasy (468).

4. Together Wilde and Wells strike at the heart of two traditions of Victorian self-fashioning, the myth of the self-cultivating aesthete and the myth of the self-made businessman. While mainstream Victorian fiction is itself rife with failures whose stories debunk or demystify these iconic figures of Culture and Commerce, few manage so systematically to foreground the broken compromise between aesthetic education and capitalist necessity.

5. The short circuit between aestheticism and an intensifying commodity culture in the late Victorian period has been, of course, addressed in detail by critics before. See Birken and Gagnier, for example. Rita Felski, too, notes in Wilde the "aesthete's continuing dependency on the commodity culture against which he appears to position himself" (*Gender* 99).

6. Naturally all novels mix descriptive summary and plot delays with scenic action and plot advances; some novels in the fabulist tradition of Sterne's *Tristram Shandy* even make a central aesthetic principle out of the ludic possibilities inherent in the balancing act of delay-and-advance. But Wilde's text assimilates and sensationalizes the dilatory and antidevelopmental logic of youth to the point of warping the biographical-time conceit that was a bedrock of mainstream realist presentation. So much is obvious at the level of the novel's plot, but it is also present at the level of style, as episode, vignette, dialogue, and epigram tend to break the continuity of narration in *Dorian Gray*.

7. The text fairly demands that critics locate it within and against the developmental fictions of the nineteenth century. Nils Clausson, for example, has explored *Dorian Gray* as a lapsed bildungsroman, noting that the novel modulates disjunctively between gothic degeneration and a Paterian model of cultivation. Jan B. Gordon observes that Wilde "inverts some of the traditional features of the nineteenth-century developmental novel: the maturation of the parent-less hero; his assumption of a viable religious attitude; and the recognition of identity within a vocation" (355). Lawrence Danson concentrates on Wilde's challenge both to progressive thinking and autonomous individuality, the two key and interlocking elements of the classic bildungsroman; Danson also underscores the hollowing out of Dorian's subjectivity as he becomes an aesthetic object. Stephen Arata points out that Wilde tends to unsettle "humanist ideologies of identity," that is, those that project an

essential and continuous self, the developing subject produced by the classic bildungsroman (59). Arata sees Wilde as challenging Herbert Spencer's evolutionary thought: "Where Spencer saw growth in terms of the coherent and directed realization of a potential latent in (and thus essential to) the individual, Wilde views it in terms of an undirected and largely alogical process of accretion" (61).

8. The passage just cited continues to use Orientalism as a motif for consumption without production as it turns to mythic tales about gems and jewels: emeralds grown on snakes in the vale of Jordan and a plague-curing bezoar "found in the heart of the Arabian deer" (167). Such treasures of the East are stock colonial commodities in the fiction of adventure, especially insofar as they represent the glamour of imperial wealth minus the unbecoming aspects of conquest, expropriation, and the global division of labor.

9. Jim Hansen usefully summarizes Wilde's concept of bourgeois individualism: "Wilde defends a radical social agenda by fitting it within the accepted ends of capitalist conceptions of individualism. He has imagined from within the moral and social program of liberal capitalist democracy a way to make Socialism into the purest realization of Adam Smith's invisible hand. In such a society, Wilde explains, people will be free to generate their own styles, their own minds, and their own personas without having to 'meddle with others,' and, furthermore, such self-interest will create a more colorful, differentiated, vibrantly liberated, and, finally, moral world. Socialism, then, would affirm rather than deny the personal and cultural achievements of bourgeois society" (Hansen 69).

10. In "Soul of Man," Wilde writes that "evolution is the law of life" and that wherever "this tendency is not expressed, it is a case of artificially arrested growth, or of disease, or of death" (1101). As Terry Eagleton notes, Wilde also insists in "The Critic as Artist" that "through constant change, and through constant change alone, will [the individual] find his true unity" (336). Wilde derives some of his ideas on self-cultivation, via Pater, from the classic German tradition of *Bildung*. Indeed Pater, in his influential *Bookman* review of *Dorian Gray*, notes that Wilde either flouts or fails the standard of "harmonious development" enshrined by that tradition (qtd. in James Eli Adams 218).

11. Terry Eagleton has proposed that Wilde's special capacity to open up the "gap between consciousness and action"—so central to the complication of progressive narrative time in *Dorian Gray*—derives from a particular Irish sense of the "discrepancy between rhetoric and reality" (333). With emphasis shading in the direction not of subtextual Irishness but of overtly parodic Englishness, Kiberd too embeds Wilde's key aesthetic maneuvers in the explanatory context of the Anglo-Irish encounter (33–50). Along similar lines, Maureen O'Connor proposes that Dorian's breakdown refers obliquely to "colonial Ireland's traumatic relationship to a history that defies linear models of progress" (463).

12. Declan Kiberd has observed the importance of the Flaubertian influence on Joyce and Bowen, particularly with regard to the figure of the hero who "permits the world to overwhelm him" (377).

13. As Wilde's spokesman and surrogate, Gilbert, avers in "The Critic as Artist," "there has been no material improvement that has not spirtualised the world" (1023). Mary C. King has argued that *Dorian Gray*, though clearly shaped by an interest in Irish myths of origin, also works to preempt an Irish revivalist logic that would pit the spiritualized Celt against the rationalist Anglo-Saxon.

14. Many critics would view Joyce and Bowen, for instance, as falling to either side of the colonial divide, in terms of family background and political sympathies. Given the complexity, though, of these writers' (and Wilde's) relation to Irishness, and given the structural peculiarities of what Joseph Valente has described as the "metrocolonial" situation of modern Ireland (3–4), it is probably best not to adopt a hard-line analytical separation of so-called colonizer and colonized identities. Although deeply interested in the cultural politics of the Anglo-Irish encounter, and strongly motivated by a sense that their own relations to the English language and English culture were those of outsiders, both Wilde and Joyce were wary of strong Irish nationalism. As for Bowen, as we will see in chapter 6, it was almost impossible for her to imagine aligning herself with either the Irish or the English given that her political horizon was defined by the dying hybridity of Anglo-Irishness.

15. Critics have long and fully treated the moral (even moralizing) dimensions of Wilde's experiment, the way it visits judgments upon its trio of main characters. As Jim Hansen notes, *Dorian Gray* "certainly entertains personal experimentation, narcissism, and non-conformity at the level of content" but also "seems to be profoundly moralistic in tone" (64). For more on the problem of a strictly antimaterialist reading of *Dorian Gray*, see Mao 84–86.

16. Dorian gives himself over to an aesthetic code and to a set of extrinsic values, offering, as Kathy Psomiades notes, "complete cooperation rather than stubborn resistance" (187). Psomiades observes that Dorian is an improper educational subject because he takes the lessons of his elders all too literally (187). His story omits, or compresses almost to the point of omission, the narration of struggle toward some kind of compromise between autonomy and authority, and his utter objectification is the logical (if supernatural) result.

17. Wilde and Wells pick up the standard bildungsroman motif of describing the hero's formation through reading. However, as was also the case in both *African Farm* and *Lord Jim*, that version of self-tutelage has become in these texts a deforming and disabling romanticism, beyond the capacity of bourgeois socialization to assimilate. Thus Dorian's encounter with Huysmans is a fatal one: "For years, Dorian Gray could not free himself from the influence of this book" (158).

18. Just as Conrad replaces Marlow as narrator quite suddenly toward the end of *Lord Jim*, Wilde surprises readers in chapter 11 by dramatizing the narrator's distance from the focalizing power of Lord Henry: "Even the cardinal virtues cannot atone for half-cold entrées, as Lord Henry remarked once, in a discussion on the subject; and there is possibly a good deal to be said for his view" (174). As Joseph Bristow has noted, one of the crucial aspects of Walter Pater's celebrated review of *Dorian Gray* was his uncertainty about how seriously to take Lord Henry (xxx). Indeed, it remains difficult to gauge the novel's stance on Lord Henry, though clearly his volubility and his strained attempt at detachment from sincere emotion make him as open to ironic scrutiny as that voluble crypto-sentimentalist Marlow.

19. But see Richard Ruppel for an account of Wildean resonances in the homoerotic and homosocial content in Conrad's fiction.

20. As James Eli Adams has noted, Wilde's text "represents a triangle of men caught up in an eminently middle-class struggle for charismatic 'influence'" (217–18). I would call this an apt description, too, of the central drive in *Lord Jim*: to find a grounding logic for male honor and influence outside the disenchanted laws of the marketplace—laws that

are nakedly exposed (despite Marlow's mystifying rhetoric and nostalgic wishes) in the colonial-maritime arena.

21. One interesting frame of comparison for Wilde (and for Conrad) might be the strikingly modern 1881 Brazilian novel *The Posthumous Memoirs of Brás Cubas*, in which a decadent aristocratic figure in the colonial contact zone of 1880s Brazil performs an equally determined upending of realist time conventions in a kind of antibildungsro-man: Brás Cubas writes from the grave and perversely refuses any mode of progress or experiential deepening. In Roberto Schwarz's bravura reading of the text, we can see Machado's masterpiece as a late nineteenth-century anti-novel that, like *Dorian Gray*, violates realist time. As Schwarz puts it, in what could have been a gloss on Wilde, "Where caprice seems to reign, causality is in fact in charge" (33). For Wilde, as for Schreiner and Conrad, the caprice of a plot in which ordinary or organic time is arrested or reversed must in the end come up against the return of temporal destiny, a reality principle often (though not always) figured as sudden death. Schwarz goes on to describe the text in terms that might well apply to Wilde and to Conrad: "We can say that the *Memoirs* com-bines a certain aestheticist view of reality—unusual and daring in its unconformity with bourgeois utilitarianism—an analytic psychology that privilege cannot penetrate, and a framework of realist fiction, in which social conflict redefines the totality of subjective pretensions and puts them in their place" (118). Speaking of the main character's charming eloquence, Schwarz writes: "The volubility undoes the rule of the clock, of conventionally sequential chains of events, of the ordering that is indispensable to active existence, but it does so in vain, for time reemerges inside the movements of volubility itself, which are impregnated with a complex, differentiated temporality, only to be found in the greatest literature" (135).

22. During his endless summer of the mind, Dorian Gray "never fell into the error of arresting his intellectual development by any formal acceptance of creed or system" (164). This is the anti-ideological fantasy of Dorian's youth, which figures the unsustainable but lovely idea of a permanently uncommitted intellectual, a free bohemian relieved of the limi-tations of a specific social viewpoint.

23. Christine Ferguson cogently argues that despite the novel's apparent foreclosure of the "decadent quest" at the end, *Dorian Gray*'s meaning still inheres in its commitment to "triumphal experimentalism" (471).

24. The performative gestures and ironic contraptions that make *Dorian Gray* such an influential text can be referred not just to Wilde's spectacular challenge to identitarian thinking, but also to the economic and national questions that cluster around antidevel-opmental fictions at the end of the nineteenth century. To the Conrad-Wilde pairing we might add a different triangulating text: Melville's *Billy Budd*, a homosocial and homoerotic experimental fiction written during the same years as *Dorian Gray* (it was left unfinished at Melville's death in 1891). Melville anticipates Conrad in his ornate impressionist style and in the theme of the redoubtably innocent sailor boy with a "lingering adolescent expression" (299). Moreover, Melville explicitly embeds his story in the historical context of a shift from liberal imperialism to the New Imperialism as tracked by British jurisprudence and prevail-ing concepts of heroic agency. In the text, this context translates into a fundamental shift from a self-governing, self-shaping male hero to one who must subordinate his "private conscience" to the "imperial one" (362). Even more precisely, Melville's imagery and diction

frame Billy Budd's frozen adolescence and radical innocence as a "savage" or "barbaric" challenge to national-imperial laws of order and progress (373, 372).

25. Gagnier has suggested that Wilde's story reflects a larger shift from discourses of production to discourses of consumption in both aesthetic and economic registers of late Victorian culture. Gagnier's periodization of this shift complements the Lukács-Arendt line of analysis in the sense that they all converge on the idea of flagging bourgeois dynamism after 1870, an idea framed by Gagnier in terms of the production-consumption shift (17). Gagnier's model is implicitly qualified and modified by Catherine Gallagher's *The Body Economic*, which suggests the coexistence in mid-Victorian texts of economic regimes based on production *and* consumption, on large-scale systems of output and on specific bodily experiences of input.

26. Gagnier's research reveals that several influential economic thinkers of the later nineteenth century viewed market society as effectively the end of history, so that capitalism itself was supposed to have reached a certain kind of self-fulfillment, with further changes to be minor rather than transformational. The novels under analysis here, however, appear to me to view capitalism as a more or less permanently revolutionary force, always in tension with those human sciences (like economics) or political discourses (like nationalism) that wish to stabilize its endless forward motion.

27. If we think about Wells's *Dr. Moreau* in relation to Wilde, we can see that both of these writers had their gothic imaginations fired by a problem that Gagnier describes as pervasive in late Victorian culture: the biologization of the division of labor (Gagnier 97). For more on Wilde's place in gothic traditions, see Arata, Hansen, and Riquelme ("Wilde's Gothic").

28. For a convincing case that *Tono-Bungay* is a modernist, metageneric experiment designed to mimic at the level of style the general economic substitution of waste for value, see Kupinse 64–70. The modernist ambition to write a book-of-the-world, evident in so many texts from Joyce's *Ulysses* and Pound's *Cantos* to Stein's *The Making of Americans*, finds a rational and didactic (rather than symbolic or mythic) form in Wells's novels. These are the terms in which Edward Mendelson describes *Tono-Bungay* as a modernist masterpiece: "It is a profoundly unsettling novel, epic in scope and encyclopedic in content, yet always disturbingly aware of its own fictional quality" (xiii). Robert Caserio also argues forcefully for Wells as a major experimental writer of the period. Caserio describes Wells's achievement as a particular and vital brand of essayistic fiction in which ideological statement is neither subsumed to narrative totality nor embedded within the mystifying devices of the protagonist. Wells's fiction, in other words, "refuses its own spontaneous presence" ("Novel as a Novel Experiment" 90). Even more to the point, Caserio suggests that Wells displaces the traditional model of protagonist for something like a "heuristic persona." No doubt that displacement allows Wells to organize *Tono-Bungay* as a met-abildungsroman: Freed from the constraints of psychological verisimilitude, Ponderevo becomes a more flexible device for commenting on the peculiarities of social and novelistic conventions. Perhaps *Tono-Bungay* retains its place as the one twentieth-century Wells novel still commonly taught (a fact lamented by Caserio) in part because it is in this novel that Wells dramatizes (via the motif of failed apprenticeship) precisely the displacement of the fictional subject that Caserio takes as the hallmark of Wells's best work after 1910 (90–94).

29. As Benita Parry puts it, this novel shows us England, "reordered and unsettled by capitalism-as-imperialism" (150).

30. Rachel Bowlby offers one of the more thorough treatments of *Dorian Gray*'s saturation by the logic of modern advertising and commodification. Jeff Nunokawa expands on her reading, noting that the "ephemerality of individual desires" in the novel seems to register the broad expansion of advertising and consumer desire in the later nineteenth century (83–84).

31. George's immaturity also manifests itself in the contradictory nature of his social commentary; Benita Parry notes, for example, that George "applauds technological advance" yet laments the "consequent disintegration of traditional social forms" (154).

32. In this sense, David Lodge's observation that England is the "central character" of the novel is right, but only up to a point (218). As Bryan Cheyette observes, the novel elegizes the condition-of-England genre; "for the twentieth-century novelist, there was no longer a settled England . . . to depict" (xx). Cheyette cites Wells's *Autobiography* on this point: "Throughout the broad smooth flow of nineteenth-century life in Great Britain, the art of fiction floated on the same assumption of social fixity" (qtd. in Cheyette xx–xxi).

33. Uncle Edward Ponderevo often becomes giddy at the thought of being a force in the colonial world economy. He praises George and himself as "big growing people," representing, "Anglo-Saxon energy." "That's it, George—energy," says Edward. "It's put things in our grip—threads, wires, stretching out and out, George, from that little office of ours, out to West Africa, out to Egypt, out to Inja, out east, west, north, and south. Running the world practically. Running it faster and faster" (282).

34. Published in 1911 on the heels of *Tono-Bungay*, *The New Machiavelli* features a protagonist-narrator (a successful politician named Remington) who describes change run amok in England: "It was a sort of progress that had bolted; it was change out of hand, and going at an unprecedented pace nowhere in particular" (41). Remington is recurrently frustrated by the fact that his society—so committed to modernization in the economic sphere—maintains such hidebound and Victorian sexual attitudes. Most of all, he protests the idea that monogamous marriage—patent lunacy to him—is seen as a reasonable way to manage love, sex, reproduction, property rights, and platonic intimacy in one holy social device.

35. As Edward Mendelson notes, Wells himself thought he was writing a novel "on Dickens-Thackeray lines" (xxvii).

36. In the quap episode, the decay of George's character is revealed alongside the contradiction between an imperialist rhetoric of worldwide development and the actual practice of colonial wealth-extraction. Parry sees Wells as offering a fairly muted criticism of empire per se (the text "refrains from repudiating the west's assumption of its right to colonial resources") but as nonetheless signifying (in the quap episode) "a frustration of imperialism's ambitions" (159).

37. There is one final prescient Wellsian subplot worth mentioning here because it cinches George's estrangement from national identity. Having developed a strategic commodity, the X2 rocket-torpedo, George is rebuffed by the British state and declares himself more or less a stateless subject, a nomad of technocapitalism: "X2 isn't intended for the empire, or indeed for the hands of any European power. We offered it to our own people first, but they would have nothing to do with me, and I have long ceased to trouble much

about such questions. I have come to see myself from the outside, my country from the outside—without illusions" (388). This declaration of the "illusions perdues" theme takes on a particularly far-reaching significance in that it illustrates a stage of disillusionment explicitly beyond the bounds of the nineteenth-century national paradigm: The self is cut adrift even from the tradition of the fiction of disillusionment.

38. Both Wilde and Wells, then, find ways to assimilate the trope of bad infinity into their conjoined depiction of an endless adolescence and a distended national frame. Compare, in this connection, Fredric Jameson's account of Forster's *Howards End* (published in 1910, the year after *Tono-Bungay*), another condition-of-England novel rescripted for the age of empire: "It is Empire which stretches the roads out to infinity, beyond the bounds and borders of the national state, Empire which leaves London behind it as a new kind of spatial agglomeration or disease" ("Modernism and Imperialism" 57). Jameson's commentary fits *Tono-Bungay* as neatly as—perhaps more neatly than—it fits *Howards End*; both novels present a structural tension between the humanist or traditionalist core culture of English elites on the one hand and the vital, supporting economic force (sourced in African commodities) on the other.

39. As Edward Mendelson summarizes the historical and economic backdrop of *Tono-Bungay*, the novel presents and reflects "a society whose wealth is built partly on the imagery of advertising, partly on the exploitation of technology, partly on piratical commerce on an international scale" (xxvii).

Chapter 5: Tropics of Youth in Woolf and Joyce

1. Kathy J. Phillips offers the most thorough presentation of this general view in *Virginia Woolf against Empire*. Her broad thesis is persuasive, though as the title suggests, Phillips tends to see the case mostly in terms of Woolf's criticism of, rather than implication in, colonialist modes of thought and forms of cultural appropriation.

2. McGee's political formalism produces similar conclusions to Raymond Williams's biographical essay on Woolf and the Bloomsbury group, in which Williams suggests that these liberal intellectuals were both beneficiaries and critics of British imperial power (*Problems in Materialism*). At a formal level, McGee argues against shunting the "negative aspects" of imperial politics onto Woolf's characters (such as Bernard in *The Waves*) in order to argue for the author's own detached perspective on the corruption of imperial patriarchy (635). Mark Wollaeger offers a similar reading of *The Voyage Out*, suggesting that the novel's anti-imperial elements must be weighed against its representation of native women as mere object-symbols of global patriarchy ("Woolf, Postcards" 44).

3. As Joe Cleary observes on the general matter of comparing British and Irish history, say industrialization and famine in the mid-nineteenth century, these can be viewed as "two altogether alien and disjunctive histories" but also as "two divergent vectors of the same modernization process" (78–79). For certain critical arguments, the level of analytical resolution requires the disjunctive model, but for others, the comparative frame of divergent stories within a larger narrative of modernization proves more apt. For an argument that emphasizes different adaptations of the English and Irish bildungsroman in the modernist period, see Gregory Castle, who states convincingly that the English variant remains a good deal more committed to socially pragmatic processes of growth and adjustment (24).

4. More precisely, Lloyd puts Joyce's fiction in critical relation to "the developmental historicism that structures nineteenth-century realism"; Joyce, Lloyd argues, allows medieval temporal forms into the narrative in ways that "make space for the disjunctive times of colonial Ireland" (*Irish Times* 94).

5. For recent treatments of the generic precedents for *Portrait*, see Castle and Boes, "A Portrait."

6. Both writers tried many different techniques to avoid writing a conventional novel. Woolf begins with the inverted *bildungsromane* of *The Voyage Out* and *Jacob's Room*, moves to the lyrical, elegiac, and pictorial novels of her celebrated midcareer, then tries her hand at various hybrid forms (group-novel, essay-novel, and pageant-novel) in the 1930s. And Joyce has his famous four variants in off-novel composition: the short-story cycle, the inverted bildungsroman, the compendium of mythic form and stylistic pastiche, and the *roman fleuve* of pure language.

7. For examples of feminist interpretation, see Froula, "Out of the Chrysalis," and Friedman, "Spatialization." For recent studies that emphasize travel and colonialism while integrating feminist insights, see Karen Lawrence, *Penelope Voyages* (154–79), and Wollaeger, "Woolf, Postcards."

8. Taking his cue from a key line found in both draft versions of *Portrait* and in *Stephen Hero* ("Is the mind of boyhood medieval . . . ?"), David Lloyd proposes that Stephen's identification with medieval thought defines the novel's inner language of resistance to capitalist rationality (*Irish Times* 83–100).

9. With regard to the links between *The Voyage Out* and *Heart of Darkness*, Vincent Sherry observes a parallel encounter in the two texts between rational discourse and "the unspeakable, insurgent Otherness of that intransigent locale" (251).

10. For more on the *bildungsheld* as "semantic void," see Moretti, *Way* 11.

11. As outlined in chapter 3, Conrad also took pains to depict his colonial outpost as a place of uneven development: "Seventeenth-century traders went there for pepper," followed by a long phase of colonial and economic neglect. Then, "somehow, after a century of chequered intercourse, the country seems to drop gradually out of the trade. . . . Nobody cares for it now" (*Lord Jim* 209–10). Similarly, in "Ireland, Island of Saints and Sages," Joyce understands Ireland as a place once located at the cusp of an advancing civilization, then thrust by the unfolding of European imperialism to a marginal or peripheral place.

12. Where Bakhtin's Goethe can see progressive time inscribed virtually everywhere—in sedimented landscapes, in wrinkled faces, in arboreal rings, Woolf's characters almost always seem to be apprehending the signs of regressive time. For a thorough reading of Woolf's generalized skepticism about developmental narratives, see Beer 13ff.

13. Since Woolf's novel revises the classic bildungsroman of Jane Austen, it makes sense that her heroine Rachel sees Austen as "so—so—well, so like a tight plait" (49).

14. As Marianne DeKoven (among others) points out, Rachel seems averse to a certain rigid set of social expectations and institutional arrangements associated with marriage, but she is not especially averse to heterosexual experience itself (127).

15. Although the plot of failed self-possession dominates the text, it is nevertheless punctuated by moments of traditional self-awareness and self-cultivation: "The vision of her own personality, of herself as a real everlasting thing, different from anything else, unmergeable,

like the sea or the wind, flashed into Rachel's mind, and she became profoundly excited at the thought of living" (75).

16. On this point, see Froula, "Out of the Chrysalis" 63, and Friedman, "Spatialization" 131.

17. Jameson, "Modernism and Imperialism" 52–58.

18. In *The Voyage Out*, Mr. Dalloway crystallizes a certain ruling-class gender ideology that appears to be intensified in a colonial setting where the masculine sphere of action is rigorously separated from the feminine sphere of contemplation. Dalloway expatiates on this principle to Rachel: "I never allow my wife to talk politics. . . . For this reason. It is impossible for human beings, constituted as they are, both to fight and to have ideals" (56).

19. Mark Wollaeger rightly notes that this episode is the scene on which "the entire narrative hinges," where the uncanny stares of the native women "bring home to [Rachel] the pressures of domestication and normalization" ("The Woolfs in the Jungle" 52 and 62).

20. That book's editor, Joseph Valente, argues that homoeroticism in *Portrait* operates "neither as a simple alternative to, nor an anomalous deviation from, some naturalized heteroerotic incitement, but as an element uncannily symbiotic with that incitement and menacing to its normalization" ("Thrilled by His Touch" 59). For Valente, Stephen's "phobic denial" of undeniable homosexual energies in his story represents a "fundamental determinant" of the narrative form of *Portrait* (49).

21. Maud Ellmann provides a sensitive close reading of the novel's "economy of flow" (158–65).

22. Deane has in mind a distinctive kind of provincializing process, though, in which Joyce's major fictions, especially *Ulysses*, turn tables to underscore the provincialism of the English domestic novel tradition.

23. In his essay on the "cubist *Portrait*," Kenner lays out the patterns that recur within each chapter; following him, a number of critics have anatomized the serial and repetitive nature of the novel. Levenson, for example, observes that "a leading pattern in the novel is the *series*, which depends not on movement toward an end but on the recurrence of identities and similarities" (1020).

24. In a different interpretive key, but along similar lines, Franco Moretti has argued that Joyce fails in *Portrait* to reconcile the movement between significant narrative "kernels" and insignificant narrative "satellites" (*Way* 241–45). In other words, the novel mixes meaningful and meaningless events rather than establishing an extended narrative around key events (as in the traditional bildungsroman) or converting the meaninglessness of everyday life into meaning (as in *Ulysses*).

25. For a useful outline of the novel's structure and symmetry, see Riquelme, *Teller* 58–64 and 232–34. On pure potentiality, see Kenner: "In the mind of Joyce there hung a radiant field of multiple possibilities" (179). Seamus Deane likewise observes that Joyce operates in a field of open possibility: "The unfinished and the uncreated culture provided the opportunity for the most comprehensive, the most finished, the most boundlessly possible art. The colonial culture produced imperial art" (*Celtic Revivals* 97).

26. Tobias Boes has recently explored the novel's use of repetition to cut progress, citing Joyce's own concept of the "individuating rhythm" to describe what Boes calls a "structural compromise between cyclical and progressive elements" ("*A Portrait of the Artist*" 770).

27. Traditional criticism of *Portrait* has been, in my view, likely to err, at least in emphasis, in the direction of seeing the novel as a continuation rather than a dramatic revision of the bildungsroman template. Breon Mitchell, for example, allows that the novel "contains an implicit critique of the *Bildungsroman*," but focuses on the way that Joyce's narrative conforms to the generic expectations set by Goethe (72). And Jerome Buckley notes that "Joyce sums up, even as he transforms, the traditions of the nineteenth-century *Bildungsroman*" (226). The summing up may be a more critical act than Buckley allows in his discussion. A more recent interpretation that accords more with my own sense of the novel's relationship to genre conventions is Jessica Berman's: "The end of *Portrait* signifies neither the hero's triumph, maturation, nor his reincorporation into society; but rather the explosion of the conventional *Bildungsroman* along with its enforcement of liberal subjectivity, its insistence on a unified perspective, and its insistence on language as a transparent expression of that perspective" (477).

28. Vicki Mahaffey observes that a combination of psychoanalytic effects—Lacanian "père-version" and what she counter-punningly terms "im-mère-sion"—works in *Portrait* both to hasten and to retard the aging process; Mahaffey rightly traces this set of effects from Joyce back through to Wilde, reading both as participants in a joint study of "unnatural youthfulness" linked not just to tender aestheticism, but to a half-articulated sense of Irish underdevelopment (81, 53).

29. On the "extreme form of the tension" that Stephen experiences between self-determination and social determination, see Pericles Lewis 30–31.

30. Seamus Deane makes the point clearly: "It was at such moments in his fiction that Joyce rewrote the idea of national character and replaced it by the idea of a character in search of a nation to which he (Joyce-Stephen) could belong" (*Strange* 96).

31. Along these lines, David Lloyd describes the Irish subject's peculiar relation to history: "Where the colonizer in his modernity appears able to dismiss the past with the easy forgetting of a historicist consciousness, the colonized is always in the position of having too much history, a history that detains and divides him" (*Irish Times* 90). The detaining and dividing interrupt the allegorical subsumption of historicist logic into the body of the *bildungsheld* so that Joyce's adolescent subject cannot square a linear sequence of youth/adulthood with a teleological model of national self-fulfillment.

32. Klein states the comparison clearly: "Scott's ambivalent acceptance of historical inevitability tied to nationalist pride finds an analog in Joyce's youthful despair at his nation's collusion in its own political surrender" (1025). This is especially apropos in that Scott is the locus classicus for fiction that chronicles the inevitable historical force of modernization via the imperial state (British in his case, too). In the *Waverley* model, which continues to resonate through all of the novels examined in this study, the developing protagonist embodies a complicated dialectical process in which youth and nationalism are partially eclipsed, partially recuperated by the advance of the multinational Anglophone empire.

33. Declan Kiberd has observed that the Baudelairean figure of the dandy was crucial to several Irish writers, including the three examined in this study, Wilde, Joyce, and Elizabeth Bowen. The decadent or dandy strain within Irish modernism marks the interpolation of a historical crisis centered in and symbolized by the failure of development/progress at the site of the colonial encounter with British culture and literary tradition. Within modern Irish literature, from Wilde to Joyce, Greg Dobbins has recently offered a striking account

of the mode of idleness as a resistance to a certain kind of labor regime associated with modernity, capitalism, and empire.

34. In *James Joyce and Nationalism*, Emer Nolan offers an excellent account of "the uncertain, divided consciousness of the colonial subject, which [Joyce] is unable to articulate in its full complexity outside his fiction" (130). Colonial self-alienation was something Joyce understood as central to Irish culture at large; he wrote that Ireland "entered the British dominion without forming an integral part of it. It almost entirely abandoned its language and accepted the language of the conqueror without being able to assimilate its culture or adapt itself to the mentality of which this language is the vehicle" (*Occasional* 159).

35. Christine Froula offers a succinct and critical account of the ways in which Stephen arrogates to himself the feminist critique of patriarchal institutions in Ireland (*Modernism's Body* 66–72).

36. For a further account of uneven development and cultural anachronism in modern Irish literature, see Terry Eagleton's description of the "archaic avant-garde" (273–319).

37. Just as *Portrait* updates in practice the novel-of-inaction as exemplified by, say, *Lord Jim* or *Dorian Gray*, Stephen updates in theory the aesthetic principle of inaction that Wilde's Lord Henry has already aphorized: "Art has no influence upon action. It annihilates the desire to act. It is superbly sterile" (*Dorian Gray* 257).

38. As Rebecca Walkowitz points out, the "syntax of 'while' captures the wandering of Stephen's mind" and keeps the temporality of the novel at a pitch of irresolution (68).

39. Pericles Lewis assesses the function of Stephen as a national redeemer, arguing that "in embracing his moral unity with the Irish race, he will reconcile his ethical self with his socially constructed identity"; however, Lewis goes on to note that "Joyce's own attitude towards this ideal [of the individual who redeems the nation] seems to have been more complex and ambivalent than Stephen's" (48). I would emphasize the second portion of that interpretive stance, and suggest that Joyce's ironization of Stephen reveals the hubris of Stephen's epigenetic conception of himself as the self-made redeemer of a new nation.

40. Patricia Spacks offers a forceful account of the novel as a failed bildungsroman in which Stephen progresses very little: "Stephen yields nothing of his youthful romanticism, he grows out of nothing. Instead, he grows more fully into a self of boyish ardency, boyish self-absorption, boyish conviction of infinite possibility. He refuses to grow up. Should we deplore or applaud?" (254–55).

Chapter 6: Virgins of Empire: The Antidevelopmental Plot in Rhys and Bowen

1. Katherine Mansfield shared with Rhys and Bowen an expatriate's interest in the theme of unsettlement and, not incidentally, understood herself as unequipped for writing novel-length story lines. Consider, for example, her comment that Jane Austen, that institution of English fiction, makes "modern episodic people like me . . . look very incompetent ninnies" (qtd. in Lorna Sage vii)

2. Julia Kristeva, in an influential essay, frames the problem of "women's time" in terms of the nation, suggesting that the "national problematic" is the basis of historical thinking for generations of women intellectuals invested in a linear model of time—that is, women whose cosmopolitan concerns are nonetheless rooted in a national-progressive model of

history stemming from nineteenth-century models of development (188–90). But there is an alternative lineage, Kristeva notes, in which women pose cyclical or nonlinear time against that older model; for a persuasive adaptation of this point to a reading of Jean Rhys's fiction, see Mary Lou Emery (95).

3. It is possible to argue that for feminist thought in general, and perhaps for a woman writer like Jean Rhys in particular, the critique of the representative individual as a symbol of progress is a critique of an essentially patriarchal concept. In *Provincializing Europe*, for example, Dipesh Chakrabarty suggests that there is a natural alliance between feminist suspicion of the modern (liberal) individual and postcolonial suspicion of developmentalist or historicist modes of thinking associated with European liberalism (42). Chakrabarty cites Carolyn Pateman's *Sexual Contract* as a book that establishes the patriarchal foundations of modern individualism. The genealogy of women novelists in the present study—from Eliot through to Rhys and Bowen—would tend to support the idea that the challenge to allegorical fictions of individual/national progress is itself animated and energized by a feminist critique of male destiny when the latter is taken as the definitive sign of social improvement.

4. Naturally, one would need to stipulate a number of key historical and historiographical differences between the early modern establishment of landed estates in Ireland (with its associated tenant farmer system) and the growth of plantation economies in the new world (with their slave labor systems), but it is also possible to recognize a comparable (though certainly not equivalent in degree or coeval) distance between these societies on the one hand and the industrialized zones of Europe and North America on the other.

5. In her 1952 preface to *The Last September*, Bowen notes that her protagonist Lois was "niece always, never child, of that house" (*Mulberry Tree* 126). Likewise, in both *Voyage in the Dark* and *Wide Sargasso Sea*, Rhys's disinherited protagonists have only tenuous connections to their fathers and mothers, connections that are mediated by uncles, stepmothers, servants, and other proxy parents.

6. Deborah Parsons is one of the few recent scholars to identify the strong resonances between Rhys and Bowen; her approach emphasizes their shared themes of urban wandering, dislocation, and dispossession.

7. See also Said, *Beginnings* 81–88.

8. Carine Mardorossian offers an even more detailed account of this basic divide among recent critics of *Wide Sargasso Sea*, listing Handley, Hulme, and several others who have generally supported the contention that the novel is latently or explicitly affiliated with the ideology of the deposed planter class (155–156). Mardorossian herself, like Benita Parry, views the novel as offering a postcolonial (i.e., anticolonial) rejoinder to a set of ideological givens, and in particular argues that the discourse of *obeah* produces a screen, or opaque boundary, that describes the limits of colonial knowledge about native or non-European culture.

9. Mary Lou Emery's book remains the standard work on this topic; it accounts for Rhys's fiction as tracing "the dissolution of 'character' and its reconstitution in fragmented and multiplicitous forms"—a recurrent plot that challenges familial, imperial, and patriarchal models of inheritance and cultural transmission (91). For an exemplary recent discussion of the novel's challenge to inherited gender categories and to "the center/periphery structure of empire" see Andrea Lewis 83–85. Lewis notes correctly that Emery's original work made

it possible for us to look in Rhys's novels for ways to understand the "subjective position of the novel's protagonist as shaped by the dynamics of global conquest" (93). Jordan Stouck follows more or less in Emery's line combining feminist and postcolonial approaches; Delia Konzett develops an updated and useful model of Rhys's "esthetics of dislocation" and offers a thorough analysis of commodity logic in Rhys's work (129–66).

10. Judith Dearlove has established the basic thematic problem of "the failure of the bildungsroman" in *Voyage in the Dark*, noting that Rhys displaces the plot of self-formation with a tragic account of commodified souls, bodies, and values (25). Dearlove notes that Rhys removes the external narrative voice or retrospective point of view by which a novel like Joyce's *Portrait* generates sympathetic yet ironic evaluative commentary on the young protagonist. Here there is no narrative distance to situate Anna's suffering in a comforting trajectory of future adjustment or adaptation.

11. As Robert Caserio observes, the novel links Anna's "economically determined modernity to an earlier stage of world imperialism" (*Novel in England* 184).

12. To take a longer view of Rhys's career, one might say that she begins by using naturalism to defamiliarize realist conventions, as in *Voyage in the Dark*, where she appears to objectify the standard motifs of the self-fashioning hero and his progressive social destiny. Deborah Parsons has suggested that by the time of *Good Morning, Midnight* (1938), Rhys has begun to suspend the naturalist paradigm by laying it bare and exposing "the vagaries of determinism" (145).

13. Molly Hite makes it clear that Rhys wishes to emphasize the fact that freedom and agency in the literary world of the bildungsroman are social privileges just as they are in actual processes of socialization: "One of Rhys's most powerful insights is that categories of literary and social determination interpenetrate. If major characters [in the mainstream English realist tradition] tend to be 'round' and thus not wholly predictable, they also tend to have privileges derived from some combination of gender, class, and racial factors that give them the scope to be masters of their fates" (27).

14. In a discussion of *The Castle* and *Wide Sargasso Sea*, David Lloyd offers the following suggestive account of the overlapping dimensions of Kafka's and Rhys's aesthetic: "Neither narrative leads anywhere, while at the same time it is the very retention of a project aimed at securing identity that in both cases creates a disjunction between the desire of the characters and the effect of the text" (*Nationalism* 22). The value of Lloyd's insight here is precisely that there remain elements of a subject-formation plot within a novel otherwise organized to displace and objectify it. Even more to the point, Lloyd situates Rhys with Kafka in a strain of parodic minor literature designed to challenge the major literatures of the European tradition from a position on the modern(ist) semi-periphery.

15. Here my reading of Rhys veers away from the critical consensus set by Mary Lou Emery and those writing in her vein. Emery suggests that the motif of the carnival/masquerade in *Voyage* establishes an atypical and non-European model of subject formation, highlighting the fact that Anna is shaped less by psychological data and more by social forces and communal sources of identity (68). In my view, this aspect of "colonial difference"—the socially shaped self versus the autonomous European individual—is not so starkly drawn. This novel at least does not emphasize the communal sources of Anna's identity as positive elements against a given Western model of psychological realism. Instead, it offers a negative model of subject formation—not the individual collectivized and indigenized, but

the individual taken apart and turned inside out. It is in this sense that I propose reading semicolonial modernist texts like Rhys's not according to "alternative" categories *outside* the Eurocentric or the high canonical, but as critical and parodic negations—from within—of genres and categories long naturalized as part of a European literature of enlightenment, global progress, and liberal individualism.

16. Rhys implies (here and elsewhere) a particular critical assessment of the sexual puritanism and hypocrisy of the English middle class. As the Frenchwoman Germaine observes in *Voyage*, there are pretty English girls but few pretty English women—an effect of their suffering from the fact that "most Englishmen don't care a damn about women" (82).

17. As Urmila Seshagiri puts it, when Anna proclaims herself West Indian, she is trying to inhabit "an identity that history has robbed of meaning" (489).

18. Although I have claimed that Rhys (like Woolf) eschews the logic of a woman-native allegory, it is also true that *Voyage in the Dark* (like *The Voyage Out*) experiments with framing the symbolic innocence of its girl protagonist in terms of the virgin lands of the New World. Such metaphors cast modernization and imperialism as tragic processes analogous to the fall from girlhood into adulthood. When Anna begins to see that English men often take an exploitative and condescending view of her sexuality, she remembers a flower-scented evening back in Dominica, when she was a child living next to the "forest where nobody had ever been—virgin forest" (83).

19. The abortion underscores, as Mary Lou Emery suggests, the power of male authority to pathologize and manipulate women's bodies, coding them as dangerous (and cyclical) threats to institutional authority and social order (23, 94). Seshagiri elaborates on the meaning of the abortion scene: The "coexistence of literary forms in Rhys's 1934 novel is unproductive, indeed, as the protagonist's abortion suggests, antiproductive" (492).

20. On Schreiner's original title, see Showalter 199.

21. On the point that Anna's difficult but meliorable class situation gives way in the novel to more fixed, biological categories of social difference such as sex and race, see Emery 22. For an example of modernist cultural history that describes the growing importance of biological categories in the understanding of social difference, see Jean-Michel Rabaté's discussion of Walter Heape's influential 1913 treatise, *Sex Antagonism*. Heape sees class antagonism (à la Marx) as a root source of social unrest, but also insists on sex and race as crucial factors to be reckoned with (Rabaté 213).

22. Carine Mardorossian notes that *Wide Sargasso Sea* is a narrative of "arrested development" designed to redress the "progressive narrative form of the bildungsroman" featured in *Jane Eyre* (89)

23. Nancy Armstrong's *How Novels Think* gives a recent and compelling overview of the long entwined history between the gothic and mainstream realism, noting that the former tends to erupt within the latter in order to destabilize its tendency to emphasize "an all-encompassing narrative of growth and development" (22). On the split of realist and gothic impulses in Irish writing in particular, see Eagleton 147–54. For more on the gothic dimensions of *The Last September*, see Corcoran 324–32.

24. For a recent discussion of the broader category of plantocratic culture, see George Handley's account of "Plantation America" (14). In a connection that is especially relevant to Faulkner's and, indeed, Rhys's presentation of post-plantation anachronisms and gothic residua, Handley writes: "As a result of modernization, the ideologies of the plantocracy

escaped dissolution because they were integrated into the very institutional fabric of postslavery societies, and their contradictions were heightened" (113).

25. Bowen's idiosyncratic management of plot and pacing has become a key point of stylistic analysis for most critics. See, for example, Corcoran's discussion of the plot of *The Last September* as being "not so much of event as of interim, a long drawn-out waiting" (316). Bennet and Royle offer a detailed and compelling account of Bowen's "dissolution of the novel," a phrase they use to emphasize catalepsis and other states of suspension or stilled life as a characteristic principle of her novels' construction (4).

26. To fold Wilde, Joyce, and Bowen into one frame of literary-historical analysis risks, of course, not just a generational but a political lumping-together of writers with significantly different attitudes toward Irish nationalism, British imperialism, and the process of decolonization. Many critics, for instance, would view Joyce and Bowen as falling to either side of the colonial divide, at least in terms of family background and associated political climate. Given the complexity, though, of all three writers' relation to Irishness and, moreover, given the structural peculiarities of what Joseph Valente has described as the "metrocolonial" situation of modern Ireland (*Dracula's Crypt* 3–4), it is probably best not to adopt a hard-line analytical separation of so-called colonizer and colonized identities in this case. Moreover, the point of conducting a more strictly formal—rather than intentionalist—approach to this set of Irish Anglophone fictions is to emphasize not so much the imagined or imputed political allegiances of Wilde, Joyce, and Bowen, but the capacity of their texts to capture—in symbolic form—some of the deeper historical conditions and structural contradictions that bear on the Anglo-Irish colonial encounter.

27. Julia McElhattan Williams and Margot Backus have recently countered Deane, too, by describing the Anglo-Irish in the novel as perforce historically passive; Backus questions Deane's lumping of Bowen (and others) into a Yeatsian tradition of "aristocratic enthusiasms" (174).

28. For an extended and compelling account of the Proustian motif of "lost time" in *The Last September*, see DiBattista 234–37. Lois the virgin and Laurence the lazy man emblematize not just the passiveness of their class in a time of troubles, but the specific kind of imperviousness to historical change that the Anglo-Irish have come to represent. More to the political point, Declan Kiberd has suggested, Bowen captures the passivity of a class that "failed to justify its privilege by service" (365).

29. For a substantial and pertinent analysis of the place of children and childhood in the history and literature of the Anglo-Irish "colonial order," see Backus 77–96.

30. Lois in fact stands out as one in a series of deliberately unbounded characters at the center of Bowen novels; as Susan Osborn notes, Bowen's "protagonists—in love and out—are typically vague and uncertain, diffuse blanks where one expects to see the representation of condensed matter" (191).

31. Robert Caserio notes succinctly that women in this novel may be inhibited from an overt or candid kind of feminist self-declaration because of their implication in colonial power: "Were Lady Naylor or Lois Farquar to assert their need or their desire for independence *as women*, they would find themselves in a position analogous to the Irish rebels" (*The Novel in England* 251). Caserio also rightly points out that the Anglo-Irish fear that they are a parasitic caste, "distant from the work of authentic social production and significance,

which Schreiner diagnoses as women's predicament" (253). Here Caserio cinches a key point of affinity between Bowen and Schreiner as colonial women writers.

32. As Bowen puts it in "The Big House" (1940): "The big house people were handicapped, shadowed and to an extent queered—by their pride, by their indignation at their decline and by their divorce from the countryside in whose heart their struggle was carried on" (*Mulberry* 27).

33. Gertrude Stein, in her inimitable account of English style, suggests that the holding of an empire made English literary culture more and more centered on explanation: "You have to explain the inside to the inside and the owning of the outside to the inside that has to be explained to the inside life and the owning of the outside has to be explained to the outside" (43). For Stein, the explaining clamor is the death-knell of English literary style; Laurence, though, seems to view the explaining clamor as the very stuff of art.

34. For more on the post–World War I ascension of the nation-state system and the devolutionary logic behind it, see Benedict Anderson (113).

35. John Coates views Laurence's speech as epitomizing a certain strain of 1920s "rationalist, hedonist" thinking that Bowen more or less repudiates (211). Coates goes on to argue that Gerald's doubts about Laurence's rationalist views are confirmed in the end, but in fact I think the novel, with its Flaubertian ethos of restraint, never does affirm Gerald's pious notion of the civilizing mission. The novel may ironize Laurence's waspish, Oxonian rationalism, but his insistence on manners over feelings and the impersonal distance implied by his notion of civilization are closer to the novel's own ethos than is Gerald's sentimentalism.

Chapter 7: Conclusion

1. For a useful overview of the difference/development debate, see Kraniauskas.

2. One should not casually lump together Marxist and liberal conceptions of historical development; still, as Martin Jay observes: "Although Marxism would later challenge the ahistorical homogenization of mankind implicit in the Enlightenment view of progress, there would be enough of an evolutionary bias left in its own assumptions to warrant a comparison" (31).

3. For Chakrabarty, the central ruse of imperial reason—the perpetual deferral of the colony's modernity and autonomy—is written into the protocols of historicism itself (8). For a similar account of the "hegemony of Eurochronology," see Appadurai 30.

4. Along these more or less Derridean lines, Ian Baucom has conducted a subtle and powerful inquiry into the archival traces of Atlantic history, construed antipositivistically as a "melancholy refusal of empire from within" (300). As Lloyd elaborates the point in a different theoretical idiom: "Formations that are recalcitrant to capitalist logic and therefore targeted for destruction are in the first place not backward remainders of outmoded traditions, but already adaptations and modifications of older formations in response to previous confrontations with earlier forms of modernization. What that implies is, in the second place, that modernity does not replace tradition, but that modern forms and institutions emerge always in differential relation to their nonmodern and recalcitrant counterparts" (*Irish Times* 4).

5. For a good illustration of the committed use of spatial theory in modernist studies, see Friedman, "Definitional Excursions." On the other side, Harootunian offers a strong and, by this point, perhaps salutary critique of the spatial turn across the disciplines.

6. Nicholas Brown argues vigorously that "a Marxist framework is not only not Eurocentric, but the only conceptual framework that potentially avoids the pitfalls of both Eurocentrism and of the paradoxically Eurocentric refusal of Eurocentrism" (5). Brown aptly identifies the problem, and the need to seek dialectical rather than counterdiscursive or alternative lines of critique from outside the chronotope of modernity. David Scott, too, notes that the project of "unmasking or correcting" Eurocentrism can gain or lose value in different critical contexts or problem-spaces, and thus should not remain the sole center of gravity in postcolonial studies (104–7).

7. For a marvelously candid account of the near-impossibility of breaking out of the dialectical machinery of Hegelian historicism, see Derrida's celebrated reading of Bataille.

8. Benjamin remains a slippery figure in this arena of inquiry (and therefore the most recruited into various, often competing, theoretical and ideological camps). Cesare Casarino, in summarizing Tony Negri's skepticism about Benjamin, makes a decisive point in reviewing the long-term impact of Benjamin's interest in various kinds of interruptive time-concepts designed to challenge dialectical historicism: "Far from being disruptive of the bourgeois myth of progress, the *Jetztzeit* . . . is flattened back into the relentless march of progress precisely because it was only a flash" (191).

9. Many of the avant-gardist movements (Vorticism, Dada, Futurism, Surrealism) were either implicitly or explicitly formed as counter-Hegelian projects; even when not so overtly arrayed against Hegel, experiments in collapsing the temporal dimensions of literature—even of prose narrative itself (as in cases like Breton's *Nadja* or Stein's *Three Lives*—gained their non-linear, looping force from a radical confrontation with the developmental historicism implied in conventional plot and syntax.

10. Timothy Brennan likewise argues that the pendulum of critical thinking has swung too far away from the "Hegelian notion of a progressive telos" and that this is indeed borne out in widespread "metaphors of spatiality" (136). He offers a systemically skeptical view of Heidegger-derived theoretical paradigms that absolutize difference (38). For a powerful statement of dissent from this position, see Gayatri Spivak, who anticipates, and rejects, the claim of a strong philosophical continuity from the historical avant-gardes, through post-structuralism, to contemporary postcolonial theory rooted in spatialized difference (313).

11. This is the passage that seems dismissive: "The answer is simple: you talk about 'alternate' or 'alternative' modernities. Everyone knows the formula by now: this means that there can be a modernity for everybody which is different from the standard or hegemonic Anglo-Saxon model. Whatever you dislike about the latter, including the subaltern position it leaves you in, can be effaced by the reassuring and 'cultural' notion that you can fashion your own modernity differently, so that there can be a Latin-American kind, or an Indian kind, or an African kind, and so forth" (*Singular Modernity* 12).

12. Ferguson elaborates his point: "One can well understand the urge to de-provincialize the notions of modernity at work in the variously Eurocentric versions of modernization theory that dominated social theory through most of the late twentieth century. And there is certainly a good deal to be gained by contemplating the 'alternative modernities' that may contest dominant Eurocentric cultural practices in the name, not of tradition, but of different configurations of the modern. . . . But what is lost in the overly easy extension of an ideal equality to 'modernities' in the plural are the all too real inequalities that leave most Africans today excluded and abjected from the economic and institutional conditions

that they themselves regard as modern" ("Decomposing" 167). In an earlier work, Ferguson makes it clear that no merely theoretical dismissal of developmental discourse is sufficient: "The subordinate position ascribed to the third world in development discourse was therefore not a figment of the imagination or a mere Eurocentric illusion but reflected an intractable political-economic reality that could not, and cannot, be wished or relabeled away" (*Expectations* 248).

13. Zhang extends these arguments in "Political Philosophy and Comparison" 96ff.

14. Peter Galison frames the question this way: "But is the alternative to such nineteenth-century *Wissenschaftlich* ideals a splintering particularism? Are we really left with no more than a relentless historicism and therefore a Hobson's choice between grand narratives of progress and a curio display of scholarly diggings?" (381).

15. Laura Chrisman likewise raises the possibility that the critique of development has perhaps gone too far in its "veneration of a principle of difference" (127–35). In her forthcoming book, *The Victorian Geopolitical Aesthetic*, Lauren M. E. Goodlad succinctly captures the keywords animating and, to some extent, polarizing this general field of debate: "Revisiting modernity's history may mitigate the impulse to pit universality against alterity, globality against locality, temporal against spatial difference, and, as a result, left politics against postmodern ethics—a tendency exemplified by recent debates over 'singular' and 'alternative' theories of modernity."

16. This pragmatic compromise was memorably advanced to me by Luke Gibbons. Along similar lines, Enrique Dussel sensibly proposes that we use a vocabulary of two paradigms of modernity, one Eurocentric, one planetary (3).

17. To privilege realist and biographical plot in this sense is to give conceptual priority to narrative itself, and to recognize in the process the deeply existential substrates of such theoretical touchstones as Jameson and Osborne, and even Paul de Man. In "Literary History and Literary Modernity," de Man rejects most forms of periodizing logic or strong historicism, and insists instead on the peculiar value of literary discourse to recognize the inauthenticity of revolutionary modernist negations of the past (149). De Man's main point of emphasis here is the special quality of the literary as a knowing rhetoric of temporality among deluded historical discourses. Literature is always and essentially modern in that it tries to fulfill itself immanently yet recognizes the impossibility of its own temporal fulfillment. In its ironic awareness of its inevitable belatedness, the literary object is permanently and preeminently modern.

18. Joe Cleary makes a similar point about Irish postcolonial studies that are invested in the category of alternative modernities: "However valuable such exercises may be," Cleary writes, "they translate poorly into the praxis-orientated world of the public sphere where the language of modernization governs almost all discussion of social change" (6).

19. Adorno observes that an artwork, unlike a propositional statement, "only becomes knowledge when taken as a totality, i.e. through all its mediations, not through its individual intentions" ("Reconciliation" 168). For an apposite discussion of narrative as a "concordant discordance" that can operate as a "living dialectic," see Ricoeur 66ff; my thanks to Jesse Matz for reminding me of the relevance of Ricoeur on this point.

20. Gregory Castle cites Beckett's fiction as a limit-case where "generic resistance" to the conventions of the bildungsroman ("biographical narrative, problems of socialization, the influence of mentors and 'instrumental' women, the problem of vocation") reaches an

extreme point (4). Patrick Bixby, too, has recently reconsidered Beckett's novels (particularly his work of the 1950s) as a kind of full-scale inversion of the logic of *Bildung* that operates as a postcolonial challenge to "the evolutionary narrative of modernity at large" (28).

21. Riotously playful though his world may be, Murphy takes a fatal turn in London that resonates quite significantly with the figure of the Jean Rhys heroine, a déclassé Anglophone émigré for whom the metropolis is not much more than a brutal triangulation of bordello, abattoir, and prison. These binational novelists bear witness to the sexual and economic bottom lines of the urban marketplace, to the commodification of cultural difference, and to a cold biopolitical regime of abortion chambers (Rhys) and mental clinics (Beckett).

22. For recent treatments of Rushdie's parodic inversions of national allegory and national-historical time, see Kuchta, Reder, and Cooppan (41–53).

23. Saleem's suffering of course also comes with the paranormal privilege of being attuned to India through the minds of all children born on August 15, 1947. The novel thus harkens back to our first text, Kipling's *Kim*, and the privileged vantage point of a youthful hero who manages to see, and to traverse, all of India. Neither Saleem nor Kim can age into an integrated adulthood representative of a fixed and stable Indian destiny; neither anticolonial nor postcolonial Indian nationalism, in these texts at least, can map onto a smooth and harmonic process of collective development.

24. For exemplary work in this vein, see Christopher Hill on the naturalist "fallen woman" plot in French and Japanese literature, where the act of translation and imitation is already immanent to the European form, not a special liability of some non-Western copy (102).

25. Leela Gandhi makes a strong and straightforward claim about the relation of European to postcolonial bildungsroman: "The only difference is this: in its European transmission, the narrative and ideology of Bildung aims to produce citizens; on its colonial travels, however, it aims, somewhat differently, to produce subjects" (60).

26. As Patricia Spacks observes of Martha Quest, she "belongs to a society in which adolescents do not necessarily grow up at all, they only grow older; and growing up is not necessarily an improvement" (51).

27. Robbins: "The incongruities between narratives of upward mobility and the static or declining state of the world cannot be corrected by some voluntary gesture of self-discipline whereby narrative would henceforth allow no image of fulfilled desire not statistically guaranteed by actual improvement on the part of X thousands or millions of people. For narratives, including metanarratives, are obliged to make use of desire, and there is no politics without them." ("Secularism" 33).

28. On the place of *The Kite Runner* in the literary world-system, see Joseph Slaughter's exemplary analysis in *Human Rights, Inc.* (320–24).

Works Cited

Abel, Elizabeth, Marianne Hirsch, and Elizabeth Langland. *The Voyage In: Fictions of Female Development*. Hanover, N.H.: University Press of New England, 1983.

Abu-Lughod, Janet L. *Before European Hegemony*. Oxford: Oxford University Press, 1989.

Adams, James Eli. *Dandies and Desert Saints: Styles of Victorian Masculinity*. Ithaca, N.Y.: Cornell University Press, 1995.

Adorno, Theodor W. *Aesthetic Theory*. Trans. Robert Hullot-Kentor. Minneapolis: University of Minnesota Press, 1997.

———. *Prisms*. Trans. Shierry Weber Nicholson and Samuel Weber. Cambridge, Mass.: MIT Press, 1983.

———. "Reconciliation under Duress." In *Aesthetics and Politics*. London: Verso, 1983.

Alain-Fournier. *Le Grand Meaulnes* (1913). Trans. Frank Davison. London: Penguin, 1966.

Alryyes, Ala. *Original Subjects: The Child, the Novel, and the Nation*. Cambridge, Mass.: Harvard University Press, 2001.

Anderson, Benedict. *Imagined Communities: Reflections on the Origin and Spread of Nationalism*. London: Verso, 1983.

Anderson, Perry. *English Questions*. London: Verso, 1992.

Annan, Noel. "Kipling's Place in the History of Ideas." *Victorian Studies* 3.4 (June 1960): 323–48.

Appadurai, Arjun. *Modernity at Large: Cultural Dimensions of Globalization*. Minneapolis: University of Minnesota Press, 1996.

Arata, Stephen. *Fictions of Loss in the Victorian Fin de Siècle*. Cambridge: Cambridge University Press, 1996.

Arendt, Hannah. *The Origins of Totalitarianism* (1951). San Diego, Calif.: Harcourt, 1968.

Armstrong, Nancy. *Desire and Domestic Fiction*. New York: Oxford University Press, 1987.

———. "Emily's Ghost: The Cultural Politics of Victorian Fiction, Folklore, and Photography." *Novel* 25 (Spring 1992): 245–67.

———. *How Novels Think: The Limits of British Individualism from 1719–1900*. New York: Columbia University Press, 2005.

de Assis, Machado. *The Posthumous Memoirs of Brás Cubas* (1881). Trans. Gregory Rabassa. New York: Oxford University Press, 1997.

Attridge, Derek, and Marjorie Howes. *Semicolonial Joyce*. Cambridge: Cambridge University Press, 2000.

Backus, Margot Gayle. *The Gothic Family Romance: Heterosexuality, Child Sacrifice, and the Anglo-Irish Colonial Order*. Durham, N.C.: Duke University Press, 1999.

Bakhtin, M. M. "The *Bildungsroman* and Its Significance in the History of Realism: Toward a Historical Typology of the Novel." In *Speech Genres and Other Late Essays*. Trans. Vern W. McGee. Austin: University of Texas Press, 1986.

———. *The Dialogic Imagination*. Ed. Michael Holquist. Trans. Caryl Emerson and Michael Holquist. Austin: University of Texas Press, 1981.

Barnard, Rita. "Tsotsis: On Law, the Outlaw, and the Postcolonial State." *Contemporary Literature* 49 (2008): 541–72.

Barney, Richard A. "Subjectivity, the Novel, and the Bildung Blocks of Critical Theory." *Genre* 26 (Winter 1993): 359–75.

Baucom, Ian. *Spectres of the Atlantic: Finance Capital, Slavery, and the Philosophy of History*. Durham, N.C.: Duke University Press, 2005.

Beer, Gillian. *Virginia Woolf: The Common Ground*. Edinburgh: Edinburgh University Press, 1996.

Begam, Richard, and Michael Valdez Moses, eds. *Modernism and Colonialism: British and Irish Literature, 1899–1939*. Durham, N.C.: Duke University Press, 2007.

Benjamin, Walter. "The Storyteller." In *Illuminations*, ed. Hannah Arendt. Trans. Harry Zohn. New York: Schocken, 1968.

Bennet, Andrew, and Nicholas Royle. *Elizabeth Bowen and the Dissolution of the Novel: Still Lives*. New York: St. Martin's, 1995.

Berman, Jessica. "Comparative Colonialisms: Joyce, Anand, and the Question of Engagement." *Modernism/Modernity* 13.3 (2006): 465–85.

Berman, Marshall. *All That Is Solid Melts into Air*. New York: Simon and Schuster, 1982.

Bhabha, Homi K., ed. *Nation and Narration*. New York: Routledge, 1990.

Birken, Lawrence. *Consuming Desire: Sexual Science and the Emergence of a Culture of Abundance, 1871-1914*. Ithaca, N.Y.: Cornell University Press, 1988.

Bixby, Patrick. *Samuel Beckett and the Postcolonial Novel*. Cambridge: Cambridge University Press, 2009.

Boes, Tobias. "Apprenticeship of the Novel: The *Bildungsroman* and the Invention of History, ca. 1770–1820." *Comparative Literature Studies* 45.3 (2008): 269–88.

———. "*A Portrait of the Artist as a Young Man* and the 'Individuating Rhythm' of Modernity." *ELH* 75 (2008): 767–85.

Bongie, Chris. *Exotic Memories: Literature, Colonialism, and the Fin De Siècle*. Stanford, Calif.: Stanford University Press, 1991.

Bowen, Elizabeth. *The Last September* (1929). New York: Anchor, 2000.

———. *The Mulberry Tree: Writings of Elizabeth Bowen*, ed. Hermione Lee. San Diego, Calif.: Harcourt, 1986.

———. *Pictures and Conversations*. New York: Knopf, 1975.

Bowlby, Rachel, "Promoting Dorian Gray." In Bowlby, *Shopping with Freud*, pp. 7–24. New York: Routledge, 1993.

Boym, Svetlana. *The Future of Nostalgia*. New York: Basic, 2001.

Brennan, Timothy. *Wars of Position: The Cultural Politics of Left and Right*. New York: Columbia University Press, 2006.

Bristow, Joseph. "Introduction." *The Picture of Dorian Gray*, by Oscar Wilde. Oxford: Oxford University Press, 2006.

Brown, Nicholas. *Utopian Generations: The Political Horizon of Twentieth-Century Literature*. Princeton, N.J.: Princeton University Press, 2005.

Bruford, W. H. *The German Tradition of Self-Cultivation*. London: Cambridge University Press, 1975.

Buckley, Jerome. *Season of Youth: The Bildungsroman from Dickens to Golding*. Cambridge, Mass.: Harvard University Press, 1974.

Burdett, Carolyn. *Olive Schreiner and the Progress of Feminism: Evolution, Gender, Empire*. New York: Palgrave, 2001.

Bürger, Peter. *The Decline of Modernism*. Trans. Nicholas Walker. University Park: Pennsylvania State University Press, 1992.

Buzard, James. *Disorienting Fiction: The Autoethnographic Work of Nineteenth-Century British Novels*. Princeton, N.J.: Princeton University Press, 2005.

Casanova, Pascale. *The World Republic of Letters*. Trans. M. B. DeBevoise. Cambridge, Mass.: Harvard University Press, 2005.

Casarino, Cesare. "Time Matters: Marx, Negri, Agamben, and the Corporeal." *Strategies* 16.2 (2003): 185–206.

Caserio, Robert. "The Novel as a Novel Experiment in Statement: The Anticanonical Example of H. G. Wells." In *Decolonizing Tradition: New Views of Twentieth-Century British Canons* (pp. 88–109), ed. Karen R. Lawrence. Urbana: University of Illinois Press, 1992.

——. *The Novel in England, 1900–1950: History and Theory*. New York: Twayne, 1999.

Castle, Gregory. *Reading the Modernist Bildungsroman*. Gainesville: University Press of Florida, 2006.

Chakrabarty, Dipesh. *Provincializing Europe: Postcolonial Thought and Historical Difference*. Princeton, N.J.: Princeton University Press, 2000.

Chalk, Bridget. "'I Am Not England': Narrative and National Identity in *Aaron's Rod* and *Sea and Sardinia*." *Journal of Modern Literature* 31 (2008): 54–70.

Cheah, Pheng. *Spectral Nationality: Passages of Freedom from Kant to Postcolonial Literatures of Liberation*. New York: Columbia University Press, 2003.

Cheng, Vincent. *Joyce, Race, and Empire*. Cambridge: Cambridge University Press, 1995.

Cheyette, Bryan. "Introduction." *Tono-Bungay*, by H. G. Wells. Oxford: Oxford University Press, 1997.

Chrisman, Laura. *Postcolonial Contraventions: Cultural Readings of Race, Imperialism, and Transnationalism*. Manchester: Manchester University Press, 2003.

Chu, Patricia E. *Race, Nationalism and the State in British and American Modernism*. Cambridge: Cambridge University Press, 2006.

Clausson, Nils. "'Culture and Corruption': Paterian Self-Development versus Gothic Degeneration in Oscar Wilde's *The Picture of Dorian Gray*." *Papers on Language and Literature* 39.4 (Fall 2003): 339–64.

Cleary, Joe. *Outrageous Fortune: Capital and Culture in Modern Ireland*. Dublin: Field Day, 2007.

Clifford, James. *The Predicament of Culture: Twentieth-Century Ethnography, Literature, and Art*. Cambridge, Mass.: Harvard University Press, 1988.

Coates, John. "Elizabeth Bowen's *The Last September*: The Loss of the Past and the Modern Consciousness." *Durham University Journal* 51.2 (July 1990): 205–16.

Coetzee, J. M. *White Writing*. New Haven, Conn.: Yale University Press, 1988.

Cohen, Scott. "'Get Out!': Empire Migration and Human Traffic in *Lord Jim*." *Novel* 36 (Summer 2003): 374–97.

Cole, Sarah Rose. "National Histories, International Genre: Thackeray, Balzac, and the Franco-British Bildungsroman." *Romanticism and Victorianism on the Net* 48 (2007): 1–20.

Coleridge, Samuel Taylor. *On the Constitution of the Church and State, According to the Idea of Each*. 4th ed. London: Edward Moxon, 1852.

Comentale, Edward P. *Modernism, Cultural Production, and the British Avant-Garde*. Cambridge: Cambridge University Press, 2004.

Conrad, Joseph. *Lord Jim* (1900). New York: Penguin, 1986.

———. *Nostromo* (1904). New York: Penguin, 1986.

———. *Youth/Heart of Darkness/The End of the Tether*. New York: Penguin, 1995.

Cooper, Frederick, and Ann Stoler. "Tensions of Empire: Colonial Control and Visions of Rule." *American Ethnologist* 16.4 (November 1989): 609–21.

Cooppan, Vilashini. *Worlds within: National Narratives and Global Connections in Postcolonial Writing*. Stanford, Calif.: Stanford University Press, 2009.

Corcoran, Neil. "Discovery of a Lack: History and Ellipsis in Elizabeth Bowen's *The Last September*." *Irish University Review* 31.2 (2001): 315–33.

Crosby, Christina. *The Ends of History: Victorians and "The Woman Question."* New York: Routledge, 1991.

Danson, Lawrence. "'Each Man Kills the Thing He Loves': The Impermanence of Personality in Oscar Wilde." In *Rediscovering Oscar Wilde* (pp. 82–93), ed. C. George Sandulescu. Colin Smythe, 1994.

Deane, Seamus. *Celtic Revivals*. Winston-Salem, N.C.: Wake Forest University Press, 1987.

———. "Dead Ends: Joyce's Finest Moments." In *Semicolonial Joyce* (pp. 21–36), ed. Derek Attridge and Marjorie Howes. Cambridge: Cambridge University Press, 2000.

———. *A Short History of Irish Literature*. South Bend, Ind.: University of Notre Dame Press, 1986.

———. *Strange Country: Modernity and Nationhood in Irish Writing since 1790*. Oxford: Oxford University Press, 1997.

Dearlove, Judith E. "The Failure of the *Bildungsroman*: Jean Rhys and *Voyage in the Dark*." *Jean Rhys Review* 8.1–2 (1997): 24–30.

DeKoven, Marianne. *Rich and Strange: Gender, History, Modernism*. Princeton, N.J.: Princeton University Press, 1991.

de Man, Paul. "Literary History and Literary Modernity." In *Blindness and Insight: Essays in the Rhetoric of Contemporary Criticism*. Minneapolis: University of Minnesota Press, 1983.

Derrida, Jacques. "From Restricted to General Economy: A Hegelianism with Reserve." In *Writing and Difference* (pp. 251–77), trans. Alan Bass. Chicago: University of Chicago Press, 1978.

DiBattista, Maria. "Elizabeth Bowen's Troubled Modernism." In *Modernism and Colonialism: British and Irish Literature, 1899–1939* (pp. 226–45), ed. Richard Begam and Michael Valdez Moses. Durham, N.C.: Duke University Press, 2007.

Dickens, Charles. *David Copperfield*. New York: Penguin, 1997.

———. *Great Expectations*. New York: Penguin, 1996.

Dimock, Wai Chee. *Through Other Continents: American Literature across Deep Time*. Princeton, N.J.: Princeton University Press, 2006.

Dobbins, Gregory. *Lazy Idle Schemers: Irish Modernism and the Cultural Politics of Idleness*. South Bend, Ind.: Field Day/University of Notre Dame Press, 2010.

Doyle, Laura, and Laura Winkiel. *Geomodernisms: Race, Modernism, Modernity*. Bloomington: Indiana University Press, 2005.

Duffy, Enda. *The Subaltern Ulysses*. Minneapolis: University of Minnesota Press, 1994.

Duncan, Ian. *Modern Romance and Transformations of the Novel: The Gothic, Scott, Dickens*. Cambridge: Cambridge University Press, 1992.

DuPlessis, Rachel Blau. *Writing beyond the Ending: Narrative Strategies of Twentieth-Century Women Writers*. Bloomington: Indiana University Press, 1985.

Dussel, Enrique. "Beyond Eurocentrism: The World-System and the Limits of Modernity." In *The Cultures of Globalization* (pp. 3–31), ed. Fredric Jameson and Masao Miyoshi. Durham, N.C.: Duke University Press, 1998.

Eagleton, Terry. *Heathcliff and the Great Hunger*. London: Verso, 1995.

Edelman, Lee. *No Future: Queer Theory and the Death Drive*. Durham, N.C.: Duke University Press, 2004.

Eliot, George. *Middlemarch*. Boston: Houghton Mifflin, 1956.

———. *The Mill on the Floss*, ed. A. S. Byatt. London: Penguin, 1979.

Ellmann, Maud. "The Name and the Scar: Identity in *The Odyssey* and *A Portrait of the Artist as a Young Man*." In *James Joyce's* A Portrait of the Artist as a Young Man: *A Casebook*, ed. Mark A. Wollaeger. New York: Oxford University Press, 2003.

Emery, Mary Lou. *Jean Rhys at "World's End": Novels of Colonial and Sexual Exile*. Austin: University of Texas Press, 1990.

Eysteinsson, Astradur. *The Concept of Modernism*. Ithaca, N.Y.: Cornell University Press, 1990.

Fabian, Johannes. *Time and the Other: How Anthropology Makes Its Object*. New York: Columbia University Press, 1983

Fanon, Frantz. *The Wretched of the Earth*, trans. Constance Farrington. New York: Grove, 1963.

Felski, Rita. *Beyond Feminist Aesthetics*. Cambridge, Mass.: Harvard University Press, 1989.

———. *The Gender of Modernity*. Cambridge, Mass.: Harvard University Press, 1995.

Ferguson, Christine. "Decadence as Scientific Fulfillment." *PMLA* 117.3 (2002): 465–78.

Ferguson, James. "Decomposing Modernity: History and Hierarchy after Development." In *Postcolonial Studies and Beyond*, ed. Ania Loomba, Suvir Kaul, Matti Bunzl, Antoinette Burton, and Jed Esty. Durham, N.C.: Duke University Press, 2005.

———. *Expectations of Modernity: Myths and Meanings of Urban Life on the Zambian Copperbelt*. Berkeley: University of California Press, 1999.

Fleishman, Avrom. *Conrad's Politics*. Baltimore, Md.: Johns Hopkins University Press, 1967.

Fleissner, Jennifer L. *Women, Compulsion, Modernity: The Moment of American Naturalism.* Chicago: University of Chicago Press, 2004.

Fraiman, Susan. *Unbecoming Women: British Women Writers and the Novel of Development.* New York: Columbia University Press, 1993.

Frank, Andre Gunder. *ReORIENT: Global Economy in the Asian Age.* Berkeley: University of California Press, 1998.

Friedman, Susan Stanford. "'Beyond' Gynocriticism and Gynesis: The Geographics of Identity and the Future of Feminist Criticism." *Tulsa Studies in Women's Literature* 15.1 (Spring 1996): 13–40.

———. "Definitional Excursions: The Meanings of Modern/Modernity/Modernism." *Modernism/Modernity* 8.3 (2001): 493–513.

———. "Spatialization, Narrative Theory, and Virginia Woolf's *The Voyage Out.*" In *Ambiguous Discourse: Feminist Narratology and British Women Writers* (pp. 109–36), ed. Kathy Mezei. Chapel Hill: University of North Carolina Press, 1996.

Froula, Christine. *Modernism's Body: Sex, Culture, and Joyce.* New York: Columbia University Press, 1996.

———. "Out of the Chrysalis: Female Initiation and Female Authority in Virginia Woolf's *The Voyage Out.*" *Tulsa Studies in Women's Literature* 5.1 (Spring 1986): 63–90.

Gadamer, Hans-Georg. *Truth and Method*, trans. Joel Weinsheimer and Donald G. Marshall. London: Continuum, 1975.

Gagnier, Regenia. *The Insatiability of Human Wants: Economics and Aesthetics in Market Society.* Chicago: University of Chicago Press, 2000.

Galison, Peter. "Specific Theory." *Critical Inquiry* 30.2 (2004): 379–83.

Gambrell, Alice. *Women Intellectuals, Modernism, and Difference: Transatlantic Culture, 1919–1945.* Cambridge: Cambridge University Press, 1997.

Gandhi, Leela. "'Learning Me Your Language': England in the Postcolonial Bildungsroman." In *England through Colonial Eyes in Twentieth-Century Fiction* (pp. 56–75), by Ann Blake, Leela Gandhi, and Sue Thomas. New York: Palgrave, 2001.

Gaonkar, Dilip Parameshwar, ed. *Alternative Modernities.* Durham, N.C.: Duke University Press, 2001.

Giddens, Anthony. *Modernity and Self-Identity: Self and Society in the Late Modern Age.* Stanford, Calif.: Stanford University Press, 1991.

Gikandi, Simon. *Maps of Englishness: Writing Identity in the Culture of Colonialism.* New York: Columbia University Press, 1996.

Gilbert, Sandra M., and Susan Gubar. *The Madwoman in the Attic.* New Haven, Conn.: Yale University Press, 1979.

———. *No Man's Land*, vol. 2: *Sexchanges.* New Haven, Conn.: Yale University Press, 1989.

Gilroy, Paul. *Against Race: Imagining Political Culture Beyond the Color Line.* Cambridge, Mass.: Harvard University Press, 2000.

Goethe, Johann Wolfgang von. *Wilhelm Meister's Apprenticeship*, ed. and trans. Eric A. Blackall in cooperation with Victor Lange. Princeton, N.J.: Princeton University Press, 1989.

GoGwilt, Christopher. *The Fiction of Geopolitics: Afterimages of Culture, from Wilkie Collins to Alfred Hitchcock.* Stanford, Calif.: Stanford University Press, 2000.

Goodlad, Lauren M. E. *Victorian Literature and the Victorian State*. Baltimore, Md.: Johns Hopkins University Press, 2003.

Gordon, Jan B. "'Parody as Initiation': The Sad Education of 'Dorian Gray.'" *Criticism* 9 (1967): 355–71.

Handley, George B. *Postslavery Literatures in the Americas: Family Portraits in Black and White*. Charlottesville: University Press of Virginia, 2000.

Hansen, Jim. *Terror and Irish Modernism: The Gothic Tradition from Burke to Beckett*. Albany: SUNY Press, 2009.

Harpham, Geoffrey Galt. "Conrad's Global Homeland." *Raritan* 21.1 (2001): 20–33.

Harootunian, Harry. "Some Thoughts on Comparability and the Space-Time Problem." *boundary 2* 32.2 (2005): 23–52.

Hart, Matthew, and Jim Hansen. "Introduction: Contemporary Literature and the State." *Contemporary Literature* (2008): 491–513.

Heise, Ursula. *Chronoschisms*. Cambridge: Cambridge University Press, 1997.

Henry, Nancy. *George Eliot and the British Empire*. Cambridge: Cambridge University Press, 2002.

Herder, Johann Gottfried von. *Reflections on the Philosophy of the History of Mankind* (1784–1791), trans. T. O. Churchill, ed. Frank E. Manuel. Chicago: University of Chicago Press, 1968.

Hill, Christopher. "Nana in the World: Novel, Gender, and Transnational Form." *MLQ* 72.1 (2011): 75–105.

Hirsch, Marianne. "Spiritual Bildung: The Beautiful Soul as Paradigm." In *The Voyage In: Fictions of Female Development* (pp. 23–48), ed. Elizabeth Abel, Marianne Hirsch, and Elizabeth Langland. Hanover, N.H.: University Press of New England, 1983.

Hitchcock, Peter. *The Long Space: Transnationalism and Postcolonial Form*. Stanford, Calif.: Stanford University Press, 2010.

Hite, Molly. *The Other Side of the Story: Structures and Strategies of Contemporary Feminist Narrative*. Ithaca, N.Y.: Cornell University Press, 1989.

Hoad, Neville. "Arrested Development or the Queerness of Savages: Resisting Evolutionary Narratives of Difference." *Postcolonial Studies* 3 (2000): 133–58.

Hobsbawm, E. J. *The Age of Empire 1875–1914*. New York: Random House, 1987.

Homans, Margaret. "Dinah's Blush, Maggie's Arm: Class, Gender and Sexuality in George Eliot's Early Novels." *Victorian Studies* (Winter 1993): 155–78.

Howe, Irving. "The Pleasures of *Kim*." In *Art, Politics and Will: Essays in Honor of Lionel Trilling* (pp. 145–58), ed. Quentin Anderson, Stephen Donadio, and Steven Marcus. New York: Basic, 1977.

Howe, Susanne. *Wilhelm Meister and His English Kinsmen: Apprentices to Life*. New York: AMS Press, 1966.

Hutchins, Francis G. *The Illusion of Permanence: British Imperialism in India*. Princeton, N.J.: Princeton University Press, 1967.

Israel, Nico. *Outlandish: Writing between Exile and Diaspora*. Stanford, Calif.: Stanford University Press, 2000.

Jacobus, Mary. "The Question of Language: Men of Maxims and *The Mill on the Floss*." *Critical Inquiry* 8 (1981): 207–22.

James, Henry. *Daisy Miller* (1878). London: Penguin, 1986.

Jameson, Fredric. "The End of Temporality." *Critical Inquiry* 29.4 (2003): 695-718.

———. *Fables of Aggression: Wyndham Lewis, the Modernist as Fascist*. Berkeley: University of California Press, 1979.

———, "Modernism and Imperialism." In *Nationalism, Colonialism, and Literature* (pp. 43–68). Derry: Field Day, 1988.

———. *The Political Unconscious: Narrative as a Socially Symbolic Act*. Ithaca, N.Y.: Cornell University Press, 1981.

———. *A Singular Modernity: Essay on the Ontology of the Present*. London: Verso, 2002.

Jameson, Fredric, and Masao Miyoshi, eds. *The Cultures of Globalization*. Durham, N.C.: Duke University Press, 1998.

Jay, Martin. *Marxism and Totality: The Adventures of a Concept from Lukács to Habermas*. Berkeley: University of California Press, 1984.

Jeffers, Thomas L. *Apprenticeships: A Study of the Bildungsroman from Goethe to Santayana*. New York: Palgrave, 2005.

Jones, Gareth Stedman. "The Marxism of the Early Lukács." In *Western Marxism: A Critical Reader* (pp. 11–60), ed. New Left Review. London: New Left Review, 1977.

Jonsson, Stefan. *Subject without Nation: Robert Musil and the History of Modern Identity*. Durham, N.C.: Duke University Press, 2000.

Joyce, James. *Occasional, Critical and Political Writing*, ed. Kevin Barry. Oxford: Oxford University Press, 2000.

———. *A Portrait of the Artist as a Young Man* (1916). New York: Penguin, 1992.

Katz, Tamar. *Impressionist Subjects: Gender, Interiority, and Modernist Fiction in England*. Urbana: University of Illinois Press, 2000.

Kaul, Suvir. "*Kim*, or How to Be Young, Male, and British in Kipling's India." In *Kim*, ed. Zohreh T. Sullivan. New York: Norton Critical Edition, 2002.

Kenner, Hugh. "The Cubist *Portrait*." In *Approaches to Joyce's Portrait: Ten Essays* (pp. 171–84), ed. Thomas F. Staley and Bernard Benstock. Pittsburgh, Penn.: University of Pittsburgh Press, 1976.

Kermode, Frank. *The Sense of an Ending*. New York: Oxford University Press, 1967.

Kiberd, Declan. *Inventing Ireland*. Cambridge, Mass.: Harvard University Press, 1995.

King, Mary C. "Typing *Dorian Gray*: Wilde and the Interpellated Text." *Irish Studies Review* 9.1 (2001): 15–24.

Kipling, Rudyard. *Kim* (1901). New York: Norton Critical Edition, 2002.

Kirschner, Paul. "Conrad, Goethe, and Stein: The Romantic Fate in *Lord Jim*." *Ariel* 10 (1979): 65–81.

Klein, Scott W. "National Histories, National Fictions: Joyce's *A Portrait of the Artist as a Young Man* and Scott's *The Bride of Lammermoor*." *ELH* 65.4 (1998): 1017–38.

Kontje, Todd. "The German *Bildungsroman* as Metafiction." *Michigan Germanic Studies* 13.2 (1987): 140–55.

Konzett, Delia Caparoso. *Ethnic Modernisms*. New York: Palgrave, 2002.

Kraniauskas, John, "Difference against Development: Spiritual Accumulation and the Politics of Freedom." *boundary 2* 32.2 (2005): 53–80.

Kreilkamp, Vera. *The Anglo-Irish Novel and the Big House*. Syracuse, N.Y.: Syracuse University Press, 1998.

Kreisel, Deanna. "Superfluity and Suction: The Problem with Saving in *The Mill on the Floss*." *Novel* 35.1 (2001): 69–103.

Krishnan, Sanjay. "'Seeing the Animal': Colonial Space and Movement in Joseph Conrad's *Lord Jim*." *Novel* (Summer 2004): 326–51.

Kristeva, Julia. "Women's Time" (1979). In *The Kristeva Reader* (pp. 187–213), ed. Toril Moi. New York: Columbia University Press, 1986.

Kuchta, Todd M. "Allegorizing the Emergency: Rushdie's *Midnight's Children* and Benjamin's Theory of Allegory." In *Critical Essays on Salman Rushdie* (pp. 205–24), ed. M. Keith Booker. New York: G. K. Hall, 1999.

Kucich, John. "Olive Schreiner, Masochism, and Omnipotence: Strategies of a Preoedipal Politics." *Novel* 36.1 (Fall 2002): 79–109.

———. "Sadomasochism and the Magical Group: Kipling's Middle-Class Imperialism." *Victorian Studies* 46.1 (2003): 33–68.

Kupinse, William. "Wasted Value: The Serial Logic of H. G. Wells's *Tono-Bungay*." *Novel* 33.1 (Fall 1999): 51–72.

Lacoue-Labarthe, Philippe, and Jean-Luc Nancy. *The Literary Absolute: The Theory of Literature in German Romanticism*, trans. Philip Barnard and Cheryl Lester. Albany: SUNY Press, 1988.

Lane, Christopher. *The Burdens of Intimacy: Psychoanalysis and Victorian Masculinity*. Chicago: University of Chicago Press, 1999.

Lawrence, D. H. *Study of Thomas Hardy and Other Essays*. Cambridge: Cambridge University Press, 1985.

Lawrence, Karen. *Penelope Voyages: Women and Travel in the British Literary Tradition*. Ithaca, N.Y.: Cornell University Press, 1994.

Leavis, F. R. *The Great Tradition*. New York: George M. Stewart, Inc., 1949.

Lee, Hermione. Preface to Elizabeth Bowen, *The Mulberry Tree: Writings of Elizabeth Bowen*, ed. Hermione Lee. San Diego, Calif.: Harcourt, 1986.

Lenin, V. I. *Imperialism: The Highest Stage of Capitalism*. New York: International Publishers, 1933.

Levenson, Michael. *Modernism and the Fate of Individuality: Character and Novelistic Form from Conrad to Woolf*. Cambridge: Cambridge University Press, 1991.

———. "Stephen's Diary in Joyce's *Portrait*: The Shape of Life." *ELH* 52.4 (Winter 1985): 1017–35.

Lewis, Andrea. "Immigrants, Prostitutes, and Chorus Girls: National Identity in the Early Novels of Jean Rhys." *Journal of Commonwealth and Postcolonial Studies* 6.2 (Spring 1999): 82–95.

Lewis, Pericles. *Modernism, Nationalism, and the Novel*. Cambridge: Cambridge University Press, 2000.

Lima, Maria Helena. "Decolonizing Genre: Jamaica Kincaid and the Bildungsroman." *Genre* 26.4 (Winter 1993): 431–59.

Lloyd, David. "Arnold, Ferguson, Schiller: Aesthetic Culture and the Politics of Aesthetics." *Cultural Critique* 2 (1985–1986): 137–69.

———. *Ireland after History*. South Bend, Ind.: University of Notre Dame Press, 1999.

———. *Irish Times: Temporalities of Modernity*. Dublin: Field Day, 2008.

————. *Nationalism and Minor Literature: James Clarence Mangan and the Emergence of Irish Cultural Nationalism*. Berkeley: University of California Press, 1987.

Lodge, David. *The Language of Fiction*. London: Routledge and Kegan Paul, 1966.

Love, Heather. *Feeling Backward: Loss and the Politics of Queer History*. Cambridge, Mass.: Harvard University Press, 2007.

Løvlie, Lars, Klaus Mortensen, and Sven Erik Nordenbo. *Educating Humanity: Bildung in Postmodernity*. Oxford: Blackwell, 2003.

Lukács, Georg. *Goethe and His Age*, trans. Robert Anchor. London: Merlin Press, 1968.

————. *The Historical Novel*, trans. Hannah Mitchell and Stanley Mitchell. Boston: Beacon Press, 1962.

————. *The Theory of the Novel* (1916), trans. Anna Bostock. Cambridge: MIT Press, 1971.

Lunn, Eugene. *Marxism and Modernism: An Historical Study of Lukács, Brecht, Benjamin, and Adorno*. Berkeley: University of California Press, 1982.

Lyon, Janet. "Gadže Modernism." In *Geomodernisms: Race, Modernism, Modernity* (pp. 187–205), ed. Laura Doyle and Laura Winkiel. Bloomington: Indiana University Press, 2005.

Mahaffey, Vicki. *States of Desire: Wilde, Yeats, Joyce, and the Irish Experiment*. New York: Oxford University Press, 1998.

Mallios, Peter. "Undiscovering the Country: Conrad, Fitzgerald, and Meta-National Form." *Modern Fiction Studies* 47.2 (2001): 356–90.

Manganiello, Dominic. *Joyce's Politics*. London: Routledge, 1980.

Mao, Douglas. *Fateful Beauty: Aesthetic Environments, Juvenile Development, and Literature 1860–1960*. Princeton, N.J.: Princeton University Press, 2008.

Marcus, Jane. "Britannia Rules *The Waves*." In *Decolonizing Tradition: New Views of Twentieth-Century "British" Literary Canons*, ed. Karen Lawrence. Urbana: University of Illinois Press, 1992.

Mardorossian, Carine. *Reclaiming Difference: Caribbean Women Rewrite Postcolonialism*. Charlottesville: University of Virginia Press, 2005.

Martin, Wayne M. "In Defense of Bad Infinity." *Bulletin of the Hegel Society of Great Britain* 55/56 (2007): 168–87.

Marx, John. *The Modernist Novel and the Decline of Empire*. Cambridge: Cambridge University Press, 2005.

Marx, Karl, and Frederick Engels. *The Communist Manifesto: A Modern Edition*, trans. Samuel Moore. London: Verso, 1998.

Mattelart, Armand. *Networking the World 1794–2000*, trans. Liz Carey-Libbrecht and James A. Cohen. Minneapolis: University of Minnesota Press, 1996.

Matz, Jesse. *Literary Impressionism and Modernist Aesthetics*. Cambridge: Cambridge University Press, 2002.

————. "T. E. Hulme, Henri Bergson, and the Cultural Politics of Psychologism." In *The Mind of Modernism: Medicine, Psychology and the Cultural Arts in Europe*, ed. Mark S. Micale. Stanford, Calif.: Stanford University Press, 2004.

Maugham, W. Somerset. *Of Human Bondage* (1915). New York: Penguin, 1992.

MacCabe, Colin. *James Joyce and the Revolution of the Word*. New York: Barnes and Noble, 1979.

McClintock, Anne. *Imperial Leather: Race, Gender, and Sexuality in the Colonial Contest.* New York: Routledge, 1995.

McClure, John A. *Kipling and Conrad: The Colonial Fiction.* Cambridge, Mass.: Harvard University Press, 1981.

McCracken, Scott. "Stages of Sand and Blood: The Performance of Gendered Subjectivity in Olive Schreiner's Colonial Allegories." In *Rereading Victorian Fiction* (pp. 145–58), ed. Alice Jenkins and Juliet John. New York: St. Martin's, 2000.

McEwan, Ian. *Saturday.* New York: Anchor, 2006.

McGee, Patrick. "The Politics of Modernist Form; or, Who Rules *The Waves?*" *Modern Fiction Studies* 38.3 (Autumn 1992): 631–50.

Melas, Natalie. "*Brides of Opportunity: Figurations of Women and Colonial Territory in* Lord Jim." *Qui Parle* 3.2 (1989): 54–75.

Memmi, Albert. *The Colonizer and the Colonized* (1957), trans. Howard Greenfield. Boston: Beacon Press, 1991.

Mendelson, Edward. "Introduction." *Tono-Bungay* by H. G. Wells. London: Penguin, 2005.

Michaels, Walter Benn. "Absalom, Absalom!: The Difference between White Men and White Men." In *Faulkner in the Twenty-First Century: Faulkner and Yoknapatawpha, 2000* (pp. 137–53), ed. Robert W. Hamblin and Ann J. Abadie. Jackson: University Press of Mississippi, 2003.

———. "Local Colors." *Modern Language Notes* 113.4 (1998): 734–56.

Mignolo, Walter. *Local History/Global Designs: Coloniality, Subaltern Knowledges, and Border Thinking.* Princeton, N.J.: Princeton University Press, 2000.

Miller, J. Hillis. *Fiction and Repetition.* Cambridge, Mass.: Harvard University Press, 1985.

Miller, Nancy K. *Getting Personal.* New York: Routledge, 1991.

Mitchell, Breon, "A *Portrait* and the Bildungsroman Tradition." In *Approaches to Joyce's Portrait: Ten Essays*, ed. Thomas F. Staley and Bernard Benstock. Pittsburgh, Penn.: University of Pittsburgh Press, 1976.

Mitchell, Timothy. *Colonising Egypt.* Berkeley: University of California Press, 1991.

Mohanty, S. P. "Kipling's Children and the Colour Line." *Race and Class* 31 (1989): 21–40.

Moreiras, Alberto. *The Exhaustion of Difference: The Politics of Latin American Cultural Studies.* Durham, N.C.: Duke University Press, 2001.

Moretti, Franco. *Modern Epic: The World-System from Goethe to García-Márquez*, trans. Quentin Hoare. London: Verso, 1996.

———. *The Way of the World: The* Bildungsroman *in European Culture* (1987), trans. Albert Sbraglia. London: Verso, 2000.

Moses, Michael Valdez. "Disorientalism: Conrad and the Imperial Origins of Modernist Aesthetics." In *Modernism and Colonialism: British and Irish Literature, 1899–1939* (pp. 43–69), ed. Richard Begam and Michael Valdez Moses. Durham, N.C.: Duke University Press, 2007.

———. *The Novel and the Globalization of Culture.* New York: Oxford University Press, 1995

Mulhern, Francis. *Culture/Metaculture.* London: Routledge, 2000.

———. "English Reading." In *Nation and Narration*, ed. Homi K. Bhabha. New York: Routledge, 1990.

————. *The Present Lasts a Long Time*. South Bend, Ind.: University of Notre Dame Press, 1999.

Nairn, Tom. *The Break-up of Britain*. London: Verso, 1981.

Neubauer, John. *The Fin-de-Siècle Culture of Adolescence*. New Haven, Conn.: Yale University Press, 1992.

Nietzsche, Friedrich. *Untimely Meditations*, trans. R. J. Hollingdale. Cambridge: Cambridge University Press, 1983.

Nolan, Emer. *James Joyce and Nationalism*. London: Routledge, 1995.

Nordenbo, Sven Erik. "*Bildung* and the Thinking of *Bildung*." In *Educating Humanity: Bildung in Postmodernity* (pp. 25–36), ed. Lars Løvlie, Klaus Mortensen, and Sven Erik Nordenbo. Oxford: Blackwell, 2003.

Nunokawa, Jeff. *Tame Passions of Wilde: The Styles of Manageable Desire*. Princeton, N.J.: Princeton University Press, 2003.

O'Connor, Maureen. "The Picture of Dorian Gray as Irish National Tale." In *The Picture of Dorian Gray* by Oscar Wilde (pp. 454–70), ed. Michael Patrick Gillespie. New York: Norton, 2007.

Orwell, George. *The Orwell Reader*. San Diego, Calif.: Harcourt, 1956.

Osborn, Susan. "Reconsidering Elizabeth Bowen." *Modern Fiction Studies* 52.1 (Spring 2006): 187–97.

Osborne, Peter. *The Politics of Time: Modernity and Avant-Garde*. London: Verso, 1995.

Parry, Benita. *Postcolonial Studies: A Materialist Critique*. New York: Routledge, 2004.

Parsons, Deborah L. *Streetwalking the Metropolis: Women, the City, and Modernity*. Oxford: Oxford University Press, 2000.

Peppis, Paul. *Literature, Politics, and the English Avant-Garde*. Cambridge: Cambridge University Press, 2000.

Pfau, Thomas. "From Mediation to Medium: Aesthetic and Anthropological Dimensions of the Image (*Bild*) and the Crisis of *Bildung* in German Modernism." *Modernist Cultures* 1.2 (2005): 141–80.

Phillips, Kathy J. *Virginia Woolf against Empire*. Knoxville: University of Tennessee Press, 1994.

Plotz, John. *Portable Property: Victorian Culture on the Move*. Princeton, N.J.: Princeton University Press, 2008.

Poovey, Mary. *Uneven Developments: The Ideological Work of Gender in Mid-Victorian England*. Chicago: University of Chicago Press, 1988.

Pratt, Mary Louise. *Imperial Eyes: Travel Writing and Transculturation*. London: Routledge, 1992.

Psomiades, Kathy. *Beauty's Body: Femininity and Representation in British Aestheticism*. Stanford, Calif.: Stanford University Press, 1997.

Rabaté, Jean-Michel. *1913: The Cradle of Modernism*. Malden: Blackwell, 2007.

Ramazani, Jahan. "Modernist Bricolage, Postcolonial Hybridity." In *Modernism and Colonialism: British and Irish Literature, 1899–1939* (pp. 288–313), ed. Richard Begam and Michael Valdez Moses. Durham, N.C.: Duke University Press, 2007.

Ramos, Julio. *Divergent Modernities: Culture and Politics in Nineteenth-Century Latin America*, trans. John D. Blanco. Duke University Press, 2001.

Randall, Don. *Kipling's Imperial Boy: Adolescence and Cultural Hybridity*. Houndmills: Palgrave, 2000.

Reder, Michael. "Rewriting History and Identity: The Reinvention of Myth, Epic, and Allegory in Salman Rushdie's *Midnight's Children*." In *Critical Essays on Salman Rushdie* (pp. 205–24), ed. M. Keith Booker. New York: G. K. Hall, 1999.

Redfield, Marc. *Phantom Formations: Aesthetic Ideology and the Bildungsroman*. Ithaca, N.Y.: Cornell University Press, 1996.

Rhys, Jean. *Voyage in the Dark* (1934). New York: Norton, 1982.

Ricoeur, Paul. *Time and Narrative*, vol. 1, trans. Kathleen McLaughlin and David Pellauer. Chicago: University of Chicago Press, 1984.

Riquelme, John Paul. "Oscar Wilde's Aesthetic Gothic: Walter Pater, Dark Enlightenment, and *The Picture of Dorian Gray*." *Modern Fiction Studies* 46.3 (Fall 2000): 609–31.

———. *Teller and Tale in Joyce's Fiction: Oscillating Perspectives*. Baltimore, Md.: Johns Hopkins University Press, 1983.

Robbins, Bruce. "Secularism, Elitism, Progress, and Other Transgressions: On Edward Said's 'Voyage In.'" *Social Text* 40 (Fall 1994): 25–38.

———. *Upward Mobility and the Common Good: Toward a Literary History of the Welfare State*. Princeton, N.J.: Princeton University Press, 2007.

Rose, Jacqueline. *The Case of Peter Pan, or The Impossibility of Children's Fiction*. Philadelphia: University of Pennsylvania Press, 1984.

Rosenthal, Michael. *The Character Factory: Baden-Powell and the Origins of the Boy Scout Movement*. New York: Pantheon Books, 1986.

Ross, Stephen. *Conrad and Empire*. Columbia: University of Missouri Press, 2004.

Rubenstein, Michael. *Public Works: Infrastructure, Irish Modernism, and the Postcolonial*. South Bend, Ind.: University of Notre Dame Press, 2010.

Ruppel, Richard. "Joseph Conrad and the Ghost of Oscar Wilde." *The Conradian* 23.1 (Spring 1998): 19–36.

Rushdie, Salman. Introduction to *Soldiers Three* and *In Black and White* by Rudyard Kipling. London: Penguin, 1993.

———. *Midnight's Children*. New York: Penguin, 1981.

———. *The Moor's Last Sigh*. New York: Vintage, 1997.

Sage, Lorna. Introduction to *The Garden Party and Other Stories* by Katharine Mansfield. New York: Penguin, 1997.

Sage, Victor. *Le Fanu's Gothic: The Rhetoric of Darkness*. New York: Palgrave, 2004.

Said, Edward W. *Beginnings: Intention and Method*. New York: Columbia University Press, 1975.

———. *Culture and Imperialism*. New York: Vintage, 1994.

———. Introduction to *Kim* by Rudyard Kipling. New York: Penguin, 1987.

———. *Reflections on Exile and Other Essays*. Cambridge, Mass.: Harvard University Press, 2003.

———. *The World, the Text and the Critic*. Cambridge, Mass.: Harvard University Press, 1983.

Saldaña-Portillo, María Josefina. *The Revolutionary Imagination in the Americas and the Age of Development*. Durham, N.C.: Duke University Press, 2003.

Sammons, Jeffrey L. "The Mystery of the Missing Bildungsroman, or: What Happened to *Wilhelm Meister's* Legacy?" Genre 14 (1981): 229–46.

Sanders, Mark. *Complicities: The Intellectual and Apartheid.* Durham, N.C.: Duke University Press, 2002.

Schiller, Friedrich. *On the Aesthetic Education of Man* (1795), ed. and trans. Elizabeth M. Wilkinson and L. A. Willoughby. Oxford: Clarendon, 1967.

Schorske, Carl E. *Thinking with History: Explorations in the Passage to Modernism.* Princeton, N.J.: Princeton University Press, 1998.

Schreiner, Olive. *My Other Self: The Letters of Olive Schreiner and Havelock Ellis 1884–1920,* ed. Yaffa Claire Draznin. New York: Peter Lang, 1992.

———. *The Story of an African Farm* (1883). London: Penguin, 1995.

Schwarz, Roberto. *A Master on the Periphery of Capitalism: Machado de Assis,* trans. John Gledson. Durham, N.C.: Duke University Press, 2001.

Scott, David. *Conscripts of Modernity: The Tragedy of Colonial Enlightenment.* Durham, N.C.: Duke University Press, 2004.

Sedgwick, Eve Kosofsky. *Between Men: English Literature and Male Homosocial Desire.* New York: Columbia University Press, 1985.

Seshagiri, Urmila. "Modernist Ashes, PostColonial Phoenix: Jean Rhys and the Evolution of the English in the Twentieth Century." *Modernism/Modernity* 13.3 (2006): 487–505.

Sherry, Vincent. *The Great War and the Language of Modernism.* New York: Oxford University Press, 2003.

Shohat, Ella, and Robert Stam. *Unthinking Eurocentrism: Multiculturalism and the Media.* London: Routledge, 1994.

Showalter, Elaine. *A Literature of Their Own: British Women Novelists from Brontë to Lessing.* Princeton, N.J.: Princeton University Press, 1977.

Slaughter, Joseph R. *Human Rights, Inc: The World Novel, Narrative Form, and International Law.* New York: Fordham University Press, 2007.

Smith, John H. "Cultivating Gender: Sexual Difference, *Bildung,* and the *Bildungsroman,*" in *Michigan Germanic Studies* 13.2 (1987): 206–25.

Soja, Edward W. *Postmodern Geographies: The Reassertion of Space in Critical Social Theory.* London: Verso, 1989.

Spacks, Patricia Meyer. *The Adolescent Idea: Myths of Youth and the Adult Imagination.* New York: Basic Books, 1981.

Spark, Muriel. *The Prime of Miss Jean Brodie* (1961). New York: Harper, 1994.

Spivak, Gayatri Chakravorty. *A Critique of Postcolonial Reason.* Cambridge, Mass.: Harvard University Press, 1999.

Stouck, Jordan. "Alternative Narratives of Race, Time and Gender: Jean Rhys' *Voyage in the Dark.*" *Journal of Commonwealth and Postcolonial Studies* 3.1 (Fall 1995): 53–59.

Stokes, John, ed. *Fin de siècle/fin du globe: Fears and Fantasies of the Late Nineteenth Century.* London: Macmillan, 1992.

Suleri, Sara. *The Rhetoric of English India.* Chicago: University of Chicago Press, 1992.

Sullivan, Zohreh T. *Narratives of Empire: The Fictions of Rudyard Kipling.* Cambridge: Cambridge University Press, 1993.

Szalay, Michael. *New Deal Modernism: American Literature and the Invention of the Welfare State.* Durham, N.C.: Duke University Press, 2000.

Taylor, Charles. "Two Theories of Modernity." In *Alternative Modernities*, ed. Dilip Parameshwar Gaonkar. Durham, N.C.: Duke University Press, 2001.

Tratner, Michael. *Modernism and Mass Politics: Joyce, Woolf, Eliot, Yeats*. Stanford, Calif.: Stanford University Press, 1995.

Trilling, Lionel. *The Moral Obligation to Be Intelligent: Selected Essays*, ed. Leon Wieseltier. New York: Farrar Straus Giroux, 2000.

Trumpener, Katie. *Bardic Nationalism: The Romantic Novel and the British Empire*. Princeton, N.J.: Princeton University Press, 1997.

Valente, Joseph. *Dracula's Crypt: Bram Stoker, Irishness, and the Question of Blood*. Urbana: University of Illinois Press, 2002.

———. *James Joyce and the Problem of Justice: Negotiating Sexual and Colonial Difference*. Cambridge: Cambridge University Press, 1995.

———. "Thrilled by His Touch: The Aestheticizing of Homosexual Panic in *A Portrait of the Artist as a Young Man*." In *Quare Joyce* (pp. 47–76), ed. Joseph Valente. Ann Arbor: University of Michigan Press, 1998.

Valente, Joseph, ed. *Quare Joyce*. Ann Arbor: University of Michigan Press, 1998.

Walkowitz, Rebecca. *Cosmopolitan Style: Modernism beyond the Nation*. New York: Columbia University Press, 2006.

Warner, Michael. "Introduction: Fear of a Queer Planet." *Social Text* 29 (1991): 3–17.

Watt, Ian. *Conrad in the Nineteenth Century*. Berkeley: University of California Press, 1979.

Watts, Cedric. Introduction to Joseph Conrad's *Lord Jim*. New York: Penguin, 1986.

Wegner, Phillip E. "'Life as He Would Have It': The Invention of India in Kipling's *Kim*." *Cultural Critique* 26 (Winter 1993–1994): 129–59.

Wells, H. G. *The New Machiavelli* (1911). New York: Penguin, 2005.

———. *Tono-Bungay* (1909). Oxford: Oxford University Press, 1997.

Welsh, Alexander. *Hamlet in His Modern Guises*. Princeton, N.J.: Princeton University Press, 2001.

Wiener, Martin J. *English Culture and the Decline of the Industrial Spirit, 1850–1980*. Cambridge: Cambridge University Press, 1981.

Wilde, Oscar. *The Picture of Dorian Gray* (1891). London: Penguin, 1985.

———. "The Soul of Man under Socialism." *The Complete Works of Oscar Wilde* (pp. 1079–1104). New York: Harper, 1989.

Williams, Julia McElhattan. "'Fiction with the Texture of History': Elizabeth Bowen's *The Last September*." *Modern Fiction Studies* 41.2 (1995): 219–42.

Williams, Raymond. *Problems in Materialism and Culture*. London: New Left Books, 1980.

———. *The Country and the City*. Oxford: Oxford University Press, 1973.

———. *Culture and Society 1780–1950* (1958). New York: Columbia University Press, 1983.

———. *The Politics of Modernism*. London: Verso, 1989.

Wollaeger, Mark. *Joseph Conrad and the Fictions of Skepticism*. Stanford, Calif.: Stanford University Press, 1990.

———. "Woolf, Postcards, and the Elision of Race: Colonizing Women in *The Voyage Out*." *Modernism/Modernity* 8.1 (January 2001): 43–76.

———. "The Woolfs in the Jungle: Intertextuality, Sexuality, and the Emergence of Female Modernism in *The Voyage Out*, *The Village in the Jungle*, and *Heart of Darkness*." *MLQ* 64.1 (March 2003): 33–69.

Woloch, Alex. *The One vs. the Many: Minor Characters and the Space of the Protagonist in the Novel*. Princeton, N.J.: Princeton University Press, 2003.

Woolf, Virginia. *To the Lighthouse* (1927). San Diego, Calif.: Harcourt, 1990.

———. *The Voyage Out* (1915). London: Penguin, 1992.

Yudice, George. "Rethinking the Theory of the Avant-Garde from the Periphery." In *Modernism and Its Margins: Reinscribing Cultural Modernity from Spain and Latin America* (pp. 52–80), ed. Anthony L. Geist and José B. Monléon. New York: Garland, 1999.

Zhang, Xudong. "Modernity as Cultural Politics: Jameson and China." In *Fredric Jameson: A Critical Reader* (pp. 169–94), ed. Douglas Kellner and Sean Homer. New York: Palgrave, 2004.

———. "Political Philosophy and Comparison: Bourgeois Identity and the Narrative of the Universal." *boundary 2* 32.2 (2005): 81–107.

Index

CPSIA information can be obtained at www.ICGtesting.com
Printed in the USA
LVOW08s0126160715

446323LV00003B/17/P

9 780199 307234